# THE GEOGRAPHIES OF THREAT AND THE PRODUCTION OF VIOLENCE

*The Geographies of Threat and the Production of Violence* exposes the spatial processes of racialising, gendering, and classifying populations through the encoded urban infrastructure – from highways cleaving neighbourhoods to laws and policies fortifying even more unbreachable boundaries. This synthesis of narrative and theory resurrects neglected episodes of state violence and reveals how the built environment continues to enable it today within a range of cities throughout the world. Examples and discussions pull from colonial pasts and presents, of old strategic settlements turned major modern cities in the United States and elsewhere that link to the physical and legal structures concentrating a populace into neighbourhoods that prep them for a lifetime of conscripted and carceral service to the State.

**Rasul A. Mowatt, Ph.D.,** is just a son of Chicago and a subject of empire, while dwelling within notions of statelessness, settler colonial mentality, and anti-capitalism. He also functions in the State as a Professor in the Departments of American Studies and Geography in the College of Arts + Sciences at Indiana University, and soon will be a Department Head in the College of Natural Resources at North Carolina State University.

"With rage and vision and in a language all his own, Mowatt paints an immersive reading experience that is both hard-hitting and deeply personal, not only powerful but vulnerable, and lyrical as well as historical."

–Micol Seigel, author, *Violence Work: State Power and the Limits of Police*

"From vulnerable bodies, to city control, to the power of the state, Mowatt's prescient book carefully excavates spatial violence in the ways the state maps, classifies and identifies those deemed disposable."

–Julian Agyeman, co-author, *Just Sustainabilities: Development in an Unequal World*

"…[M]akes a compelling case for social activists to consider physical spaces and social structures in their scholarly analyses and abolitionist praxes."

–Lynell L. Thomas, author, *Desire and Disaster in New Orleans: Tourism, Race, and Historical Memory*

"…[A]n action bubble POW! The book's power derives from a globe-trotting analysis of white colonial settler states that is also rich in detail."

–Marissa Moorman, author, *Powerful Frequencies: Radio, State Power, and the Cold War in Angola, 1931–2002*

"Truly the book for our times"

–Karl Spracklen, co-author, *Protests as Events*

# THE GEOGRAPHIES OF THREAT AND THE PRODUCTION OF VIOLENCE

## THE STATE AND THE CITY BETWEEN US

RASUL A. MOWATT

Routledge
Taylor & Francis Group

NEW YORK AND LONDON

First published 2022
by Routledge
605 Third Avenue, New York, NY 10158

and by Routledge
2 Park Square, Milton Park, Abingdon, Oxon, OX14 4RN

*Routledge is an imprint of the Taylor & Francis Group, an informa business*

Library of Congress Cataloging in Publication Data
Names: Mowatt, Rasul A., author.
Title: The geographics of threat and the production of violence : the state and the city between us / Rasul A. Mowatt.
Description: New York, NY : Routledge, 2022. | Includes bibliographical references and index.
Identifiers: LCCN 2021019627 (print) | LCCN 2021019628 (ebook) | ISBN 9780367708948 (paperback) | ISBN 9780367711542 (hardback) | ISBN 9781003149545 (ebook)
Subjects: LCSH: City planning--Moral and ethical aspects--United States. | Urban policy--Moral and ethical aspects--United States. | Ethnic neighborhoods--United States. | Violence--United States. | Race discrimination--United States.
Classification: LCC HT167 .M69 2022 (print) |
LCC HT167 (ebook) | DDC 307.1/2160973--dc23
LC record available at https://lccn.loc.gov/2021019627
LC ebook record available at https://lccn.loc.gov/2021019628

ISBN: 978-0-367-71154-2 (hbk)
ISBN: 978-0-367-70894-8 (pbk)
ISBN: 978-1-003-14954-5 (ebk)

DOI: 10.1201/9781003149545

Typeset in WeidemannStd-Book
by MPS Limited, Dehradun

# CONTENTS

# ACKNOWLEDGEMENTS

To my mother, Leatrice McClain Mowatt, who made me care about the streets, the people within them, and the ways to be proximate to their issues and their day-to-day struggles.

To my father, Andrew Duffus Mowatt, who made me work the land, made me stay close to the soil, and gave me a sense of how important long histories and perceptions of home really are.

To my aunt, Leanita McClain, who wrote the word, worked at grave costs to her life, and modeled working within worlds that one can never belong to.

To a city, Chicago/Shikaakwa, that I was born within. The lives lived, the lives lost, and the risk to my own life if it were not for music, books, friends, elders, and this place that will never be home again.

# 1.
# THE STATE BETWEEN US: AN INTRODUCTION

**Fig 1.1** My Mother, Brother, and I (Walking Staunchly With a "Sippy" Cup) Picketing Outside the South Shore (Now South Shore Cultural Center), 1977. (Photo Credit: Author)

"In town
In town
In town
Something in the way of things
Something that will quit and won't start
Something you know but can't stand
Can't know
Get along with, like death".
– Amiri Baraka, February 21, 2009 "Something in the Way of Things (In Town)" Sanctuary for Independent Media in Troy, New York.

"I have a foot in each world, but I cannot fool myself about either. I can see the transparent deceptions of some whites and the bitter hopelessness of some blacks. I know how tenuous my grip on one way of life is, and how strangling the grip of the other way of life can be".
– Leanita McClain (Aunt), October 13, 1980 "The Middle-Class Blacks Burden" in *Newsweek* and later in *A Foot In Each World*

DOI: 10.1201/9781003149545-1

It was 1977, a five-year-old me was walking in a picket line, likely oblivious of the seriousness of the moment, the issue, and its implications. Yet, there I was walking staunchly, clenched fist, mimicking what I felt around me, the anger of what was happening (see Fig. 1.1). No sense of knowing what the combined forces of what comprised the State, as a political organisation and entity, had in store for any of us. The State as the configuration of the power of government, corporate interests, classes of elites, and upper levels of a bureaucratic management class that implements the ruling class' goals and aims that sits atop an accumulated economic base. The State as the pseudo-territorial expression of the dominion over land, property, natural resource, mobilities, and identities tied to that designated territory. The State as the Creator that strengthens and reinforces gender as sex and Race as ethnicity that coincides with that pseudo-territorial expression of the State in order to create imagined nationhood, nationalism, and fabricated societies. The State as the great lord of the mental terrain that constructs our cognition of how we see the world, what we do in it, and the constant generator of our social condition.

So, of course, I did not know the magnitude of what was happening or why this protest was important to them, to me, or to us. The importance of why this small strip of concrete on a sidewalk was part and parcel of a greater system called a city, one of the primary political imaginations and articulations of the State. But the protest was small yet palpable enough for a five-year-old to understand the feeling without understanding the point. What was happening and what was the basis of that anger? You see, the anger of what had been happening over the span of many years was also on the sidewalk among the picketers at this protest coordinated by the Coalition to Save South Shore Country Club – a coalition that comprised the families of various ethnic populations that had been historically relegated to the neighbourhood area of Chicago, South Shore, but also remained in South Shore despite opportunities of "upward" mobility. Some were Irish, several were Jewish, and many were Black residents of the South Side of Chicago. This coalition of peoples alongside the various socio-political and community-based organisations that represented an equally multi-ethnic and political assembly of members and missions sought to fight a city, a State.

## 1.1 Palaces for the People

All were in for the fight of what was being deemed as "A Palace for the People", because many felt if this building, the South Shore Country Club, and the land around it fell to the whims of the official administration of the City of Chicago it would be designated for demolition that would thereby shutter any potential hope or any future possibilities in South Shore, and the greater Chicago South Side. Demolished buildings and abandoned properties are not what makes a healthy, safe, and viable neighbourhood and community. And this action, this potential and likely action, had to be stopped. Because you see, Chicago saw (and still sees) its South Side as being less than. A negative. An eyesore. A now forgotten land of hope and wondrous activity. And the people of this geographical space are one and the same with this forgotten colonised land. This protest was near the beginning of the contemporary narrative of the South Side as the location where gun shots rained down on everyone, and bodies dropped on the daily. The objectionable names for the land and specific areas within it would come later, "Terrortown", "The Wild 100s", "Dodge City", and "Chi-raq", but the sentiments and narrative originated then. The narrative of South Side another twenty years later in the 1990s, was where cars got jacked, and people were savagely robbed. The narrative of the South Side another twenty plus years later in 2020, as I draft this introduction, would now become that land where people walked around exposing others to a global disease, and hospital emergency rooms were overrun with irresponsible people. But returning back to 1977, it was still the time before crack cocaine, it was still a period in which the energy was less frenetic, and it was the era before the unbridled abandonment of neighbourhoods in cities by the State. And the people on this picket line did not know of all of this, of what was to come, but they felt something was coming, something was in the way of the futures that they each hoped for. Something was in the way of the basis for so many to invest in their homes.

Something was in the way of reasons why many slaved in occupations and started families. Something was in the way of the future for their children, and it was not each other; it was the State. Why else would one exert all of this energy to move to a neighbourhood, to start a family, and to call a place home? Why else would one exert all of this energy to protest?

My mother was a child born out of refuge, of parents who fled the South. And there she was, the matriarch of one of the many families on the picket line, my mom, a working mother, a Chicago Public School teacher assigned to a West Side school that required her to drive some immeasurable hours and miles away because none of the schools in the area would take her. There she was, just four years removed from being shot by a student in a West Side school parking lot, her very first school assignment. While my father was absent from the image, he was not absent from my life, like Louis Till, father of Emmett Till, who never returned home from war to see his wife or his son due to being lynched in Germany (Wideman, 2016). My father was not an absentee parent as some readers may have begun to thought, he merely absent from the protest; yet, he made those signs that my mother and my brother were carrying. The power of imagery to foster notions of absence where there wasn't. The power of imagery to confirm or deny old and new narratives. This image appeared in a feature in *The Chicago Tribune* on the protest, but none of the protestors were truly featured or given complete lives and stories. So, where was he, and what was his story? He was likely working somewhere else or getting some rest. He worked a second job as a late-night supervisor for the U.S. Postal Service. At this age, all I knew of him was this older man who would come into our house and sleep and leave for work. Because, you see, in order for my parents to move into South Shore, there were many sacrifices, concessions, and negotiations that had to be made. Who would do what? For how long? In what way? Immediate celebrations of marriage, purchase of a home, and a birth of a child had to be placed on hold for the future, a future. As some may say, money was tight to not only live (for basic needs) but to also be alive (for aspirational desires).

My father grew up as a colonial subject in Jamaica. Like my mother, my father also worked as a Chicago Public School teacher, and in fact, that was where they met and dated, taking classes to receive their teaching certificates. No, there is no further story that needs to be told, some common story that may fulfil many readers of this book on the trials and tribulations of a Black single parent home. Homes are homes, with people in them who are doing the best they can to make sense of the fabricated-Society that has been crafted for them. These contextual excerpts that I am providing are not a presented story to curry your favour, to appeal to your sense of another Black boy growing up on hard times on the South Side of Chicago. What we like to hear, to see, and to read are the hard times of the commonly believed and naturally occurring cycle of poverty, not the hard times as a deliberate consequence of State dominion that creates and maintains these cycles and also creates those myths that engineer conceptions of nature and not by design. I make this point, not because there is something wrong with single parent homes, or something magnificent with dual parent homes. We live how we live. We live how we have to live. Because if we don't, we die. It is just that the narrative of such a story serves to quench the thirst for a certain reader who wants to be drawn into the supposed emotionality of a story and to think and do nothing.

Instead of me being sucked into your lies of empathy that lead to these sorts of empty calls of care for my well-being. Instead of me being sucked into your need to relate, as if a personal story can make any of us fully relatable. I choose not elaborate. Because if we truly did relate, we would rather stand more in the way of the somethings that prevent many in the settler colony of the United States to ever thrive and fully become human. We would stand in the way of the somethings that will come for us all at some point or another. That something is not the presence of a natural death, the force that is part of our shared humanity. That something is the reality of an artificial death – the death that consigns certain people to subsistence housing conditions, unsafe working conditions, historical discriminatory treatment, exclusionary State-sanctioned violence, hyper-inequitable exposure to harmful vectors for disease, the undue provision of toxicity in water and air, and the absence of protections from harm and the absence of provisions of safety. This consignment guarantees the existence of "crime" and justifies abandonment. This idea or conception that has been rumbling through my head in conceiving this book during a pandemic straightforwardly cannot be shaken loose. With pandemic on my mind, how did so many people become exposed and become sick? Why did so many people start to die? Why were some people more than others likely to become both? From this pandemic on my mind, why did the city become the site for the increased effects of State failure and State power? Without the physical use of a city, the management of the social order in any and every nation-state would crumble. The State really must regulate all sites, locations, places, and spaces. The State must regulate where its populace resides, engages in trade, seeks and performs work, re-creates, etc. The State must regulate via policy to establish a rule of law, whether it abides to those laws itself or not. The State must regulate via force to dictate and control behaviour. The State must regulate via coercion the social acceptance of policy as *lawfare* (the protection of State actions and interests, and not the citizenry) and the social acceptance of the force as *warfare* (the use of State and State-sanctioned violence upon the citizenry). Without this abandonment and regulation, we, the citizenry would come up with our own version of a society instead of the fabricated-Society that is given. Self-determination threatens consignment.

This consignment produced the criminal because the existence of "crime" due to abandonment resulted in an over-dependency of "crime" since many other employment opportunities had long since been foreclosed. The demolition and abandonment of buildings are the demolition and abandonment of places to live and to work. This consignment that established racialised and gendered victimhood as "crime" was only allowed in "free to crime" zones and not in "crime-free" zones. This consignment instigated the protest in 1977 because those who did not seek to "crime" and did not accept the role of the "criminal" sought to challenge the conditions that produced "crime", granted the "criminal" free reign, and enabled the

State theft of profits, people, and property. This consignment also then justified the repression onto protestors whether you protested this consigned reality or were complicit in its insidious schemes. So no, I am not going where some of you as readers may want me to go. The need for relatability and the appeals for empathy lull us away from a true clarity that informs action. If something threatens either of us then responses of warm hugs that are devoid of emotional depth; that are rife with the giving away of gift cards to consume away our misery; that are empty postings of sympathy necessitated by an incentive-driven performance on a socially-mediated platform; that are convoluted offerings of well-being vacations as cleverly disguised plans for permanent retreats; and that are the preponderance of hollow proclamations of self-care, each and all would seem to be counter to the seriousness of the threat and the violence that comes to squelch those who are deemed threatening supposedly on behalf of those who represent the threatened. The partial story of the image that contains my family, and contains an image of me, is merely a faint, an intentional distraction with a purpose to draw some of the readers in further whereas other readers may have been ready from the start.

While there are picketers in this image, there is the side of a building, an entryway, and signage. There is one example of signage that we could focus on in 1977 that said, "South Shore Country Club" but in 2020 says "South Shore Cultural Center". And there is another example of signage that says "Closed", which could very well have said "Open" back in 1977, but there were forces that made the "Closed" not only a statement of operation but also a statement of reality. Besides the building, there are sidewalks and adjoining streets also depicted in the image. There is one example of a street sign with "71st St." in 1977; a 7-mile stretch of this street would later be named Emmett Till Road, for the same aforementioned Emmett Till, the 14-year-old Black Chicagoan murdered when he visited family in Mississippi during the summer of 1955. There are other street signs and stop lights also in the image. There are a variety of other things and parts of the infrastructure that established a social order for transport and traffic flow like stop lights, but there are also various other things and parts of the infrastructure that safeguarded a Co-relational social order, a classed, gendered, and racial order. We see an image of people. We see an image of my family. And most would see the people, and most would be drawn into a discussion of that family and not the infrastructure. This is telling that our first inclination would be the story of the people absent of the infrastructure that consigned and constricted them.

So, with this in mind, enough about my family, per se, and on to the point of this book. I am taking you where I want to take you. I am not here for your feelings. I am not concerned with how you feel. I am concerned with what you and I will think and do. There was something in the way things were. There is something in the way things are. There is a State that lies between us. Each of us needs to be the (counter) something in the way of things that maintain the status quo and the social order. The point of this introduction is to not even begin a story. The point of this introduction is to posit an analysis. It is to indict a system. It is to shed light on the greater machinations of what a society does with people who they consider to be threats. But I am getting ahead of myself.

## 1.2 The World Is Coming to an End

The potential demolition of the South Shore Country Club was part and parcel of a slow abandonment of the South Side that was engineered by City of Chicago officials and the social acceptance of many Chicagoans in other parts of the city. By the 1970s, White flight damn near destroyed South Shore, moving a viable tax base elsewhere and reducing the viability of schools, parks, and city services in its wake. This was also the same White flight that allowed my parents to buy a house at a fire sale price because many of the last remaining Irish Chicagoans, who were now White, were also running as far away as possible. But this is not the first time that White flight occurred; it was just the latest, and the "final", one. Many of us, at least in the United States, have seen this movie before. The previous version of this dreadful movie involved the Irish moving in; those seeing themselves more so of English descent panicked and fled. This was later followed up with

another version when Jewish residents came in greater numbers to the area, and the upper middle-class Irish Chicagoans, out of concern and disgust, likewise fled. A swath of Black families began to eye property in South Shore from the late 60s onwards, and some of the remnants of the Irish enclaves and some of the upper middle-class Jewish residents fled to the north side and to Hyde Park, respectively. But little did those Black families know that the fears of riot, crime, vice, etc., were being heaped upon them with such fortitude that the very sight of a moving truck filled with their stuff, that stuff being uploaded from said truck, and the occupants of that truck would trigger a series of actions evolving into newly minted White families vacating their properties *en masse* (Rotella, 2019).

"The world [was] always coming to an end in South Shore", according to Allan B. Hamilton, a real estate broker of several properties in South Shore who was interviewed in 1969 for *The Chicago Daily News* (Palmer, 1969); in particular, he owned property along 71st Street, where my parents would move to in 1970, a year after he decided to abandon all of his properties. And the evidence that the world was truly coming to an end in South Shore in the 1960s was that it was once 90% White, but by the 1980s it had become 95% Black. The flight was real. But how was the world coming to an end? The end was an end of the continuous and sequential flipping of racially classified populations. The end was an end of yet another potential opportunity to build a culturally and economically diverse neighbourhood. Neighbourhoods with a thriving and diverse tax base to shore up the allocation of resources. Neighbourhoods with lawyers, doctors, and teachers with toilets. Neighbourhoods also with architects, furnishers, and designers who installed those toilets. And neighbourhoods with contractors, plumbers, and cleaners who worked with those toilets in some way. Much like what often goes into the toilets, the newcomers were feared to be bringing their literal "shit" with them to destroy the place. But instead of a neighbourhood moving toward these types of community-controlled economic ends, the neighbourhood was moving toward an end. This end was an end, but not *the* end, at least not yet.

Black families were the latest in a line of

successions, but in this particular case there was not quite the same possibility of another wave to occur after the arrival of these families. Who and what comes after Black people? Black families brought with them the fear of the "end of days". Instead of being seen as the newest set of people who just wanted a home to raise a family, to pursue work, and to enjoy a retirement, this newest set of arrivals were seen as threats. They were the harbingers of a coming doom. They were the carrion coming to pick at any pieces of flesh they could find. For the newly minted White residents of South Shore that fled, they were the something that was in the way of their thing, their comfort, and their way of life. White family flight turned into White business flight that turned into White bank flight that would then turn into City of Chicago resource flight.

The year of 1969, the year of the interview with the fleeing property owner, brings us back to the opening image in 1977. The predominantly White country club was leaving, as most of their clientele no longer wanted to maintain their membership around "The Blacks", especially since they had to drive from miles away to enjoy the pleasure of their gated golf club, tennis courts, horse stables, and beach front. This open space was for private use only. This private space was for a selected public, and instead of this private space – as it was closing – being released to the public, it served other needs and ends. Ironically, the first public use of the space after a transfer from this private club to the City of Chicago was for the Chicago Police Mounted Patrol Unit. The notion of a fort-style structure with police officers on horses invoked thoughts of having the appropriate delivery of force to curtail an unruly Black populace hiding a protesting Black mass. City patrols on horseback are likened to slave patrols on horseback. With the Club's abandonment, the City, who ran and operated the shoreline, was also the same City that planned to demolish the historic building on the property and level the area. But residents, Irish and Jewish families who chose not to flee, joined with their new Black neighbours to challenge this move. Why? To present the decay that had already ensued after the organized abandonment of resources to these neighbourhoods in other parts of the South Side of the City from coming to this part

of the South Side. When large greenspace and historic landmarks were removed, there would only be one type of future: ruin.

So, the signs of protest that read, "Preserve the Buildings" carried by someone who looked like a White woman in front of us in the picket line, and the other signs "…The Future of South Shore" and "Don't Remove" that were carried by two White men just behind us, reflected this collective fight. But then there were our signs, made by my pops, my moms, looking like a scholastic fashion apparel model, holding up a sign that read, "Don't Destroy the Buildings. Save South Shore. The Future", and my older brother with his own sign that read "Don't Bulldoze the Buildings or The People of South Shore". Don't bulldoze the buildings or THE PEOPLE of South Shore. The concern for the reality that was being shown in these signs and this contemporary counter-history that buildings and property mattered over a Black life after a riot are both at odds with our notions of that same reality. Black residents had (and have) concern for buildings and property. But it is also evident to many of those same residents that there was (and is) little concern for the Black lives that dwelled in those buildings. In the era just before crack cocaine, myths had not yet become as stable and fixed as they are now. Now, unequivocally, buildings matter over Black lives, unless Black lives are in them. But also buildings matter less if Black lives are near them, as those lives (and the buildings that houses them) need to be bulldozed. And with this new-ish reality, then those building can be ordered for demolition. It was only at this moment in 1977, another moment decades later, the moment of 2020, the moment of crafting a book on the geographies of threat, identifying populations to be dealt with in some startlingly insidious ways, that I realise the additional levels of deepness in the meanings of these signs. In the summer of 2020, buildings were set on fire from the various forms of riot in response to both the ongoing visual triggers of state-sanctioned violence but also the sheer governmental and economic abandonment of everyday people amid a pandemic. Yet, the overwhelming response from many in the colony of the United States was on the act of riot, a response to the looting and the destruction of property, not a

**Fig 1.2** Tanks of the Mexican Army Roll Through Neighbourhoods With Tank Guns Pointed Up and Into the Various Apartment Buildings in the Northern Section of Ciudad de México on October 3, 1968. (Photo Credit: Associated Press)

response to the destruction of 781 people – 781 people, at the time of drafting this introduction, that one by one died by way of the police – nor the destruction of people from a disease that was just under 200,000 deaths in the United States (Mapping Police Violence, 2020; National Center for Health Statistics, 2020).

## 1.3 Don't Bulldoze People!

My brother's sign said "Don't bulldoze THE PEOPLE", but people are often bulldozed with little to no concern. At least three Olympics in their planning and execution have legacies of doing just that, the bulldozing of people. And many more planned and hosted Olympics have legacies that lead to forced displacement. The Olympics, an event that lights a torch of unity and that releases a dole of doves representing peace, are often conceived and built upon bodies, blood, and sorrow. In 1968, a year before the world was coming to an end on the South Side of Chicago, residents, students, and other protestors were massacred at the Plaza de Las Tres Culturas (Three Cultures Square) that was within the Tlatelolco housing complex in Ciudad de México, a

modernist government-funded housing development that just opened in 1964. An estimated 10,000 people came to a planned demonstration to prevent the destruction of a series of homes and businesses for the sake of the 1968 Olympic Games in Ciudad de México. Two hundred tanks with thousands of solders littered the plaza area (see Fig. 1.2). Shots rang out from the guns of those soldiers, tanks, and swirling overhead helicopters, with another set of violence workers firing upon the demonstration. While buildings were bulldozed by tanks, mounds of bodies were also bulldozed by those same tanks. Official records initially indicated only 4 dead due to the State action, with the final count arriving at 40 dead with another 1,000 injured. Yet, the count among those who opposed the Olympics' construction of stadia and the military occupation of a neighbourhood indicated the number of deaths were closer to 3,000, with zero deaths among the State actors, despite official accounts that student protestors had fired first. Historians have found records of orders dispatching members of the Presidential Guard sniper units onto the rooftop of buildings as well as holdings orders to fire at the army to instigate the State violence that would ensue.

Protestors chanted, "¡No queremos Olimpíadas, queremos revolución!" ("We don't want Olympics, we want revolution!") because the Olympics were enabling long-term city plans to expand parts of Ciudad de México for tourism and for the wealth. Ciudad de México and the greater colony of México made use of the violence for their politico-economic ends off the publicity and success of hosting the 1968 Games but at the detriment of those who were living in conditions that were worsened by job loss, the closing of educational opportunities, and now the destruction of their homes. The Tlatelolco Massacre on October 2, 1968 remains a meagrely noted and obscure bit of history, but the Games and the Black Power salute are what we now maintain as an acceptably public memory of these times, despite John Carlos' insistence on us remembering the death of these students and residents prior to their historic moment (Carlos & Zirin, 2011). What we know or choose to know is what happened on that particular medal stand on October 16, 1968. The iconography is only what counts; the imagery of that moment is all that matters now. The iconography of the people, not the iconography of what the people were drawing our attention to and the infrastructure around them. After winning their respective track heats, Tommie Smith and John Carlos later received gold and bronze medals. Joined by Peter Norman of Australia, they made a stand in solidarity of global human rights while elevating the violations of human rights for millions of Black Americans back in the colony of the United States under the coalition of athletes and scholars of the Olympic Project for Human Rights.

Tommie Smith not only won gold but set a then world record. He was brought over to a young rising sports announcer, Howard Cosell, who asked him to explain to television viewers in the United States what he just did and why he did it (referring not the world record but to the protest action). In my view, such an open-ended question would have led me to ask, "Just did what?" Winning gold or winning the moment for protesting? Smith promptly responded with a lesson rather than a sound bite, a decoding of protest rather than protest branding, a declaration of conviction rather than propping oneself as figurehead of a movement,

First of all, Howard, I would like to say I'm very happy to have won the gold medal here in Mexico City…the right glove that I wore on my right hand signified the power in black America. The left glove my teammate John Carlos wore on his left hand made an arc, my right hand to his left hand, also signifying black unity. The scarf that was worn around my neck signified blackness. John Carlos and me wore socks, black socks, without shoes, to also signify our poverty. (Hoffer, 2009, p. 177)

Later in the broadcast, Cosell in reflecting back on his exchange with Smith stated,

And, so, the Olympic Games for the United States have become a kind of America in microcosm, a country torn apart. Where will it all end? Don't ask the U.S. Olympic Committee, they've been too busy preparing for a VIP cocktail party next Monday night in the lush new Camino Real. Howard Cosell reporting from Mexico City. (Vogan, 2018, p. 90)

Cosell's remarks alluded to some semblance of a class unity in the moment. These young college students were running for free at the behest of wealthy elites who ran the International Olympic Committee (IOC) in partnership with governments who cared little for the likely communities that most of the athletes came from and the communities that the very stadia were built upon. To think that a massacre of hundreds, if not thousands, occurred days before and still the 1968 Olympics began without a hitch. This successful execution of an event only meant that there was a concerted effort to ensure that the torch was going to be lit at all cost. A parade of athletes had come out to appear on TV as a spectacle of achievement for the then Mexican government, the TV broadcasters, and the IOC. Even the guns of the Olympic Battalion, the official security force of the IOC, also opened fire on local protestors just 16 days before the medal stand. But only the 1968 Olympics and the image of the salute were in our view, now and then. Viewers in the United States sought escape from what was happening in their streets but were confronted by it with the protest of Smith, Carlos, and other U.S. athletes.

The disgust was not immediate, as more attention was placed upon the awarding of medals and the setting of records, but the disgust at the action of the protesting athletes came soon enough. In a broader global context, however, especially in what was happening locally in Ciudad de México, the idea of protest and the protestors had to be snuffed out.

Just days before one historic act of protest about the lived conditions of people who were deemed a threat in the colony of the United States, a massacre of thousands who were deemed a threat had just taken place. But this massacre was preceded by other State actions, as bazookas were also fired into buildings where students fled to for safety at the National Preparatory School in San Ildefonso. This action only galvanised those students who organised and protested against the violent work of the police under the National Strike Council (Consejo Nacional de Huelga) that was composed of some 70 university and preparatory schools in México. A July fight between rival student gangs at two vocational schools was responded to with exceptionally repressive actions by police forces in Ciudad de México. This was followed by a peaceful demonstration of 50,000 student at the National Autonomous University of Mexico (UNAM) in August, which was in response to the police repression and was responded to by the Mexican Army with a compete takeover of UNAM. This led to the aforementioned incident at Plaza de Las Tres Culturas. Protests were violently pacified in México, much like the pacification of the favelas in Rio de Janeiro in anticipation of the 2016 Summer Games decades later – another Olympic Games with demolition of property, displacement of people, and use of public funds, this time a total cost of $12 billion in public funds. The 2016 Games were merely the cover for the need for mass displacement of people and buildings for the creation of a "new playground" for the Rio-based elites and aspiring classes. Many of the displaced were given remote, temporarily pleasing dwellings in Parque Carioca, but even this appeared to be a payoff instead of a socially responsive solution, as the displaced were now out of sight and out of mind. Those who are in sight or in view, such as those in the "neighbourhood" area of Maré quite near the International Airport, were overlooked.

Rio had been using a series of mega-events to successfully make these plans happen through the 2007 Pan American Games, 2011 Military Games, 2012 Earth Summit, 2013 FIFA Confederations Cups, 2014 FIFA World Cup, and of course, the 2016 Olympic and Paralympic Games. With each successive event, more and more democracy could be suspended, curtailed, or eliminated for the sake of a "cosmopolitan awakening" in a Rio of the future for the few. Another example was hosting of the Games in 2008 in Beijing, which prompted the eviction of 1.5 million people in a historic neighbourhood near the edges of Tiananmen Square (Beck, 2007). The hosting of the 1988 Olympics in Seoul and the 1996 Olympics in Atlanta led to the respective forced displacement of 720,000 and 30,000 people (Centre on Housing Rights and Evictions, 2007). The Games often bring despair and misery. The bright and spangled splendour of the parade of athletes; the incredible feats of physical prowess; and the pride of imperial nation-states, settler colonies, and tenuously secured countries of recent independence movements competing against one another, all overshadow the populace that was robbed during such an undertaking as hosting of the Games. In their 2007 report, the Centre on Housing Rights and Evictions (CHRE) noted,

> A decade ago, the UN Centre for Human Settlements (UNCHS) identified that more than one in seven massive evictions worldwide were related to mega-events, and that "beautification" projects related to these events served as the most common justification for slum clearance programmes.

CHRE further stated, based on studying the Olympics since 1988, patterns of forced evictions preceding the hosting of the Olympic Games are virtually fundamental to Olympic bidding, planning, and execution (Mowatt & Travis, 2015). The active displacement of people that was brought on by the frequency and propensity of coerced buyouts, subversive increases to rent and utilities, slum clearance, and forcible removal cannot mean that these are imitative accidents, but instead shared policies on land grabs and property theft in places where everyday people inhabit. These people, a certain people, were threats that had to be dealt with.

But what happens to those who challenge these tactics, challenge these exertions of power? Political participation, at least in the United States, can at many times be summarised within two realms: the dissenting public thesis and the engaged citizen thesis. Under the dissenting public thesis, political expression using a range of tactics in public space and virtual spaces can be regarded as forms of social activism and organising against a perceived status quo. Based on seminal literature about anti-system protest participation (e.g., Davies, 1962; Gurr, 1970; Lipset, 1960), dissenting public thesis is the work of individuals through collective action engaged in public and online political discourse while undergoing their own political disaffection and social disadvantaging. This can be viewed through engagement with calls for public participation by community residents to State actors during the failed Chicago 2016 Olympic bidding process, and the lack of transparency and failure of community engagement (Mowatt & Travis, 2015).

On the other hand, the engaged citizen thesis is the personal resource and engagement model of participation (e.g., Inglehart, 1997; Putnam, 2000; Verba et al., 1995) that suggests that public and online political expression are key elements of conventional political participation. This can be viewed through the sustained engagement in opposing the Chicago Olympic bid, within both domestic and international spaces, to ensure the voice of dissent was heard by official Olympic deliberation bodies. The position of the citizen engaged thesis is that it was then likely for activists and organisers to be influenced by their own resources, their own motivations for political engagement, and their own social networks in order to sustain dissent of any type. But just maybe, without knowing it, those activists and organisers were influenced by State socio-political restrictions that would curb their imaginations and constrict their activities. It is expected that people who express their ideas in both public and online spaces are politically engaged and socially well connected, in addition to being composed of both disadvantaged and advantaged individuals. To break from those potential State restrictions, recognition of

the work of No Games – Chicago, the work to oppose the bid was an arduous endeavour that led to the successful disruption of the bid and the sullying of the perception of Chicago to official deliberators. In studying and chronicling within spaces allowed for community-minded scholars to broaden scholarship on mega-events, specifically the Olympics, the combination of a dissenting public and the engaged citizenry are some ways that defiance, opposition, and dissent of State power can lead to engagement of growing oppositional power (Hiller & Wanner, 2016; Lenskyj, 2009). Class-based statuses of the populace fail to insulate the ruptures in the socio-geographical fabric of neighbourhoods and communities, as both have been identified as service populations to the State and will be deemed as threats that have to be dealt with.

## 1.4 "Crime", Disease, and a City for the Elites

But what is the nature of a threat? On the surface, "crime" and disease are most often raised as the concerns from supposed collectives of "concerned" citizens who are often the only ongoing attendees of city council meetings. They relay what is happening on their block from their stoop or porch. They make the call for what needs to be done in their neighbourhoods. They become the sole voice for their communities. And they aid and abet the machinations of the State, knowingly or unknowingly. They decry the "criminals" who engage in "crime" in their homes. But the concerns from the "concerned" citizen are only the useful opening to an eagerly awaiting city council. Those concerns justify the council's already strategically planned assault onto the geographies of the city, into the geographies where the threats are most immediate, and where the opportunity for more accumulation of capital can be extracted. In order to be safe, "crime" and disease must be eliminated. But this does not mean the actual prevention of "crime" with the proffering of quality employment and the end of disease with high-quality health care. This means the removal of people most often associated with the "crime" and the disease. And with their eventual and hastened removal, the true intent of the city should be revealed to us. No other city administration action

**Fig 1.3** Rio Olympics Opening Ceremony in Maracana Stadium With Mangueira Favela in the Foreground, May 8, 2016. (Photo Credit: Alamy)

moves with such swiftness. Snow removal in a hazardous blizzard, dangerously dilapidating public schools, overgrown grass that hides syringes in parks proximate to disposable people, or someone in an abandoned part of the city dialing 911 to receive protection. None of this garners speed, competence, or accuracy. But the construction of a stadium and events in the midst of strapped budgets also warrant swift actions like those applied to the elimination of "elements" in society that engage in "crime" and spread disease. Yet, "crime" and disease are never removed, just people, a certain type of people – people of a certain kind of threat, as threats to a certain kind of order.

And what is a threat? Threats obstruct opportunities and assurances – threats to profit, to person, and to property. In thinking about profit with the 2016 Summer Games in Rio, the neighbourhood area of Barra de Tijuca needed to be developed to an acceptable level but at the cost of the favelas of disposable populations and of the low-income

housing projects near Vila Autódromo. Golf courses built for the Olympics would become golf courses for the condo projects that soon followed the end of the Games. Logic was (and is) not the order of the day for these actions, as in Rio many of the buildings and facilities of the 2016 Olympics (and the 2014 World Cup) still lay vacant and unused even to present day (see Fig. 1.3). But all of this was done in order to bring Barra to "a level that only kings have previously had" (Watts, 2015). The developer further noted that,

> We think that if the standards were lowered, we would be taking away from what the city – the new city – could represent on the global scene as *a city of the elite, of good taste* [emphasis added]. For this reason, it needed to be noble housing, not housing for the poor. (Watts, 2015)

For then and still mayor of Rio, Eduardo Paes, the people of "crime" and disease and where they dwelled were in the way of making Rio "the city of the future", as he described Rio in a TED Talk to a live and later online audience who ignored the true cost of this vision (Paes, 2012). Even TED provided a misleading and obscuring description to Paes' city of Rio on their website, "a sprawling, complicated, beautiful city of 6.5 million". Complicated? Such an interesting word for the suffering of some and the entertainment of others, the Cariocas. But there the word is on their website, a mask to a lecture that also masked ongoing corruption and the faint shades of a (ethnic) cleansing. Within the talk, Paes stated to a usually complacent TED audience that there were four "basic commandments, you can really get cities to be a great, great place to live. I want you all to imagine Rio", and they were: 1) a city of the future had to be environmentally friendly (create open spaces); 2) a city of the future had to deal with mobility and integration (mass, public transportation); 3) a city of the future had to be socially integrated ("Favelas are not always a problem... Favelas can sometimes really be a solution"); and 4) a city of the future had to use technology to be present (working with U.S.-based tech firms to create a mobile command centre). The complacent TED audience became the complicit TED audience in their round of applause at the talk's conclusion.

Paes delivered on none of these things, per se and per quod. Open space was cleared and made possible through land theft and removal. Public transportation allowed police forces to move more rapidly throughout the massive city to institute their shoot-to-kill policy. Favelas, comprising 1.4 million inhabitants, were (and still are) brutally pacified into submission. And with the mobile command centre, Rio was now the most surveilled city in South America. But couched within this talk, Paes accidentally slipped and revealed his hand when he stated that "Rio has the aim, by 2020, to have all its Favelas completely urbanized", and as it is now 2020 that I am crafting this introduction, we know a great deal more that "urbanised" actually meant eliminated. But in re-listening to the TED Talk, post World Cup and Olympics, the hidden hand of what we now know has been revealed. The promise of abundance is always at the cost of abandonment. The destruction of the Favelas, the theft of public

funds for little actual need (health care, clean water, schools), the mobility and rapid deployment of police power, and more importantly, the ubiquity of State surveillance were the true outgrowths of the four commandments that Paes articulated (Cuadros, 2016). The last commandment he discussed was the mobile command centre to "help with traffic flow", but it was a U.S.-based company created surveillance system – a budding partnership between States and their cities' function. This, to me, was just another indicator that much-heralded and celebrated buzz-words like "smart cities", "new urbanism", "sustainability", "resilience", "green cities", etc., are all terms, concepts, and structures that are bankrupt of the necessary philosophies and struggle for anti-imperialist and anti-colonialist life-sustaining States and cities. We are nothing more than intellectual crocks if we embrace those buzzwords without such a philosophical foundation and socio-political reckoning.

We are crocks in the sense that we, as either academics or practitioners, are (conveniently) naïve, (dangerously) oblivious, or (insidiously) corrupt. The promulgation of these buzzwords, the construction of infrastructure, and the actualised realities from their use is virtually the same in every city in every nation-state, country, or colony. These "brilliant" ideas only seem to expand State power's control on its population and never, ever seem to give life to the entirety of the people. We cheer for these concepts at the expense of the people who are on the ground experiencing the most subjugation from those concepts. The complacent complicity of TED audiences can be extended to scholars and lovers of all things "green", sustainable, and energy sufficient. They delightfully gloss over a slum for production and use of electric buses. Children on the street without food or education are glossed over for privatised recycling initiatives. The absence of clean water and adequate health care are glossed over for the niche availability of home solar panels. The forced closure of schools is glossed over for the promotion of goat farms. The crisis of "crime" and disease, and the capitalistic opportunity of the World Cup and Olympic Games, granted Rio the opportunity to become a city of a certain future (see Fig. 1.4).

**Fig 1.4** Brazilian Flag Waves on the Top of a Building in the Vila Autodromo Favela, Next to Olympic Park Barra and the Main Press Center. Only 20 of 700 Families Were Able to Remain Due to Protesting. The Building and the Favela Were a Key Area of Resistance to the 2016 Olympic Games, August 4, 2016. (Photo Credit: Associated Press)

The crisis of pestilence, much like war, is simply an excuse to exercise a shock doctrine onto a populace. Crises are critical, as they are merely opportunities to exploit and more rapidly expand State power. Events are useful, as they proffer a more appealing and amiable social acceptance to manage crises. Crisis and moral panics are the

> principal forms of ideological consciousness by means of which a "silent majority" is won over to the support of increasingly coercive measures on the part of the state, and lends its legitimacy to a "more than usual" exercise of control. (Hall et al., 1978, p. 221)

Couched within the nationalistic fervour of hosting mega-events like the Olympics and the World Cup was/is the opportunity to wholesale rid a city of a populace utilising the backdrop of "crime" reduction and disease elimination, and many of the contemporary Games since Greece in 2004 to the planned Qatari Games in 2022 have taken advantage of this opportunity that was effectively taught to

nation-states with the planning and hosting of the 1968 Mexico City Summer Games (Oliver & Lauermann, 2017; Zirin, 2009). The lessons that were taught by the 1968 Games in the bulldozing of people and their buildings was that the bigger the distraction, the more effective it is to generate the social acceptance of eliminating the unfavourable. Those people of "crime" and disease are in the way of (economic) growth, the future. The threat to profit, person, and property, reveals the hand of capitalism through disaster production (Klein, 2007). The crisis at the level of the State supersedes the crisis at the local level, and instead of the concerns of one portion of the populace. The crisis

> of the ruling class's hegemony, which occurs either because the ruling class has failed in some major political undertaking for which it has requested, or forcibly imposed, the consent of the broad masses (war, for example), or because huge masses (especially of peasants and petit-bourgeois intellectuals) have passed suddenly from a state of political passivity to a certain activity, and put forward demands which in

their disorganic whole constitute revolution. A "crisis of authority" is spoken of, and this is precisely the crisis of hegemony, or general crisis of the state. (Gramsci, 1975, p. 1603)

The State will use the local moment of crisis to better address its own concerns of crisis, because,

> The state apparatus is far more resistant than it is often possible to believe and it manages, in moments of crisis, to organize greater forces loyal to the regime than the depth of the crisis might lead one to suppose. This is especially true of the more important capitalist states. (Gramsci, 1971, p. 113–124)

The State will inform us that those people of "crime" and disease will expose us to their sickness. In sequential order, after a threat to profit comes the threat to personhood. Baltimore created restrictive covenants in 1910 based on newspaper accounts in 1892 that stoked the fear of the,

> villainous looking negroes who loiter and sleep around the street corners and never work; vile and vicious women…, that's "Pigtown". (Crooks, 1968, p. 20)

Pigtown was a condemned ghetto that White Baltimoreans took flight from, and the burgeoning Black Baltimorean bourgeoisie wanted to distance themselves in respect to the "disreputable and vicious neighbourhoods of their own race" (Haynes, 1913, p. 111). Those people of "crime" and disease were in the way of social growth. While this class of Black Baltimoreans thought they could distinguish themselves from their racialised Black working and poorer classed fellow residents, the process of racialisation associated the "crime" and disease with Race and not class. But it also represented early (aspiring and elite) class protection of what had been "earned" from their accumulation of wealth by way of appeals to the State for that protection. They failed to realise that Black excess wealth and Black access of opportunity still curried White animosity and hostilities just as much as Black "crime" and Black disease. The Black elite and aspiring middle class moved out and away, and their new proximity to the

White elites and middle class ruffled feathers and raised concerns. Neighbourhoods beyond "Pigtown" started to become "darker".

Something still had to be done about the smell coming from "Pigtown" and other downtrodden locations of the City, but something also had to be done with the Black hoity-toity class who still had the stench of "Pigtown" upon them since they had only come into favourable income just mere "days-a-go" relative to the creation of White wealth notions of time. This should have been an early sign that the role of ownership of property would never attain any form of independent liberation. Thus, precipitated the need and conception for restrictive housing throughout the city of Baltimore, the first restrictive covenants in the entire United States. In 1911, Baltimore Mayor Mahool, a noted champion of social justice, signed into law, quote,

> [a]n ordinance for preserving peace, preventing conflict and ill feeling between the White and Colored races in Baltimore city, and promoting the general welfare of the [Baltimore] city by providing, so far as practicable, for the use of separate blocks by White and Colored People for residences, churches and schools. (City of Baltimore, 1911)

Those people of "crime" and disease would most assuredly destroy property (values). And in continued sequential order, threats to profit and to person gave way to threats to property. And this brings us back to the 2020 narrative of fear brought on by riot and looting that occurred during riot.

The fear that was also indicative of the end of the world in 1969 Chicago after the 1968 riots in the city. In April 1968, Chicago, like many other cities, responded in an uproar to the 1968 assassination of Martin Luther King, Jr., that represented the last hope of peaceful change. The riot, also turned rebellion, caused an estimated then $50 million in damage, and

> Where then Mayor Richard J. Daley the Elder afterwards issued the infamous order to, Shoot to kill any arsonist or anyone with a Molotov cocktail in their hand in Chicago. To fire a

building because [the buildings'] potential murder and to issue a police order to shoot, to maim or cripple anyone looting any stores in our city and above all the crime of arson to me is the most hideous and worst crime of any and should be dealt with in this fashion. (Davis, 1968)

Throughout this introduction, looting is not being praised or given some elevated status. Looting is just another activity that merits study, merits explanation, and also merits analysis when you consider the responses to looting that occur within a city. Why do looting and any of the other related actions happen? Are these "criminals" waiting for an opportunity? Today, they are robbing the Gap, H&M, or Banana Republic in some shopping district, and tomorrow they will rob you in your home – these are the likely connections that readers, viewers, and listeners of the news are supposed to make. The looters cannot satisfy their desire for other people's stuff. They need to be put down. Well, a critical analysis would make note that any of these conclusions do not sound like an adult's reasoning and mature thought process about things that occur in the world around them. If looting is no different from theft or robbery, why not just call looting "mass shoplifting" since a supposed "crime" is happening? Think about it. We don't call it that; no one does, including the State. We are selective in assigning and distancing ourselves from criminality, "crime", and in this case, looting. We steal staplers, printer paper, gift cards, computers, tool belts, cars, food, and time from our own workplaces in ways that are beyond unethical. We excuse these minor infractions of theft.

But in looking at the fine print of our employment contracts, we have committed a "crime" that could lead to termination of employment, to arrest, and in many cases, to incarceration. However, we then balk at the act of looting, the alleged mass theft, even though we all have individually stolen. The difference between us and them was our own triflingness that was revealed in the basis for our thievery and in the basis for their looting. Our individual infractions are personally motivated, so what then lies in the motivations of the looting crowd?

While a boy's body laid on the ground for four hours after being shot and killed by a police officer, outcries justifying the shooting pointed to the theft of items at a nearby market minutes earlier (Michael Brown of Ferguson, MO, in 2014). Similarly, supporters noted that individuals were shot in the head at a convenience store by a store owner over candy (Latasha Harlins of Los Angeles, CA, in 1991), were killed after selling bootleg CDs and DVDs in the parking lot of a food mart (Alton Sterling of Baton Rouge, LA, in 2016), or were kneeled upon by a police owner after being arrested for using an alleged counterfeit $20 bill at a small grocery store (George Floyd of Minneapolis, MN, in 2020). These are the articulated bases for the protestors who loot, who engage in acts of collective theft. To decide to loot as a form of protest, a base response to the lived conditions rather than to steal, is a form of "crime". And in our disgust for looting and our condemnation of these "thieves" who had it coming to them, we cognitively exempt ourselves from the possibility of our own demise if we are also caught in our own individual and unmeritorious acts of thievery. The shoot-to-kill orders of Mayor Daley the Elder in the 1960s are only augmented by the permission to kill of then governor Ronald Reagan of California in stating "if it takes a bloodbath, let's get it over with, no more appeasement[s]" in the 1970s, and later echoed by a clearance to shoot to kill from governors Haley Barbour of Mississippi and Kathleen Blanco of Louisiana during Hurricane Katrina of 2005. But preceding all of these was the shoot-to-kill orders by Mayor Eugene E. Schmitz during the imposition of martial law for the San Francisco Earthquake of 1906. Property was/is to be protected; property was/is to be mourned. But who would mourn any of us, protest our death that came from an individual act of theft? The looters to some degree, and the actors of protest to a greater degree. Injured people (injured by the State) rise up, cause damage to the infrastructure, and injure buildings, and they are blamed for that injury. They are then injured yet again by the agents of the State that further their *violence work* of maiming and injuring.

Remarkably, the order from Mayor Daley the Elder was issued after peace and calm had been restored, thereby suggesting the intent to use the

image of looting and buildings ablaze was to cultivate the experience of the riot as threatening to
everyday citizens to his advantage, to suppress any
political dissent that was to come, and to maximise a
certain kind of urban development (Chandler,
2002). The dissent would come later that same year
with the riot of police in response to the protests of
the August 1968 Democratic Convention.
Incidentally, the riots of 1966 in and along Division
Street and the ones on the West Side of Chicago
were in response to the collapsing economic infrastructure and conditions in neighbourhoods. The
State-sanctioned violence that spurned the riot were
denounced by Martin Luther King, Jr., and led to his
own consideration of Chicago as a site for civil rights
work around fair housing. Ironically, Daley the Elder
refused to label these activities as riot and often referred to them in reports and in the press as little
more than "juvenile disturbances" – but the concerns were clear, and there were no concerns for the
welfare of those living in under-resourced communities. The concerns were not even articulated to the
alleged acts of depravity upon "good" citizens, as
there was insufficient evidence that those who engaged in riot sought to cause harm to any person.
The concern was and is always on the damage to
property and the future reputation of a city.

## 1.5 Don't Destroy the Buildings…Preserve the Future!

Returning back to the initial 1977 protest image and
seeing the messages on the signs, "Preserve the
Building!?" and "…The Future", I am sure that my
mom and others did not mean it in the context of
how it could read or be perceived during Summer
2020 (see Fig. 1.1). What future were they talking
about? The building and the social club were
founded and built on racial exclusion in 1906. White
Protestants were replaced by the socially mobile Irish
Catholics of the South Side, who were now in a
better position to flex their muscles after decades of
being excluded from other social circles throughout
the city of Chicago. As mentioned, the post-World
War II Chicago South Side transitioned to a predominantly Jewish area; yet, the Club maintained its
exclusionary practises instead of broadening its
membership base. By the time of the aforementioned
1960s, the Club no longer had a significant membership to maintain itself since it disregarded the
influx of Jewish and later Black Chicagoans. The
Club's Board of Directors refurbished the building in
1967 to only turn around and completely abandon it
seven years later. The riots of 1966 of Chicago were
followed by the 1967 riots of Red Summer
throughout the United States, but they especially
were felt in Chicago.

A perception of Black riot was cultivated into a
narrative of Black terror that was unleashed upon
cities. Black families moving into neighbourhoods
around the Club only raised anxieties for the wanton
destruction of their jewel on the lake. Then came
1968, which ushered in two more major riots, and
the growth of the "militant" Illinois Chapter of the
Black Panther Party, the Black Arts Movement, the
Congress of African People, the Young Lords, and the
Young Patriots. This was too concerning for the
highbrow tastes of the aspiring and actual elites of the
city. The influx of new Black "immigrants" was placing the members and the Board of the Club far too
proximate to the undesirables just outside the flimsy
green chain-linked fence that lined most of its peri-
meter. Instead of growing its dwindling membership
even further, a membership that was now at a historic
low of only 731 members, leaders and members of
the Club held one last hoorah, a dance in 1974, and
shuttered the place. Even in closing its doors, the
Club directors chose to sell its assets rather than hand
them over to any potential Black buyers.

Under the leadership of Warith Deen Muhammad,
the Nation of Islam underwent a process of reformation
that would develop it into momentarily becoming the
World Community of Islam in the West. It attempted to
purchase the property to convert it into, among other
things, a community hospital. I recall rumours stating
that a briefcase of $2 million in cash was offered due to
Islamic abstention of usury and credit. Whether this
was true or not, the rumour also reflected another point
or sentiment of those who helped spread the rumour,
the South Shore Country Club was never going to
entertain selling the property to anybody Black. The
Chicago Park District eventually acquired it for $10
million and swiftly made plans to demolish the large
clubhouse building. No townhall meetings were

conducted to make any official plans known to residents. No community meetings on the South Side were ever held. No notices were posted throughout the district, ward, or area. I suppose when it came down to it, that building (the large clubhouse) did not ever matter. But I also suppose that certain buildings that would also likely service certain population never should matter. By 1980, the building demolition plans were withdrawn, and although in disrepair, part of the property was featured in *The Blues Brothers* movie released later that year. In the sole on-site scene in the movie, the clubhouse was used as a stand-in for the fictional Palace Hotel and Ballroom. The Palace, an in-movie legendary venue for music, was to hold the performance by the Godfather of Soul, James Brown. It is ironic that even in fiction the South Side could not be promoted, praised, or mentioned in any mode of reverence. Instead of the South Shore Country Club, it was the Palace Hotel and Ballroom. Instead of being on the South Side, the scene was set geographically somewhere else in the City. Instead of remotely reflecting the real relationship with Black people that the halls and stages of the Club actually had (one of service), it was given the honour of being some mythical place that Black people and their art was always welcomed. In the culminating concert scene that ultimately lands Elwood and Jack Blues in jail, all of the on-screen antagonists, which included the Chicago Police Department, the American Socialist White People's Party/the Illinois Nazis, and the Good Ole Boys country band, descended upon the Brothers with extreme fury.

We rooted for the Brothers against these forces in fiction, but in real life we seem to only root for those forces that are against the "Brothers", would-be heroes, and the people. And despite its historical and cultural significance, even in the present day as a renamed and repurposed South Shore Cultural Center, it still must fight to stay afloat and remain fully functional due to the lack of financial support from the City and the state of Illinois. A former Club and park on 64 acres of land that is along the shoreline and beachfront of Lake Michigan, is in a now predominantly Black neighbourhood and is not something to ever preserve. A building that was worthy of landmark designation on the National Registry for Historic Places that was acquired in 1905 and constructed in 1906, is now in a

predominantly Black neighbourhood and is not something to conserve. Even its historic association with the architectural firm, Marshall and Fox (Benjamin E. Marshall and Charles Fox, that built numerous prestigious hotels and apartments throughout the City), cannot save it (Bachrach, 2001). Its visitation by U.S. Presidents, U.S. Presidential candidates, future Presidents (including the 1992 wedding of 44th President and FLOTUS), European nobility, famed artisans, and significant mayors is insignificant to saving it. The building and its property remain within the mindset from the years of not allowing scores of Black people to ever visit.

This once great "Playground for the Rich" up to the 1950s, with its 2,000-person dining hall, horseback riding fields, skeet shooting range, and outdoor pavilion, became just "A Palace for the People" since the 1980s, a different people. "The People" were and are composed of beer-drinking blues listeners, African drum ensembles, kinara-lighting Kwanzaa celebrators, and little soaking Black kids wet from splashing in the waters of Lake Michigan. It is almost as if you could hear in its hallways the recording of "Sing, Sing, Sing" by Benny Goodman and Band (who was from Chicago and who frequently returned to play in Chicago throughout the 1930s) scratch and skip to the tumultuous sound of "The Day the N\*ggaz Took Over" by Dr. Dre (who best reflected the sonic imagery of the supposed gang culture in Los Angeles, even though the song is in reference to the L.A. Riots of 1992). "The world is coming to an end" when the Blacks move in. "When music goes around, Everybody goes to town/But here is one thing you should know...", the up-tempo Goodman hit that later added lyrics to it was now jarringly mixed in with the chaotic "...Dem wonder why mi violent, dem no really understand/For de reason why mi take mi law in mi own hand". As it was in 1969 Chicago with the moving in of so many more Black families, so it remained. As long as they (those Black people) were around this wonderful estate on the lake, that same estate can fall to the wayside. A prestigious and exclusive social Club was willing to shutter its doors. A city was willing to demolish a nationally registered landmark. A people were disposable enough to foreclose all futures. And the only momentary glimmer of hope came with the 1983 election and administration of Chicago's first Black Mayor, Harold Washington, who designated $10 million for a restoration that most prominently became the terracotta hue that still bathes over the entire premises.

But prior to that momentary glimmer, the sentiments for the property in the heart of a predominantly Black community were best expressed by Ed Kelly, the then Chicago Park District Superintendent in the 1970s, who commented, "Oh, they [Black people] don't need that [fancy building] down there [the South Side]". "They": Chicago taxpayers and homeowners turned into the racial "Other". "Down there": a location within the same city, at best 5–10 miles away from the District's main office, referred to as if it was in the heart of Mississippi, some distant land beyond the true City borders according to this city official. Those people in that distant land had no value or culture worth catering to and serving. And although the building was placed on the National Registry back in the 1970s, it was not awarded the City's own Chicago Landmarks Commission designation until 2004. I suppose it was better to be late in acknowledging the protection of its significance than never coming through with such a designation, unless that lateness was a part of a long list of snubs, slights, and slurs. How remarkable could it have been if the South Shore Cultural Center was designated and renovated back in the 1970s? Instead of picketing families, scores of families entering its premises to see their arts and culture on stage. In what ways could such a designation and facilities have made South Shore thrive and prosper?

And why did the people even have to protest to keep the property? Why did the people have to fight to make it open and accessible? Why do the people even now have to keep preventing the lights from being turned off (Chicago Public Library, 1997; Cholke, 2015; Lieberman, 2019)? Preserving the future, but what future? What type of future is being talked about in the present moment of 2020? The picket sign wording runs up against the discourse during the Summer of 2020 and the civil unrest in numerous cities, at least in the United States. It is hard to read the wording of "buildings" and "preserve" used in any context and to not think it. After all, "Buildings Matter, Too" was the headline on the front page of the June 2, 2020, *The Philadelphia Inquirer*. The op-ed, while lending support to protestors, focused on the property damage as the point of contention and not the basis of the unrest, which was the killing of George Floyd. The response from the public and the nearly 40 staff members at *The Inquirer* led to calls in outrage and the forced departure of a veteran editor and staff member of nearly 20 years (Wise, 2020). But buildings did not matter to Wilson Goode, Mayor of Philadelphia, and others some more than 35 years ago when a building was bombed, and an entire neighbourhood area was allowed to burn from the fire of the blast (see Figs. 1.5 and 1.6). And the lives of John Africa, Rhonda Africa, Theresa Africa, Frank Africa, Conrad Africa, Tree Africa, Delisha Africa, Netta Africa, Tomaso Africa, Raymond Africa, and Little Phil Africa, the 11 people within those buildings, not mater.

But this is where we have come to in the Summer of 2020: buildings and property damage become the order of the day. The "fire of a building", invoking the words of Daley the Elder, is a cause for State actors to shoot to kill and for citizens to join in the protection of that property, but the basis for the fire is never addressed or remedied. Seventeen-year-old Kyle Rittenhouse of Antioch, Illinois (just an hour north of Chicago), was so primed to protect property that he headed to Kenosha, Wisconsin, driven by his mom and armed with an assault rifle. He shot three people and killed two, Joseph Rosenbaum and Anthony Huber (Wood, 2020). "Violence pertains to the State alone" (Anderson, 1976, p. 32); legitimate violence is determined solely by the State. So, violence is defined solely by the State, and responses to that defined violence are enacted by the State unless,

> The State is not seen to be fulfilling this basic function, in the face of a serious and sustained upsurge of violence – either criminal or political – we can be sure of one thing: that sooner or later, ordinary citizens will take the law into their own hands or will be disposed to support a new form of government better equipped to deal with the threat. (Moss, 1976, p. 226)

**Fig 1.5** A View of Osage Avenue in Philadelphia, Pennsylvania, Showing the Remnants From a Shootout and Bombing of the Residence of Members of MOVE (a Black Liberation Movement Organization) by the Police Department Upon Orders of the Mayor for a Forced Eviction. Subsequently, a Fire Spread and Was Never Extinguished by the Fire Department and Allowed to Spread, Destroying Some 61 Homes, 18 May 1985. (Photo Credit: Bettmann/Getty Images)

**Fig 1.6** A Barren Expanse of Dirt Is All That Remains on the West Philadelphia Neighborhood From the 13 May Siege of the Residence of MOVE, 10 June 1985. (Photo Credit: Amy Sancetta/AP Photos)

The cause célèbre are the actions of the looters and rioters and not the actions of the State that have led to nearly 8,000 people killed by police in the United States since 2013. And while the fanfare keeps us within the scope of the camera lenses that eye those looters and rioters, particularly those Black and Brown ones, we miss when Black and Brown communities are continuously looted of funding that is owed to them, and we have long missed the indigenous lands that this entire enterprise occurs on. What is owed to them is not reflected by watered-down notions of reparations (i.e., acts of kindness, sympathy, syllabus inclusion, even checks).

What is owed to them from a real investigative consideration is inherent in the study of State repair and restitution. What is owed is based on the standards that have been developed by and of a national registry and city landmark distinction. What is owed comes from the very idea of TIF (tax increment financing) funds that were allegedly created to re-develop communities like South Shore, but also other Chicago communities on the other wrong side of wealth like Albany Park, Archer Heights, Armour Square, Ashburn, Auburn Gresham, Austin, Avalon Park, Avondale, Back of the Yards, Belmont Cragin, Brighton Park, Bridgeport, Bronzeville, Burnside, Calumet Heights, Chatham, Chicago Lawn, Clearing, Douglas, Dunning, East Garfield Park, East Side, Edison Park, Fuller Park, Gage Park, Garfield Ridge, Grand Boulevard, Greater Grand Crossing, Hegewisch, Hermosa, Humboldt Park, Jefferson Park, Kenwood, Logan Square, Lower West Side, McKinley Park, Montclare, Near West Side, New City, North Lawndale, Norwood Park, Oakland, Portage Park, Pullman, Riverdale, Roseland, South Chicago, South Deering, South Lawndale, Washington Park, West Eisdon, West Garfield Park, West Lawn, West Pullman, West Town, Woodlawn, and especially, West Englewood and Englewood (see Fig. 1.7).

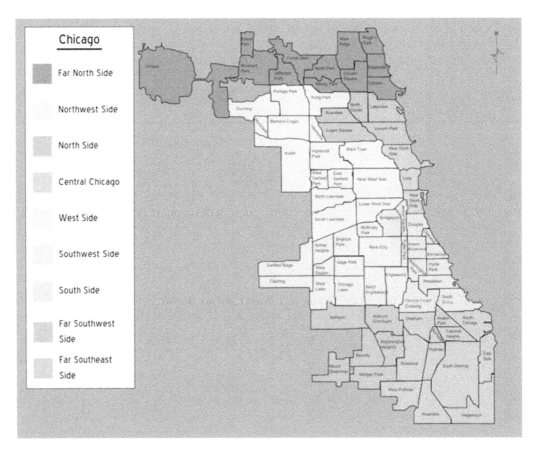

**Fig 1.7** Map of the Neighbourhood Areas and Geographic Regions in Chicago. (Wiki Commons/Public Domain)

In response to the shooting of an Englewood man on the Chicago South Side, some sought a swift and decisive response to the looting in the downtown area – looting that was in direct response to the shooting. Mayor Lightfoot in a press conference stated,

Whether it's in our downtown commercial district or in one of our other 77 neighbourhoods, there can never be any place in Chicago where businesses are afraid to open, where residents and visitors are afraid to travel and shop. (D'Onofrio & Wall, 2020)

But nearly occurring concurrent to the looting was the increase in TIF funds allotted to subsidise redevelopment and infrastructure within the City, particularly funds given to projects aimed at improving any of the communities mentioned that were given to projects in communities that did not need the subsidy. The projected future property tax revenue could be directed toward present-day spending on improvement initiatives. The rhetorical explanation for TIFs has always been redevelopment, but it ought to be for deteriorating areas of a given city. TIFs create and incentivise partnerships between developers and City government since public improvement project costs are incurred solely by the developer or the costs for such projects are often far higher if undertaken without the subsidy. An area must be clearly designated as substandard, if not blighted, in order to be intended as the site for development. The decay caused by supposed excessive levels of "crime" and disease spread would merit such a designation. Through this process, property values are technically frozen until the TIF is fully underway. And while the freezing of property values prevents wealth generation among homeowners, it also prevents devaluation of homes and property. The successful redevelopment should eventually foster increased property values, once the project is completed. And through that property valuation increase, revenues from the property tax should replace the public funds that were used to initiate the process – a process that on paper reads as if the

buildings of the disposable, and the disposable themselves, could be valued.

TIF-funded projects must be completed within a 15-year window. However, the budget for the projects is never quite transparent, and the decision making on what projects are funded or even considered remains intentionally hazy. Additionally, the designated TIF districts tend to skirt the line of being substandard. Many projects are proximate to downtown areas rather than in the heart of long-abandoned neighbourhoods. As mentioned, while under 100 Chicagoans ransacked downtown stores during the Summer of 2020, areas like those just "west of Lincoln Park, [that] barely qualified for a record subsidy of up to $1.3 billion" received TIF funding while areas like Englewood have never been considered through the programme (Dardick, 2020). "Crime" and disease are never really eliminated; they are two constructs that are maintained, used, and wielded by the State. The emphasis in the news was on the stores that were vandalised by those 100 Chicagoans, the items that were stolen, who the looters were, and what neighbourhoods they likely came from – neighbourhoods prior to their own abandonment were once thriving (see Figs. 1.8 and 1.9). And who the looters were and where they were from only intensified the public's reaction to what they did, since the South Side of Chicago has been permanently grafted with a narrative. In response, there was not only increased police presence and social media investigations that lasted until mid-Fall 2020, but also the literal drawing of the bridges barring those from the South Side from entering the luxurious parts of the Chicago Loop, Near North, and the greater North Side.

The infrastructure of the city was deployed as the social control mechanism for protest, riot, and looting, something that was done fictionally in both 2005 *Batman Begins* and 2008 *The Dark Knight,* when Chicago was used as a stand-in for Gotham City. In order to protect itself from the chaos-infused machinations of Liam Neeson's Ra's Al Ghul and Heath Ledger's The Joker, bridges were raised to protect the property of downtown, not the populace of the city. Not to necessarily praise the Joker's terror upon a fictional Gotham City/real-life Chicago, but

**Fig 1.8** The Heart of the Englewood Shopping District on Chicago's South Side, 63rd and Halsted Ave., 1929. (Photo Credit: Getty Images)

**Fig 1.9** Pedestrian Crossing, and Shopping in Englewood on Chicago's South Side, 63rd and Halsted Ave., c. 1962. (Photo Credit: Alamy)

you only have a sense that the terror that he was inflicting was upon Gotham City's elites and city officials. They were the ones who needed to be protected. Neighbourhoods of Gotham were never filmed, and were never truly the focus; they were thereby left unscathed by the Joker's wrath. But as a viewer of the movie, you are left with a notion that the terror the Joker could cause could be levied upon all of us. But all of whom? Certainly, nobody on the South and West Side of fictional Gotham City/real-life Chicago. Joker's likely despotism was going to be applied to the wealthy and the powerful. As a consequence, and at all costs, he had to be stopped, or at least prevented, from reaching further into the seats and pockets of power. Those bridges had to be drawn to keep him away, and to keep the wealthy in power, and their respective property protected – leaving the rest of the city to fend for itself. Even in fiction, buildings matter the most.

But this fiction showed the last display of the drawing of bridges from "criminals", provided by the city to Christopher Nolan's production crew; the last time this actual tactic was used upon the City's citizenry was the Lager Beer Riot of 1855. The riots were equally predicated upon racialised sentiments of "native-born" Chicagoans versus the newer German and Irish immigrants (Keefe, 1971; Mortice, 2020). On February 26, 1855, the *Chicago Tribune* published Nativist's sentiments that questioned,

> Who does not know that the most depraved, debased, worthless and irredeemable drunkards and sots which curse the community, are Irish Catholic? Who does not know that five-eighths of the cases brought up every day before the Mayor for drunkenness and consequent crime are Irish Catholics?. ("Irish-Rule", 1855)

The aftermath of the 1855 Riot led to the professionalisation of the police force in Chicago in spite of concerns from many residents that such a force would be like an occupying army deployed in order to establish a certain social order from time to time, for

> An ordinance creating a new police department squeaked by on a council vote of eight to seven.

Every North Side alderman, whose wards contained substantial German populations, voted against the measure. To them, as well as their constituents, the police represented a repressive institution, a tool of the Puritan elite to keep working people from enjoying life as they saw fit. Memories were still fresh of policemen closing taverns on Sunday and arresting the proprietors. A policeman was someone who was all too quick to arrest a man for having one too many, while more serious offenses went ignored. (Hogan & Brady, 2015, p. 88)

What will those 2020 "riots" of Michigan Avenue's businesses lead to? Increased privacy law violations on social media and the expansive use of facial recognition software via street cameras. A system and network of cameras that will increase Chicago's notoriety as the most surveilled city in the United States, if not North America, with more than 50,000 cameras feeding both state and private surveillance appetites (see Figs. 1.10, 1.11, and 1.12). It is important to note that Englewood is among a cluster of communities that are not a part of such a vast network of surveillance cameras despite having the

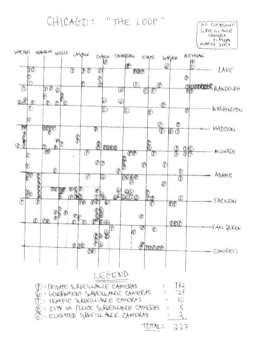

**Fig 1.10** A 2003 Artist Sketch of the Number of Cameras Just in the Chicago Loop Area. (no copyright)

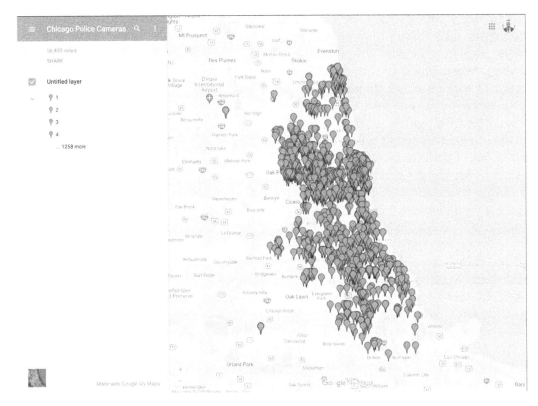

**Fig 1.11** A Screenshot of the Blue Chicago Police Department Police PODs (Police Observation Devices) in the City of Chicago. (Screenshot from Google Maps; no copyright)

highest number of homicides in the entire city (see Figs. 1.13 and 1.14). Yet, there were enough cameras to refute the false claims of actor Jussie Smollet in early 2019, but not enough to protect citizens from murder, their alleged purpose. Englewood, the insultingly labelled murder capital of Chicago and the basis for the equally derogatory term "Chi-raq" used by outsiders, had an average of 70 murders per year but had a clearance rate of under 17% in solving said murders. Yet, Chicago also reported a clearance rate of more than 50% of murders in other parts of the city, especially if the victim was White. There was and is nothing to ever watch in Englewood, because no one and no thing is worth watching. But the stores, residencies, properties, and reputation all along Michigan Avenue were and are always very worthy of being watched. The concerns of property damage-related "crimes" in the City yet again are given as the reason for extending State institutional repression of dissent and everyday-ness.

## 1.6 Riot, Protest, and Dissent

Chicago has a considerable history of riot, protest, and dissent. However, many of us who are aware of these actions and incidents do not view them in a critically spatial way. Riots, protests, and acts of dissent are seen as separate types of occurrences, each with its own import and rationale instead of being understood as relational to each other and in relation to other factors. In viewing them separately, each receives its own merit of praise and disgust. But this is an error in analysis, and in committing that error, we fail to see the similar factors that lead to them as well as seeing the ways that the State uniquely responds to each but uses each for the same ends. Within this vein, the already-discussed 1855 Lager Beer Riot is utterly forgotten in the memory of most Chicagoans and the memory of anti-immigrant sentiments (for Irish and German immigrants) that came from Chicago-based Nativists and members of the Temperance Movement.

**Fig 1.12** A Screenshot of the Red Light Photo Enforced and Traffic Cameras in the City of Chicago. (Photo Credit: www.photoenforced.com)

Within this same context, the aforementioned 1966 Riot (that was actually two distinct riots on Division Street in June and then on the West Side in July) is not even remembered in the same cognitive space as the two 1968 Chicago Riots (one in April in response to the assassination to Martin Luther King, Jr., and the other months later at the Democratic National Convention in August). The State, through its bureaucratic administrations of control and meaning making, are always "active in defining situations, in selecting targets" and by doing so and never governing for life are also, "advertently and inadvertently, [amplifying] the deviancy they seem so absolutely committed to controlling" (Hall et al., 1978, p. 52). The 200-page report on the April 1968 Chicago Riot from the Chicago Riot Study Committee (1968) that was appointed by Daley the Elder, indicated that "the majority of Blacks in the riot was a spontaneous overflow of pent-up aggressions" (p. 72).

Pent-up aggressions over what? Dissent that evolves in protest is telling us something. But what? And are we listening accurately? Some scholars who have cursively looked at protest, riot, strikes, rebellions, and revolts typically mention or even situate the basis for protest in the worsening of the lived conditions of everyday citizens. This was as true in 1820 as it was in 1920, and as it is now in 2020. Protest is just as it implies and as it exists. Protest is a refutation and an act of dissent. Protest may be the response to the failures of governance, but protest is also a response to being governed. Since Democracy is the form of governance in the United States, then protest is a response to the policies, politicians, and policing of/by the State. But once again, conditions arising from stagnant economic growth, exclusionary state (sanctioned) violence, and the uprisings of those left without reserves are telling us something. Protest can be marches and rallies, and they can be riots and strikes. And looting can occur. The moments and the conditions dictate what we will see, whether it is marches, rallies, demonstrations, strikes, riots, or rebellions. But how and why? And why now in the Spring and Summer of 2020? And why at other times throughout history? Why does protest take certain forms at certain points in history? For the sake of the focus of this book, the *Geographies of Threat, Cities of Violence*, how and why does

**Fig 1.13** A Screenshot of the Blue Light Chicago Police Department Police PODs (Police Observation Devices) in the Englewood Neighbourhood of the City of Chicago. (Google Maps Screenshot; No Copyright)

protest and State response take their respective forms within the landscape of cities?

In the early 1800s, riots and insurrections were prominent due to the exploitations that were inherent in capitalism for the poorly paid labourer and the enslaved labourer. In the 1820s, Denmark Vesey's conspiracy for revolt took place in the city of Charleston, South Carolina. Also in the 1820s and 1830s, some of the most prominent strikes were of immigrant women working in mills in the Northeast United States in cities like Lowell, Massachusetts. The selling of labour instead of a product offered capitalism an effective means to accumulate greater quantities of wealth. In 1920, on the island of Oahu, a multiracial strike of three labour unions rallied against sugar plantation owners. Just the year before, the Great Steel Strike of 1919, which began in September but ended in January 1920, only represented 100 years of capitalism evolving and

becoming more efficient in extracting. Not to mention the ongoing Race riots – riots levied at Black citizenry on an ongoing basis, beginning in East St. Louis in 1917 to 1921 with the Tulsa Race Massacre. They oftentimes had labour issues like job loss, shrinking wages, and unattainable wealth as backdrops that precipitated a useful rallying of State-sanctioned actors in stabilising any challenge to the order and restricting any access to the city government coffers. In Chicago's own history of riots, the 1919 Chicago Race Riot during the year-long nationwide "Red Summer" is oftentimes not added to the official record of civil unrest in the city, especially when disdain for the act of riot is delivered and is articulated by the various mayoral administration.

On July 27, 1919, at Chicago's 29th Street Beach, 14-year-old Eugene Williams swam across a dividing line in the segregated waters of Chicago's Lake Michigan, the same lake and shoreline that the

**Fig 1.14** A Screenshot of the Red Light Photo Enforced and Traffic Cameras in the Englewood Neighbourhood of the City of Chicago. (Photo Credit: www.photoenforced.com)

South Shore Country Club of my childhood sits just a few miles southward. His trespassing did not lead to racialised taunts or even an unlawful arrest. It resulted in a stoning that eventually led to his death by drowning as the White assailants prevented him from returning to any beach area. The incident represented the tensions of an economically rising Black population and the coalescing of an institutionally significant Irish population, with a greater White, non-Irish population waiting in the background (Coit, 2012; Tuttle, 1996). This Irish population was distinct from the aforementioned upwardly mobile Irish population that was in South Shore and dominated the South Shore Country Club and Park. This population was poorer and far more dependent on the scant working-class occupations within the city, but they did aspire for a greater foothold in the city. But those limited lines of employment were also impacted by the demographic effects of those fleeing the reign of lynching terror in the South through the Great Migration to the North, with over 500,000 Black citizens of the United State making the exodus. The city of Chicago's Black population grew from an estimated 44,000 to 110,000 between 1910 and 1920. This Irish population and their wealthier counterparts were becoming more and more accepted as White at the same time as the South Side was becoming a hell of lot Blacker (see Figs. 1.15, 1.16, and 1.17).

As cities grew and greater economic mobility occurred, people vied for their space, and the State dictated the spatial arrangements of those people. Cities allow the State the ability to cultivate and execute its power in very specific ways that directly impact the citizenry that is bounded under the various facets of its control (policy, force, and coercion). Ethnic consciousness is spatial and territorial. The plots of land that are allocated and the populations contained within its boundaries can become useful tools in leveraging support and/or instigating strife. City governance is the localised version of the State that is proximate to the regulated lived experiences the populace has been placed within. Home rule is just one philosophy of many that eases the management of that population by granting discretionary decision making to local representatives of the State

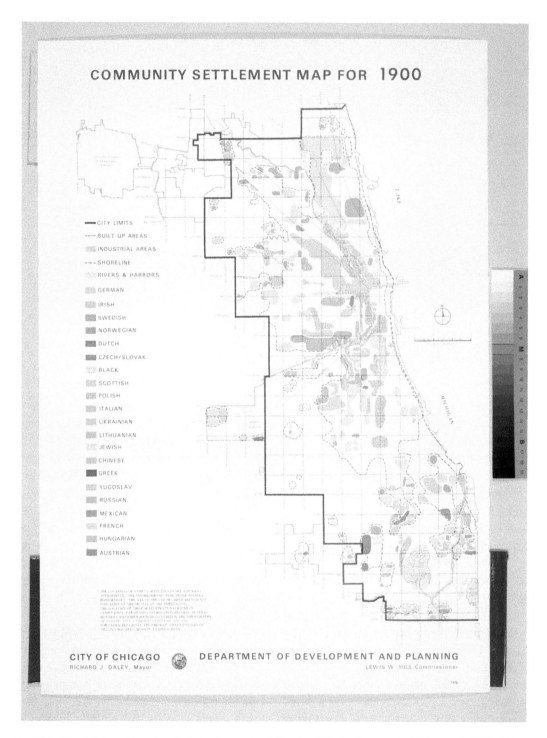

**Fig 1.15** City of Chicago Department of Development and Planning (Ethnic) Community Settlement in 1900. (The Chicago History Museum)

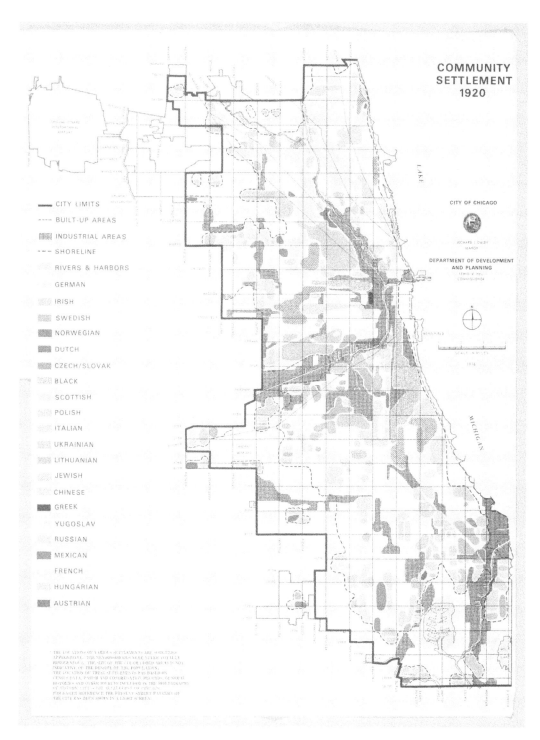

**Fig 1.16** City of Chicago Department of Development and Planning (Ethnic) Community Settlement in 1920. (The Chicago History Museum)

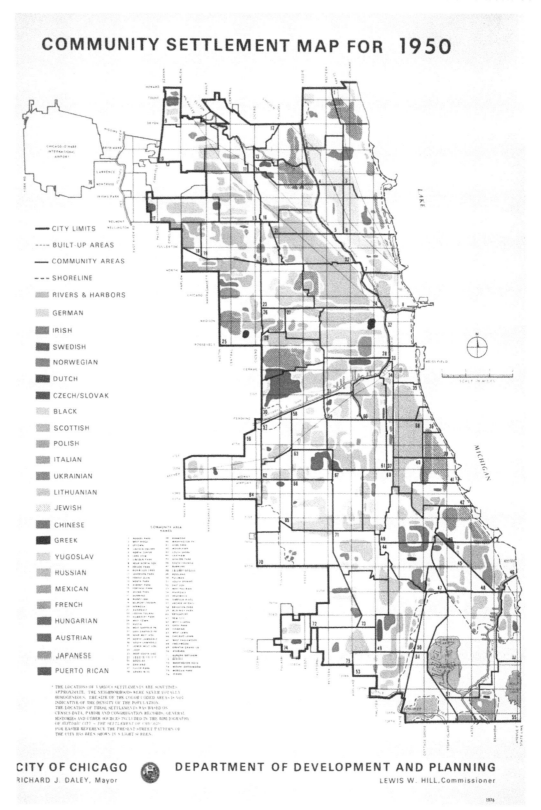

**Fig 1.17** City of Chicago Department of Development and Planning (Ethnic) Community Settlement in 1950. (The Chicago History Museum)

(the police officer at the micro-level and the city council/city administration at the macro-level). Cities assert and exert power, and they never share it with their residents. Free movement and the mobility of a population was (and is) insufferable and must be curtailed and regulated. And this (first) encroachment of Black people to parts of the South Side in 1919, before the next massive demographic that would come in the 1960s and 1970s that brought people like my parents, was intolerable. Chicago instituted policies of Restrictive Racial Covenants, through which the Chicago Real Estate Board and City Council could enforce the racial segregation of the city through all of the properties within the city limits, including recreation centres, churches, social clubs, and professional associations (Jones-Correa, 2000). The Irish, while flourishing in the city, were still relegated to a status not fitting their perceived role in business and commerce, city administration, and law enforcement. According to Gotham (2000), these covenants "were contractual agreements between property owners and neighbourhood associations that prohibited the sale, occupancy or lease of property and land to certain racial groups, especially Black [people, however not exclusively either]" (p. 617) that in more official ways made racism "a permanent and ineradicable feature of American society" (p. 616). Legalised housing restrictions kept the undesirables in Chicago at bay throughout the city. Since the 1855 Lager Beer Riots, Irish and German Chicagoans were still discriminated against but did enjoy some measure of mobility that the Jewish, Italian, Czech, Polish, and Black Chicagoans did not. The competition for housing and opportunity for jobs became fierce. While Restrictive Racial Covenants legally segregated and kept the racialised "Other" in their place, leisure and recreation spaces socially and unofficially served to reinforce this legislation.

The need to socially maintain racialised spaces was so strong that a single White man was observed throwing rocks, one of which hit Eugene in the head as he attempted to tread water with a railroad tyre. Immediately after Eugene Williams was killed, the police officer on duty did not arrest this man, but instead arrested a Black man who breached the colour line in anger at what took place. The police

were becoming an even more effective tool for White Supremacy in the city of Chicago in this particular way at the time, both in looking the other way when a crime was committed upon someone Black and in making an arrest when someone racialised as Black did something remotely illegal. The violence escalated at the beach to the point that one man was immediately shot by police, but this violence swiftly moved to the neighbourhood areas in "The Black Belt", the predominantly Black South Side of Chicago. The defence, as much defence as could be possible from the legions of vigilantes, police, and military actors of this neighbourhood, fell into the hands of many of the Black veterans of World War I. The offence to those neighbourhoods was through the organised activities of working-class Irish teens and adults of the ethnic social clubs who entered the Black Belt to kill and to destroy property, and who performed the vast majority of the riotous actions (see Figs. 1.18 and 1.19). Many of these clubs functioned as "street gangs" sponsored by the heavily Irish-represented police for the sake of youth outreach, mentorship, and guidance. Of the many gangs that were involved, one was the Hamburg Social and Athletic Club, in which a future mayor, the then 19-year-old Richard Daley the Elder, was a member. The beach and the Lake were contested spaces where Black people transgressed where they shouldn't have and incited "pure" and newly accepted White anger and violence (Chicago Commission on Race Relations, 1923; Johnson, 1922; Sandburg, 1919).

An official city commission was formed, and a report was published. Within the 722-page *The Negro in Chicago* report, a South Park commission unequivocally stated, "the parents were opposed to race contacts in swimming and wading-pools. "Not 10% of the families will allow contact with Negroes in the pools…" (p. 288). The commission also acknowledged that "voluntary racial groupings and serious clashes are found mainly at places of recreation…large parks, beaches, and recreation centers" (p. 297). And lastly, the commission recommended "1) additional facilities in Negro areas, particularly recreation centers…[and] 4) efforts by such directors to repress and remove any racial antagonism that may arise in the neighborhood

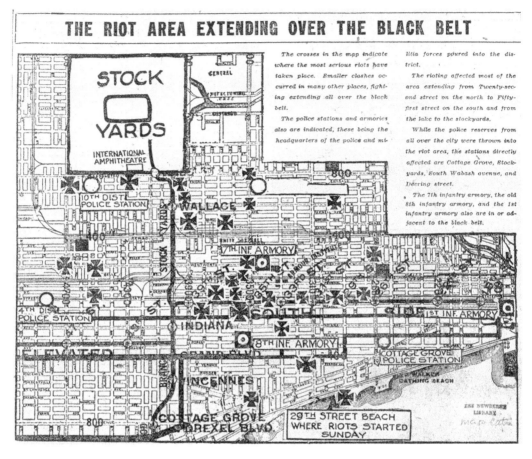

**Fig 1.18** The Riot Area in the Black Belt During the 1919 Chicago Race Riot. (The Newberry Library)

about the park" (p. 297). The commission, the Mayor William Hale Thompson, and Illinois Governor Frank Lowden failed to address the actual reason for the riots by limiting the focus of the entire report on the actions of unnamed White hoodlums and Black transgressors from named parts of the city.

The report also failed to capture the electoral politics and rivalries that were also occurring during the time between Thompson and Lowden. Lowden, a Republican, was attempting to extend his party's control over the city of Chicago as well as bolster his personal aspirations for the 1920 U.S. Presidential election. The riot was also used by Thompson to sully Lowden's reputation by pretending that the Illinois Army National Guard never arrived when they should have. In reality, they were never called, and Thompson watched as his city was on fire and bodies laid on the ground. "Big Bill" Thompson, also

a Republican and the last Republican mayor that Chicago has had (and will likely ever see), sought to block Lowden's rise and nomination, and was ultimately successful by raising the question if "Governor Lowden was a 100 per cent American" ("Mayor Thompson", 1919). The report made no mention of these factors, aims, and subplots and spent far more time creating a narrative of a new type of segregated Chicago in order to keep people ethnically safe and in their confined areas. The only remedy or recommendation was to construct more racially segregated facilities and to heap the entire responsibility of curbing racial violence on potentially sympathetic recreation directors.

The increased construction of segregated facilities and sites was far more important than the reconciliatory and reparatory work of rebuilding Black communities that had been devastated first by the

**Fig 1.19** The Locations Throughout the City, Well Beyond the Black Belt Where Violence Took Place During the 1919 Chicago Race Riot. (The Chicago History Museum)

vigilante acts of White citizenry and second by failed official government administration. Just as the police were used as a tool of White Supremacy, so too were the riots. The racial order had to be maintained at all costs. Thus, space, if conceived in the Mazúr and Urbánek (1983) way as an emptiness or something that requires filling in, becomes a supplement to power. Space is something to enhance power, its qualities, and the authors of its control and conscription. Space and land are the locations in which the execution of power can be planned out. People are arranged into a space through various forms of management. People are granted permissions and clearances to move through that space through various forms of privilege and enforcement. People are grafted with allegiances to conceptions of that space through various forms of mediated imaginations. Even the notion that space begins with an emptiness indicates the power and expression of the State to render something from nothing. There was something before it, there can be something that exists alongside it, and there could be something else in its place. But the State wipes these realities away and begins with the space as some empty land awaiting dominion. Space is a locational schema to be used as an instrument to make the State and State power real. The Space produces this, our reality, and then reproduces it over and over again with every red light in traffic, every rental agreement that is signed, every curb cut planned on the street, every building constructed, every footstep of the populace going to and from work, and every dead body that lays on the ground and is outlined with chalk or tape. Space is the constitutive element of our lived experience that dictates what our identities are through the roles and behaviours that are acted and enacted in its spatiality. Space deconstructs who we could have been in order to construct us into who we should be, and for what purpose we serve that is in the best interest of the State. Through the space of the city, "the state has strengthened and reinforced ethnicity by creating a shared ethnic consciousness to coincide with the territory covered by the State itself" (Slowe, 1990, p. 91).

It is filled with the politics of Race and the legalities in maintaining the racial order. Space, in the form of the waters of Lake Michigan, is a site for the socially constructed force of Race to be wielded, preserved, and made tragically punitive. The erection of the signage to articulate this power does not go away with the signage's removal. The city used a riot to create new markers for the divisions in the city. Where the Chicago River was once the dividing line for Irish and German immigrants from their Protestant and Nativist fellow Chicagoans, now the line was moved down to 22$^{nd}$ Street or 29th Street, where the McCormick Place now stands. The line would move again during the 1960s even further south. The line helped to determine where development and abandonment would be managed and orchestrated. Where equitable resources went to Hyde Park's growth, the neighbourhoods around were strangled. Where equitable resources went to the North Side's prosperity, the neighbourhoods of the South and West Side were hastened to poverty. During the 1919 Chicago Riots, it is estimated that while 38 people were killed with 537 injured, thousands more lost homes – damage to property that was sometimes due to children with their adult scholastic mistresses from settlement houses supervising their damage as a seemingly experiential city field trip (see Fig. 1.20).

Municipal resources that were inequitably distributed, employment opportunities that were now facing closure, exclusionary policing that led to inequitable arrests, bias in court deliberations that certified property claims that could never develop into the return of certain neighbourhoods, and the relegation to underfunded public education had all become hallmarks of the City, but most importantly, via the use of the 1919 Chicago Race Riot and a new type of spatial arrangement it devised (a spatial arrangement legacy that is being challenged principally by the present-day Chicago 1919 Race Riot Commmission and its memory work through tours, public education campaigns, and memorialisation initiatives). And this is what is lost with our public memory, analysis, and understanding of the 1919 Chicago Race Riot; it isn't so much an example of forgotten history as much as it is an example of a perverted history. The background of the intentionally stoked ethnic divisions, the State sanctioning of selective violence, and the use of the violence for both personal gains and policy enforcement are never in our conception of the historical event of the 1919 Riot. The 1919 Chicago Race Riot teaches us the lesson of the 1855 Lager Beer Riot in creating the professional police force in the city that leveraged the aspirations of an all-too-willing Irish immigrant in assimilation. The 1919 Chicago Race Riot also teaches us of what would become the lesson of the use of the two 1966 and the two 1968 Chicago Riots to engage in stronger intelligence-derived enforcement strategies in cultivating and knowing a populace. But the 1919 Chicago Race Riot teaches us to also situate the Chicago Railroad Strike of 1877, the Haymarket Massacre, the Pullman Strike of 1894, and the Memorial Day Massacre of 1937 as the basis for clearance to use deadly force on those who strike, were present at a strike, and were representatives of a striking populace. The 1919 Chicago Race Riot

teaches us, by re-thinking the Airport Homes Race Riots of 1946, Fernwood Park Race Riot of 1947, Englewood Race Riot, Humboldt Park Riot of 1977, and the aforementioned Division Street and Chicago West Side Riots of 1966, that neighbourhoods are the distilled site of conflicts, and they will either be abandoned or protected at all costs depending on the value of property within those neighbourhoods or what is near them. And lastly, the 1919 Chicago Race Riot teaches us, by the political protests in the 1968 Democratic National Convention Police Riot, the Days of Rage in 1969, the Chicago NATO Summit Protests of 2012, and what are now labelled as the George Floyd Protests of the Summer of 2020 in Chicago, that to fight back against violence and repression will cost you dearly (see Fig. 1.21 and Fig. 1.22).

**Fig 1.20** White Children and Adults Outside the Home of a Black Family They Had Set on Fire During the Chicago Race Riot of 1919. (The Chicago History Museum)

## 1.7 A Geography of Threat

Was the 1977 protest over the closure and potential demolition of the South Shore Country Club and Park successful in its aims? Eh…maybe. In some ways, it galvanised a group of citizens and community organisations to challenge private and public interests. In other ways, it provided that group of citizens with the possibilities of their own will and moral indignation. The buildings and space did become public spaces through their acquisition by the Chicago Park District, and eventually the Club was turned into the rightly heralded South Shore Cultural Center. But is a protest ever truly successful? Not really. Not in the direct way that a State power listens, responds favourably, or ostensibly changes hands in terms of power over the fate or future of a city. In this regard, the protest also lost, as you can read thoughts and opinions of present-day viewers on the YouTube posting of Daley the Elder's 1968 press conference. Posted comments from the Summer of 2020 hailed Daley the Elder and called for his resurrection as the type of mayor to handle the protestors and rioters that disgusted them in Summer 2020. The same Daley, who at age 19 ran

with his police-sponsored social club and rioted upon Black families and their homes, became president of this same social club only three years later, and he slowly became a virtual king of Chicago and "kingmaker" to U.S. Presidents.

But the 1977 protest was successful in that it gave us – it gave me – a glimmer of hope to begin to think enough was enough at a stomping young age. Everyday people have long cared about the places that they inhabit, that the State has dictated where they could inhabit. This care, that is both a human need and an implied role of the citizen, also opens an alternative thinking than what is set by the State. But it is how those places and spaces are managed that dictates what their condition will be and not the wishes and whims of those everyday people who may occupy those spaces. This authority falls not into the hands of residents, but into the hands of bureaucrats, city administrators, political representatives, business interests, and chambers of commerce. A beautified neighbourhood and a ravaged neighbourhood are designed spatial outcomes located on a map that is placed on a table in some dusty board room, not the marks of intelligently or unintelligently responsible citizenry. And their

**Fig 1.21** George Floyd Memorial at the Intersection of Chicago Ave. and E 38th St. in Minneapolis, MN, June 18, 2020. (Photo Credit: Lorie Shaull of St. Paul/ Wiki Creative Commons)

purposes are to reify the social order through bene-volence or violence onto the territory of the natural and built environment.

A geography of threat receives the violence that is dispatched with impunity. A change of group and geography begets different reactions and actions. Criminality begs for the call for lethality, from the public, the media, or the government. Criminality and lethality are the ways Orlando Patterson (1982) and Lisa Cacho (2012) describe how the State distinctively takes on *social death* functions. Policing beyond just traffic stops, helicopters and heavy assault units are deployed with precision. The street stop and the detaining of individuals if they are within certain communities is the State controlling the behaviour of its populace. The detaining of individuals who do not belong by both State actors and sanctioned vigilantes can be seen through the case of the violent assault of Sureshbhai Patel of India in Madison, AL, in 2015 and the tragic death of Trayvon Martin of Stanford, FL, in 2012 after being stalked under the auspices of the National Neighborhood Watch. The search and seizure and the raid are merely offshoots of the stop and detention in a public space. The search and seizure is a violent work in a private space. The use of raid tactics upon Remarley Graham of New York, NY, in 2012 in the bathroom; Aiyana Stanley-Jones of Detroit, MI, in 2010 while laying on the couch probably waiting for her grandmother to bring some Kool-Aid; and Breonna Taylor of Louisville, KY, in 2020 after having been awakened in bed, after a long day at work or being intimate with her partner, each reflect more than the actions of officers but rather targeting of a neighbourhood for a certain type of policing and a certain type of governance – and the serving of an order for eviction with force, as was the case of Eleanor Bumpurs of Bronx, NY, in 1984. The violence in policing that has caught our attention has been the geographies of in-between places or places that have already undergone gentrification-based changes. The police have long been dispatching people to otherworldly lands of Valhalla and Tartarus for years in their segregated neighbourhoods away from the general public eye. The reality and fiction of "crime" and disease call for repressive reaction and action.

How do we conceptualise a geography that is intended to be threatened and is most pronounced within cities? Moving past a focus on these incidences of exclusionary and selective state-sanctioned violence from the vantage point of the victim, the focus moves toward the working mechanisms in a city that commits the violence. This focus as well as engagement with a range of connected and seemingly not connected cities proffered a consideration that in cities operated within a "contrapuntal geographical" landscape – where exchanges in methods, techniques, resources, and even personnel were shared in efforts to maintain their respective order – crises and the realities of "crime" and disease at the local level were replaced with a greater emphasis on those manufactured and scripted manifestations at the global level, across cities and States. The moral panic of September 11, 2001, and now COVID-19 beginning in late Fall 2019, came to represent nearly 10 years of a shifting geo-political landscape between States bracing for a period of water shortages, shrinking resources, decreased capital, and crumbling infrastructure. A lone geographer, Rupal Orza (2007), incorporated Edward Said's (1993) close analysis of a shared U.S., British, and French hegemonic dominion of a global swatch of territories as "contrapuntal". However, instead of outright seizing territories and forcing developing States to capitulate, Orza (2007) theorised in this global "War on Terror" that the use of the crisis had created new "contrapuntal geographies of threat and security" to manage opposition while managing surplus populations and the joint global extraction mechanism.

This "contrapuntal geography of threat and security" rests on the legacy of "geographies of deracination" (Gahman & Hjalmarson, 2019). As Vergara-Figueroa (2018) explained, *deracination* is the political foundation that encompasses "diasporas, exiles, holocausts, cleansings, and genocides that different societies have known through their histories" (p. 17). Gahman and Hjalmarson (2019) situated this explanation of deracination "as a socio-spatial process of (de)territorialization and forced (dis)location that operates...as a social relation of domination" (p. 109). Through a political scientist lens, Ashley Dawson (2006) centred Mike Davis's

(1998) "ecology of fear" that had been orchestrated within Los Angeles and placed it within the international setting of the cities in South Africa. Where a notion of a "geography of crime" has long been a discussion within the field of geography and elsewhere in academia, the philosophical basis of what "crime" is has always been flawed, so researchers chart the geographies of arrests and the deployment of force, which has always been racialised and gendered (with the additionally false idea that there is a societal consensus to this fear throughout the edited volume of Evans & Herbert, 1989). Additionally, some of those same researchers admit to a propensity for studies to label certain behaviours and populations as deviant, which thus legitimises actions within an even more problematic "geographies of social control" (Lowman, 1989).

Opposition from a dissenting populace can be isolated into hinterlands, but it is best to engage in constant dispossession and re-concentration tactics within borders, territories, and city limits as geographies of fear under strict and exclusionary rule of law (Dawson, 2006). Warfare should be avoided in favour of administrative oversight of managed organised abandonment to strangle opposition through regulated violence work that secures extraction. Where Orza (2007) read across three particular States (the United States, Israel, and India), the work here is to read across a larger grouping of cities of the world and their respective histories. This commitment to committing violence is steeped in history through geography, the killing spaces that are high lighted in *Geographies of Violence* (Doel, 2017). And where Dawson (2006), within conceptions of a "Geography of Fear", highlighted the need to examine the network of cities within a State, the work here is to examine such a network within and beyond any given State. However, under this rule of the State through its cities of domination there lies a possibility, a hope that comes from the transnational solidarities of struggle against suffering and misery in the cities of dispossession and extraction (Erakat, 2020). In considering each of these cities and their respective histories of managing threats, a clustering of significantly radical and/or critical books on the particular formation of cities provided additional insight into particular cities and their functioning as

colonial, imperial, and apartheid cities. But even more importantly, this clustering of radical and/or critical city texts in geography, city and urban planning, urban design, architecture, anthropology, sociology, law, and history aided in confirming the need for such a conceptualisation across cities.

The insights of the historical-political legacy of cities were gleaned from various texts and highlighted: the necessary biopolitical concentration of peoples as a form of management in a city in Daniel Nemser's (2019) *Infrastructures of Race: Concentration and Biopolitics in Colonial Mexico*; the racialised basis for architecturally designed and city planned use of infrastructure in Irene Cheng, Charles Davis, and Mabel Wilson's (2020)*Race and Modern Architecture*; the systematic and government-conceived use of techniques to use segregated populations as forms of urban dispossession in Carl Nightingale's (2012) *Segregation*; Robert Adelman and Christopher Mele's (2015) *Race, Space, and Exclusion*, and Richard Rothstein's (2017) *The Color of Law*; the gendered shifting of access and mobility within cities in Chris Booth, Jane Darke, and Susan Yeandle's (1996) *Changing Places: Women's Lives in the City* and in Leslie Kern's (2020) *Feminist City*; the limited and specific role of the city in Richard Schragger's (2016) *City Power,* and the expansive and schematic project of the State in James Scott's (1999) *Seeing Like a State*; fostered by greater global desires for extraction, the intentional creation of megacities and megaslums in Mike Davis' (2017) *Planet of Slums*; within the very policies of the cities, whether explicitly or implicitly, the plans for crushing neighbourhoods for the sake of the idealised Society in Jane Jacobs' (1961) *The Death and Life of Great American Cities*; examination of the long, fraught, and violent histories of cities in their founding, growth, and continued functioning in Walter Johnson's (2020)*The Broken Heart of America: St. Louis and the Violence History of the United States*; the suppression of dissent and transgressions in Daniela Gandolfo's (2009) *The City at its Limits*; and, the realities of a long and protracted road in challenging present-day social formations of death-dealing in favour of emancipatory social forms of life-giving in David Harvey's (2009)*Social Justice and the City* and Don Mitchell's (2003) *The Right to the City*. But all roads of such city-level insights and interests begin with Du Bois' seminal text, *The Philadelphia Negro: A Social Study*, for me. This ambitious and nigh Herculean effort sought out to study the quality of life of nearly 40,000 Black residents of Philadelphia in 1899. And while it is principally a field-influencing sociological study in which 9,675 Black Philadelphians in over 2,500 households were interviewed, it begins with pages upon pages with rich historical archive work charting the history of the city and its organising of the Black neighbourhood areas in the 7th ward. It concludes with a positing of the meaning of all of this, that the class, gender, and Race problematic realities of the city are truly "the old world questions of ignorance, poverty, crime, and the dislike of the stranger" (Du Bois, 1899, p. 385).

Each of these texts formed the foundation of a tabulation of cities that an ideological connection could be conceived to then re-examine those texts and other texts on specific topics of colonialism, imperialism, state violence, and other areas of study to pose a conceptual linking thread. The geographic and spatial arrangement of the populace within cities and the responses to that populace reveal contrapuntal practises of demographic management through carefully identified populations; that are then skilfully associated with cultivated crises, moral panics, and other types of ginned-up threatening concerns; and coalesce into seemingly isolated methods of violence onto selected populations, once a historical and macro-level perspective had been removed. Cities have a story to tell, but they are not the stories of individualised upbringings in the conditions that have crafted through intentional design, organised abandonment, and selective and exclusive violence.

## 1.8 Geographies of Threat, Cities of Violence

During the bustling day, and the slumbering night, cities breathe their deep breaths. The living city is not a fictional Gotham filled with a caped crusader and other heroes defending it from the likes of petty criminals, mob bosses, and psychopathic arch villains. Nor is the living city an innocent happenstance marvel of the engines of ingenuity. People work and live within the city, but the construct of the city does not serve the people. It breathes and exhales whether the people do or not. In fact, it seemingly thrives off that precarity, the business bustle and the baton beating. The city serves the State. The living city is a product of the exercising of State power to focus potential, whereupon its geographic reach maps the lives and lived experiences of its diverse residents. But the living city is also the location in which State power is exercised upon and through its citizenry, where within its geographic boundaries (and non-boundaries) those same diverse residents are subjected to or protected from the violence of maintaining the social order. Thus, the endeavour here begins with the city as the cultural text of study: how does it feel, how does it function, and what does it mean (in its experience and operation)? Walking on pavement, observations of policing, and the social interactions between the housed and the unhoused all become lines on pages, images to capture, or activities to make note of, in order for the city to be read. The city, a city, and cities are all read as a singular socio-political historical formation. And in this study of the city as the text, dispossession and extraction are read upon its infrastructure, conception, and cultural form.

Why the focus on cities? Cities serve the arguments in this conceptual journey in *Geographies of Threat, Cities of Violence* in two ways. First, the city that is inclusive of the idea of a city (small cities, big cities, port cities, administrative centres, metropolises, and capitols) is used as a governing concept for the organisation of spatial arrangements and social structures in the public sphere (streetscapes, parks, schools, hospitals, businesses, and residences). These social structures exist as well in the suburb, village, town, or township/berg at a reduced scale, but the development and usage of each of these reduced geographic arrangements are done in consultation with the idea of the city. And while this first basis is clear and potentially more obvious, it is the other basis for the use of the city in this book that is most relevant. The city is the primary objective of any nation-state; the city is the ultimate articulation of the State. In my opinion, suburbanisation is clearly the creative attempt to create "new cities" away from or place proximate to old cities in order to si-phon resources away from cities that have been overpopulated by undesirable, disposable, and surplus populations and to consolidate power (and not just organise social structures) in that suburb, temporarily. Consider cities like Atlanta that transitioned from "The City Too Busy to Hate" to "The City Too Busy Moving to Hate" in the matter of a decade, as thousands of White Atlantans moved their families, taxes, and resources to the suburbs and diverted State resources to those same suburbs and away from the city (Kruse, 2005). Additionally, the maintenance of rurality in settlements, like the village and town beyond the city, also indicates a subscription of preventing those locations from ever building enough power to became focal points for State power, and thus they remain in a form of pseudo-Stateless reliance (the need for manufacturing companies or prisons to be proximate to them in order to prevent decimation). Lastly, the city as it is conceived provides a working structure for a concentration of populations that functions under an authority and power of governance. This is why Ruth Wilson Gilmore's (2008) discussion of prisons as constructed dead cities is vital or why military bases and compounds are often organised as closed cities with an adjoining military town to serve them (Touchton & Ashley, 2019). A city is both the cause and the effect of the material conditions of our realities. Cities are the forts of White Supremacy that provides the space for the citadels of patriarchy.

What power does the city have? The city regime is the militarised budget of the State. Power to levy and collect taxes, to manage revenues from the modes of production, to organise labour in living quarters for daily work, to discipline labour from ever striking at ownership, and to contract and expand its reach and physical presence into the landscape of the natural environment. While this expansion via consolidation or suburbanisation can be looked upon as an issue of sprawl, what is also occurring is the strangling of resources in the "old" city and the "old" city residence (disposable populations). The "new" city is invested in until the "old" one has been strangled enough to force the disposable population down through generational policing and displacement. The "new" city is

unambiguously a temporary space, because the "old" city still rests on years of city capacities and infrastructure (sewage, public works, proximity to seats of authority). The city is the pseudo-territorial State that governs settlements whether they are real, imagined, or self-determined. With the city, capital

> did not need to have a representation of itself laid out upon the ground in bricks and mortar, or inscribed as a map in the minds of its city dwellers…it preferred the city not be an image – not to have form, not be accessible to the imagination, to readings and misreadings, to a conflict of claims on its space – in order that it might mass-produce an image of its own to put in the place of those it destroyed. (Clark, 1984, p. 32)

The city is the final imagination of dispossession and extraction that began with the occupation of indigenous lands (in a colonial context) and the lands of the commoners (in an imperial context). With the occupation of land, land became a territory under dominion and authority. Indigenous and commoner populations are "removed" and reconstituted as free and unfree labourers for the purposes of extracting resources as capital is accumulated. The settlement is the next thread in imaginative destruction of the physical world, where the occupation has been sustained and expanded into a thriving, designed society. The settlement grows, and grows, and grows and becomes village, then town, and then eventually the city. And the lessons of the oldest "manual" for this sequence in domination, the 1573 *Laws of the Indies*, become the primary text of study and analysis that directs the logic in articulating what a geographic arrangement and management of threats is, as best represented by the production of the city. The city, the city planning process, and the general plan in administering a city heavily derives from this text as it formed the process to engage in discovery, settlement, and pacification (Mundigo & Crouch, 1977).

With a city, the State can generate the energy (materials produced, revenue from taxation, levying federal funds, attracting big business) that determines the reasons why violence is used upon populations that are deemed threatening to its social functioning. The urban infrastructure is bank-rolled in a way that can establish segregated housing, employ 24-hour policing of that housing with a police force, and construct locations to direct and not direct resources. The stakes are greater in the State than in a suburb, village, town, or township/berg; thus, the social control manifests itself in more vicious ways. Extending the logic of Joy James' (2007) *Warfare in the American Homeland* and Micol Seigel's (2018) *Violence Work: State Power and the Limits of Police* as the impetus of warfare-based policy enforcement in cities and applying a critical re-interpretation of Orde Kittrie's (2016) *Lawfare: Law as Weapon of War*, the State uses lawfare to legitimise violence through the creation of a particular classification of workers but within the geographies and contours of society. Violence workers do violence, but they mostly operate with the threat that they can muster through the authority given to them and they are allowed to exercise through the effectiveness of legalistic lawfare to protect those actions without the need for outright warfare. The State employs a class of workers as police from the potentially dissenting populace, with the perception that they are but servants of the modern civil society. But these violence workers instead function as officers of the State that, once deployed, solely serve the State in opposition to the ideals of a civil society. For these violence workers, the city is simultaneously the canvas of a map and the factory floor for them to work their craft. Through the legalities of lawfare, the city is the locus of the delegitimising of a population through legislation and legal systems in order to repress dissent in civil society in opposition to oppression. It is the intentional dysfunction of city management that leads to exposure to toxic waterways; the organised abandonment of identified areas of a city that develops into the decrease or absence of city services; and the exclusive use of police forces upon selected neighbourhoods, all under legislative and legalistic protections.

My extension of these conceptualisations is the spatial examination and discussion of this lawfare and warfare, and what I am calling "The Geographies of Threat" in order to use that same geography to do their abandonment and violence. I extend violence work because that line of work needs the threat to profit, person, and property for the escalation of that type of work to happen. It happens on a small scale or in incremental effects in response to the threats to profit, person, and property. As Gahman and Hjalmarson (2019) indicated, an analysis of deracination is "socio-spatially contingent and context dependent, and must be mindful of time (history), place (geography), and the politics of alterity/difference (identity) (p. 109)." However, this analysis is from the perspectives of the effect of such geographies onto peoples of the world. The analysis here is to conceptualise the affective function of the geography of a city. The conceptual structure of **The Geographies of Threat** is, thus, threefold:

1. **The Identification of Populations**

- Maps, census and demographic data, and other categorisations that report and notate a classification of a population provide seemingly benign indicators of income range, household worth, racial composition, ethnic demography, language clusters, and gender percentage. Yet, maps, data, and other categorisations serve as the tools to identify, categorise, and concentrate the populace.
  Examples include historical maps of the colonial cities and the cloistering of populations in imperial cities. Maps in the present day also show the continued usefulness of this knowledge and identification as shown in the maps commissioned by Daley the Elder of the different ethnic settlements living in conclaves in the city of Chicago from 1870 up to 1950 (see Figs. 1.14, 1.15, and 1.16).

2. **The Identification of Threats**

- Maps turn into policies and statements that direct zoning actions in/for spaces that will instil submission, acceptance, and cooperation. These policies and statements reflect the combination of private and public interest in curtailing certain segments of a population, and from cutting those geographic concentrations from city services when plans for clearance and removal have been determined.

    ◦  Examples include the use of coded language of "dirty", "unsafe", "violent", "savage", "beastly", etc., where threats are identified and forces are deployed in zoning ordinances, surveillance methods, and strategic planning implementations over the span of decades by the works of leading architects and city planners at the behest of city councils. The maintenance of coded language continues to crop up in gentrification and new urban development initiatives that never result in favourable outcomes of selected neighbourhood areas.

## 3.  The Identification for Violence

• The social acceptance of policies grants the State additional authority in issuing orders to quell revolt, silence dissent, and exploitatively manage costly dereliction and disorder because the specifically identified portions of the populace have been identified as a threat. Once a group has been culturally identified as the "Other" through both media practises, policy declarations, and the outcries of the conditioned public, the deployed forces have been given clearance and discretion to do a range of actions with the use of a range of tools. But immediate force deployment ensues quick death; slow death requires a violence from the pen.

    ◦  Examples include the public housing unit, the ghetto, the reservation, the Favela, the Mediterranean strips of land, the township, and the settlement as locations for management of violence work, the execution of lawfare, and management of current and future riots. Just as the press conference of Daley the Elder after the April 1968 Chicago Riots gave the order to "shoot, maim, or injure" anyone and anywhere who sought to fire a building (see Figs. 1.15, 1.16, and 1.17).

The abolition of slavery (the "first abolition") prompted an evolution that turned a slave into a criminal (the 13th amendment to the Constitution). The 13th Amendment discontinued the enslavement of abducted Africans and breeding of African Americans, but also prevented any other group from being placed in forced bondage, which would have been a likely future if slavery had not ended. The Black Codes, debt peonage, convict leasing, and mass incarceration solidified Black criminality but warranted a police state for all citizenry as the tools for fostering that myth of criminality (the inheritably genetic psycho-social structures of Race) birth eugenics that justified sterilisation and population control of any labelled undesirable trait population. So, from Reconstruction up to 2020, the settler colony of the United States has been in the long struggle of the second abolition, from criminal to a citizen or the abolition of criminality – the abolition of lethality in society, to finally make amends for the wrongs of society in developing a system of threat identification for the sake of violence. Part of this effort is legislative, and another part of it is in infrastructure, which forms the basis for studying the geography of State power. But this is getting way ahead of myself.

    This violence that must be abolished is actualised for those deemed disposable (the basis of class), oppositional (the basis for gendering), and "criminal" (the basis for racialisation). The disposable, oppositional, and "criminal" are threats that must be regulated or eliminated at all costs for the rightful social order and proper functioning of the State. For the classed "Other", the city itself manages their disease, dirt, and stink from highbrow noses of the bourgeoisie, petite bourgeoisie, and bourgeoisie-aspiring working class. It is best to keep the refuse among the refuse. The gendered "Other", the very nature of domination, invokes a masculine principle that necessitates the constant suppression of those who physically represent the oppositional principle, even if they work to support the status quo of the State. Hidden corners, dark parking lots, and long alleyways encourage the busy and chilling work of assault. And the "criminal" "Other" must be identified, surveilled, detained, arrested, caged, and killed, with killing always an option to jump to at a moment's notice. For this racial "Other", the police are always lurking somewhere in the geography of a city – lurking to do their work of violence.

The concept of "The Geographies of Threat" is based on the ways that the State (government, political appointees, private interest) constructs the space of a city to do the work of classifying, racialising, and gendering a population. On one hand, it is to dictate the mobility and actions outside of work hours and the abiding citizen conduct to ensure proper production of materials inside work hours. And when society produces excess, surplus people who are not needed in the limited available of forms of labour, surplus people have to be tended to. This surplus population is a threat to the functioning of society because they drain the already limited resources that are available. And in their lack of productive and usefulness they also become dangerous threats to the social order since they have no order to govern them. But on the other hand, space is used to regulate the formation of unions between workers by enhancing the perceived differences with residential difference. This unification is also a threat to the social order. Violence is used as a tool to dictate and regulate through the maintenance of spatial separation and public congregation.

Class, conceived as the combination of income, occupation, education, and lifestyle, modulates the violence. Wealth migrates violence away from happening to you, and poverty ensures it is always directed toward you. Karl Marx once articulated that the engines and landscapes of capitalism turned "the Black" into a slave (Robinson, 1983). The extraction of labour depends on some form of authority and oversight; thus, capitalism requires constant command to instruct and guide that labour to create surplus value and accumulate greater amounts of capital. Marx posed the conception that capitalism is contingent in its existence because it is, and since it is, it can be defeated. It is contingent upon a real, living history and not contingent upon the supernatural, the vague, and the impossible. It is contingent upon the social arrangements in society, and because of this, it can be broken. But the site of that breaking point is also the site of governance and repression. The dependency on labour is its lust, dependency, and undoing. Friedrich Engels (1972) extended this and explained that the intentionality of

enslaving societies with agrarian and matrilineal traditions was at the initiation of the patrimonial engines that produced capitalism and the Industrial Revolution with colonialism and slavery. The sites or geography of class conflict are not just the factory floor and the factory, but the very land that the factory has been built upon and now occupies.

Gender is not organised geographically in the same way as Race. Neighbourhoods are not cordoned off like for income and Race, but while it is not organised geographically, it is organised in the schema of the geography. Types of employment are and can be gendered, and as a consequence, neighbourhoods could overwhelmingly spatially be comprised of specific types of gendered women (working class single parent, women-headed household based on income, older/senior homeowners, or women of colour). Thinking intersectionally must be far more than representational identity, but instead the very real and very dangerous histories and geographies of colonialism, capitalism, and patriarchy. The city is a State container for various properties, both in the infrastructure of buildings and other facilities and of the body that is in possession of those gendered as men. Thus, buildings and people are both commodities, servicing and serving purposes of extraction and wealth accumulation. The experience of a gendered woman in a city is one of constant assailing appropriation – appropriation of one's conduct, one's look, one's body, and one's life. Patricia Hill Collins's (2000)*Matrix of Domination,* while oftentimes understood as a precursor to Kimberlé Crenshaw's (1995)*Intersectionality*, puts the emphasis on the experience of being dominated through a matrix of domination (Race, Gender, and Social Class), or interlocking systems of oppression, that may serve as analyses for self-empowerment but also require us to begin with the point and nature of oppression and not the identity that is being oppressed. There is one structure of domination, and this articulation focuses our analysis on performance of domination rather than focusing on separate systems that are dominant through individual experiences.

Domination also calls upon nuanced responses to that domination, whether it is to fight for survival (protest, riot, and strike), to flee for survival (i.e., the Great Migration), or to mediate/negotiate survival

(Joy James' concept of the *Captive Maternal*). Each of these responses are never seen as feminine and maternal responses to domination; they are for defence and not for offence. And this response reflects a guiding principle in the ways to understand the function of gender as opposed to reflecting on gender experience specificity. The captive maternal was my mother modelling a form of protesting against the demolition of self-determined important infrastructure on my brother, my father and my behalf. The captive maternal was also my father working two jobs in order for us to live and survive long enough to awaken ourselves to respond to our condition. The captive maternal also was my mother and my father being in an early cohort of Black residents moving into South Shore for improved opportunity while risking safety from White homeowners and risking dignity from their discrimination. Notions of mothering is gender non-conforming for subjugated populations, as "those most vulnerable to violence, war, poverty, police, and captivity; those whose very existence enables the possessive empire that claims and dispossesses them.[…]Captive Maternals can be either biological females or those feminised into caretaking and consumption" (James, 2016, p. 255).

Cities are gendered, because patriarchy has gendered them. Cities are not self-gendering social arrangements that result in a (fabricated) Society of sexism. The city is space filled with property and filled with zoned restrictions based on the expectations of familial production and gendered divisions of labour. The city provides the State with an accommodating site to produce and construct a Society, a fabricated-Society, that aids the continued ethnic consciousness of the populace but also in the assigned gendered expectations of each individual in the Society. The single-family unit and mortgage co-signer are not work of the actors within real estate agencies or banking institutions. For the problem of sexism in the fabric and geography of the city, "lay neither (or rather not solely) in the gender composition of its practitioners nor in the gender blindness of its subject matter but at the theoretical and analytical level" (McDowell, 1993, p. 161). Control, access, and ownership dictate the ways in which the gendered woman moves through spaces and moves through cities. Women as labour producers and the producers of people only further intensify the subjugation of the body and womb, not just as commodities that are made at the site of production. And as divisions of labour lean upon the surplus production of the racial "Other", the children of colour born from mothers are relegated at birth into positions of service unless they are bestowed with traits that garner their advancement to elite and ruling classes. Cities are gendered, but they are also racialised, and for indigenous women, Black women, and other women of colour, this means both specific and varied types of restrictions and affordances (Watson & Scraton, 1998). The concept of *spatialised feminism* extends dimensions of radical feminism in response to power and within the collective action of dissent in the geography of a city. As Aitchison (1999) explained,

> spatialized feminism refers to feminist analysis which identifies and explains the spatial dimensions of power relations between the sexes. Spatial dimensions can be viewed as including the differential use, control, power and domination of space, place and landscape for social, economic and environmental purposes. (p. 25)

Stuart Hall et al. in 1978's *Policing the Crisis* succinctly posited that Race is the modality in which class is experienced, and the divisions of labour can be expanded. Slavery was a class position that came to define a racial position, commodities producing commodities. Race is always relational, but it also has always been geographical. The distance between us must be physically created and brutally enforced. And the State must legislate and enforce that distance. Thus, the State is between us. A control of the means of production is the control of land, because land is the location or space for production. However, this control became most effective once the labourer no longer controlled the production of their craft and thus the value of the product. Once labour itself was what was priced, then the wage regulated the value of the person. The means of production was now in the control of the shop owner, the landowner, and the State. This is even the case in the contemporary illusionary tech industry. Regardless of the perceived digital and virtual world, those worlds still need a programmer sitting in a chair and a server housed in a building on a plot of land that is acquired by a company owner, sold by a real estate agency, financed by a bank, and zoned by a city. Power works through the control of production, property, and the land in which it needs to extract wealth. By extension, gender is also a modality for the experience of class as well, but it is also a modality for the management of class. How I situate such an understanding within the conceptual structure of the "Geographies of Threat" is that class is far more than the combination of lifestyle, education, and income from work. Race and gender flushes out what we understand class to be in the workplace and marketplace conditions, the public and private spheres of a fabricated-Society. Race and gender are the reason why class assists in furthering the conflict at the site and crux of the divisions of labour (between owners and workers). It is insufficient to simply have wealth and income representing the dividing line, as the mere division of a paycheck could be overcome and assist in the unification among the broad working-class citizenry (since the majority of the populace works). However, if racial and gender and differences are exacerbated and used as buffer classes, then unification will always be tenuous, and so a re-imagined union is nearly impossible to attain. Thus, the presence of the State is also in us and works within our imagination of the fabricated-Society that has been given rather than the one that can be imagined. The intersections of oppressions are also the intersections of murders that become intersections of memorials, when we need the intersections and the oppressions removed (see Fig. 1.21).

The problem with the 20th century is the colour line, as described by Du Bois. But this is not a symbolic line, but a literal line in the physical space. Rituals of Race performance occur in the geography of a city. As such, this discussion is to postulate that the items of urban and cultural geography (parks, schools, streets, and art districts, etc.) are sites of *racecraft*: 1) the articulation of power; 2) the erection of places of demarcation; and 3) reification of the Racial order. This discussion serves as "an interdisciplinary [analysis] of the relationships between people, places, and environment" that is needed in looking at the racialised, gendered, and classist geographies in the built and nature environment managed by people (Aitchison, 1999, p. 21). Race, as articulated by Karen and Barbara Fields in their 2012 seminal work *Racecraft: The Soul of Inequality in American Life*, "race stands for the conception or the doctrine that nature produced humankind in distinct groups" even if the science of natural selection, biological order, and genetic heredity was flawed and proved false (p. 16). Children learn how to colour, but colourism is not racism. Colourism just allows for the future ease to process racism as actors on behalf of the State, to locate tools for splitting cities, and to effectively hoard wealth based on selective criteria. Adults, and not children, construct the real-world lines in the colouring book of the city and insert the numbers of what colour to use for every block, neighbourhood, and community.

"Racism refers to the theory and the practise of applying a social, civic or legal double standard based on ancestry (Race), and to the ideology of such a double standard", which is both cold and emotionless (absent of hate) in operation because it is a collective social action not an individual act of preference (p. 17), thus making *racecraft* the "mental terrain and pervasive belief" (p. 18) that is the "social alchemy... that transforms racism into race" (p. 262). *Racecraft's* purpose is achieved through concealing the connection between structural inequality and racism and "disguising collective practise as inborn individual traits", the focus on the racist as opposed to a system and processes of power (p. 262). While bodies are rendered racially, it is the spaces they inhabit that are demarcated for dispossession and extraction as the truer articulation of racism; it is within the perceptions of space and place that the domains of *racecraft* are best understood (Mowatt, 2019). Racial discrimination, contemporary and historical, only gets at the point of refusal and the time of mistreatment in work and daily life. Racial discrimination does not (nor can it) reckon with the disproportionate "death by cop" of Black, Brown, and indigenous people while also overlooking the sheer amount of death by cops of any and all citizens, including cops. The inherent failure in these definitions is that the repetitive use of racism (so defined) makes Race look real (biologically, naturally, and historically). But racism is not power and privilege, prejudice and belief, or treatment and discrimination. Racism is, and ought to be, conceived in the "Geographies of Threat" in three parts:

1.  To create and maintain socio-political division (and to prevent collective organising and action). This can be seen most especially in the very creation of the police/professional police in England and the United States between 1825 and 1855 in response to a) the needs in the colonies to suppress unionising and force work (Brogden, 1987; Vitalie, 2017); b) labour riots and strikes in the early mills and factories (Harring, 2017; Miller, 1977); and c) insurrections of enslaved peoples (Muhammad, 2019; Websdale, 2001);

2.  To create and maintain Whiteness as a functionary position based on a colour metaphor as Blackness/"Negro" is for criminality, Red/"Indian" is for savagery, White is for dominance ("Indian" throughout the book is only used for native or indigenous peoples of the Americas when sources or known laws specifically use the term, otherwise Native is used. East Indian and Indian without quotations is used in reference to peoples in the southern Asian continent). The very creation of eugenics for selective breeding for growth of those with desirable traits, and for the curtailing of birth rates of those with undesirable traits. Myths of criminality and savagery had to be created to justify mass incarceration and all that comes before and thereafter (Gilroy, 1982; Muhammad, 2019); and,

3.  To create and maintain slavery (forced work conditions) to ensure a steady flow of production; separation within and between the divisions of labour and ownership; and the furthest maximisation of revenues for personhood, profits, and property claims (Gilmore, 2007; Robinson, 1983). There is an economic basis for the state repression of Black people, not a racial basis. If it were racial, it would happen every day until Black people simply do not exist. It instead rears its head when economic interest is threatened (property) and economic development becomes threatening (growth). Blackness attracts the surplus extraction of value. Black is

classification of domination, and Black is a response to being dominated. The domination revolves around the modes of production and the material reality of the state. But all populations can become surplus due to the shrinking availability of jobs due to revenue greed.

Racialisation intensifies in its identification of different populations with the increase of the modes of production and rise of capitalism (re: Census categories). Race pictured by the individual subject is real, but this isn't an individual reality; it is a collective one. And therein lies the machinery of the programme. And that programme obscures an understanding of racism. A person who is racialised as White is not automatically supreme, since Race is not a natural occurring fact. The Irish were not in power in Chicago during the aforementioned 1919 Race Riot. Their role in the riot was just their membership fee to join the White Race because their role in the 1855 Lager Beer Riot reflected a different social status. Their membership was provisional, as it is for anybody that affirms the order.

But class produces a socio-historic bloc that can assume non-White populations in support of sustained dominance. Race transforms the action of racism into the aspect of the target (i.e., a person is killed based on the supposed "colour of their skin"). Race is an illusion resource because it keeps us looking at skin and other phenotypic features and not looking at space, the sites of labour, the restrictions in mobility, and the policies of extraction and dispossession. It can be leveraged by anyone to steer us away from the persons in authority, the profits that are being accrued, and the properties being seized and sold.

Where Race reifies the social order and racialisation intensifies in identifying a different population with the increase of the modes of production and rise of capitalism, sex regulates individual bodies to assigned roles of functionality and productivity, and gendering grows as space of the modes of production and division of labour expands. The conception of gender and the assigning of gender roles change across time, across societies, but also in response to the spaces that those societies take shape. But more importantly, the State and not the fabricated-Society (the social arrangements filled with customs of culture) is the true determiner of gender. This provides the impetus for the development of patriarchy, thought of here as the set of institutional structures (the ownership of property, property rights, the control of property, access to power, the holding of positions of power, the relationship to wealth, and the relationship to sources of income and the modes of production) that requires a dichotomous and unequal categorisation of gendered persons according to the early writings of Harriet Martineau and Anna Julia Cooper (Giles, 2006; Logan, 2007). Patriarchy is, in the conception of Acker (1989), the dual systematic oppression of women and the systematic elimination of outgroup men. The emphasis on the system begs us to locate the policies, enforcements, and coercions that make gender so. If the State is the determiner of gender, then the ways in which gender functions can be viewed through the populace's relationship with property, the spatiality of a city, and the mobilities of groups of individuals.

At the crux of this feminist spatial analysis of power lies the maintenance of the racial order of space and the protection of the White home. The violence in many ways is the maintenance of a spatial order and the maintenance of the extractive accumulation of wealth. And at the heart of these arguments was a stance that would give White women greater power outside of the home but at the cost of Black and other non-White lives. White women were imparted the cult of domesticity to feminise agrarian and home labour and remove this block of women in ethnic immigrant groups from allying more strongly with their gendered male counterparts and Black and other people of colour. In many ways, Race is what is gendered. Women of colour were never afforded such a "cult" because their ongoing labour in the public sphere necessitated their continued work in both spheres. But if they were included in the creation of the cult of domesticity then another form of unity could have ensued a rupturing of the home and the factory. Instead, White domesticity sets up new allies to affirm the power of the State, as it was seen the rallying cries of White suffragettes who lobbied against the would-be Black Lyncher as Ida B. Wells noted in the late 1800s to the early 20th Century (Wells, 1894). Within the colony of the United States, only "Black women listened, organised, and acted on the theses…" of Ida B. Wells and others, according to Carby (1985),

> …but very few White women responded to their social critiques…a transformed woman's movement, purged of racism, would have provided a liberating experience for White women themselves. But racism led to concession, to segregated organizations, and, outside the antilynching movement, to a resounding silence about – and therefore complicity in – the attempt to eliminate Black people politically, economically, and indeed, physically. (p. 272)

In the eyes of some gendered women, the protection of the home and property was/is far more important than the destruction of patriarchy. White women and others have been conditioned to see the wrong of White women being placed into forced reproductive labour in the fictional *Handmaid's Tale,* not the near extinction of Black people and the extermination of Indigenous peoples, while also the mass displacement, incarceration, and enslavement of Black people, particularly Black women as a security force for the handmaid's in the book is utterly absent in the TV Show based on the Atwood novel. In the present day, much attention is given to the travails of Greta Thunberg on the issue of climate change. While this work of speaking to various entities throughout the world is just and necessary, our ascribed singular narrative focus fails to acknowledge the numerous other youth and adults, particularly of colour, who do the same without focus or fanfare but also with more serious realities to environmental racism and ethnic cleansing. What is masked in the fanfare is the serious risk that gendered girls and women of colour face in challenging systems that benefit from oppression, in thinking of the 2016 assassination of the Honduran environmental activist and organiser Berta Cáceres and twelve others since 2014. The direct threat to extraction of natural resources, capital accumulation, and the control of natural spaces was the basis for the State-sanctioned response to Cáceres and others.

The 1800s division of the types and places of work in the private sphere of home chores and in the public sphere is of factory work, eliminated the ability of two labourers to pool and combine incomes for a range of opportunities (greater social mobility, creation of an independent business, unified home vote for elections). During the late 1700s, the census articulation of a racial category of slave and White assisted in splitting the efforts of insurrections and rebellions that were against the private interest of factory and farm owners as well as the growing State. In the present day, it is lost on us that low wage work is predominantly comprised of women labourers, and thus low-income neighbourhoods are also predominantly comprised of women (single, single mothers, women-led homes based on job). As James (2016) pointed out,

> In transitioning a colony through a republic into a representative democracy with imperial might, the emergent United States grew a womb, it took on the generative properties of the maternals it held captive. Western democracy, based in American Exceptionalism, merged Enlightenment ideologies with Western theories to birth a new nation (a nasecent empire) that fed on black frames... Still, it is not their victimization that marks them; it is their productivity and its consumption. Throughout history, Captive Maternals provided the reproductive and productive labor to stabilize cultural and wealth. (p. 256)

Despite this collective reality, gender is elusive to collective organising against the State as the co-optation of any collective reaction and organising of women are often blocked by class divisions of labour occupation (income and status attainment) and the other modality of class, Race. Policing is performed out of a need to maintain the division of gender (sodomy laws, miscegenation, immigrant women labour strikes, women suffrage activists, class hierarchy, racism hierarchy) but at the individual level between the racial "Other" and those who may consider Race suicide (not birthing, not mothering, not wedding for the promulgation of the "Race"). Power and rulership in society, especially State power and city home rule that manages the lives of women often evolve into reductionist accounts of everyday social life that seem to stand outside the

operations of White Supremacy, patriarchy, imperialism, settler colonialism, and capitalism, and this is what this ideological conceptualisation of "The Geographies of Threat" is also attempting to reconcile.

## 1.9 A Conclusion

If Race and gender are truly social constructions then they are neither the preferences of individuals nor the arbitrary classifications of a small group of people, no matter how influential they may be. Yes, the social constructions of Race and gender are the stuff of systems, as Du Bois taught us in the late 18th Century. But what is argued here is that those social constructions are utterly dependent on the way that space is produced to make those social constructions true functional realities and long-serving histories. *Geographies of Threat, Cities of Violence* (the book) and "The Geographies of Threat" (the threefold conceptual structure) through three chapters focus on the history, the design, and the society of the city and how each serves as the basis for what lies between people along the long road in the abolition of our present reality and in re-imagining new socio-political practises that can foster the democratic possibilities that have always been denied to so many by the prevailing geographies of threat. However, upon greater scrutiny, abolition is insufficient in dealing with a colonial legacy and a colonial present. The book dwells within the confines of anti-colonialism. The book aims to examine and question the purposes of the occupation of space and exertion of force within the space of a city. The book seeks to situate violence performed by State actors (police shootings/deaths) and civilians (lynchings/Race "riots") in the context of the structures, streets, and public spaces of a city. The book pursues a possible thread of logic that connects these functions and the roles that they have played in maintaining instability in living complete lives for those deemed disposable, "criminal", and oppositional to the State.

Lefebvre's (1991) *spatial triad* alludes to the second type of space: space of the conceived (*l'espace conçu*, "representations of space") that is composed of both the governed and the imagined, the institutionalised and the othered. This effort,

being undertaken through the ideological conceptualisation of "The Geographies of Threat",
serves to expand the field of geography but also the
articulated geo-spatial function of class, gender, and
Race. This effort takes Neil Smith's (1990, 2005)
notion of *deep space* into the intended non-
geographical socio-spatial theories that then re-
spatialises what class, gender, and Race really are in
the fabricated-Society, the basis for the creation of
threats with the intended purpose of violence to
maintain the order. This results in more intense
population management, first through organised
abandonment and State repression. Threats in geography – articulated explicitly as such – have only
recently been invoked in literature in the field of
geography but in relationship to the analysis of State
discourse on dealing with racialised religious populations (Orza, 2007) and with the geospatial constitution of subjugation within transnational
relationship through the use of border restrictions
imposed by borders, and the struggle against borders
(Mitchell & Kallio, 2017).

Without being situated in space, the realities of
class, gender, and Race would wither away or remain the stuff of ideas. Without the reaffirming
powers of physical space, the processes of classification, racialisation, and gendering would not
work. They would just be ideas that would drift
away nearly as quickly as they are conceived and
uttered. But with these processes that are affirmed
in concrete cement, mortar, and brick, they gain
permanence and power over our life experiences.
They are the cages that shackle any liberating
imagination. But in my opinion, this is the something that is missing in our analysis of geography,
urban planning, and place-making as well as our
analysis of class, gender, and Race. Just as Baldwin
made us think about how it feels to be around
"White" folk, I do not want to get at how it feels to
be in "White" cities/spaces but to instead arrive at
how those "White" cities want us to feel, move,
function, and die. We go to a rally, and then we go
home to our subjugated territories, and if the physical space remains, so too does our oppression.
What was introduced here will be explored as we
move throughout the book. Women should not be
seen outside the home. People of colour should not
be seen on the streets. The poor should not be seen
at all. The empty street or road, the deserted
parking lot or park, the dimly lit alley or stairwell –
what we consider to be public life belongs to gendered men. What we consider to be public space
belongs to racialised White people. What we consider to be public-produced good belongs to the
State. People love the stuff of conspiracy theories in
fantasising big things that dictate our lives and
disrupt our free will. But people do not love the
study of the minutia in the use of highways, roads,
streetlights, alleys, parks, cul de sacs, and country
clubs for power. In 1977, the minutia was present
in the image of a protest, but the long history of
State power was very much there in that image as
well. And to think, all of our worries, our concerns,
our issues, our problems, and our suffering is by
design and not by nature. Something is between us.
Between the possibilities of a world that can be
imagined by the populace and not the State.
Something is most emphatically in the way of things
in my town, in your town, in any of our towns and
cities (see Fig. 1.22).

"Abolition geography starts from the homely
premise that freedom is a place".
– Ruth Wilson Gilmore, 2017, from "Abolition
Geography and the Problem of Innocence" in
Johnson and Lubin's Futures of Black
Radicalism, p. 227.

"..., in Salvador
where the blood will never soak
into the ground, everywhere and always
go after that which is lost.
There is a cyclone fence
between ourselves and the slaughter and
behind it
we hover in a calm protected world like
netted fish, exactly like netted fish.
It is either the beginning or the end
of the world, and the choice is ourselves
or nothing."
– Carolyn Forché, 1981, from "Ourselves or
Nothing" in *The Country Between Us*,
pp. 58–59.

**Fig 1.22** "My Kind of Town", Taken During the Protests to the 2012 NATO Summit That Occurred in Chicago, IL. (Photograph Taken by James Watkins of Jim Watkins Photography)

## References

Acker, J. (1989). The problem with patriarchy. *Sociology, 23*(2), 235–240. 10.1177/0038038589023002005

Adelman, R. & Mele, C. (2015). *Race, space, and exclusion: Segregation and beyond in metropolitan American.* Routledge.

Aitchison, C. (1999). New cultural geographies: The spatiality of leisure, gender and sexuality. *Leisure Studies, 18*(1), 19–39. 10.1080/026143699375032

Anderson, P. (1976). The antimonies of Antonio Gramsci. *New Left Review, 100,* 5–78.

Bachrach, J. S. (2001). *The city in a garden: A photographic history of Chicago's Parks.* Center for American Places and the Chicago Park District.

Beck, L. (2007, June 5). Beijing to evict 1.5 million for Olympics. *Reuters.* https://www.reuters.com/article/us-olympics-beijing-housing/beijing-to-evict-1-5-million-for-olympics-group-idUSPEK12263220070605

Brogden, M. (1987). The emergence of the police—The colonial dimension. *The British Journal of Criminology, 27*(1), 4–14. http://www.jstor.org/stable/23637268

Booth, C., Darke, J., & Yeandle, S. (Eds.), (1996). *Changing places: Women's lives in the city.* Sage.

Cacho, L. M. (2012). *Social death. Racialized rightlessness and the criminalization of the unprotected.* New York University Press.

Carby, H. V. (1985). "On the threshold of Women's era": Lynching, empire, and sexuality in Black feminist theory. *Critical Inquiry, 12*(1), 262–277. https://www.jstor.org/stable/1343470

Carlos, J. & Zirin, D. (2011). *The John Carlos story: The sports moment that changed the world.* Haymarket Books.

Centre on Housing Rights and Evictions. (2007, June 5). *Mega-events, forced evictions and displacements.* The Centre on Housing Rights and Evictions.

Chandler, C. (2002, April 4). Shoot to kill…shoot to main. *The Chicago Reader.* https://www.chicagoreader.com/chicago/shoot-to-kill---shoot-to-maim/Content?oid=908163

Cheng, I., Dais, C. L. & Wilson, M. O. (2020). *Race and modern architecture: A critical history from the Enlightenment to the present.* University of Pittsburgh Press.

Chicago Commission on Race Relations. (1922). *The Negro in Chicago: A study of Race relations and a Race Riot,* Map. The Newberry Library Collections.

Chicago Commission on Race Relations. (1923). *The Negro in Chicago: A study of Race relations and a Race riot.* The University of Chicago Press.

Chicago Public Library. (1997, September). *Coalition to Save the South Shore Country Club* Archives. City of Chicago. Chicago, IL. https://www.chipublib.org/archival_post/coalition-to-save-the-south-shore-country-club-archives/

Chicago Riot Study Committee. (1968, August 1). *Report of the Chicago Riot Study Committee to the Hon. Richard J. Daley*. City of Chicago, Office of the Mayor. Chicago, IL.

Cholke, S. (2015, March 17). Funds to restore "Blues Brothers" filming site nixed by Gov. Rauner. *DNA Info*. https://www.dnainfo.com/chicago/2015031 7/south-shore/south-shore-cultural-center-loses-25m-restoration-work-from-state-cuts/

City of Baltimore. (1911, May 15). *Ordinance 692*. The City of Baltimore.

Clark, T. J. (1984). *The painting of modern life: Paris in the art of Manet and his followers*. Thames and Hudson.

Coit, J. S. (2012). Our changed attitude: Armed defense and the new Negro in the 1919 Chicago Race Riot. *Journal of the Gilded Age and Progressive Era*, *11*(2), 225–256. 10.1017/S1537781412000035

Collins, P. H. (2000). *Black feminist thought: Knowledge, consciousness, and the politics of empowerment* (2nd ed.). Routledge.

Crenshaw, K. W. (1995). The intersection of race and gender. In K. Crensaw, N. Gotanda, G. Peller, & K. Thomas (Eds.), *Critical race theory: Key writings that formed the movement* (pp. 357–383). New Press.

Crooks, J. B. (1968). *Crooks, politics, & progress: The rise of urban progressivism in Baltimore 1895 to 1911*. Louisiana State University Press.

Cuadros, A. (2016, August 1). The broken promise of the Rio Olympics. *The Atlantic*. https://www.theatlantic.com/international/archive/2016/08/building-barra-rio-olympics-brazil/493697/

Dardick, H. (2020, August 6). Record $926 million flows into controversial Chicago TIF districts, more than a third of city property taxes. *Chicago Tribune*. https://www.chicagotribune.com/politics/ct-cook-county-chicago-tif-district-report-20200806-7wh5 hc7mxzctfackoi4nkefjsq-story.html

Davies, J. C. (1962). Toward a theory of revolution. *American Sociological Review*, *27*, 5–19.

Davis, M. (1998). *Ecology of fear: Los Angeles and the imagination of disaster*. Henry Holt.

Davis, M. (2017). *Planet of slums*. Verso.

Davis, P. (1968, April 15). Mayor Richard J Daley's "shoot to kill" comment to reporters. Getty Images. https://www.gettyimages.com/detail/video/after-the-chicago-riots-following-the-murder-of-martin-news-footage/665646748

Dawson, A. (2006). Geography of fear: Crime and the transformation of public space in post-apartheid South Africa. In S. Low & N. Smith (Eds.), *The politics of public space* (pp. 123–142). Routledge.

D'Onofrio, J. & Wall, C. (2020, August 14). Chicago police flood downtown with 1k officers this weekend; Lightfoot releases plan to protect businesses, neighborhoods after looting. *ABC 7 Chicago*. https://abc7chicago.com/chicago-looting-police-mayor-lori-lightfoot-cpd/6370260/

Drucker, P. (1999). *Management challenges for the 21st Century*. HaperCollins Books.

Du Bois, W. E. B. (1899). *The Philadelphia Negro: A social study*. University of Pennsylvania Press.

Engels, F. (1972). *The origin of the family, private property and the State*. In E. B. Leacock (ed). International Publishers.

Erakat, N. (2020). Geographies of intimacy: Contemporary renewals of Black-Palestinian solidarity. *American Quarterly*, *72*(2), 417–496.

Evans, D. J. & Herbert, D. T. (Eds.). (1989). *The geography of crime*. Routledge.

Fields, K. & Fields, B. J. (2012). *Racecraft: The soul of inequality in American life*. Verso.

Forché, C. (1981). *The country between us*. HarperCollins Publishers.

Gahman, L. & Hjalmarson, E. (2019). Border imperialism, racial capitalism, and geographies of deracination. *ACME: An International Journal for Critical Geographies*, *18*(1), 107–129.

Gandolfo, D. (2009). *The city at its limits: Taboo, transgression, and urban renewal in Lima*. University of Chicago Press.

Giles, M. S. (2006). Special focus: Dr. Anna Julia Cooper, 1858–1964: Teacher, scholar, and timeless womanist. *The Journal of Negro Education*, *75*(4), 621–634.

Gilmore, R. W. (2007). *Golden gulag: Prisons, surplus, crisis, and opposition in globalizing California*. University of California Press.

Gilmore, R. W. (2008). Forgotten places and the seeds of grassroots planning. In C. R. Hale (Ed.), *Engaging contradictions: Theory, politics, and methods of activist scholarship* (pp. 31–61). University of California Press.

Gilroy, P. (1982). The myth of Black criminality. In E. Martin & D. Musson (Eds.), *The Socialist Register* (pp. 19–19). Merlin Press.

Gotham, K. F. (2000). Urban space, restrictive covenants and the origins of racial residential segregation in a US city, 1900-50. *International Journal of Urban and Regional Research*, *24*(3), 616–633.

Gramsci, A. (1971). *La costruzione del Partito comunista 1923-1926*. Einaudi.

Gramsci, A. (1975). *Quaderni del carcere*. In V. Gerratana (Eds.), Einaudi.

Gurr, T. (1970). *Why men rebel*. Princeton University Press.

Hall, S., Critcher, C., Jefferson, T., Clarke, J., & Roberts, B. (1978). *Policing the crisis: Mugging, the state, and law and order*. Palgrave.

Harring, S. L. (2017). *Policing a class society: The experience of American cities, 1865–1915*. Haymarket Books.

Harvey, D. (2009). *Social justice and the city*. The University of Georgia Press.

Haynes, G. E. (1913). Condition among Negroes in the cities. *The ANNALS of the American Academy of Political and Social Science, 49*(1), 105–119. 10.11 77/000271621304900113

Hiller, H. H. & Wanner, R. A. (2016). Public opinion in Olympic cities: From bidding to retrospection. *Urban Affairs Review, 54*(5), 962–993.

Hoffer, R. (2009). *Something in the air: American passion and defiance in the 1968 Mexico City Olympics*. Free Press.

Hogan, J. F. & Brady, J. E. (2015). *The Great Chicago Beer Riot: How lager struck a blow for liberty*. The History Press.

Inglehart, R. (1997). *Modernization and postmodernization: Cultural, economic, and political change in 43 societies*. Princeton University Press.

(1855, February 26). Irish-rule, whiskey, Jesuitism, Pauperism, and crime. *Chicago Tribune*.

Jacobs, J. (1961). *The death and life of great American cities*. Random House and Vintage Books.

James, J. (Ed.). (2007). *Warfare in the American homeland: Policing and prison in a penal democracy*. Duke University.

James, J. (2016). The womb of Western theory: Trauma, time theft, and the captive maternal. In P. Zurn & A. Dilts (Eds.), *Challenging the punitive society: The carceral notebook, volume 12* (pp. 253–296). Columbia University.

Johnson, C. S. (1922). *The Negro in Chicago: A study of race relations and a race riot*. The University of Chicago Press.

Johnson, W. (2020). *The broken heart of America: St. Louis and the violence history of the United States*. Basic Books.

Jones-Correa, M. (2000-2001). The origins and diffusions of racial restrictive covenants. *Political Science Quarterly, 115*(4), 541–568. http://www.jstor.org/stable/2657609.

Keefe, T. M. (1971, September). Chicago's flirtation with political nativism, 1854-1856. *Records of the American Catholic Historical Society of Philadelphia, 81*(3), 131–158. http://www.jstor.org/stable/44210773

Kern, L. (2020). *Feminist city: Claiming space in the man-made world*. Verso.

Kittrie, O. F. (2016). *Lawfare: Law as weapon of war*. Oxford University Press.

Klein, N. (2007). *The shock doctrine: The rise of disaster capitalism*. Knopf Canada.

Kruse, K. M. (2005). *White flight: Atlanta and the making of modern conservatism*. Princeton University Press.

Lefebvre, H. (1991). *The production of space*. Blackwell.

Lenskyj, H. J. (2009). *Olympic industry resistance: Challenging Olympic power and propaganda*. State University of New York Press.

Lieberman, J. (2019, February 12). A palace for the people. *The South Side Weekly*. https://southsideweekly.com/a-palace-for-the-people-south-shore-cultural-center/

Lipset, S. M. (1960). *Political man: The social bases of politics*. Anchor Books.

Logan, D. A. (Ed.). (2007). *The collected letters of Harriet Martineau*. Pickering and Chatto.

Lowman, J. (1989). The geography of social control: Clarifying some themes. In D. J. Evans & D. T. Herbert (Eds.), *The geography of crime* (pp. 228–259). Routledge.

Mapping Police Violence. (2020, September 6). Police have killed 781 people in 2020. *Mapping Police Violence*. https://mappingpoliceviolence.org/

(1919, December 13). Mayor Thompson dubious on Lowden. *The New York Times*, 6.

Mazúr, E. & Urbánek, J. (1983). Space in geography. *Geojournal, 7*(2), 139–143. https://doi.org/10.1007/BF00185159

McDowell, L. (1993). Space, place and gender relations: Part I. Feminist empiricism and the geography of social relations. *Progress in Human Geography 17*(2), 157–179.

Miller, W. R. (1977). *Cops and bobbies: Police authority in New York and London, 1830-1870*. University of Chicago Press.

Mitchell, D. (2003). *The right to the city: Social justice and the fight for public space*. Guilford Press.

Mitchell, K. & Kallio, K. P. (2017). Spaces of the geosocial: Exploring transnational topologies. *Geopolitics, 22*(1), 1–14. 10.1080/14650045.2016.1226809

Mortice, Z. (2020, August 14). Chicago's 1855 "Beer Riot" is a bridge to the unrest of 2020. *Bloomberg City Lab*. https://www.bloomberg.com/news/articles/2020-08-14/in-chicago-unrest-echoes-of-a-1855-beer-riot

Moss, R. (1976). *The collapse of democracy*. Temple-Smith.

Mowatt, R. A., & Travis, J. (2015). Event planning, public participation & failure: A 2016 Olympic bid case study. *Revue Loisir et Societe - Leisure and Society*, *38*(2), 249–267.

Mowatt, R. A. (2019). A people's history of leisure studies: Leisure, a tool of Racecraft. *Leisure Sciences*, *40*(7), 663–674. 10.1080/01490400.2018.1534622

Muhammad, K. G. (2019). *The condemnation of Blackness: Race, crime, and the making of modern urban America*. Harvard University Press.

Mundigo, A. I. & Crouch, D. P. (1977). The city planning ordinances of the Laws of the Indies revisited. Part I: Their philosophy and implications. *The Town Planning Review*, *48*(3), 247–268. https://www.jstor.org/stable/40103542

National Center for Health Statistics. (2020, September 9). Weekly updates by select demographic and geographic characteristics. *Centers for Disease Control and Prevention*. https://www.cdc.gov/nchs/nvss/vsrr/covid_weekly/index.htm

Nemser, D. (2019). *Infrastructures of Race: Concentration and biopolitics in colonial*. University of Texas Press.

Nightingale, C. H. (2012). *Segregation: A global history of divided cities*. The University of Chicago Press.

Oliver, R. & Lauermann J. (2017). *Failed Olympic bids and the transformation of urban space: Lasting legacies?*. Palgrave MacMillan.

Orza, R. (2007). Contrapuntal geographies of threat and security: The United States, India, and Israel. *Environment and Planning D: Society and Space*, *25*(1), 9–32. 10.1068/d1404

Paes, E. (2012, February). The 4 commandments of cities. *TED*. https://www.ted.com/talks/eduardo_paes_the_4_commandments_of_cities?language=en

Palmer, L. F. (1969, February 26). South Shore divisions run deep. *Chicago Daily News*, 3–4.

Patterson, O. (1982). *Slavery and social death: A comparative study*. Harvard University Press.

Putnam, R. (2000). *Bowling alone: The collapse and renewal of American community*. Simon & Schuster.

Robinson, C. J. (1983). *Black Marxism*. The University of North Carolina Press.

Rotella, C. (2019). *The world is always coming to an end: Pulling together and apart in a Chicago neighborhood*. University of Chicago Press.

Rothstein, R. (2017). *The color of law: A forgotten history of how our government segregated America*. Liveright Publishing Corporation.

Said, E. (1993). *Culture and imperialism*. Alfred A Knopf.

Sandburg, C. (1919). *The Chicago Race Riots, July 1919*. Harcourt, Brace and Howe.

Scott, J. C. (1999). *Seeing like a state: How certain schemes to improve the human condition have failed*. Yale University Press.

Schragger, R. (2016). *City power: Urban governance in a global age*. Oxford University Press.

Seigel, M. (2018). *Violence work: State power and the limits of police*. Duke University Press.

Slowe, P. E. (1990). *Geography and political power: The Geography of nations and states*. Routledge.

Smith, N. (1990). Geography redux? The history and theory of geography. *Progress in Human Geography*, *14*(4), 547–559.

Smith, N. (2005). Geographers, empires, and victims. *Political Geography*, *24*(2), 263–266.

Touchton, M. & Ashley, A. J. (2019). *Salvaging community: How American cities rebuild closed military bases*. Cornell University.

Tuttle, W. M. (1996). *Race riot: Chicago in the Red Summer of 1919*. University of Illinois Press.

Verba, S., Schlozman, K., & Brady, H. (1995). *Voice and equality: Civic volunteerism in American politics*. Harvard University Press.

Vergara-Figueroa, A. (2018). *Afrodescendant resistance to deracination in Colombia*. Palgrave.

Vitalie, A. S. (2017). *The end of policing*. Verso Books.

Vogan, T. (2018). *ABC Sports: The rise and fall of network sports television*. University of California Press.

Watson, B. & Scraton, S. (1998). Gendered cities: Women and public leisure space in the postmodern city. *Leisure Studies*, *17*(2), 123–137.

Watts, J. (2015, August 4). The Rio property developer hoping for 1 $1bn Olympic legacy of his own. *The Guardian*. https://www.theguardian.com/sport/2015/aug/04/rio-olympic-games-2016-property-developer-carlos-carvalho-barra

Websdale, N. (2001). *Policing the poor: From slave plantation to public housing*. Northeastern University Press.

Wells, I. (1894, May 24). Sentiment against lynching. *The Parsons Weekly Blade*, 1.

Wideman, J. E. (2016). *Writing to save a life: The Louis Till file*. Scribner.

Wise, J. (2020, June 4). *Philadelphia Inquirer* reporters skip work after paper publishes "Buildings Matter, Too" headline. *The Hill*. https://thehill.com/homenews/media/501136-philadelphia-inquirer-reporters-skip-work-buildings-matter-too-headline

Wood, G. (2020, August 28). Kyle Rittenhouse, Kenosha, and the sheepdog mentality. *The Atlantic*. https://www.theatlantic.com/ideas/archive/2020/08/kyle-rittenhouse-kenosha-and-sheepdog-mentality/615805/

Zirin, D. (2009). *Brazil's dance with the devil: The World Cup, The Olympics, and the fight for democra*. Haymarket Books.

# 2.
# THE HISTORY OF THE CITY: THE IDENTIFICATION OF POPULATIONS

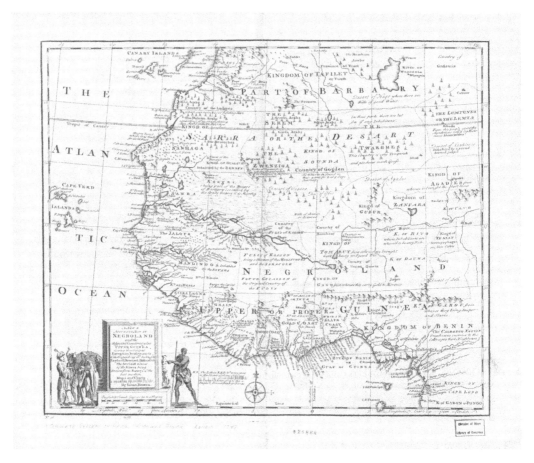

**Fig 2.1** "Negroland", as Identified on a Map of Settlements of Europe, 1747. (U.S. Library of Congress' Geography & Map Division – Digital ID g8735.ct010405/Public Domain)

"The census, the map, and the museum: together, they profoundly shaped the way in which the colonial state imagined its dominion – the nature of the human beings it ruled, the geography of its domain, and the legitimacy of its ancestry".
– Benedict Richard O'Gorman Anderson's (1983) *Imagined Communities*, p. 164.

DOI: 10.1201/9781003149545-2

"The map is the perfect symbol of the state."
– Monmonier, 1991 in *How to Lie with Maps,* p. 88.

It is often said that history has a way of repeating itself.

But why is this said? What truth is there to this statement? Or, an even better question, why do we cast aside a sense of truth for saying such things?

Our memories of the past, any past, are obscured by the salience of our present. In some way, we are looking for meaning to what we are presently experiencing. In another way, we are always looking for answers from others who might have experienced what we believe we are experiencing in the now. If we look back into the past, we think we see recurrences, and this validates our notion of the repetition of the cultural conception of time (Trompf, 1979). After all, "time does repeat itself". But this notion actually validates inaction, as we can simply "wait out the storm until it passes". Repetition also means there is a futility in acting, as what we are experiencing is bound to happen and is bound to (soon) be over. A notion of the cyclical nature of history satiates us and is appealing because it satisfies and instils in us thoughts that "this too shall pass". The "this" is whatever our current predicament may be – existential predicaments of mundanity, banality, inefficacy, incapacity, poverty, and carcerality. We are...

Sitting, rocking away on the top deck in the hull of a slave ship across the Atlantic.

Reading the newspaper as you see smoke from the fire coming from an entire district of your city in Tulsa, Oklahoma.

Cutting your hair and shopping for assimilation attire while massacres are happening in the Canadian provinces.

Rolling your eyes at the inability of someone to remember their address like you did as you filed into the cue at the entrance of a segregated ghetto in Berlin.

Turning away to catch a baseball as you can hear the screams from a family member in the distant barracks of a camp in Nanjing.

Adjusting the wiring of your TV set to catch the latest soccer match at the same time as gunshots can be heard at the check point into Gaza.

Shaking your head in admonition of someone else being tasered for not obeying the rules that you distinctively follow as you cross a border from México.

These things, all of these things, shall pass because they merely reflect history "repeating itself". Yes, they are terrible, but confronting them is a far more terrible idea to even consider. But I contend here that the comfort of historical recurrence is an engineered intent and a necessitated cognitive condition by the State that instils a sense of comfort in experiencing the worst of history through spatial arrangements that produce social acceptance and complicity. Whatever the State does today, no matter how harmful it is onto its populace, its populace will go back to their lives and to their work to maintain the order. And what is inherent in this notion of historical recurrence is that "the more things change, the more they stay the same". This breeds a logic of futility in the present through a pedestrian interpretation of history. Despite all our stories of great men and great women of the past, the present nor future needs them. Why waste one's time being more than what is needed? Mistakes cannot be avoided. Social positions cannot be reversed. Power cannot be transferred.

But power can be transferred. Social positions can be reversed. And mistakes can be avoided.

History does not repeat itself; it merely echoes. And this echo is not the confirmation that historical recurrence is real; it is confirmation that a power has yet again sought to maintain itself. This power, State power, that holds dominion over its populace is always concerned with maintaining its foothold on the control of its people. The very notion of historical recurrence is not the foretelling of ever-subjugated people of the past conveying to newly subjugated people of the present and a possible future, that everything will be alright because you must make the best of it. Historical recurrence is a tome that has pages upon pages, and footnotes within footnotes, added to it from the knowledge base of previous States that have passed on to current and future States in order to provide guidance in governance. As Harvey (2003) contended, "no social order can change without the lineaments of the new already being present in the existing state of things" (p. 16).

States and their power are tenuously temporary despite their expansive territorial awe displayed in map depictions of dominion, depictions that invoke a far reach and a merciless response to opposition. An old order gives way to a new order, and that change of hands or transfer of power is never pleasant and steady. Peer States that have been in competition will make transfer difficult because the pride that is lost while facing decline is embarrassing, but the true challenge comes from the masses of people who begin to respond to being violently and brutally governed.

History does not repeat itself, but the power of dominion always wants to repeat itself by maintaining itself. So, there is a caution with trying to understand and making contemporary analogies with historical events. There are no blueprint solutions in the past that we can glean and directly use for our current predicament. There are no blueprint solutions from the past that can easily deter us from plainly complying with our circumstance in the present. Through analysis and interpretation, by staying close to the texts of and about history, and staying close to the data of a source, we can arrive at a set of information, empirical indicators, or nodes of intersection. Thus, this chapter will create a conversation between past and present in order to further define the conceptualisation of the "Geographies of Threat", or more specifically the first stage in that conceptualisation, the **identification of populations** as understood through the history of settlements and cities – settlements of the colonial and later imperial powers of the world, settlements that will become eventual cities that these colonial and later imperial powers will deploy their best thinkers, best technologies, and best innovations to dispossess various populaces and extract untold amounts of resources (as depicted in the 1747 map of Western Africa; see Fig. 2.1).

Before we can locate and move through the other two stages of the **identification of threats** and the **identification for violence**, the **identification of populations** situates how we come to see distinctive groups in a population that will inform how they shall be managed and dealt with by the State ("Negroland"; see Fig. 2.1). This **identification of populations** can be seen through the processes and traditions of map making that were often sponsored by government and corporate interests. The **identification of populations** can be demonstrated by the collection of State census collections whether for just benign population enumerations, religious congregation donations, or for malicious population control measures. There is always a population problem rather than a governance problem, a wealth-distribution problem, or an access-to-resource problem. Population problems are naturally occurring phenomena that population studies "need" to solve (Carr-Saunders, 1922) without ever solving the State systems that make population growth untenable. And further, this **identification of populations** through map making and census gathering is created as a mechanism for categorical reporting that sets into motion methods to indicate occupational types, income and earnings, household numbers, and worth alongside the affirming of arbitrary racialised and gendered compositions of groups that were extended to other cultural markers of language and religion. This data, the percentages that are derived from it, and the areas of concentration formed from it, led to power maintenance. (State) Power repeats itself, not history.

But in the maps of European antiquity lie manifestations of power maintenance that have trickled down throughout the centuries. In the new maps of the current age lie old ontologies of the world and old ontologies of the people in it. State power lies in both of these historical lines of reality; it is the essence of the map in the making of the map, the use of the map, and the sharing of the map. How do we situate those who are within the locus of State power and those who are beyond it (and the lands that they occupy)? It is a bit naïve to perceive the maps of European antiquity as truly articulating curiosity or fears about the unknown – scared men with their scary maps that were setting out for the great, unexplored unknown. Instead, it is best to view the maps of European antiquity as representing the anxieties in marvelling at what was at the time controlled while also pursuing what was desired just beyond the reach of the colonial, and later imperial, State. The map did not bring the explorer onto shores, shivering in fear that then only haphazardly led to colonialism. The map served a practical role in guiding explorers of feudal-turned-colonial-turned-imperial States during uncertainty in journeys of conquest and served a symbolic role of identifying the known unknown to the heads of State to inspire further funding for these schemes of conquest.

## 2.1 Here There Be Dragons

But one particular map set the stage for serving both the practical and symbolic roles, the 1504 Mundus Novus (New World). Carved into an ostrich egg, this globe marked lands that had been charted from years of trade and engagement. This globe also bears one distinct warning in Latin, *HC SVNT DRACONES* ("Here Be Dragons" or "Here Lie Dragons"). We have told ourselves that this depiction of wild beasts and mythical creatures was from the imagination of cartographers who articulated the fears of sailors who returned from perilous voyages and of sponsoring orders of religiosity. We have told ourselves that these were meaningless embellishments of the overly religious and supremely superstitious – as we will tell ourselves anything in order to avoid an analysis of State power. Yet, throughout European antiquity from the Dark Ages to the Enlightenment this supposed warning failed to curb exploration and the conquest that followed. What is contended here is that "Here Be Dragons" was an early note of the

preparation for arms against the identified "Other". If one travelled there, one should be prepared for danger. Or, if one travelled there (some other land), one should do so to conquer those "dragons". The maps and globes reflected what had been conquered, and the edges of the maps with the inscription "Here Be Dragons" was an indication of where conquering had yet to occur (but conquering had to be done). The second oldest globe in European and United Kingdom tradition, the Hunt-Lenox Globe c. 1510 drew our attention to the earliest depictions of the newly encountered lands in what would be called the Caribbean, Central, and South America. Known for its artistry and detail, the globe is full of distinct information that could only have been contributed by interactions with sailors on numerous voyages. "Fear" had not stopped the sailors; it only drove them onward. The Latin phrase appeared in the Southeast Asian region on the globe (see Fig. 2.2). This descriptive function of the language that was used on these globes should draw our critical and radical criticism in the present. As Turnbull (2003) posed, globes and maps are an "argumentative system of statements" that reflect a cognitive schema. To think this cognition was the stuff of superstition in the past is to then dilute the political intent in their conception in the present. When a

**Fig 2.2** The Hunt-Lenox Globe With the Inscription "HC SVNT DRACONES", Here Be Dragons. c. 1510. (Photo Credit: New York Public Library)

globe was made (and are still made), a relationship was asserted between States, populations, and geo-historical phenomena.

The lingering meaningfulness of "Here Be Dragons" has still made its way into contemporary times and, in similar contexts, even into fiction. Season Two, episode 11, of the streaming sci-fi show, *The Expanse*, was titled "Here There Be Dragons". In the episode, two spacefarers were discussing what to do next when faced with the unknown territory, *terra incognita*, of a known unknown entity that could threaten human civilisation throughout the solar system. One character commented, "You know what sailors used to say when their ships past the end of their maps…time for a new map!", and the other character retorted, "no…here be dragons". The push for exploration for the sake of the Empire was met with caution about the things that could topple that mighty Empire. This was the fear of the end of the Empire, not the confrontation of wild beasts. Globes and maps provided control and order, albeit with the uncertainty of meeting a comparable force. A globe ordered the world under an Order. Globes and maps put all of nature in order, noting geological land masses and geographical landscapes. Nation-states, colonies, cities, and settlements were now placed alongside the wilderness, the wild, the desert, and the jungle. And like Turnbull (2003), the contention here was that globes and maps reflected a theory for that order. Globes and maps were (and are) not re-presentations of territory, but rather the representation of a conception of the territory, a "graphic representation that facilitate a spatial understanding of things, concepts, conditions, processes, or events in the human world" (Harley & Woodward, 1987, p. xvi). Maps turn land into territory. Even in the depiction of satirical blankness (see Fig. 2.3), a map can still convey meaning and challenge meaning. No "dragons" depicted, but there are "dragons" ima-gined. We struggle in viewing such a thing in our minds by filling it with what should be acceptable items littered across its empty space. Such a map conveys our cognitive conditioning by the State of what should be in a map that more profoundly reveals what is a map. A map is order.

Preceding the Hunt-Lenox Globe were maps that featured more dragons and more warnings

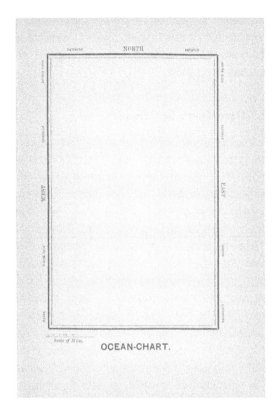

**Fig 2.3**  The "Bellman's Map" Ocean-chart from Lewis Carroll's 1874 *The Hunting of the Snark*. (Cornell University Library)

(Gods blowing merciless winds, great tusked mam-mals, people with faces in their stomachs). But yet again, these "fears" and "warnings" did not curb or end this period of exploitative exploration that was happening and would continue to happen for several more centuries. The Borgia Map (c. 1430) high-lighted dragons in Asia with warnings of the people who dwelled there, "*Hic etiam homines magna cornua habentes longitudine quatuor pedum, et sunt etiam serpentes tante magnitudinis, ut unum bovem comedant integrum*" ("Here there are even men who have large four-foot horns, and there are even serpents so large that they could eat an ox whole"). Other non-Christianised people were simi-larly depicted, whether from regions in present-day Ethiopia or the broader Middle East. Housed in the Vatican library and commissioned by the Vatican before Christopher Columbus, the map reflected the presumed warning alongside the indication of a sentiment of a population of people. A sentiment of non-human descriptors of peoples laid the ground-work for the need to seek conquest as they could become threats to the realm. Named after Cardinal Stefano Borgia, who was one of the key leaders in the Papal conclave of 1800 that also oversaw one of the final transfers of State power from the Papacy to the (Military) Nobility, the map was a part of a vast personal collection that the church had amassed. The outcome of the 1800 conclave also led to the crowning of Napoléon as emperor by Pope Pius VII and to the confiscation of the property of the church by French forces that was bolstered by the France dominion of Europe and beyond. The globe, alongside numerous other documents, was part of Borgia's personal collection centuries later, and the proximity and role in this eventual transfer of power should not be overlooked in this discussion of the relationship with these globes, maps, and State power.

Even predating the Borgia Map, the T and O Psalter World Map associated dragons as representations of sin (see Fig. 2.4, Fig. 2.5, and Fig. 2.6). In employing the biblical psalms as early as the 7th century, these maps would later add the names of Noah's three sons, Shem, Japheth, and Ham, in relationship with the three respective continents of Asia, Europe, and Africa. The

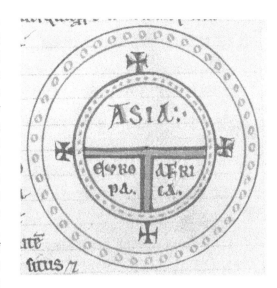

**Fig 2.5** (Middle) 12th Century Designed by the Bishop of Seville.

**Fig 2.6** (Right) Radkarte des Mittelaiters ("Circle Map of the Middle Ages") c. 1885. (Wiki Commons/Public Domain).

**Fig 2.4** Three Cropped Version of the T and O Psalter Maps: (Left) *Mappa Mundi* ("Map of the known World") in 1472.

three sons, and later the people descended from them after the Great Flood, were given designations:

Shem means "renowned", ...[Ham] means, "warm", and ...Japheth means "width", for from him were both the pagan nations.... (Isidore of Seville, 2006, pp.16–18)

Three continents held a position on the map orientated to the East (for Paradise) and not the North, with bodies of water around the continents and rivers forming the cross that divided this geography. With this map, we see even more intentionality in identifying populations and ascribing them with noted features and histories for later use. All lands were within the bounds of the royal-religious-nobility State.

The biblical Book of Genesis conveyed a story of how Ham saw his father, Noah, sleeping unclothed and chose to cover him after consuming wine and becoming drunk from the celebration for surviving the flood. Noah awakened in a fit of rage and cursed his son, and this curse henceforth left the mark of "Blackness" on the sons of Ham, beginning with Canaan. The passage and its interpretation would centuries later be used to justify African enslavement (Stanton, 1960), but from the 7th century up to the 13th century, it was an acknowledgement of the signified pseudo-difference of appearance of those residing in Africa. This difference would raise ire, and the curse would be extended to the designation of servitude to his brother's children (Goldenberg, 2003). This curse, and the travels of Ham and his sons into Africa, were the dominant notion that countered the other less popular idea among theologian scholars that climate and environment might have been factors for differences in complexion (Goldsmith, 1774; La Peyrère, 1655; Livingstone, 2002). de Montesquieu (1748) in particular set in motion an association and assessment within a geographical framework. His pseudo-analysis of laws and religion alongside features and customs determined that prolonged exposure to a climate left a permanent mark on the over-capabilities of the various darker "Races" to develop civilisation. Not only were a people relegated to being doomed, but also the lands that they had occupied or had come from. This moral judgement of populations and lands fostered the theoretical creation of "moral climatology" that was mobilised as a specific intellectual body of scholarship to enact processes of extraction (Livingstone, 2002). But this still rested on the

1400s foundation of limpieza de sangre (purity of blood) that socially constructed what will be Race and what to do with those people that have been racialised and stratified into a system (Israel, 1975), while the Papal Bull, as public decree initiated the entire colonisations of continents (Serrano y Sanz, 1918). Ransacking lands of certain people was the stuff of adamic-based State power, but laid within his analysis was also ransacking these lands of the stuff of those people, and that would be revisited in later years after the Church was no longer the dominant driver in State power.

In the meantime, as these debates continued, they also affirmed the strength of the period in which the Church was indeed the leading State power, and with this role the European Church geographically extended the biblical traditions to other parts of the world. Goldenberg (2003) highlighted that by the 15th century, the following was true:

> In sum, in regard to Noah's curse, four factors were at play during the first six or seven centuries of the Common Era [emphasis added]: *explanation* – an attempt to make sense of the Bible; *error* – a mistaken recollection of the biblical text [that Ham was cursed]; *environment* – a social structure in which the Black had become identified as slave; and etymology – a mistaken assumption that Ham meant "Black, dark". The combination of these factors was lethal: Ham, the [assumed] father of the Black African, was cursed with eternal slavery. The Curse of Ham was born. (p. 167)

Again, the concern or focus here is not on the sentiments of those who would create elaborate explanations of the "natural" and "factual" basis of Race, but rather the use of the signifier and identifier for more than purely indoctrination and enslavement. Many scholars have highlighted and critiqued how this passage and its interpretation served as an early justification for the racism of enslavement by forging the myth of Race. But the concern or focus here is how geography was the necessary implement used in enacting schemes. The map reveals "how Black and indigenous life...slows and interrupts White settlement" and revels in the possibility of violence that will be levied at the colonial and imperial inconvenience (King, 2019, p. 77). The geographic site of capture or enslavement to conduct the racialisation served a greater purpose, not the creation of "racist" sentiments or even the very act of enslavement. It served the purpose of an antiquated version of "extractivism": extraction of people for the purpose of wealth accumulation and extraction of resources from the lands that the people once inhabited.

The concern or focus here is on the knowledge of other lands beyond the State power of France, Spain, Portugal, and other European powers of the time, and how that knowledge evolved into increased efforts of dispossession and extraction for the purposes of accumulation. Thus, the additional concern or focus here is the usefulness of identification of those "Othered" people and their lands to execute this purpose. The *mappae mundi* from the 7th century was reproduced more than 600 times and laid the groundwork for how the world was conceived in order for it to be controlled. The engravings of Theodor de Bry furnished every explorer and conqueror with "concrete" imaginations of the Americas over a 44-year publishing period in order to "tame the savage mind" of the indigenous populations in these conquered lands (Beck, 2011). Later concepts of mestizo, Race mixture, racial deterioration, Race suicide, eugenics, and miscegenation within academic discussions found a mix of disgust and praise but also hid the usefulness of these early **identification of populations** through map making for the truer and more salient purpose of extraction and dispossession. The proclamations that these maps, these concepts, and the thinking behind them were racist is a limiting and reductionist analysis that forecloses the grander view that feudalism turned capitalism maintained the manifested power of State by making more precise the geographic viability of sites of extraction, dispossession, and ultimately wealth accumulation. It does not matter if the biblical Adam could be proven as real, much less whether he was African. Nor does it matter whether a solid argument could be found to un-justify the use of his ilk from generational servitude. Why Adam's children were placed on a map and the greater purpose for what was being done to them should be our concern. The very real actualisation of this purpose was the groundwork for the decline and

eventual end in no longer labelling faraway lands in such a way. As this decline occurred, so did the occurrence of the increased labelling of governed territorial hinterlands within the boundaries of the city and known State – and within those boundaries, the emergence of designated areas for population concentration within the settlements and cities.

In furthering the use of these cartographic tools for power maintenance, the invocation of elephants performed similarly symbolic functions to dragons as representational semiotic locations of the known unknown but also the precise locations of the racial "Other". Jonathan Swift, author of popularly known *Gulliver's Travels*, in *On Poetry: A Rhapsody* in 1733 presented another satire of the very real expression of racialisation for the purpose of continuing the theft of people and lands,

> "…So geographers, in Afric maps,
>   With savage pictures fill their gaps,
>   And o'er uninhabitable downs,
>   Place elephants for want of towns." (lines 179–182)

Just like the notion of dragons, we can equally be tricked into embracing the notion that placing elephants on maps indicated a lack of knowledge of certain continents like Africa (see Fig. 2.7) – or a wilful lack of knowledge that is performed in the produced map as the elephants are precisely over territories and subjects one ruled may not have been as necessary, so arbitrary titling sufficed. But once again, a critical lens would suggest that this was a State ploy hidden in plain sight. Oceans and seas no longer needed to be traversed as much as mountains and jungles. Even Swift in this particular excerpt conveyed more a disdain than the humorous satire that was expressed in the rest of the poem. Swift was critiquing the practice of map making by cartographers of his time, who fashioned these maps on behalf of their official sponsors. Africa was not truly unknown. Africa was already in the consciousness of elites and various European States as African enslavement had already become well actualised at this point. States were competing for the volumes of enslaved peoples they could capture. The State and business

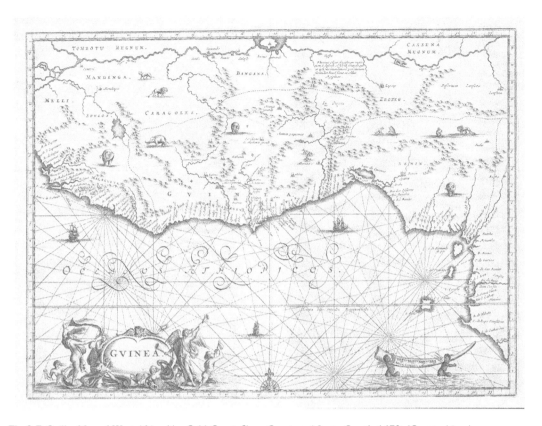

**Fig 2.7** Ogilby Map of West Africa (the Gold Coast, Slave Coast, and Ivory Coast), 1670. (Geographicus)

interests collaboratively funded construction of slave forts on the periphery of these continents and defended and secured strategic port locations for the frequent warehousing and shipping of this human commodity. The maps now aided efforts to go deeper within territories and to firm up the control of existing territories (see Fig. 2.8). The realities of privatised and State-organised commissions that wished to explore the continent further and convened to debate and discuss such matters cannot be reconciled by proponents of the unknown.

In 1790, James Rennell, a noted British cartographer, articulated to the Association for Promoting of the Discover of the Interior Parts Africa that,

But the public are not to expect, even under an improved system of African geography, that the Interior Part of that Continent will exhibit as aspect similar to the others; rich in variety; each region assuming a distinct character. On the contrary, it

**Fig 2.8** The Mitchel Map for the American Colonization Society's Map of the Liberia Colony, Depicting the Second Settlement City of Monrovia and Other State-Sponsored Colony Sites for Repatriated and Formerly Enslaved Africans, 1846. (Public Domain)

will be meagre and vacant in the extreme. The dreary expanses of [desert] which often surround the habitable sports, forbid the appearance of the usual proportion of towns...;. Little as the [Ancients] knew of the Interior Part of Africa, they appear to have understood the character of its surface; one of them comparing it to a leopard's skin. Swift also, who loses no opportunity of being witty at the [expense] of mathematicians, diverts himself and his readers both with the nakedness of the land, and the absurdity of the map makers. (Rennell, 1790, pp. 215–216)

Satire, criticism, and commentary aside, the map and the use of wild beasts in strange lands were strategic plans that foreshadowed European and British imperialism.

The dragon, the kraken, the lion, and the elephant were those beasts. The depiction of those beasts in the wild and faraway places beyond the territories of rulership, as dangers to the State, were eventually subsumed by the Empire. Those same beasts, if depicted within the kingdom, became the signs and symbols of ownership, might, and most importantly, wealth. The historical recurrence of power manifestation employed scientific accuracy in these maps merely as an additional advantage and benefit. The function of these maps and the beasts contained in them were more symbolic and theoretical, alluding to the plans of power. To maintain the State, those lands at the edges of our geography had to be explored; those beasts had to be confronted. The need to maintain the State power of any of the imperial powers had to be assured. This purpose of imperialism pre-dated Swift's satire, as elephants had been placed on maps depicting Africa since the Medieval period. To control the world, one must know it. And to know the world, one must in some way envision it by way of mapping, as Anna Neil (2002) posited that,

"savagery" is an invention of geography. Swift attacks geography as fraudulent learning, as a science that is always trying to cover the gaps and inconsistencies that it inevitably confronts by insisting on the barbarousness and barrenness of those regions about which it has little or no knowledge. Like the gaping lines of bad modern

poetry, geographers' texts are filled with fantastic figures that expose their authors' want of knowledge more than they reveal the real character of the places and peoples they purport to represent... Rather than accounting for some existing geocultural reality or providing reliable documentation about the kind of human beings to be found in a continent as enormous and unexplored as Africa, Swift points out, "savage pictures" are in fact the product of a dangerous modern ambition to map the entire globe fully and systematically. (p. 83)

## 2.2 White Town, Black Town

To map the entire globe fully and systematically is not a benign act of scientific accuracy. Precision and systematic processes aid the deployment of forces that maintain power. It is State power imagining itself in its splendour at the time of the creation of a map. And the more accurate map secured the State's future christening to the level of empire. Building from Rouse's (1987) conception of power,

Power has to do with the ways interpretations within the field reshape the field itself and thus reshape and constrain agents and their possible actions. Thus, to say that a practice involves power relations, has effects of power, or deploys power is to say that in a significant way it shapes and constrains the field of possible actions of persons within some specific social context. (pp. 210–211)

The map is a form of discourse that showcases language and symbols. In showcasing both, a signification of what the State has accepted as what is seen and known is coupled also with what the State has not tolerated as being unseen. Unknowns, empty spaces, and blank canvases cannot be tolerated. Unofficial, not sanctioned, and aboriginal names are not permissible. Indigenous names for certain lands, non-State language words for places, and non-European views on direction are encroachments to State power as they display another power. Thus, the State map in its naming, placing, and orientation is the subtle State power that is practiced in map production. The cartological and geographical documentation aided States to expand and become empire, and for those empires to control land across distance. Once again, land is turned into territory with the map. And on those lands, and in those territories, the settlement can become a city. It is this notion of the city that evolves from settlement as the arch-technique in cultivating the power of the State to eventually become an empire that supports the conceptualisation of the "Geographies of Threat". And it is with globes and maps that the settlement and the cities, and the State and the empire, are scholarly depicted, legislatively planned, and juridically managed.

If one State was not able to maintain its rulership and control, the maps passed through the hands of the fallen State to another rising State that was more than capable of controlling the faraway lands and maintaining power over populations. Law (1984) made note of the colonial lens of the world that was levied onto India by the initial power of the Portuguese State. The map was the key document to justify claims of control as well as provide guidance to emissaries venturing to and from the Empire (Tooley & Bricker, 1976). But it was the administration of the settlement-becoming-city that served, as I would contend, Law's "emissary class of device" (Diffie & Winius, 1977). While the police force, the Company army, and the Crown's military violence workers were the trained and drilled personnel to enforce law and rule (McNeill, 1982; Parry, 1963), the city was the device used to ground and actualise that law and rule. The perfecting of these three emissaries of State – documents (imperial and colonials maps), drilled people (violence workers), and device (the city of enclosure) –innovated the ways that empire-becoming States sought to grow in power (Law, 1984). Portuguese imperialism of India was divided into three administrative units in Daman (from 1559–1961), Diu (from 1535–1961), and Goa (from 1509–1961), the Estado da Índia Portugesa (the State of Indian Portuguese). The maps and administration through personnel effectively distanced and outlined the rulership of the Portuguese Empire while also making note of the competing British Empire's controlled territories and the locations of any Indian resistance. The

operations, in constructing fortifications since the 1400s, provided Portugal with a strength in managing its Empire, as it drifted away from broad land acquisition to central city form of rule over key geographical locations. Alfonso de Albuquerque, conqueror on behalf of the Portuguese Empire, made note in correspondence to the crown during the 1500s, "I beg your majesty to bear in mind that Goa is a grand place, and in the event of India being lost, it can easily be reconquered if we hold such a key [location] as Goa" (Christian, 1945, p. 141).

Some 521 miles away on the other coast of India, the British Empire was expanding and perfecting its own reach in the cities/Presidency towns of Bombay (modern day, Mumbai from 1618–1947), Calcutta (Kolkata, from 1612–1947), and Madras (modern day, Chennai, from 1640–1947) through trading companies and military force. With Madras (then known as Madraspatnam), the initial Portuguese presence through the port of Sao Tome in 1522 and later the added presence of the Dutch in 1612 in nearby Pulicat aided the British Empire once the city was taken. The British East India Company "purchased" land along the coast and slowly built a city on top of an existing city in 1639. The initial garrison, Fort St. George, protected the East India Company factory and warehouse. The economic pull of currency and employment between the Portuguese, the Dutch, and the Brits heavily favoured the British fort and factory, from which settlements-turned-villages emerged. Infrastructure, like the outside walls of major British buildings, were painted white to demarcate the area as "White Town", where all Europeans were free to roam, trade, and reside. With the increase labour force from nearby villages and the influx of others from distant Indian regions, "Black Town" was constructed to house all non-White populations (see Fig. 2.9). This colonial practice was replicated in Calcutta, with two main districts of operation (see Fig. 2.10; the grey shading is "Black Town" areas, and no shading marks the two sections of "White Town"). Even in present-day Kolkata there are the "Blacktown Walk" tours that take tourists through historic sections of the city that were early forms of in-city racial concentration and segregation. With the full establishment of "White Town" and "Black

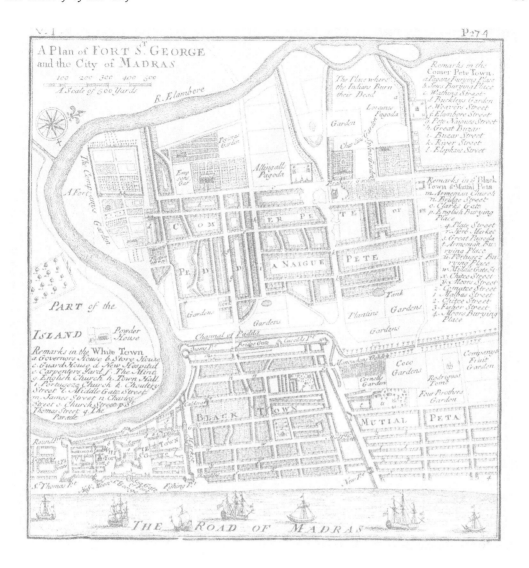

**Fig 2.9** "White Town" and "Black Town", Herman Moll Constructed Plan of Fort St. George and the City of Madras 1726. (Wiki Commons/Public Domain)

Town", Madras flourished with a population of 36,409 British military personnel, State bureaucrats, and East India Company army and staff. This presence and control continued until the 20th century as British military continued to be the principal European presence in all of India. Indian labour was cheap and steady, so unlike other colonial enterprises, there was never a need to apply anything more than lawfare and moments of violence work in India. India was a colony of exploitation rather than a colony of settlement. Unlike Kenya via the city of Nairobi as a city of settlement that sought to protect

and insulate the European settler and military class by keeping the various African indigenous populations on the periphery of the city, Indian populations were still quite close despite the segregated living quarters (Marshall, 1990).

The use of the cordoned areas like "White Towns" and "Black Towns" was duplicated in other colonial city projects (Map of Singapore depicting "Europe Town" and other racialised campongs/kampongs, see Fig. 2.11; Map of Johannesburg depicting a "Coolie Location" for extracted labour from other colonies, Fig. 2.12). Asian indigenous

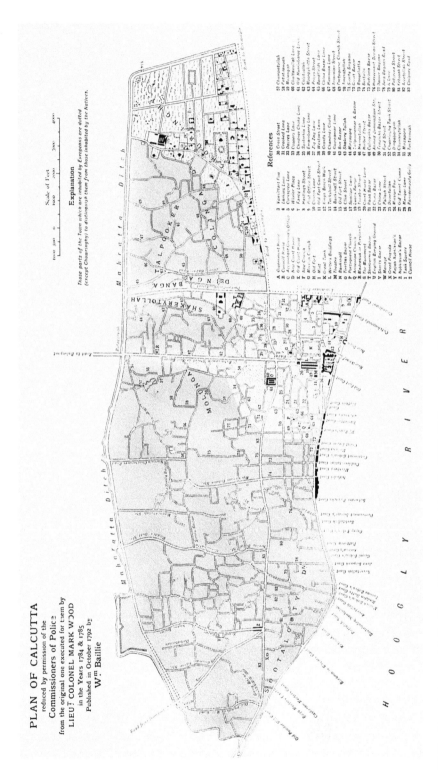

**Fig 2.10** The Commissioners of Police Plan of Calcutta (Kolkata), India, 1792. (Hulton Archive – The Print Collector/Getty Images)

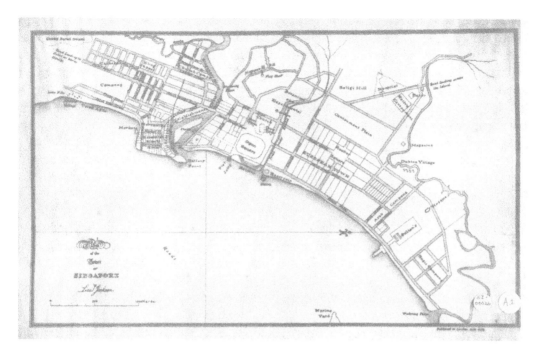

**Fig 2.11** The Jackson Plan Town Map of Singapore Under British Rule With Distinct "European Town" as Well as Chinese, Chullah, Arab, and the Relocated Bugis Campongs, c. 1822. (Wiki Commons/Public Domain)

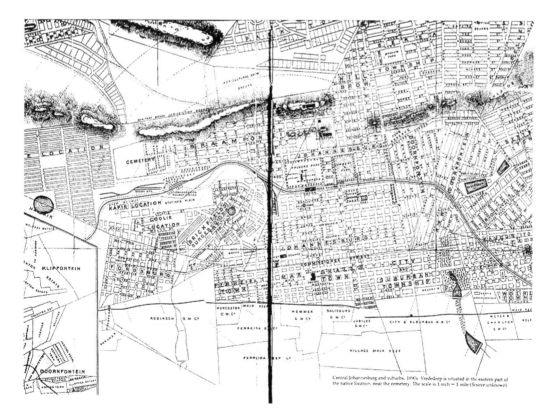

**Fig 2.12** Map of Johannesburg, South Africa, in Afrikaans, 1899. (Wiki Commons/Public Domain)

populations' open kampung or village became British, Dutch, and Portuguese fortified compounds (campongs/kampongs), enclosed for the purposes of the imperium. State power across considerable distance segregated these cities in distinct racialised and labour class lines. But unlike imperial cities in the home seat of power or in earlier failed colonial city/settlement projects, the towns within the cities of Madras and Calcutta grew at an uneven and disorganised pace and process (Scriver & Prakash, 2007). The erection of "the Government House provid[ed] the clearest assertion of Empire…not [as] a symbolic focus of national sentiment…[but as] a representation of the authority of an imperial power and the residence of that power's representative in the colony" (Metcalf, 1989, p. 9). Going further to balance the desires of the East India Company and the interests of the Crown, the two-way lines of communication and unevenly shared decision making with indigenous populations led to inefficiencies in city administration that formed two unique forms of White racialised awareness: White Imagination and White Consciousness. In Kolkata, "the spatial restructuring of Kolkata represented one of the first instances of attempting to alter the physical form of a city to improve social and political control" that was justified through racialised discourse (Sen, 2017, p. 53). The pursuit to exploit local populations and natural resources drove the Company and the Crown to these far-away locations. Once faced with the reality that there was great deal of wealth to loot and plunder, the Company and the Crown had to create semi-permanent garrisons and cities to keep the flow of wealth and capital continuing. The administration of those emerging cities found it necessary to construct physical demarcation zones for the disposed labourer who did the work of extraction, away from the emissaries of the extracting power. With previous skirmishes with the Portuguese and the Dutch settled, British control was able to embark on "major [changes that] occurred in the form and pattern of European settlement, which was to transform Calcutta into a 'city of palaces'" (Davies, 1985, p. 50).

The focus was always on the "White Towns" to keep the emissaries of the extracting power comfortable and loyal, and the condition of and in "Black Towns" could fall to the wayside. The British city in the occupied Indian landspace hid its problems behind walls and false beauty of the night sky (Kipling, 1899). Infrastructure in "White Towns" was needed to accommodate British tastes and luxuries through urban and architectural development initiatives. This included both functional accommodations as sewage and water systems, and aesthetic amenities as garden houses and park spaces. Yet, beyond the "White Town" in Calcutta, "there was another side to the city…an appalling underworld of poverty and despair which [Rudyard] Kipling [1899] [fictionally] portrayed in 'The City of dreadful Night,' where thousands of people slept each night in the gutters outside the palaces of the rich" (Davies, 1985, p. 76). The creation and beautification of "White Town" and the abandonment and dereliction in "Black Town" would come back to haunt the British and other Europeans in the city. It showcased a lasting city development strategy with an "emphasis on over-building and dilapidation, on disease, dirt and stench" (Evenson, 1989, p. 25). A "Gray Town" for "the Portuguese, Greeks and Armenians" served as a neighbourhood "buffer between Black and White town", although at first many of these populations were lumped into living in "Black Town" due to still-evolving articulations of Race via colour segregation (Sen, 2017, p. 48). With the creation of a "Gray Town", the fledging effort of elites to demarcate the racial order crumbled within:

> The landscape of colonial Calcutta was too complex to be usefully described in terms of the duality of [Black and White] towns. The city consisted of overlapping geographies and conceptions of space and territory, both indigenous and foreign, that were constantly negotiated. (Chattopadhyay, 2005, p. 157)

However, these "towns" propped up a White imagination that would be insufficient in protecting its military and company residents from the festering health conditions in "Black Town" that were intentionally produced from years of abandonment. With the Epidemic Diseases Act that was passed in 1897, the Governor General of India empowered local authorities throughout all Asian colonies to respond to epidemic outbreaks (Waring, 1868). In a nod to how many States responded to the coronavirus pandemic, particularly in the United States, the passage of the Act was accompanied with very little resources, and in the already-established racialised city structure, the emphasis in response was on the protection of the British colonialists and the Indian and other non-White labour. This meant excessive force was now applied to the long disregarded "Black Town" and any other non-White residents in the space of the city. State power in the colony and city came with harsh forms of disinfection, the forceful segregation of all infected (and potentially infected) persons, military-led evacuation, and the demolition of allegedly infected locations. State power through military force and medical inspections increased detention and general restrictions on travel. White fears of "Black" disease invoked temporary warfare (both the Company's armies and the Crown's forces) and lawfare (legislative empowerment of administrators) (Harrison, 1994; Superintendent Government, 1902). Ranking officers of the British East India Company and their administrative counterparts were generally not as familiar with epidemic management.

Losses of life due to sanitation and cholera within the colonial city project that had a functioning British hospital since 1679 in Madras, a system of hospitals in Calcutta in 1796, a decreed medical college that was established in 1835, on top of the indigenous medical system, was astronomical. The Royal Commission reported on the sanitary conditions of the Army that deteriorated from poor drainage systems for the housing area of the lower ranks in supposed White spaces, and of course within the "Black Town". With the Military Cantonments Act of 1864, the creation of a sanitary police force joined the existing violence work of the Company army and the Crown's military forces. But incompetently handled exposure impacted the Officers in the Company and the military who engaged in force upon the indigenous population, who

also began to riot and revolt with the repression unleashed by the Act. Until the 1930s, diseases like the "Blue Terror" of cholera were thought to be the diseases of the poor, dirty, and non-White, which only laid the seeds for a greater spread of the disease's effects since it went largely ignored in its early manifestations before the 1817 acknowledged outbreak (Sanitary Commissioner, 1901).

In alignment with the emphasis of a conceptualisation of the "Geographies of Threat", while racial overtures definitely exaggerated the British's understanding of the disease and led to much of its impact on Indian victims, the creation and mode of the management of abandonment allowed the disease to truly spread. In another nod to the present-day pandemic of 2020, the British themselves were the principal carriers of the disease from one city to another city in colonial India, as well as bringing it back to Britain by 1831. As it reached cities like London, cholera killed nearly 30,000 people but was a far cry from the death toll on millions of Indians still trapped in the continuously repressed "Black Towns" in the three administrative Presidency cities (Arnold, 1986; Harrison, 1994).

While White imagination constructed a city that symbolically favoured the lifestyle of a fabricated British and other European Society, among the working-class residents and those of lower military rank in the colonial city of British India, a kind of White consciousness also emerged. The notion of White was a more flexible racial categorisation in India that was predicated on the use of the English language, the practice of Christianity, along with the explicit identification of European descent. Managing a colonial city – unlike living in the base of the imperial state – meant that these lines of demarcation were often exceptionally blurred, ignored, or challenged by the on-the-ground living conditions. Race and caste were not interchangeable concepts, but they also were not fixed to the British social order. What wasn't White was more firmly defined than what was White, as well as what was supposed to be bestowed to those who received the mark of identity. The lower ranks of the military and company army did not get their garden house in Kolkata like the officers and higher up civil servants. The elites were far more "White" in code and conduct, as well as in residence and infrastructural amenities. A colonial identity emerged that challenged the foundations that had only become mainstream through the writings and lectures of the popular scholarly proponents of scientific racism. A colonial identity also emerged because the seat of the Crown was thousands of miles away and, despite the trappings of "White Town", the splendour was not for all. Even those who enjoyed some measures of its accommodations were still rather limited in the full enjoyment of the finer things. The streets in Kolkata and Chennai only went so far in proving a fidelity to the streets of London, Liverpool, Leeds, etc., in Britain (Chattopadhyay, 2000; Mizutani, 2013).

As early as the 1780s, State power in the colonies did not manufacture as efficiently an apparatus to churn out White people as it did in the streets of London, Liverpool, Leeds, etc. Assimilation necessitates a range of inclusions of a previously ostracised and marginalised population. White dispossession, while initially backing Indian dispossession, did lay the seeds of the same military forces that held up the regime of colonialism from also taking colonialism down. Besides the health risk that only worsened from being forced to police the streets of "Black Town", the White rank-in-file saw themselves as a burgeoning community with rights that were being violated. Despite Madras being a factory town, it had become an expansive city through the will of the Crown in its resources gained from other colonies. The vast majority of the White workforce were military, Company army members, and the sanitary police force, not the civil servant classes that predominated colonies in the Caribbean, South Africa, and West Africa. Work strikes turned into outright civil disobedience, and riot turned into ruminations of revolt. The State, through the India Act of 1784, gave specific mention to the handling of local offences by White personnel in the city colonial project. The White soldiers responded with the creation of a free and independent press that only fanned the flames of revolt further. Similar to what was occurring on plantations in the settler colony of the United States and in the colonies throughout the Caribbean, private and public meetings of the disgruntled spread and were repressed through court order. The only issue was that those who would enforce the order were often the convenors of the meetings.

The year 1809 brought the first officer rank mutiny against the Crown and colonial administrators, and by the 1820s,

> As the political climate in Great Britain changed, Whites in India, official or unofficial, were less and less willing to be treated as the garrison of a beleaguered city under authoritarian rule. They again began to claim rights. (Marshall, 1990, p. 32)

And similar to the labour unrest in both Britain and the settler colony of the United States, State power would never empower any of its subjects. But unlike colonial South Africa and the Caribbean, the sociopolitically awakening British did not see their Indian counterparts as rivals but instead as fellow dissenters. Some of this involved a perception of Englishness via education, some of it involved living or working in locations proximate to the racial "Other", and some of it involved the lobbying for similar rights or access to the basic functioning necessities (fair pay, health, education, and quality living conditions) that only became more tenuous with cholera. But as we are focusing on State power here, the State never relinquishes power easily. In experiencing the consistent mutinies and dereliction of duties over and over again, and also seeing a growing educated class of Indian and so-called mixed "Race" citizens, the State conceded with the creation of a new colonial multiracial elite, "British in language and sympathies, but [comprised of settlers, assimilated Indians, and people of mixed race" and this "elite would assume more and more [the] local administration, a welcome alternative to autocratic rule by remote civil servants" (Marshall, 1990, p. 38).

## 2.3 Power Maintenance Through Space

As an articulation of power maintenance and not historical recurrence, the State power that was wielded by monarchies through these colonial city projects sought to enact some aspects of *city-splitting* strategies that were conducted in the seat of the kingdoms that they ruled. Dividing, cordoning, quartering, and segregating came after the conquest, theft, annexation, and assumption of a territory. Nightingale (2012) in *Segregation: A Global History of Divided Cities* brilliantly defined and situated this approach to city governance as *city-splitting* and traced the long history of it over seventy centuries. Designated locations for shelter, religiosity, trade, education, and heath evolved over time to modern-day zoning of residential, commercial, and industrial (colonial Singapore had clearly zoned areas for residential, commercial, and civic purposes with the Jackson Plan in 1828; see Crawfurd, 1968). The designations assisted in creating another class of people who owned property to cultivate crop growth, animal domestication, boarding, and eventually commerce. As this class became increasingly wealthier, so too did the various monarchies of rulership. The State expanded its membership to religious orders and aristocratic guilds, and the city expanded.

Cities that were split in such a way assisted States to also establish more widespread and more power-efficient forms of political control like authoritarian, fascist, and technocratic governments. Cities became hubs, centres, and destinations for the official dissemination of State doctrine and ideology. The level of activity and the dependency of engaging the city for taxation transactions, trade opportunities, and employment grew the population of the city. Therefore, cities also were effective sites and locations to extravagantly spend and hoard the accumulation of wealth through capital campaigns, monumental architectural construction, and large-scale development. People and their dwellings became additional items for the State to divide through early urban planning. As States became full-fledged empires, colonies replicated the production of the colonial city as the key construct to not only organise all ways of life, but also to replicate the imprint of State power in a "new", conquered territory and in reaffirming already governed territories. Colonial cities – the ones already mentioned (and the ones that will be mentioned) – reflected this city-splitting technique of things and people as much as they reflected the intent of the colony to create settlements to proffer extraction, dispossession, and exploitation.

City-splitting no longer simply divided up cities for on-the-ground functions, revenue generation, or urban management. Cities could now be split based on ethnic group concentration based on a myriad of academically developed racial categorisations. The East Indian "White Towns", "Gray Towns", and "Black Towns"; the settler colony of the United States' Chinatowns, Native Reservations, Black "Ghettos"; Iraqi and Syrian Kurdish camps, the Southern African Black townships and Coloured settlements, the Isreali apartheid walled zones, territories, and settlements designated for Palestinians in Occupied Isreal, the Brazilian Favelas, the Middle Eastern "Bazaars", and other locations in other colonial city projects and imperial seats of power were the infrastructural articulation of racialisation. But while racial restrictive covenants, segregation, and redlining in the United States during the 20th century have been mentioned and will be mentioned again throughout this book, in this reading of Nightingale, it is important to see these as only contemporary examples of previous historical iterations of city-splitting that occurred in Beyrut/Beirut, Calcutta/Kolkata, Cape Town, Chennai/Madras, Ciudad de México, Nairobi, Rio de Janeiro, Singapore, Toronto, and other cities throughout the history of colonialism, as well as Amsterdam, Berlin, Lisbon, London, Madrid, Paris, Vienna, and other cities within the aspirations of imperialism. But in my working with Nightingale's city-splitting framework to develop the conceptualisations of the "Geographies of Threat", the racial spaces of demarcation are not outgrowths that were added later as cities evolved, but instead were (and are) the fundamental basis for creation and existence of cities to be used by State power. The origin, etymology, or history of the terminology of Race are not the focus as that distracts from the speed with which the application of the terminology is deployed. The articulations of the study on species and Race were immediately appropriated into planning and initiatives like conquest, enslavement, and colonisation. This wielding of power was not going to leave this city-splitting practice to just a process of segregating people via the **identification of populations** (re: the **identification of threats**, the **identification for violence**). The actions of conquest, enslavement, and colonisation were already being done, and the terminology only assisted with legitimising it to a greater populace that could raise concerns with their own issues of resource abandonment inside the seat of power. The actions of conquest, enslavement, and colonisation were effective in transporting the approach to new languages and in ensuring that future generations of power wielders would continue their own position and practice of power maintenance. Nightingale (2012) presented an alarming list of city-splitting tools, such as,

> walls, palisades, battlements, bastions, fences, gates, guard shacks, checkpoints, booms, railroad tracks, highways, tunnels, rivers, inlets, mountainsides and ridges, buffer zones, free-fire zones, demilitarized zones, *cordon sanitaires*, screens of trees, road blocks, violent mobs, terrorism, the police, armies, curfews, quarantines, pass laws, labor compounds, building clearances, forced removals, restrictive covenants, zoning ordinances, racial steering practices, race-infused economic incentives, segregated private and public housing developments, exclusive residential compounds, gated communities, separate municipal governments and fiscal systems, discriminatory access to land ownership and credit, complementary rural holding zones, influx control laws, and restrictions against overseas immigration. (p. 12)

There is nothing in this comprehensive listing that would allow me (or anyone) to return to some notion that cities are happenstance in their development, and that there was not a high degree of design in its application of such techniques. What I am offering here, with Nightingale's analysis and the discussion of others, namely, Daniel Nemser (2019) in *Infrastructures of Race: Concentration and Biopolitics in Colonial*, is that this question of city design and infrastructure was always about governing with dominance – despotism. For Nemser,

> What appears as infrastructure – disappears from view – necessarily does so in relation to specific subject positions or practices. What constitutes infrastructure for some, facilitating their circulation through space, may constitute an obstacle of attention for others…infrastructure are learned, and the habitual practices that congeal around them are themselves

constructive of collective norms. If familiarity can generate a shared sense of belonging to a community of users, engaging with unfamiliar infrastructures can yield the unsettling sense of being out of place. (p. 17)

To split a city also expended great quantities of power through warfare through Seigel's (2018) *violence work* in the training, equipping, and implementing force to establish and maintain the boundaries inside and outside the city. To split a city also required an immense amount of legal, legislative, and commercial effort that was backed by an investment of a great deal of capital for placemaking, unmaking, and remaking through Kittrie's (2016) *lawfare*. The warfare and lawfare in the utilitarian city of the State reveals any city's functionary role in plunder. Just as the colonial city projects directly attempted to duplicate the amenities of the seats of power, Kolkata contained features of and from the cities of Cape Town, Kingston, Nairobi, and Singapore. The State in seeking and exploring new locations for conquest duplicates itself, and thus locations and schemas are duplicated. British rule contained similar features in each of its colonies, just as the Dutch, French, German, and Spanish rule resulted in similar features within their respective colonies. The emerging social activities that comprised the fabrication of a society and later took more elaborate shape within the space of the city were at the direct behest of the State or at the very least State sanctioned (Werlen, 2005). City splitting, system segmentation for properties and people, and "territorial segmentation" are the most pernicious expressions of State power in modern nation-state governance, either imperial powers or settler colonial powers (Taylor, 1994, 1995).

This *territoriality*, according to Taylor (1994), is the form of behaviour that utilises "bounded space, a territory, as the instrument for securing a particular outcome" (p. 151). Such a behaviour can only be fully actualised by the State, a State as there are competing States within a global reference of space. And while Taylor saw that in cities, "gangs [can] lay to neighbourhoods", it is contested here that those "gangs" are only allowed to lay claim to space at the behest of a far more powerful State that allows for their controlled violence to exist in lieu of the State's own conduct of violence work. Why exert the power to suppress and repress sections of the city if others can do so at your bidding? The idea of "their" or "my" neighbourhood is a naive euphemism for claims on space at the micro-level. But so is the idea of "country" and "nation" as important examples of obscuring euphemisms by the State for its populace to adopt and employ. State rule or dominion can hide under the guise of "homeland", "citizen of", or "country of origin", giving us false senses of autonomy and agency.

Our false senses of autonomy and agency make us ignore all the signs of (limited and granted) possession and (class, gender, and Race) dispossessions that are actually occurring around us. Who possesses a State (or is associated with a State) and who does not determines their lot in all socio-political relations. But even that idea of possession is an extension of the false sense of ownership. The State possesses us, and the State can dispossess us. The State's unbridled containment of power, wealth, property, society, and culture forecloses any notion of a non-State competing possession. State power determines all space within a city unless it is: 1) space of the non-European, United Kingdom, and United States' past that was not yet colonised; 2) space that has been temporarily abandoned by various city-splitting techniques; and 3) space that has/had been liberated, and that ultimately formed the basis for another counter-free State. The State must be the sole sovereign power in a space; otherwise, the State would not exist cognitively or territorially. The State and its administrative bodies and violence workers contain space and constitute through the hierarchical and functional process of ordering, and "the domination of political practice in the world by territoriality is a consequence of this territorial link between sovereign territory and national homeland" (Taylor, 1994, p. 151). The historical recurrence that is power maintenance is a century-spanning pronouncement of power expression and power containment within the space of a map (cognitive representation of the State) and the space of a city (operational function of the State) (Giddens, 1985). States then,

not only regulate(s) the classifications of [social] activities and things [people], but also have to locate them physically, in order to control them as concrete individual bodies and their interactions. In order to fulfil this task, individual items and locations are often represented by a name or a serial number, such as in passports or addresses. (Zierhofer, 2005, p. 34)

## 2.4 State Sovereignty via Infrastructure

In remaining within this cognitive thread that it is this historical reoccurrence of power maintenance, State sovereignty is then really an articulation of dominion – a dominion over ideas, people, and land. Turning land into territory is the business of the State, and the use of people either through dispossession or reconcentration greatly expands sovereignty. People no longer occupy free space, but instead that space is ascribed with the ideas contained in maps and other documents. High walls, check points, and caged fencing above are just some of the ways to dispossess or reconcentrate, whether it was in Apartheid South Africa of the recent past or in Occupied Palestine of the long present. On sovereignty, dominion over

> The right of life and death was one of sovereignty's basic attributes...the right of sovereignty was the right to take life or let live. And then this new right is established: the right to make live and to let live. And then this new right is established: the right to make live and let die. (Foucault, 2003, pp. 240–241)

European and British State power has often been rightly characterised as having the power over life and death. But within the context of this conceptualisation of the "Geographies of Threat", State power is really nothing more about possessing the power to let people die once their use in extraction has been achieved. People, once they have served, have been used, or have been deemed disposable, are relinquished from their utility to the State. Life – giving life – was never the aim of the State nor the aim of the city. The State skilfully cultivates notions of indifference, routinely neglects, systematically overlooks, and organises the abandonment of populations. Some would situate this within the scope of Foucault's (2008) *biopower*, as the regulating of population through systems that manage everyday life as a form of governance (official policy) and governmentality (social support and enforcement of official policy). Foucault (1997) noted,

> To say that power took possession of life in the nineteenth century, or to say that power at least takes life under its care in the nineteenth century, is to say that it has, thanks to the play of technologies of discipline on the one hand and technologies of regulation on the other, succeeded in covering the whole surface that lies between the organic and the biological, between body and population. We are, then, in a power that has taken control of both the body and life or that has, if you like, taken control of life in general – with the body as one pole and the population as the other. (pp. 252–253)

Others would give a particular nod to Mbembe's (2019) *necropolitics*, as it more squarely directs our attention to the long history of the State that solely exists to wield power to subjugate populations until their death, directly or indirectly, by the hands of the State. For Mbembe (2019), "to exercise sovereignty is to exercise control over mortality and to define life as the deployment and manifestation of power" (p. 12), and the purpose and project of (State) power is "the generalized instrumentalization of human existence and the material destruction of human bodies and populations" (p. 14). Schuller (2018) adds considerations for the entangled ways that Race and gender dictate value and importance in eugenics schemas (selective birth for desirable traits, restricted births of undesirable traits). Schuller (2018) posited the twine that binds Race and gender together as a project for oppression,

> As the struggle for the rights of women coincident with the category's new ontological status [the category of woman], feminism derives its political purchase from and within the larger framework of biopolitics. If woman is the product of racial thought, nineteenth-century

feminism itself becomes a civilizational and biopolitical strategy, and not only in its explicitly imperial variant. (p. 18)

All three scholars (Foucault, Mbembe, and Schuller) begin or heavily integrate an analysis of the repercussions of the 19th century State power via colonialism and enslavement. Just "moral climatology" served one endeavour of distant people dispossession and land extraction (Livingstone, 2002); so did Malthusian theory of population that called for in-city dispossession and land extraction. Undesirable populations needed to be checked and curtailed in their birth rates and social mobility under the guise of food shortage concerns (Malthus, 1806). In Thomas Malthus's *An Essay on The Principle of Populations,* a moral judgement levied at the distant native worked in the same way as the moral restraint of the working class and immigrant city dweller in London of the 1800s. Conscription into military service, birth control, and neighbourhood cordoning were the only ways that could check the excessive growth of populations, certain populations. City splitting, location schema, territory segmentation, system segmentation, and also spatial seclusion were then other ways that colonialism and enslavement were perfected and adopted into imperial cities. Spatial enclosure (the city or desirable neighbourhood areas within a city) enabled exception or the focused management of disposable populations. The opportunity of being within the enclosure was just a happenstance benefit from the exception or seclusion. Beyond the enclosure, sovereignty over life and death was sovereignty over the right to kill and maim through violence work. Beyond the enclosure, sovereignty granted lawful clearance to misconduct, mistakes, mishaps, and malfeasances through acts of warfare.

Daniel Nemser (2019) in *Infrastructures of Race* profoundly distils and then expands the work of Foucault, Mbembe, and Schuller as articulated here. Nemser examined the history and origins of concentration as a form of biopolitics that sought (and continues to seek) to manage and structure the movement of populations in a predictable manner based on State power. Returning to an understanding of sovereignty, Nemser made the point that sovereignty's power over life was "the full extent of the sovereign's power – a negative power not over life but strictly over death" (p. 12). While this chapter has spent some time discussing British Colonial rule, and has alluded to Dutch, French, and Portuguese Colonial rule, Nemser brings to the table a long and expansive work on Spanish Colonial rule. In particular, he discusses the Spanish Colonial system's elaborate techniques to regulate populations and utilise city management to most effectively regulate those populations. The origins of the 20th century concentration camp that was most profoundly represented by the practices of Nazi-controlled Germany in its campaign of genocide upon European Jewish populations owes its creation to techniques applied by Spain during the 1895–1898 Cuban War of Independence. At the behest of the Spanish Crown, colonial officers ordered rural civilians to report to the nearest city that served as a garrison, much like the city of Madras in India under the British. What is most important in this examination was the element of power maintenance that States used by learning from the techniques of competing States and their own record of practices in dominion.

In the examination of the history of concentration, Nemser charted back to the beginning of Spanish Colonial rule in México, and the form and function that concentration took in the colonial city project of Ciudad de México. The colonial implementation of concentration produced a system of social ordering through population management. Further, the colonial implementation of concentration that was employed also assisted in the production of Race in order to improve the type of management undertaken in Spanish Colonial rule. Space was the arch tool to racialise a population, "racialization as the politics of death cannot be detached from the biopolitics of life" (Nemser, 2019, p. 12). Using some of the earliest colonial city-splitting and territory-segmentation techniques in building segregated neighbourhoods, Nemser's work also highlighted how those techniques only came after the Spanish colonial implementation of the development of centralised towns, the construction of disciplinary institutions of all sorts, and general collections for order. Just as modern-day Cape Town, Chennai, and Singapore are still impacted by their initial colonial creation, the signs buried within the

plans that constructed the 17th century organisation of Ciudad de México are still present today. And many of the ways that the 1968 Tlatelolco Massacre was devastatingly managed, as discussed in Chapter 1, are based on features and techniques of Spanish Colonial rule and the Spanish Colonial city project.

> The process of learning the lessons of Spanish Colonial State power charts back to the, beginning in the sixteenth century, at the "threshold of modernity," a new form of power, borrowing and expanding on the techniques of the Christian pastorate, began to operate in conjunction with the emergence of modern capitalism. It did so first at the level of the individual, using discipline to optimize the body's forces and integrate them effectively and efficiently into various processes of production, and later at the level of the population, intervening in abstract biological processes and rhythms in order to foster life and maximize vitality. In contrast to "taking life," the negative capacity of sovereignty, the shift to "making live" captures the productive orientation of biopolitical forms of modern power. (Nemser, 2019, p. 12)

State power is, and always has been, supreme. It is indivisible and absolute. And it is further enabled by the submission of people to the sovereign for false guarantees of profit, security of personhood, and the order that is necessary to protect property.

Yes, a Foucauldian notion of power is extended to the interactions and relationships between people, as the State "is superstructural in relation to a whole series of power networks that invest the body, sexuality, the family, kinship, knowledge, technology, and so forth" (Foucault, 1980, p. 123). These social activities are still under or within State rule, and many of these activities were derived directly from the sovereign. The State, through social control, "doesn't only weigh on us as a force that says no; it also traverses and produces things, it induces pleasure, forms of knowledge, produces discourse" through social activity (Foucault, 1980, p. 120). Social activity produced the mode of playful interactions and performances of leisure for the "common good" that are in fact "scenario [s] of obedience in which those who are subject to the sovereign's law acknowledge and comply with it"

(Nemser, 2019, p. 108). The city then offers the State to enact death dealing, but the city also allows the cultivation of an idealised image of humanity (free of the criminal and the diseased). Nemser (2019) prevents a reading that may go too far in thinking that social activity is the norm and purpose of the State, for

> the rise of an affirmative biopolitics, deeply invested in the production of life, does not mean that the negative power of sovereignty over death declines, disappears, or becomes entirely obsolete. (p. 12)

The process of racialisation and the doctrine of racism is "a way of introducing a break into the domain of life that is under power's control: the break between what must live and what must die" (Foucault, 2003, p. 254). And there is a logic, and not an irrationality, to racism that clearly understands the usefulness of social activities to foster social relations: "the biopolitical state never stops drawing on the techniques of sovereignty" (p. 12). But for many of us, we fall into Fields and Fields' (2012) cautionary trap of *racecraft* and do not see the management of populations through a prism of warfare (how to deal with identified threats). Warfare in all colonial projects was the prime framework. It was always employed and always ready to be deployed again. Since Race was and still is arbitrary, "racism [is] against the abnormal" (Foucault, 2004, p. 316). Warfare, for Nemser (2019), is described as follows:

> The ancient logic of warfare, by which one side confronts and must destroy another in order to survive in battle, is transformed into a new logic of biopower that operates on the basis of racial hierarchy, linking the elimination of inferior races with the improvement, optimization, and purification of life in its most general sense. Death is deployed, in other words, in the interest of life: "massacres have become vital". (p. 12)

And warfare achieved pacification and rule that aided city-splitting administrative techniques with,

> The relocation of native bodies – or at least the designation of their areas of residence as parts of a larger administrative grid – permitted to be identified in Spanish political and religious

terms. Resettlement and evangelization were consistently denoted by the same terms used by translation: *reducir*. To reduce a thing to its former state, to convert, to contract, to divide into small parts, to contain, to comprehend, to bring back into obedience: the multilayered definitions of *reducir* allow for a variety of contexts. It thus sums up the thrust of Spanish colonization as both a political and moral undertaking designed to reconstitute the natives as subjects to divine and royal laws. Bodies were to be "reduced" to centralized localities subject to the letter of the law...the hierarchical organization of settlements function as terminal points into which natives could be inserted and thereby reduced to the terms prescribed by law. This task in turn required the work of a certain kind of translation: the recording of names on tribute rolls, the accounting of native domiciles, and the differentiation of the populace into discrete categories...the recording of those names in administrative lists and records. The process would result, as far as the colonizers were concerned, in converting the colonized into arbitrary elements that could be made to fit into a divinely sanctioned order characterized by the hierarchization of all signs and things in the world. (Rafael, 1993, p. 90)

It is difficult to conceive our present world as it is today without the consideration that comes from this historical view and to the extent to which the present has been moulded and crafted by State power through the process of colonialism. Through warfare and occupation, States possessed people and land that then became populations and territories under the political control of that foreign State. The Portuguese and Spanish Colonial States were the first truly global empires that broadened the powers of their respective State regimes through colonialism as early as the Conquest of Ceuta in Morocco in 1415 and the occupation of the Caribbean Antilles in 1492. The overseas expansion of control by other acknowledged States came via trade occupations in West and East India in the 1500s by the Dutch Republic, military occupation of Acadia (present day Nova Scotia) by the French Colonial Empire in 1605, and full-on settler invasion of Ireland throughout the 1500s by the British Empire. All five State powers competed, collaborated, conceded, and signed treaties over their respective claims of territory and explorations throughout the charted world that appeared on maps that were purchased and exchanged between these States. Many of those treaties also structured the ways in which the various States would interact within their occupied territories (missionary work, building of a trade post, cultivation of farmland, and nautical/terrestrial protection from newer States and location unacknowledged Nations). The Spanish missions (religious), civil settlements (pueblos), and military outposts (presidios) actualised Spanish rule far away from the State Crown and seat of Empire.

The territory itself, after clearing indigenous populations, often required various institutions to make occupation creation and settlement building possible. The very nature of the topography and geology of the territory, based on the soil and climate, affected the level of wealth that could be established and extracted over an extended period of time. Those institutions of extraction had to be financed by institutions that would fund and endow the endeavour over that period. The density of the indigenous population also determined the degree to which both State and privatised military would be needed to maintain clearance. More carnage, more soldiers to pay. More carnage over an extended time, more soldiers to pay over an extended amount of time. Knowledge gained from these experiences led these Empires and other States to seek territory that was more sparsely populated than others as this would decrease the costs in offence and defence of occupation and wealth extraction. Populating these territories did not have to be financed by the State as most States (forcibly) encouraged the derelict, lower classes, debtors, and other disposable classes to re-create small farming settlements from the imperial seat in the Empire's newly acquired territories. Settlements were connected together through proximity to resource extractive factories, trade posts, military garrisons, or other fortifications. Governance would be situated through this activity centre, and the greater the activity, the larger strewn together settlements would likely re-emerge as a colonial city. Church plaza complexes became the site for festivals and for major settlement-unifying social activities. The corridors and streets from residencies and other buildings would be shaped around the plaza (see Fig. 2.13). Street patterns, neighbourhoods, and market districts were set in a grid structure, and the grid structure allowed city administrators to sell and manage property as much as it managed the populations that would/could come into possession of that property (see Fig. 2.14). The grid made the colonial settlement a new form of city rather than the resituated medieval-inspired town away from Europe.

As Stanislawski (1946) noted from the 1573 *Laws of the Indies,* under which Spanish Colonial rule was ordered and enacted,

> From the plaza shall begin four principal streets: one from the middle of each side and two streets from each corner of the plaza; the four corners of the plaza shall face the four principal winds, because of this manner, the streets running from the plaza shall not be exposed to the four principal winds which would cause much inconvenience. (p. 114)

Municipal administrations would then draft and proclaim ordinances for residency that,

> here and there in the town, smaller plazas of good proportion shall be laid out, where the temples associated with the principal church, the parish churches and the monasteries can be built, such that everything may be distributed in a good proportion for the instruction of religion. (Crouch & Mundigo, 1977, p. 255)

The *Laws of the Indies* was the consolidation of the 1512 *Leyes de Burgos* ("Laws of Burgos"; that regulated the conduct and status of Spanish subjects in the occupied territories) and the 1542 *Leyes Nuevas* ("New Laws" for the Good Treatment and Preservation of the Indians) within a plan for the spatial arrangement of those populations. The rule of the State was the basis for the land, turned territory, turned settlement, turned city in which space was turned into plazas. The plaza was the core basis for how the settlement transformed itself into a city, and the basis for a thriving colony. As noted in the

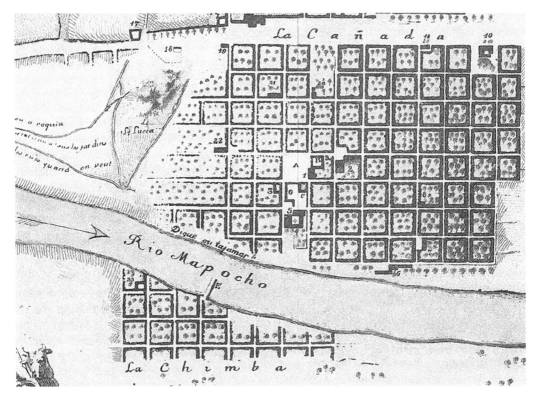

**Fig 2.13** La Chimba en Plan de la ville de Santiago, mapa de Santiago de Chile. "A" Denotes the Plaza,1756. (Public Domain)

precise instructions from royal orders that were applied to Panama City in 1519 through the Furor Domini ("Wrath of God), Pedro Arias de Ávila,

> Let the city lots be regular from the start, so once they are marked out the town will appear well ordered as to the place which is left for a plaza, the site for the church and the sequence of the streets; for in places newly established, proper order can be given from the start, and thus they remain ordered with no extra labor or cost; otherwise order will never be introduced. (cclxxxi)

All of this occured through "discovery, settlement and pacification."

Institutions to manage property claims and rights were established, and with this came the possibility of a sustainable outpost of the State to rule – the true colony. The quality of the environment, the military capabilities, and the economic models truly determined the degree of success of the colony, but the identity and experience of the colonizing State set the manner of the expression of the colony. The mercantilist approach assisted in resource extraction aims, while the market approach assisted in land and property development aims (Lange et al., 2006). In particular, where British Colonial rule would slowly prosper through seeking less populous territories and then spread outward with small-scale settlements turned cities over centuries, the Spanish Colonial rule sought more densely populated areas that already had pre-existing institutions and city-structures that they replaced with their own rule and operations. Spanish rule was articulated through full-blown predation that led to institution dysfunction and greatly stratified colonies, while British rule's slow build established localised rules, regulations, and administration. The colonial city project was the location to regulate those markets for trade commerce, to city-split along arbitrary demographic lines, and to solidify a base for political authority to erect

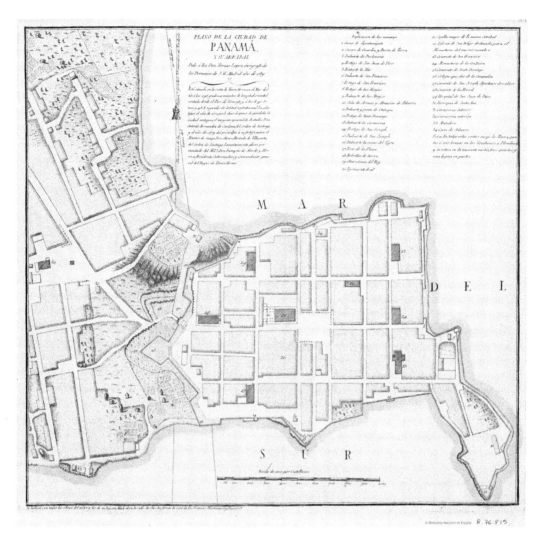

**Fig 2.14** Plano de la Ciudad de Panamá. Planos de población, 1789. (La Biblioteca Nacional de España, Madrid, ES)

the rule of law to enforce policy and manage disputes. And the site of the city, the colonial city project, through this territorial process confirmed the economic development and social development of the State through political governance. For Spanish rule, the city was the urban area and the outer areas, while under British rule, the city was principally the city centre. Nemser (2019) channelling Lefebvre (1991) viewed "the colonial city is not only an 'artificial product' but also an 'instrument of production' since it constituted part of a project aimed at facilitating new modes of extraction" (p. 18).

Crown laws were articulated and enforced through local representation, but in all things of rule beyond a certain reach, local central governments were enabled to seize opportunities to insert laws of their own. Early municipal governments were city-state governments at the allowance of the greater State. By 1534, these local forms of government under the greater Spanish-ruled Ciudad de México enforced a range of laws associated with "disease", and then later, "crime". These local edicts and discretionary notes constructed the uniformity in infrastructure of aesthetics, public hygiene, sewage and drainage, utilities, and public safety. The greater State concerned itself with the management and use of the resource and labour extraction.

Within Puebla de los Ángeles, the city functioned along the trade route and as a go-between the port city of Nuevo Veracruz and Ciudad de México in the indigenous area of Tlaxcala, Cholula, formerly under Aztec Empire rule. In Fig. 2.15, with the direction of south at the top and north at the bottom, four locations of note are presented as #1 Cathedral, #2 Palacio Episcopal, #23 San Francisco Convent, and letters "S" Quartel de Dragones and "T" Quartel deel Batallion. The first two (#1 and #2) locations overlooked the plaza where the slave market first existed until 1624 and then later moved to #23 (Sierra Silva, 2018) Figs. 2.16, 17, 18, and 19. The proximity of force ("S" and "T") remained. In the lower right corner, the block of text reads (in translation),

The very noble and very loyal city of Los Angeles was founded in the year 1531 on the 16th of April, governing Spain was the Emperor Charles V and the Catholic Church, his Holiness Alexander

VI. This city is 19°55' northern height (latitude) y at 288° of longitude. The weather is benign and gentle; the southern wind dominates. The quarters of the city are of equal extent, and beautiful, distributed in proportion, being in height 100 Castilian bars, and in width 200. The width of its streets is equal and equipped to allow free passage extending to 14 bars. The ground is firm, abundant are waters of distinct qualities, with healthy sources for baths. Neighboring amenities include hills for wood, fertile valleys which take seeds. The observance of its communities should be celebrated, as well as the subtlety of its ingenuity, the adornment and beauty of its churches, and the skill of its craftsmanship.

Delineated by Joseph Marianus a Medina.

The city extends in its widest part a league in diameter and three in circumference. According to the most prudent calculation taken in the last census it arrived at 200,000 persons, of clerics

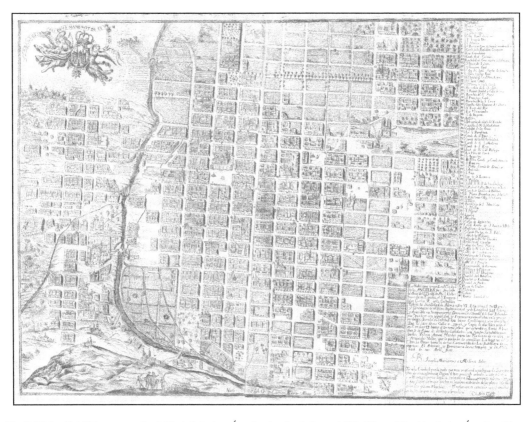

**Fig 2.15** La Nobilísima y muy Leal Ciudad de Los Ángeles fue fundada en 1531 (Map of Puebla de los Ángeles, Now Known as Puela). (Wiki Commons/ Public Domain)

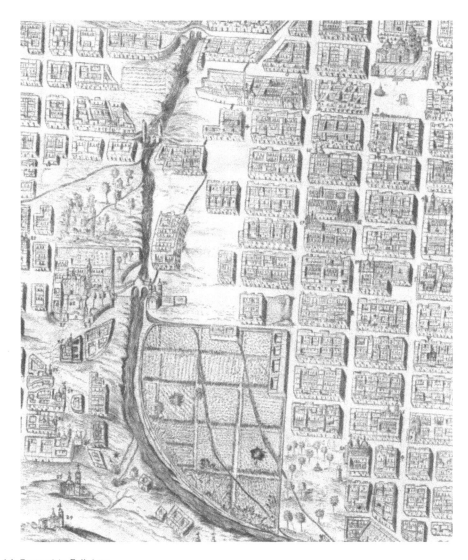

**Fig 2.16** Zoomed in Full Area.

800, not including those who help in the administration of the alms(?) and haciendas which are many. They maintain commerce and their families are for the most part on ecclesiastical incomes.

The year 1754. (Medina, c. 1754)

In annexing the nearby indigenous towns of the former Aztec Empire – Amozoc, Totimehuacán, and Cuautinchán – Puebla de los Ángeles also used another site, #49 St. Xabiel College, as the Doctrinos de Indios (Tamayo, 2010). The constructed colonial city project was space that was founded on "two urban forms":

> The city, which was conceived as the space of "civilization", of "Whites", and the people of Indians who were conceived as the rural, the peripheral. Thus, "urban space was perceived as the space of the non-indigenous population. (Herrera Ángel, 2004, p. 171)

In this spatial arrangement, two basic categories of populations emerged: 1) the colonisers and colonised,

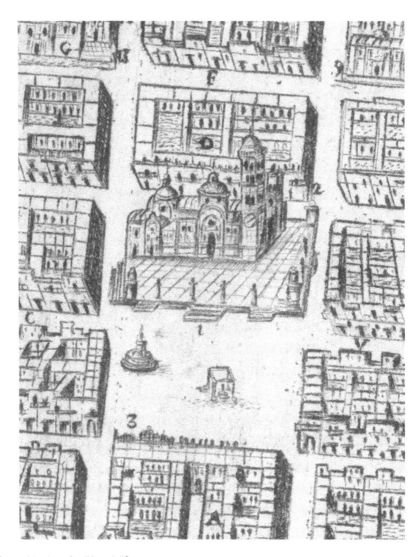

Fig 2.17 Zoomed in Area for #1 and #2.

interacting and sharing the same space; and 2) representation of the Crown and its emissaries. Social activity separation played as much of a role as spatial separations between these populations and within the first population shared by two groups. Laws applied to both colonised and coloniser as subjects of the Crown/the State head. But laws pertaining to legal equality and social equality assisted in the division of the coloniser and the colonised. Colonisers were principally those of the Church as *doctrineros* and those who worked as conquistadores but in retirement and with their grant of lands were now *encomenderos*. The encomenderos were also rewarded with labour from both indigenous

populations and enslaved Africans. The indigenous populations beyond the city would be forcibly incorporated to attack and consolide warring indigenous city-states of the Aztec Empire. Congregation of indigenous populations within cities was done initially by force but also through indoctrination as a form self-control and early governmentality. We are often mislead in thinking that indoctrination was simply learning scripture. The social activities and the plaza were both the event and setting location, the space to learn and to practice State-accepted and decreed social interactions, customs, interrelationships, etiquette, and norms. Post-indoctrination in the city, the indoctrinated indigenous

**Fig 2.18**  Zoomed in Area for S and T.

person would seek work and residence in the city, another city, or the nearer countryside. Space in the city leveraged Catholic doctrine to build manifestations of the Catholic identity, but more specifically, the Catholic identity that was forced upon colonised indigenous populations (Violich, 1962).

Tamayo (2010) outlined that the Church

prescribed that in each doctrine a place of worship (church) be built that because of its quality as a sacred space, it became the center of doctrine. Around this, the place of residence of the doctrinero (house cural), the place of instruction for the population (school), the place of care of health (hospital), the place of punishment (prison) and the place to bury the dead (cemetery). These spaces are not simple urban elements doctrine, they are, first of all, Catholic representations that they sought to contribute to the construction of the Catholic identity in the indigenous colonial. (p. 80)

The city,

was neither a capital nor a port, yet its entanglement with trans-Atlantic slaving networks is significant ... [such a reality leads to an understanding that] can and should be extended to other colonial cities with smaller Spanish and larger indigenous, African and mixed-raced populations, reduced credit markets and fewer

governmental institutions vis-à-vis colonial capitals. (Sierra Silva, 2018, p. 9)

Sierra Silva (2018) posed simple questions with relevance to Geographies of Threat: "could space define slavery? [And] if so, what can Puebla tell us about the daily negotiation of bondage in colonial Mexico?" (p. 4). But further, what are the implications of Puebla in fuelling Ciudad de México both in terms of the overall economy and labour from both enslaved Africans and the conquered indigenous population? The city shaped the trade and transit of enslaved peoples, and it indoctrinated the indigenous.

It is with this I return to Nemser (2019) and the focus on four key spaces: religious congregations, mestizo schools, urban neighbourhoods, and the city's royal gardens. The physical separation of cultural groups in the social activities of the plaza and other sites of leisure, the territorial segmentation outside the city, and city-splitting techniques in neighbourhood design implicitly is the actual basis for the creation of the subordinate status of non-White, non-Spanish, non-Christian populations. With a larger population, Ciudad de México also contended with a burgeoning mestizo population alongside the structures and statuses articulated by Herrera Ángel (2004) and Tamayo (2010), creating a paradoxical existence for the mestizo and in the segregated neighbourhoods of Ciudad de México. As New Spain (México)

**Fig 2.19** Zoomed in Area for #23.

expanded, mestizos initially served as social and physical mediators to bring the Spanish Catholic faith to indigenous populations. But with economic resources dwindling in the colonial city project, their paid status changed from doctrineros in missionaries to vagrants and street poor. They, too, like the indios and negros, had to be separated socially and structurally, and their neighbourhoods were deemed dangerous. The tools of ordering came from a broad range of fields and disciplines, and Nemser (2019) suggested that innovative Spanish understanding of botany, through the organisation of the city's botanical gardens, was the predecessor to scientific racism's ordering of people of many colonial and imperial societies beyond Spain (re: Carl Linneaus 16th century taxonomy of people with temperaments: Europæus albescens (White European as sanguine), Americanus rubescens (redish American as choleric), Asiaticus fuscus (yellow Asian as melancholic), and Africanus nigriculus (Black African as phlegmatic)).

The colonial city project was all about managing populations in carefully conceived areas of concentration. This strategy informs how modern cities still employ methods that produce a certain type of subject, animate a certain type of effect, and engage a certain type of violence onto their populations. The colonial city project is about keeping people in place. Nemser's forms of concentration – *congregation*, *enclosure*, *segregation*, and *collection* – as implemented at different times in Ciudad de México, inform the State governance of populations through the city. Congregation was the centralised town structure that was slowly built up into a city that forcibly removed indigenous populations beyond the city and then re-centralised them into this territorial structure. The modern city, and most cities of former colonies of the Empire, bear this mark in not only their older cities but also in newer cities throughout their territories. Enclosure was both the early disciplinary and carceral system, but also the educational system for indoctrination that educated mestizo populations to serve as middle management and buffering communities. The modern city design, especially employed through New Urbanism, built a series of neighbourhoods around school centres. Our contemporary period of smaller cities in the United States reflects this continued practice of building in and around prisons in order to curb their decay and sustain efforts in growth.

Segregation was the neighbourhood and district structures for the segmentation of population based on a range of demographics but most profoundly by occupation, gendered property control mechanisms, and racial categorisation. The city in current colonies, former colonies, seats of power, and independent States engages in city splitting intentionally or unintentionally, invoking its history of racialisation through space. Collection was the management of life. First, plant life served both science and leisure; the ordering of things informed and refined the other three. Imperial botanists in Ciudad de México separated plants and other flora into distinct spaces for cultivation and study and harnessed the engineering techniques of micro-climates to match each species of plant's biological characteristics. Similar to collection, a new conceptual understanding of biopolitics was developed to manage a so-called multiracial population. In the case of the Spanish Empire, the biopolitics that ordered life were expressed through the *régimen de castas* ("hierarchical racial system"; see Fig. 2.20). While some have made attempts to establish a social concreteness to such a system, it was virtually impossible

to maintain and control in everyday social practice and function. Left to their own devices, and without the power of the State monitoring their every move, individuals saw Race in everyday life as fluid.

However, the spatiality of the colonial city maintained a socio-cultural notion of Race by way of the physical infrastructure of the city that over generations became a fundamental part of political and social activities (Lefebvre, 1991). The inability of the Portuguese and Dutch to maintain a solidified cultural identity within cities as they enslaved African, Asian, and South American indigenous populations was/is enough of a lesson. The strong maintenance of old class hierarchies and status from the seats of the Empire into the colonies only lead to grift, ruin, and revolt. While the notion of the regulation of behaviour could appear to be a logical structure, it only reminded the Portuguese and Dutch lower classes of the Empires they left behind in the seat of power. The Dutch, in particular, often sought concealment of their dominance over indigenous populations over fear of having an insufficient military force to repel attacks or defend against competing Empires; they gave the illusion of just being traders and not really colonists (Vink, 2003). The Dutch Republic colonial city project replicated the social status of its members onto the building structures and styles. City walls, unbridged canals, and smaller quarters denoted areas for the segregated populations (Zandvliet, 1998). But the Dutch Republic, unlike all the other Empires, allowed for the greatest degree of equal access and mobility to all parts of the city for movement and is the most socially similar to modern cities. The city grid of Simon Stevin's "Ideal Plan for a City" promoted both egalitarianism and territorial segmentation, as access to water was throughout the colonial city but the proximity to the source of the water was reserved for the Dutch, and the Dutch of means and wealth (Stevin, 1650; 1955). The city plan integrated both old Roman features and Italian Renaissance theoretical features into European cities as they expanded or recovered from disasters (like the Great London Fire of 1666 and later the Lisbon earthquake of 1755). The Spanish Empire settlement turned city of Caracas (Santiago de León de Caracas) in present-day Venezuela was the first city among all colonial empires to employ the grid plan in 1578 (see

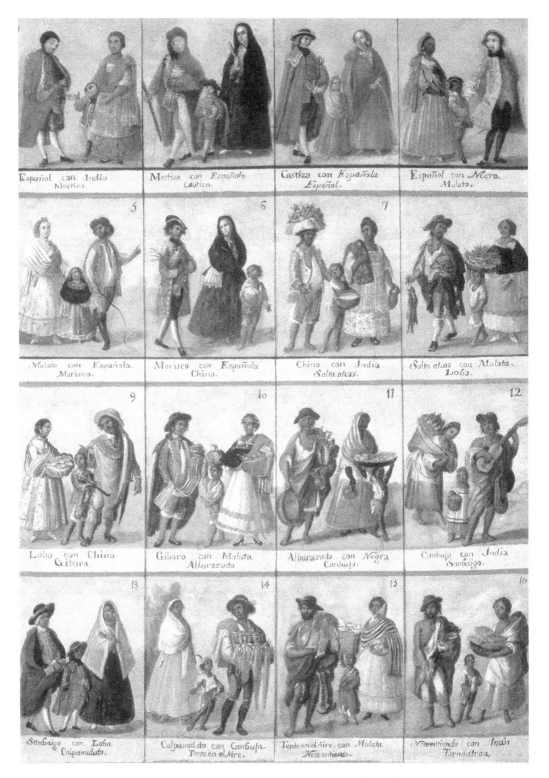

**Fig 2.20** Pintura de castas con todas las 16 combinaciones (Painting of the 16 Racial Classifications) in the Spanish Colonies of the Americas, c. 1700s. (Wiki Commons/Public Domain)

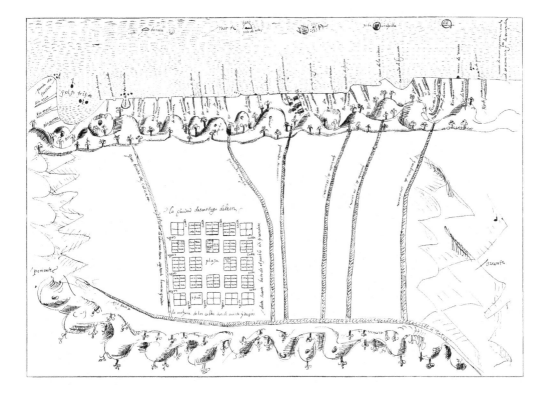

**Fig 2.21** The First Map Plan of Caracas Under Governor Juan de Pimental, 1578. (Wiki Commons/Public Domain)

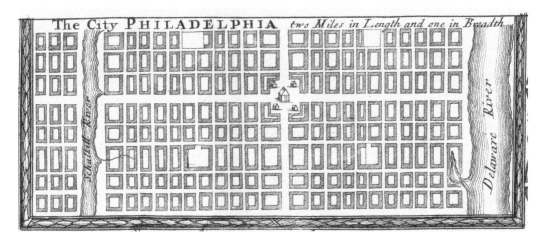

**Fig 2.22** Thomas Holme Map, "A Mapp of Ye Improved Part of Pensilvania in America Divided into Countyes Townships and Lotts" From the Offices of William Penn & Assoc. (esq.), 1687. (Public Domain)

Fig. 2.21). Specific to English-controlled North America, the grid would take root on a grand scale with William Penn and Thomas Holme's topological re-conception of Philadelphia in 1682, influenced by breaking from the Puritan "Ordering of Towns" and the medieval village design and township making (see Fig. 2.22). The first post-Renaissance European city to make use of the grid structure was Mannheim,

**Fig 2.23** Plan der Residenzstadt Mannheim, Germany, 1813. (Public Domain)

Germany, in 1758 (with fortification removed in 1813; see Fig. 2.23).

But it is contended here that the Spanish mastery of city development in its colonial settlements – referenced by the Dutch, plagiarised by the Portuguese, considered by the French, revised by the British, and enhanced by the settler colony of the United States – forms the basis of the physical world we inhabit today.

These efforts in all Empires, but most especially in returning to the Spanish, all situated Race as the material outcome of State processes. The State must extract resources to remain economically in power,

and the State must dispossess to remain territorially in power. In order to do so, the State must create occupational and income classes using Race and gender as the primary modality. Race was not the starting point. There are material practices that created Race through spatial arrangements and access, property ownership, and taxation. Groups were formed through city splitting and territorial segmentation for resource extraction, not for "preserving the Race". Further management of a city in this way re-enforced the "realness" of Race and gender, but particularly Race since it is organised in the infrastructure that then enhanced further processes of racialisation. The padrones and the census to record how many people and what type of people they were became a technique to govern and not just tax. The slave, the native, the Negro, the Indian, the Indio, Criollo, the mazombo, the insulares, the creole, the mulatto, and the mestizo all were not the original Imperial subject nor power, and all become cognitively "real" through infrastructure. Likewise, they were expanded through continued engagement and residence in that infrastructure. The ways of being were normalised via infrastructure, and over generations populations fully adopted the identities and characteristics given to them due to their comfort and familiarity with the spatial designation. Different forms of groupness were developed by these spatial arrangements and spatial restrictions. People and populations inhabited their subjectivities, and their subjugation.

Yet, infrastructure fades into the background and hides its part in creating these subjectivities. This was the lesson from the Dutch that was most salient, the lesson of discretion and concealment, not forced and apparent borders or walls. For the Dutch, these were *wingewest*, regions for making profit through land extraction and a cheap labour class. And on the matter of class, the production of space was what capitalism did. The gradual extension of capital and its investment from the seats of the Empire to the development of the faraway was what made Imperialism. The colonial period birthed capitalism and violent processes like enslavement, forced labour (removed from land and now working for wage), and the accumulation of owners (Marx's discussion of the colonisation of the Americas). Gender was the social construction to manage labour and property (reduction of competitive interest, who owns it, and most importantly, the prevention of inheritance of mestizos). Women in the seats of the Empire were summarily removed from ownership and control of property. This violently reduced them to property with the potential value of the production of a future labourer. Private property created gender. Race was a material outcome of the processes and the purpose of the city (labour, enslavement, genocide, and spatial arrangement). Infrastructure created Race. Race was/is used as a discipline of population.

Infrastructure created Race. Roads, electricity, fibre optics, and waterlines are not constructed aspects of the city that are in the forefront of our minds, and they are not seen as the aspects of a city that alienate. Where does the sewage go? Who drains the sewage? How does the sewage drain? Where does the sewage run? Is everyone's water clean? Gender functions via property. Race operates infrastructurally. Gender instigates territorialisation. Race eases extraction of resources. Gender determines and divides labour. Race enables dispossession. These are the true basis of the social construction of gender and Race. As Federici (1994) decisively posited,

> The expropriation of European workers from their means of subsistence, and the enslavement of Native Americans and Africans to the mines and plantations of the New World, were not the only means by which a world proletariat was formed and "accumulated". This process required the transformation of the body into a work-machine, and the subjugation of women to the reproduction of the work-force. Most of all, it required the destruction of the power of women which, in Europe as in America, was achieved through the extermination of witches. Primitive accumulation, then, was not simply the accumulation and concentration of exploitable workers and capital. It was also an accumulation of differences and divisions within the working class, whereby hierarchies built upon gender, as well as "race" and age became constitutive of class rule and the formation of the modern proletariat. (pp. 63–64)

While all Empires were fundamentally about extraction and dispossession, they did so with established labour-coercive institutions of free enslaved and exploited labourers. The Spanish Empire imparted to the British and other Empires, the system of social stratification and city design. Spanish Imperial rule's campaigns for colonialism were within merchantilist colonialism with the purpose of labour to establish economic self-sufficiency through natural resource accumulation/extraction and trade agreements. This was in contrast to liberalist colonialism of the British

Imperial rule that was enacted with the purpose of labour to maximise profits through free market. The British Empire imparted to new Empires the elaborate system of labour exploitation, management of markets, and capitalism accumulation. Liberalist colonialism can then be broken up into four distinct types: settler colonialism, direct colonialism, hybrid colonialism, and indirect colonialism. As mentioned before, the British Empire established itself over a longer period of time both globally and within specific regions of the ever-defined globe. Over that period, the British Empire utilised settler colonialism with the permanent transfer of British subjects from Britain that marked the distinct end of any pre-existing pre-colonial cultures and spatial arrangements in lesser populated areas (the initial colonies of the United States, Australia, New Zealand, and the Caribbean). With direct colonialism, the British Empire fully created a new colonial State over an expansive territory that promised substantial trade and installed legal and law enforcement institutions in protection of property (Hong Kong, the city of Singapore, Sri Lanka, and the British West Indies). A form of hybrid colonialism was also developed in locales that direct colonialism and indirect colonialism were both used at varying times (Malaya, South Africa overall, and the cities of Cape Town and India's Kolkata) or in different cities (India, and the cities of Kolkata in comparison to Madras). The British Empire also used indirect colonialism. When faced with a complex pre-colonial society, it employed patrimony that granted local authority continued command over their population but with taxation to the Crown and colonial administrators (the Pacific Islands, the continent of Africa overall, and specifically, Kenya's Nairobi) (Lange et al., 2006).

The settlement builds the nation-state; the city builds the Empire. The city erases the indigenous and renders it rural, even if indigenous populations no longer reside in hinterlands. But if they continue to reside in the hinterlands, it is to serve the purpose of "preserving the spaces of modernity for the White settler population", as was the case for South Africa's

Apartheid cities (Dawson, 2006, p. 126). Utilizing the rurality of the hinterlands further expands ideas of indigenous and Black savagery and tribal backwardness. However, these hinterlands could not be as far as they once were as the native and the savage have to remain close to the city as they are "an essential source of labor for an increasingly industrialised and urban economy" (Dawson, 2006, p. 126). The city encloses populations within false communities, even if there is a grid structure that grants open accessibility of space. The city segregates along demographic lines as that is the basis for the collection of demography, even if the identities in demography are arbitrary and illusionary. And the city collects and orders things for the purpose of the greater State, even if forms of government involve public participation. The city conceals the "ongoing colonial nature" of the continuing colonial city project and dominion of the State. The modern city in the ongoing colonial project of the United States, despite revolting against British rule, has continued its colonizing mission through the city. The United States, which was freed from its former Imperial subjugation, established itself as a new Empire, whereas other States like it (Australia, Canada, India, Israel, and New Zealand) have not.

The modern cities in the settler colony of the United States still bear the marks of the colonial city project, even if new States emerged over the territorial space of the old colonial city project, such as St. Louis (see Fig. 2.24 and  2.25, #14 "habitat of Negroes"). The modern city continues the city splitting and territory segmentation through concentration as the old city by way of the identification of its populations for control. Settlement mapping hides the power that placed people in their appropriate space. Settlement mapping hides the **identification of populations** and the lands that were designated for them. It hides the colonial city project's purpose in enacting the power of the State. Settlement mapping hides that people did not move around with wagons, guilelessly find a plot of land, and set up a tent turned house. And houses do not turn settlements into cities. States do. So, modern settlement mapping is a clever reimagining to put forward a myth and hide a power (also shown in Chapter 1, see Fig. 2.26; Daley the

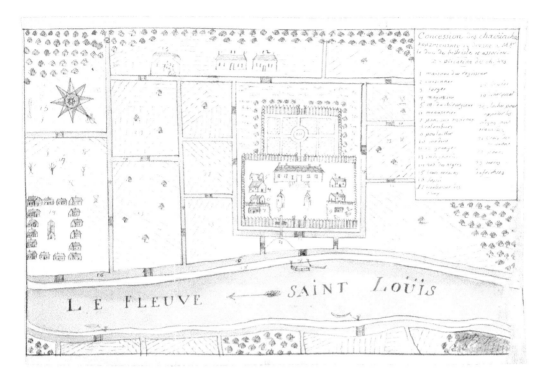

**Fig 2.24** French Colonial Officer Jean-François-Benjamin Dumont de Montigny Drew This Map of the Chaouachas Concession, a Plantation in French Louisiana, to Accompany His Memoir of His Experiences in the Region, 1747. (The Newberry Library)

Elder's 1950s re-telling of Chicago history in maps of the city for the 1900s, 1920s, and 1950s). The urban settlement, the city,

> ...in settler-colonial contexts, then, occupy a paradoxical kind of site in relationships between colonizer and colonized... Cities barely register as the actual locations of claimed lands in global land rights struggles, and yet contain the very sites where the actions of those struggles, on the streets, in Parliaments and courtrooms, materialize...The role of cities and the urbanization processes that create them in the twin tendencies of Indigenous genocide and dispossession is virtually entirely obscured from and *by* urban analysis. (Porter & Yiftachel, 2019, pp. 177–178)

## 2.5 Cities in the Seats of Power

Amsterdam, Antwerp, Berlin, Lisbon, London, Madrid, Paris, Stockholm, Vienna, and other cities in seats of

the Empire were also altered by the colonial city project and colonialism. Just as Cape Town, Ciudad de México, Chicago, Jerusalem, Mumbai, Nairobi, New York, Rio de Janeiro, Singapore, St. Louis, Sydney, Toronto, and other cities in the course of colonialism have also been altered by the work of imperialism and the Empire. There is no country, no nation. Societies are illusions. Social activities are for indoctrination. The cities are the truest expression of contact with governance but at the same time the lack of governance. The purpose of governance from an absent, distant State is solely to extract resources and wealth, and to dispossess populations. The infrastructural manifestation of the city is the infrastructural enforcement of populations.

Just as the words "colony" and "city" owe their origins to the Roman administration of its Empire, the operations of cities owe much of their conception to the Romans and to the States that began to link their histories to claims of Roman Empire descendancy. The *colonia* was literally the settlement

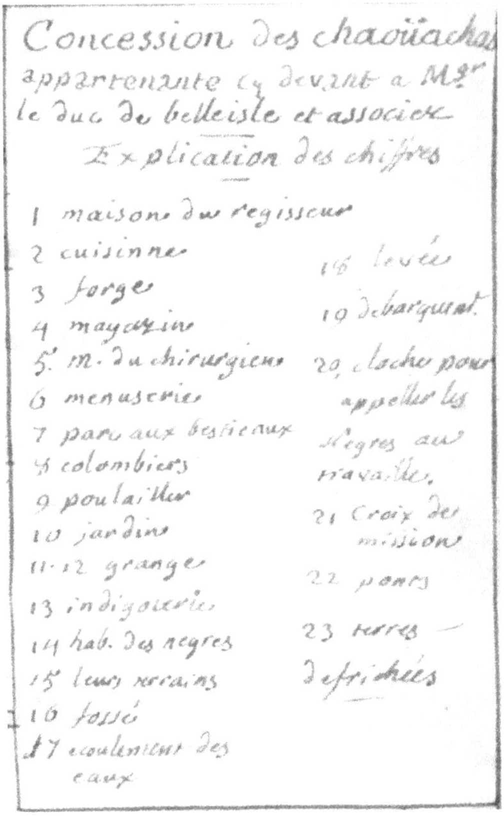

*Concession des chaouachas*
*appartenante cy devant a Mgr*
*le duc de belleisle et associés*
*Explication des chiffres*

1 maison du regisseur
2 cuisinne
3 forge
4 magazin
5 m. du chirurgien
6 menuscrie
7 parc aux bestieaux
8 colombiers
9 poulailler
10 jardins
11-12 grange
13 indigoterie
14 hab. des negres
15 leurs terrains
16 fossé
17 ecoulement des eaux
18 levée
19 Debarquent
20 cloche pour appeller les negres au travaille
21 Croix des mission
22 ponts
23 terres Defrichées

**Fig 2.25** Key of the Map of the Chaouachas Concession, Highlighting #14 "Habitat des Negres", 1747.

city away from the seat of the State, while the *polis* was the city within the seat of the State. While the explicit function of a capital city in the modern usage may have drawn upon the primacy of that city in managing all of the affairs of the State, this hid the reality that several cities served similar or vital secondary roles. The (free) imperial city (*urbs imperalis libera*) described self-ruling cities within a greater, more expansive State (an Empire) that held some measure of autonomy but were still vitally connected to the greater State based on their importance.

While it is clear that what is termed in this chapter as "colonial city projects" may have become imperial cities, many also did not. However, the vast majority of what are considered imperial cities are within seats of the Empire and have held long-standing positions within both old States and new States within the same geographic region. In fact, it was during the period of widespread warfare that resulted in conquest, enslavement, extraction, exploitation, colonialism, and dispossession from the 1400s to the 1800s that the creation of distinct definitions and understandings of the words for "town", "settlement", and "city" took place alongside the actual construction, shuffling, reconfiguration, and expansion of their infrastructural manifestation (Carey, 1967; Lederer, 1985).

The infrastructural manifestation of the city also led to the identity manifestation of the person but in association with his or her position in the State (coloniser or colonised in the colonial city project; the various class structures, statuses, racial categories, or gendering roles/functions). The rise of these particular cities, in the periods that they were birthed in, were predicated on extraction and dispossession. In the colonial city project, the natural resources and peoples were both subject to theft and exploitative uses, and those indigenous to the lands were forcibly removed and banished to distant regions of less use. In the imperial cities, extraction and dispossession still

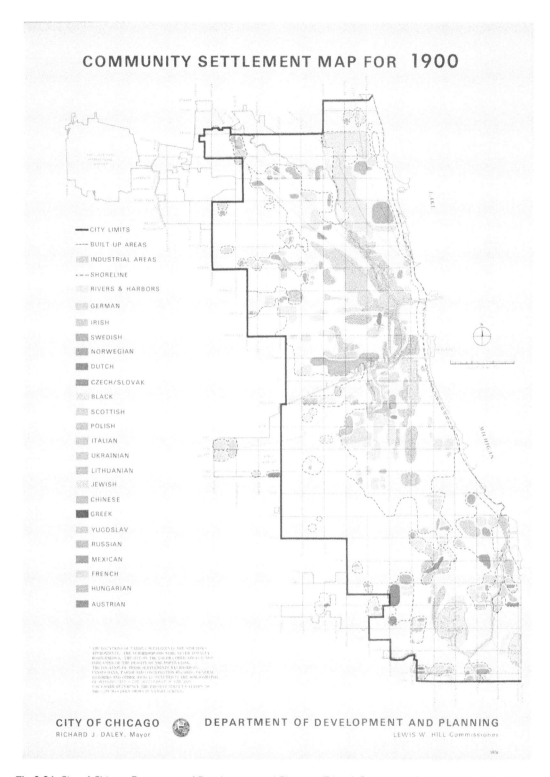

**Fig 2.26** City of Chicago Department of Development and Planning (Ethnic) Community Settlement in 1900. (The Chicago History Museum)

existed but in slightly different forms of forced and cheap labour, removal from property, and regulation to sites for marginalisation (Marx, 1976). For Ginn and Spearritt (2016),

> A city is an imperial city when its urban – its physical reality – functions exist to establish, perpetuate, and assert the power relationships of empire. Such cities are usually located at the metropole, but exclusively so. They tend to have physical elements and arrangements of space that serve as a range of imperial functions. Furthermore, such cities usually foster and are the object of a mystique, an imperial ideology, which harness the prestige of that city to the enduring (but not always long-lasting) power of the empire itself. (p. 1)

It was the city that served/serves as the site for both the indigenous and peasant to be transformed into labourer, whether that was in their territory of indigeneity or in the territory of their oppressor (Emmanuel, 1972). Further, it was the city that served/serves as the location for the accumulation of wealth by an elite class through possession of land and property and the extraction of the resources in the environment and peoples of the land/other lands. But most importantly, it was the city that served/serves as the space for ruling and governing to form and implement beyond its residence. Cities did not require the State to be present because they allowed for its constant presence. The roads, streets, cul-de-sacs, pleasances, interstates, highways, bridges, buildings, centres, parks, and squares were the State letting you know that it was there, and you must do what was expected of you in this infrastructure. The city was (and is) not the home (*domus*), the place of domestication (the maternal, of the mother). The city was (and is) the patronage (*patronus*), the place for indoctrination (the paternal, of the father). The imperial cities, along with the capital cities, governed the colonial city project. And the colonial city project fed the capital city as well as the imperial cities. Cities like Seville, New York, London, and Paris in the seats of the Empire played particular roles in bringing us to the modern era, not just in terms of city design, but also in population management as examples respectively of Nemser's *congregation, enclosure, segregation*, and *collection*.

As Chapter 1 indicated, the ideas for this book sprung from the experiences of the 2020 coronavirus pandemic, both direct (disease and policy response) and adjacent (job, rent, health), and the ongoing civil unrest due to State-sanctioned violence (policing, borders, surveillance) in 2020 and 2021. The mental space that I was in for Chapter 1 is not the same as for this chapter. At the time of the initial drafting of this chapter, weeks have passed. Indigenous People's Day was ironically occurring, and much of this chapter dealt with the myriad indigenous populations that had been extracted and dispossessed on their lands and in distant lands. The example the city of Seville serves this discussion well. Christopher Columbus, as the explorer-slaver, may have been funded by the Crown of Spain, but his capture and selling of indigenous peoples in Spain financed the vast bulk of his sails. His first return voyage in 1493 resulted in 25 indigenous people being brought into Seville. It was estimated that the total from all voyages and voyages associated with the expeditions was nearly 6,000 to Spain and Portugal. These were the first of the enslaved from and for the "new" lands of the Caribbean, North, Central, and South America. With this significant population and populations hailing from North Africa and the Baltic region, Seville, along with the cities of Cordoba and Cadiz, grew and created infrastructure for the large-scale slave marketing. The identification of slaves was arbitrary as some ledgers say *Indios* and some say *Negros*; they were not Spaniards or any other population in Europe. As the population of indigenous people escalated from increased extraction from their homelands, the city government in Seville by royal order developed a position of,

> Mayoral e Juez todos los Negros e Loros (de Zuniga, 1677, p. 374)

As the indigenous scholar Jack Forbes (1993) indicated,

> in 1475, Juan de Valladolid, an [African] of noble ancestry, was appointed as the judge and mayor of the Blacks and Loros (Browns) of the Seville area, with authority over their communal life, whether they were free or slave. (p. 28)

But as already mentioned, Seville was a destination for many enslaved peoples. Prior to Columbus' voyage, Moors and Tartars lived within the confines of the city (Pike, 1967). Indigenous populations from the Caribbean Islands and the West Coast of Africa began to be greatly represented; others from the Canary Islands and Greece as well as Slavs, Turks, Egyptians, Asians, and East Indians were part of the city population, thus the need to expand the market space. Colour-based terms were used such as the aforementioned *Loro* and *Negro*, but also *Blanco* (light), *Loro Casi Negro* (for brown, almost black), and *Indios* (for those specifically coming from the Indies) (Forbes, 1993, p. 40). Other enslaved populations with distinct identification were *Naborias*, those coming from the "useless island", like Jamaica (the island of my family), or places with no gold to extract. But this did not prevent Spain from maintaining its occupation and subjugation on "useless islands" like Jamaica, even naming the first settlement Sevilla la Nueva complete with its designated areas for "Negroes" (Hueman, 1981; see Fig. 2.27). Back in

Seville of the "Old World", each population had their designated trades and lines of work, location of residence, and levels of autonomy. They could be seen both in their slave labour and their trade work (for extra pay) along the Sevillian Arsenal, the public Squares, and wharves (see Fig. 2.28). The restrictions on policing the emerging realities and associations with "crime" were curbed by the status of the master who held the right to behaviour and autonomy of his "property". In some cases, the Sevillian enslaved were sent to conduct the affairs of their masters back in the islands of the Caribbean. Seville, a city marked once by Moorish conquest, became equally marked by the *Indios*, *Negros*, and "mulattoes" of the Caribbean and were weaved into the city life through continued enslavement, promotion, and emancipation. Through warfare upon indigenous populations, Seville flourished. War for land and war for labour.

The creation of land ownership and property rights were consequences of the phenomenon and system of enclosure. As the privatisation of land creates a physical enclosure, that then amplifies the

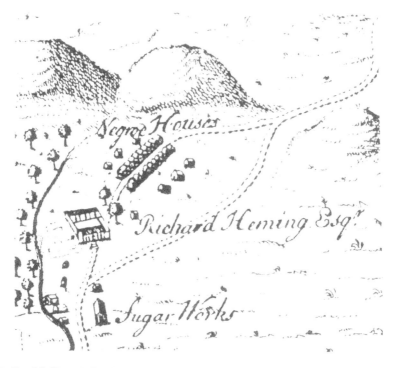

**Fig 2.27** Sevilla (Seville), Plano de Tomás López. The "House of Trade" Is Featured in Bottom Portion Left Corner of the Upper Right Quadrant of the Map. Houses for Negros and Other Population Are Scattered Throughout the City and Map Key, 1788. (Public Domain)

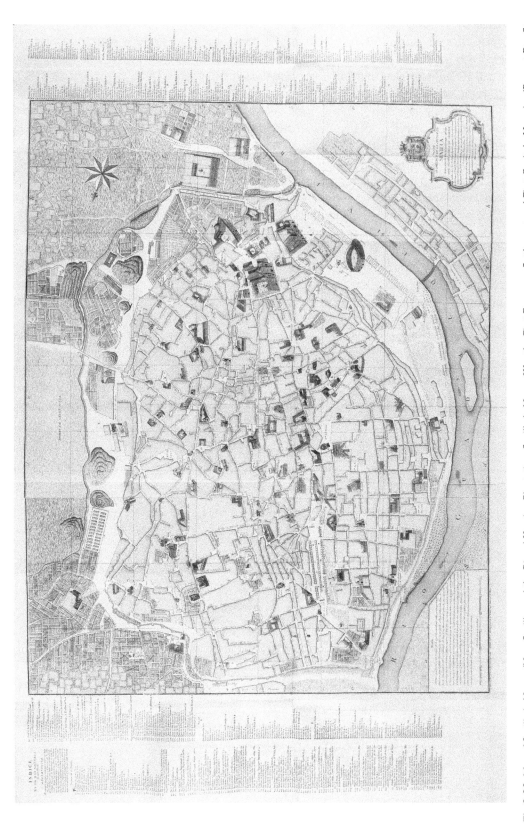

**Fig 2.28** Map of Sevilla la Neuva/New Seville, and the Ricard Heming Plantation. Sevilla la Nueva Was the First European Settlement and First Capital of Jamaica (Present Day St. Ann's Bay). 1721. (Jamaican National Library/Public Domain)

process of "social enclosure, the reproduction of workers shifting from the open field to the home, from the community to the family, from the public space (the common, the church) to the private" (Federici, 1994, p. 83). People of the land were tied to the land, but not free within it. Hodkinson (2012) described the conditions for enclosure as taking place in,

> Myriad of wars and evolved through time: [1] by "piecemeal" arrangements where landowners agreed to take small pieces of land out of the open fields or commons for their own exclusive use; [2] by the Lord of the Manor collecting all the tenancies into his own hands, not issuing new ones, or straightforward evictions; [3] by encroachment or squatting; [4] by agreement based on the common consent of all the landowners in a parish; [5] by special Royal licence; [6] by outright purchase by one owner of all common rights; [7] by "various forms of force and fraud" (Slater, 1907, p. 6); and, [8] once Crown opposition had subsided, by the state itself under act of parliament, either by a private act or under the authority of the General Enclosure Acts of 1830, 1836 and 1845 and its amending Acts, that provided enclosers with the legal powers to enclose the commons while outlawing all opposition and rebellion as punishable by jail and even the death penalty (see Hollowell, 2000; Marx, 1990 [1864]; Mingay, 1997; Slater, 1907). (p. 504)

The use of the grids that situated street placement and directions along with property placements in respect to those streets fulfilled the intent of the New York Commissioner's Plan of 1811 to regulate the development of land and the sale of it. (see Fig. 2.29). Where the Crown and its representative's ownership of land was the rule, the individual could not possess or be sold land. With the terms of the Dongan Charter of 1686, municipal ownership opened up the possibility for land to become a source of revenue for the city. The taxation of private owners alongside the initial sale of the land assisted in city growth and expansion. The 1811 Commission was given the authority and,

**Fig 2.29** The Commissioners Map of the City of New York. 1807. (Public Domain/Wiki Commons)

Exclusive power to lay out streets, roads, and public squares, of such width, extent, and direction, as to them shall seem most conducive to public good, and to shut up, or direct to be shut up, any streets or parts thereof which have been heretofore laid. (Bridges, 1811)

While the plan was fully unveiled in 1811, the Act that empowered it came in 1807, and within it an extensive articulation of streets and avenues (and explanation of their distinction) was given. Aspirational commentary on how far north (past Harlem since the Manhattan tribe had long since been displaced) that development would extend was also mentioned. Further, it provided for the placement of numerous monuments and buildings. City government, and not the State, flexed its authority over ownership with the coercion of private interests. The Spanish Empire's *Laws of the Indies* grid, which was tweaked to varying degrees in European city redevelopment and later altered by an English system, provided the best answer to maximizing the parcelling and selling of land, like modern airliner seats or sport stadium VIP seats. How many blocks along a street and avenues could mean the difference in thousands, and later millions, and even later billions, of dollars in revenue. While some contend that cities grow organically, and that enclosure is inevitable and exclusion of some peoples and land will occur, the boundaries inherent in the ideas, plan, and map dictated the enclosure rather than the already-established movement and travels of New York settlers. Rule of law was (and is) the key foundation for capital-led economic development location schema. Rule of law parcelled (and parcels) the land and certified (and certifies) the sell. It bounded (and binds) contracts and enforced (and enforces) infractions. It regulated (and regulates) construction and usage. Rule of law made (and makes) public property private property. It took (and takes) conquered land and placed (and places) it in the public domain for it to be allocated and distributed selectively. And hiding the rule of law in the public domain of open space for plazas, squares, roads, playgrounds, and parks enabled it to be used as the enemy of congestion and crowding. Rule of law removed this availability of the public domain

and the public from open spaces (eminent domain, the law that allows government to take private land for public use) (Ballon, 2013; Lankevich, 1999).

The "greatest grid" could now chart, block by block, the property to be sold and taxed, and the populations of "crime" and disease to be managed, in years to come. The grid enabled the formation of Seneca Village in 1825 and its removal in 1857 to be Central Park, "The Lungs of the City"; the grid enabled the use of the Commission-planned streets that assisted the Anti-Abolition Riots of 1834 and New York Draft Riots in 1863 (Schecter, 2005; Wall et al., 2008). In defence of property, the New York State constitution "imposed a $250 property suffrage for African American men...[and] had to fulfil a three-year residency requirement for voting" (Wall et al., 2008, p. 97). Distant and separate community settlements in the city were acts of protection from violence by making use of land still in the supposed public domain. New York's proximity along a waterway with a port should not be overlooked as a location first settled by the Dutch and British, an eventual major colonial city project, and then an imperial city once the colony of the United States ceased to be a direct colony of the British Empire.

By the 1900s, Britain had amassed the "greatest geographical empire in world history, with territories on every continent except Antarctica"; thereby, London became the "world's largest city" (Ginn & Spearritt, 2016, p. 9). London was truly "Imperial London", the administrative site for governance and "home" offices for colonial administrators as well as trade with its port, proximity to the Channel, and banking institutions (Schneer, 1999). With Britain as the Empire, cities like London and Liverpool were heavily managed, both for their wealth returns but also their labour extraction and dispossession resulting from that extraction. Similar to the religious padrones in New Spain (México) Puebla de los Ángeles, maps and records of the city formed a record of the occupation and income class to determine wage extraction through donations to the Church that the maps of Reverend Albert Hume (1858) in working with city administrators similarly determined (see Fig. 2.30),

lists of streets in their respective districts, in which outdoor relief is most uniformly

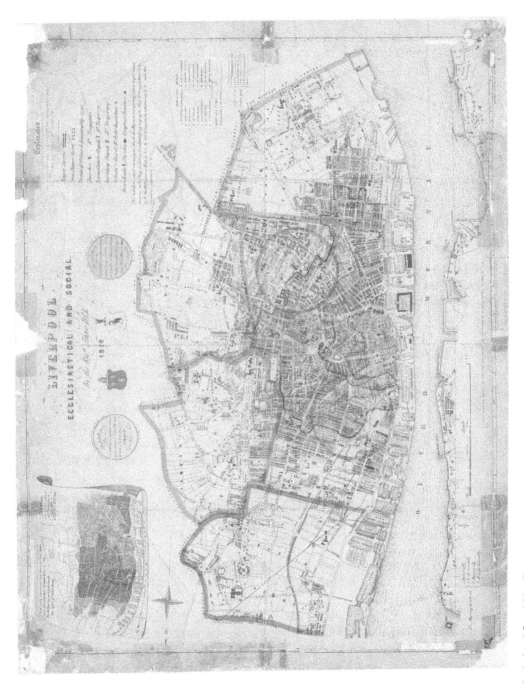

**Fig 2.30** Ecclesiastical and Social Map From Abraham Hume's "Four Maps of Liverpool: Ecclesiastical, Historical, Municipal, Moral and Social", 1854. (Courtesy of Tinho da Cruz, Department of Geography and Planning, University of Liverpool)

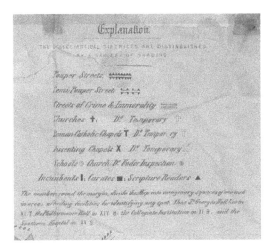

**Fig 2.31** Key of the Ecclesiastical and Social Map From Abraham Hume's "Four Maps of Liverpool: Ecclesiastical, Historical, Municipal, Moral and Social."

distributed. Each of them divided his list of streets into two classes; those which were wholly pauper, and those which were half or partially so. (p. 21)

This passage highlights their classification, and location within a section titled, "The Rich and The Poor". The passage on the preceding page is more telling, even it is naivete,

These terms are employed merely in their conventional sense; they are not used as a political economist would use them. By the rich we understand those who distribute large sums of annually; and by the poor, those who distribute small ones; though the latter may live within their names, and the former may exceed them. When we say that the poor crowd themselves upon spots gradually deserted by the rich, the statement requires a slight modification... There are large portions of the town, therefore, in which the labouring and destitute poor do not reside; and other spots, again, which they seem to monopolise. (p. 20)

The maps, the record keeping, and the notations all alluded to the narratives that emerged as the basis for city splitting. The **identification of populations** that resulted in a population's paper status as a critique, condemnation, and moral failing served as the basis for that population's utility in taxation and

wealth sharing (see Fig. 2.31). Malthus' ideas (1806) resulted in Poor Laws that re-directed cities' and State's resources, not to those areas in need but to bolster areas of affluence. The concerns tied to "crime" and immorality based on their swelling numbers in a space. The abandonment of space by the rich, and by extension the city administration that resulted in dereliction. The packing of this identified population in a small, less than viable, space for a thriving life. The dereliction opened up the possibility for city drainage systems and provisions tied to health, hygiene, and ultimately disease. Hume (1858) specifically made note of locations,

1. Violent Deaths – In the year 1857, there were 605 inquest held at the Coroner's court for the Borough; but 108 were deaths from injuries... these two wards, therefor, in the north end of the parish, constitute the region of violent deaths...
2. Unhealthy Localities – In 1847, the average duration of life in Liverpool was 20 years and five months...In 1853, the average age of all the patients who died...was fourteen years and eleven months; and the district does not embrace the lowest portion of the town. (p. 26)

Vaughn (2018) in *Mapping Society: The Spatial Dimensions of Social Cartography*, indicated that "two thousand copies of Hume's map were sold or distributed" with "one was set before the select committee of the House of Lords…[and] displayed at the National Association for the Promotion of Social Sciences meeting" (p. 67). This map making and record keeping influenced the work of Charles Booth, shipping industrialist and aspiring politician, in surveying 1880 London, employing the very same methods in gatherings and presenting the data as Hume. In the appendix of the original 1889 publishing and the introduction of the 1984 reprint, David Reeder stated,

> During the 1880s a new perception was being formed in London's social condition, growing out of spate of writings on how the poor lived by journalists and city missionaries…middle-class anxieties were fuelled by descriptions of…poor as a brutalized and degenerate race of people, the victims but also the agents of the deteriorating forces of city life. (Booth, 1994)

And similar to Hume, Booth's intent was focused on raising the "poverty question" to implore those with means and control of the city to address under- and unemployment, opening the doorway to the State to seek a solution tied to population containment and control, Nemser's *enclosure* and *collection* from the Ciudad de México plan. Booth attempted to go further with his empirical study by estimating not only the amount of people living in poverty within London, but also how many were living in a specific neighbourhood, East End (Vaughn, 2018). The location schema displayed in Booth's street study map, in my opinion, is the primary precursor to the redlining maps that would be employed in the United States some 50 years later. Employing a colour scheme, Booth noted on the maps (with Vaughn's annotations; see Figs. 2.32 and 2.33), making special note of

> Black. The lowest grade (corresponding to Class A in the statistical study), inhabited principally by occasional laborers, loafers, and semi-criminals – the elements of disorder.
> Yellow. Wealthy; hardly found in East London and little found in South London; inhabited by families who keep three or more servants, and whose houses are rated at £100 or more. (pp. 70–71)

But what is missing in the work of Hume and Booth, as well as our own present-day analysis of their work, is the political and intellectual environment that they occurred in. The colonial project of India, most particularly Kolkata, led to an earlier influx of British subjects, both indigenous immigrants and repatriating citizens born in India or returning "home". The sanitation issues that spawned the spread of cholera in India were intensified in the living conditions of London, Liverpool, and other cities. Furthermore, the return or migration of those who carried the disease with them brought on heightened fears and concerns of disease spread. Preceding their presence in London, detailed accounts of the conditions of the affected and death due to cholera were widely covered in news sources and other media. The British East India Company was freed from blame for its role in spreading the disease from one isolated region in India (a region that it was limited to for thousands of years). It was the disease of the Indian, the native, the darker "Other", and of the immigrant White poor that was the cause (see Figs. 2.34 and 2.35).

As mentioned earlier in this chapter, by 1831, cholera had killed 30,000 in Britain, with hundreds of books, graphs, charts, and maps devoted to the study of its effects and spread in the imperial city and State. Public health, and specifically epidemiology, was the intellectual tool deployed to study and curtail the spread. But in the early stages, much of the work was devoted to behavioural analysis of populations. These works were filled with not only identifications of specific populations as culprits, but also crafted narratives of their behaviours that led to such a spread. It was not until the spread of the disease had intensified those epidemiological investigations moved to population-based studies (much the same way that it played out in India, first affecting Indians with little to no concern, just judgement) (Hamlin, 2009). Racialisation of Indians accompanied racialisation of those in the White labour class (the living and sanitary conditions of immigrants, Brits born in India).

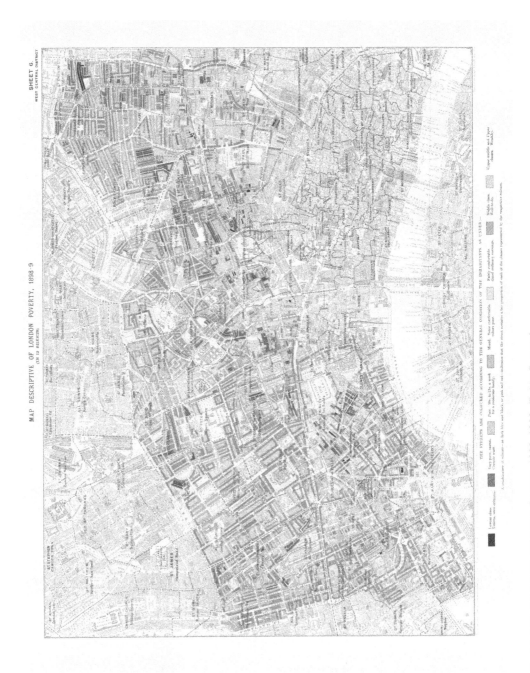

**Fig 2.32** Charles Booth's Map Descriptive of London Poverty, 1898–1899. (Public Domain)

**Fig 2.33** The Colour Key for Charles Booth's Map Descriptive of London Poverty in *Life and Labour of the People in London*, 1889. (Wiki Commons/Public Domain)

At the behest of the nephew of the French Emperor that was crowned by Pope Pius VII, Napoléon III, Baron Georges-Eugène Haussmann modernised Paris. The Imperial Capital city was re-partitioned and erected as a complex arrondissement system of 20 distinct zones. Newly designed boulevards replaced dilapidated and useless streets for the explicit purpose of fostering social order and making ample provisions to the emerging elites. City life became of new use alongside the function of work. In the 1643 map of the city, Paris can be seen with very narrow, almost crookedly designed streets which had no real structure, pattern, or direction. In the 1890 map (see Fig. 2.36), streets were transformed into monumental Boulevards while the existing neighbourhoods, containing slums, and buildings were destroyed in order to create space for them. The crooked streets were straightened and planned in such a manner that important monuments and buildings that reside in the city could be seen with no obstructions blocking the view. Furthermore, the Boulevards were decorated with elaborate street furnishings, benches, monuments, gas lights, and trees, displaying the power of the city. Another feature that

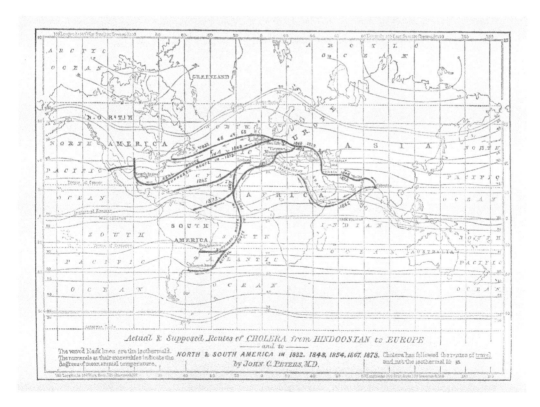

**Fig 2.34** Actual & Supposed Routes of Cholera From Hindoostan to Europe, 1832–1873. (Wellcome Images/Creative Commons)

**Fig 2.35** Cholera Map of the Metropolis of London, 1849. (Wellcome Images/Creative Commons)

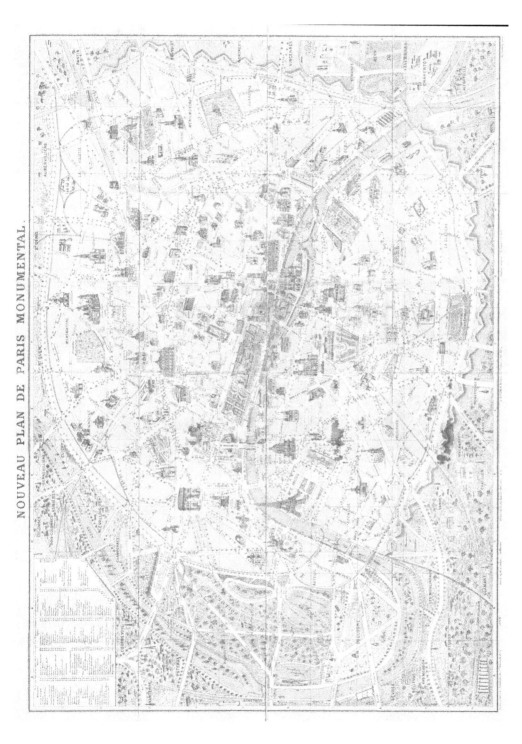

NOUVEAU PLAN DE PARIS MONUMENTAL.

**Fig 2.36** Guilmin's Nouveau Plan de Paris Monumental Featuring the Work of Georges-Eugène Haussmann's Revolutionary Modernization of Paris. 1890. (Paris Collection)

developed in the city during modernisation was the "garden squares", which were created with the notion of public spaces for the people of the city to interact with one another and to partake in leisure activities. Alongside this above-ground development, also came the development of the modern sewerage systems. During the 1800s, Paris was one of the first cities in Europe to construct an effective, clean, and safe sewerage system to mitigate hygiene-related issues that arose in London and elsewhere. Subterranean Paris also further influenced the progress and modernity for the entire city and became a social activity space for tours of amazement.

Also inspired by the grid design was the most recognised collection of the Spanish *Laws of the Indies*, the 1680 *Recopilación de las Leyes de los Reynos de las Indias* ("Compilation of the Laws of the Kingdoms of the Indies"; Lyman, 1980), but less as a literal translation and more for the allotment of space for those deemed valuable and disposable. Haussmann's finished product also inspired Latin America's ongoing transformation of colonial city projects to emerging Imperial cities, such as Ciudad de México, Buenos Aires, Santiago de Chile, and modern-day Rio de Janeiro's Olympic redevelopment plan. In fact, Ciudad de México's Paseo de la Reforma was an assumed copy of the Boulevards of Paris. Paris's redesign featured rectilinear streets that assisted State political control of its population in the event of an uprising. The broad street design would grant army wagons to travel and fire into various communities, but in day-to-day functionality was used to encourage various social classes to interact and mingle to create an allusion of social unity in the midst of dispossession. As the initial designs were implemented, slight modifications were implemented by the elites to decrease these encounters. The great spectacle of the power of money on the grands boulevards and grands magasins, and the expositions universelles, was to foster a modern conception of community. But the elites knew that too much marvelling would lead to demands for land sharing and wealth distribution and to mobs of the disposed if they were allowed to gaze too long. The social re-spatialisation of Paris was utterly for the dominance of State power

within the guise of alluring aesthetic public works. As Harvey (2003) noted,

> Public investments were organized around private gain, and public spaces appropriated for private use; exteriors became interiors for the bourgeoisie...the boulevards, lit by gas lights, dazzling shop window displays, and cafes open to the street (an innovation of the Second Empire), became corridors of homage to the power of money and commodities, play spaces for the bourgeoisie. (p. 275)

For that reason, spaces excluded the disposed of space and labour and became private space. The distance between the poor and affluency no longer intersected, and the suburb became the space for relocation. Haussmann expelled much of the labour classes from the centre, pushing them ever outward, to virtually anywhere on the map of the city, to the north and northeast of the city – the hinterlands within a city but socially beyond the city.

> That Paris was more spatially segregated in 1870 than in 1850 was only to be expected, given the manner in which flows capital were unleased to the tasks of restructuring the built environment and its spatial configuration. Much of the worker population was dispersed to the periphery...or doubled up in overcrowded, high-rent locations closer to the center. Industry likewise faced the choice of changing its labour process or suburbanizing. (Harvey, 2003, p. 95)

Haussmann continued to work on the city, especially when growing concerns from the Paris bourgeoisie often spoke about *les classes dangereuse* (the dangerous classes), not because of their "crime" or disease but because of their potential for uprising. Saint-Antoine, in particular, a suburb known for being populated by those dangerous working classes that was of concern to Napoléon as many of its residents were at the heart of the 1789 revolution, had a new boulevard cut straight through it in the fashion of the interstate and highway fracturing of neighbourhoods in the 20th century.

## 2.6 A Second Conclusion

As a European social construction, our modern views of public space and social activity as something more than material production – as space for the imagined and fabricated society filled with social interaction, leisure, and other forms of social re-creation – was founded by the emergence of these new, reimagined Spanish, "American", British, and French Empires from the early 1700s to the late 1800s. The State and its fabricated society are respectively not the same thing or composed of the same institution and processes. People inhabit the spatial ordering of the city long since predicated by the colonial and imperial city projects. The State, once again, is the combination of the ruling bodies (monarchy, elected, appointed), the bureaucratic classes (those upper-level administrators of government), the corporate elite and their companies, and the elite private interest class. The State is the entity that governs, rules, extracts, and dispossesses. The fabricated society is the illusive combination of citizenry of States, the subjects of the rule despite level of class, categorised racialisation, or manner of gendering. The State conquers, displaces, occupies, exploits, and enforces space that a small portion of it may be repurposed as temporary and symbolic public use. The fabricated society takes on that repurposed space and creates social activities and senses of meaning and attachment to those spaces either in support of the State (governmentality) or against it (rebellion). As the dominating nation-States and Empires claimed a philosophical lineage to Greece and Rome (Hemingway, 1988), they also wrestled with their own class structures through the reorganisation of their monarchies and government. The city, and the lifestyle that accompanied it, brought forth a false and illusionary articulation of a leisured society for all citizenries. The major capital campaigns, world fairs, open parks, public museums, cafés, shopping districts, and other edifices first articulated what we now see as modern leisure spaces (McClellan, 1984; Small, 2011).

Specifically, within literature concerned with the design and function of social space (leisure studies, urban planning, architectural design), little has been considered and discussed about how Trans-Atlantic Slavery, Imperial Colonialism, and Independence Debt led to the allowance of an emerging and expanding leisured class with discretionary time and income during and post-Industrial Revolution (Hunnicutt, 2006; Veblen, 1994). The ways in which this use and function of space identified a broader class of people who still maintained the aspirations, taste, and values of the ruling elite while also acquiring an increased disdain of those identified "dangerous classes" is lost to us in some cognitive respect. While some credence is given to what emerged in France, in particular that which birthed conceptions of leisure and the leisure class (Bramham & Wagg, 2014; Russell, 2017), it does not solely rest with French society nor with just becoming a leisured class. Romanticism (Campbell, 1989), Impressionism (McClellan, 1984), the aforementioned Haussmannisation of the city (Pinkney, 1955), and Benjamin's Flâneur (Lauster, 2007; Rojek, 1997) are just some of the emerging social activities that inspired periods in art, urban design, and social thought that then impacted how people function in French society and beyond. However, what has been painfully missing are the potential roles that slavery, colonialism, and debt served in funding those articulations of public space, leisure, and recreation (Hunnicutt, 2006). But these social activities and art movements were financed by spatial dominion of indigenous peoples abroad and the labouring class at home. Additionally, these social activities also reimagined these cities with the rewriting of history, the revising of city design, and the reduction (reducir) of people as subjects.

One of the underlying principles of leisure, the "freedom from the necessity to labor", is built upon holding some distinctive class position of privilege in a society and can only be created from holding such a class position (Hemingway, 1988, p. 180). Exploited service is then rendered to those classes (or those with aspirations to those classes). Very little is conceived of for those who cannot afford to play. And even less is conceived and concerned with the classes of those who have been dispossessed, first by the State and then by the leisured classes. Hemingway (1998) noted that, "we must recognise at the very least that understanding leisure is an activity extending considerably beyond the provision of services" (p. 181). However, de Grazia's (1964) critique and inquiry into the question of morality in leisure should not be confined to contemporary modes of leisure and their departure from a Greek ideal, but more so, a critique and inquiry into the period of the 1800s birthing of not only the modern use of public space, social activities, leisure, and recreation but also the modern question of the morality of leisure. Even the assumption that leisure is the highest form of the expression of freedom begs interrogation when cast alongside the slavery, colonialism, and debt incurred during the early 1700s to the late 1800s. If freedom and enlightenment are pre-conditions for leisure (Pieper, 1952), then what does it mean when one's pre-condition is subjugation and servitude? What does it mean if one's ancestry is marked by this pre-condition? What does it mean if one's pre-condition of freedom is tainted by the servitude of another? European and British States overthrew Non-European matrilineal societies through relentless savagery with the outcome of enslavement, uncompromising barbarism that resulted in colonialism, and the dominance of civilisation through the creation of indebtedness (Engels, 1909). The city produced the dispossessed and new set of dispossessors. The emerging leisured classes of Europe were not happenstance occurrences. By paying closer attention to the behaviours, lifestyles, and locations of engagement with leisure, we begin to see the leisure of the modern era (Hunnicutt, 2006; Rojek, 1985), but also the ways that the State hides its actions through the social effects of society until the violence of enforcement needs to appear to maintain order. The spatially fabricated society is built upon the indigenous, the enslaved, and that which is crafted by the labourer.

As wealth was redistributed and statuses realigned due to internal revolts, what were some of the expectations associated with those new lifestyles? And what were some of the opportunities that both the private and public sectors supplied to this leisure class? An "American" visiting Paris in 1869 remarked how the culture of seeing and being seen was taking form in the salons and cafes and was influencing the world,

> Persons of all classes sitting [in the cafés] smoking, drinking, chatting, reading journals. Here is a true democracy – the only social equality to be seen...The Senator and the

blouse sit side by side, and...rest dainty cups on the same table. (McCabe, 1869, p. 75)

However, the café scene was not new. In fact, by 1720 there were probably around 400 known cafes in Paris that quickly grew to over 40,000 by the 1880s. However, the 1800s brought forth the ideal that all in French society were welcome. (Marx first met Friedrich Engels in the Café de la Régence in the Palais Royal.) The fairs and music halls of a new London (and British countryside) were raising the question of citizenship over class. In particular, the creation of the 1867 Reform Act enabled working class (gendered men) citizens to vote. Public discourse became commonplace across classes, and recreation was thought of as a way to enlighten those dull "common people". The goal was common British-ness. By 1914, Coventry, also by an American's account, was the site of expansion and growth as,

> The people...walk quicker than other Englishmen, Everyone seems prosperous. There is a briskness in the very air of the place. Your factories are growing as fast as the factories in Detroit – and I cannot say more than that. Everyone is busy. (Beaven, 2005, p. 2)

During this same period, "cinemas, dance halls and social clubs increased in number and size in response to vitality of the local economy" (Crump, 1986, p. 261). But it is insufficient to only deduce, as Hunnicutt (2006) posited, that through these personally intimate opportunities, salons, cafés, festivals, and music halls were locations for,

> Human brutality, sexual exploitation and excess, blood "sports", public spectacles, executions and torture, political and family intrigues, and power struggles, overindulgence in food and drink, mind-numbing idleness, and the simple pleasure of dominating and bossing others around, are among the first activities that humans, newly empowered, discovered and enjoyed for their own sakes, and which remain among the most familiar leisure pursuits. (p. 60)

Through the transdisciplinary examination of extraction of natural resources and exploitation of labour, there has been an increase in knowledge of

**Fig 2.37** La Médina de Tunis. 2016. (Sami Mlouhi/Wiki Commons/Creative Commons)

how societies benefited from slavery beyond centuries of free labour, crops that were harvested, and buildings that were constructed (Harley, 2013; Tomich, 2003; Williams, 1994).

For example, New York Life (Insurance) has come forward as being one of the early insurers of enslaved Africans in the Southern United States (New York Life, 2017; Swarns, 2016b). The company's profits soared as they were able to recoup for slave owners nearly three-quarters of the value of the enslaved, rather than a complete loss if one was found dead due to exhaustion, physical abuse, or some work-related "accident". Other insurance companies followed suit, while banks allowed the enslaved to be considered collateral for all types of loans (i.e., housing, capital campaigns, small business, etc.). Universities such as Georgetown, Harvard, Brown, and the University of Virginia profited from plantations to bankroll the early construction of their campuses and payment of salaries of the early faculty (Georgetown University, 2017; Swarns, 2016a).

The identities we carry through occupations that we hold within the fabricated society give those identities value. But nonetheless, it is the State that dictates the existence of those identities and the manner and degree that those identities serve (at a greater level) the interests of the State.

Social activities, use of public space, leisure, and recreation are merely displays of control – control of one's time and the time of another. In order for there to be an identified leisured class there must be an identified dominated class somewhere to make the luxury of leisure possible (Wilensky, 1961). And where are they? On the fringe of the city limits within a native reserve, township, or indigenous reservation. Or, maybe closer to the city centre in a rundown neighbourhood area that is demarcated by street names like the Sevillian Calle des Negros, the French-controlled Tunisian Rue des Nègres (see Fig. 2.37), or Martin Luther King Blvd. in any city of the United States. Exploitation through wage theft and taxation went hand-in-hand with the promulgation of leisure in much of the European and British world (and those States that were European and British-aspiring). But financing the Crown and the State became one of the initial stopgaps prior to revolt. For example, on August 8, 1788, the royal treasury of France was declared empty as wealthy nobleman (through the Parlement of Paris) refused to back the Crown any longer through loans.

As various European (and the emerging "American") empires wrestled with actual revolution and potential rebellion, levying high taxes on their domestic and settler population was not favourable as it could incite further revolt. Thus, the taxation of non-settler colonies afforded these societies with an effective and profitable approach to generate revenue, invest in public works, and limit (and decrease) taxation within the colonizing State (Coelho, 1973; Frankema, 2010).

But taxation was not the sole route of funding an empire, which thereby funded growth of State supportive and complicit social activities (leisure), and State-aligned and complicit classes (leisure class). In 1791, following the 1790 Martinique uprising, the enslaved Africans of the French colony of Saint Domingue (present-day Haiti) revolted. By 1804, as an independent nation, Haiti struggled to maintain itself, especially after the United States and Britain refused to trade with the new nation.

In 1825, through an assembly of 14 gunships, Haiti was threatened by a financially drained France to comply with demands or face continued warfare. The new nation of freed persons could not afford a sustained engagement and agreed with King Charles X's demands of paying France 150 million gold francs, reduced to 90 million (that was estimated to be ten times the State's annual revenue; valued at $17 billion dollars in today's currency). Haiti could not pay the debt immediately and instead was forced to take out loans from the only banks that would loan them money, in France. By 1947, Haiti had only finished paying the interest, and by the 1970s, it finished paying the loan completely. Extraction and dispossession are the consistent order of the day and are the historical recurrence of the articulation of power maintenance. It is not that gender and Race are merely social constructions of the fabricated society; it is that they are produced via the production of space of the city. The city that is built on top of indigenous land must also require the removal and erasure of all things indigenous (the people, the space, the land, the culture) (Estes, 2019).

The city is the place that benefits when that extraction and dispossession of faraway places is actualised into aesthetic public work campaigns, but the city is the place that the extraction and dispossession within the space of the city also occurs. And if extraction ends due to the available resources dwindling down to amounts that no longer yield profits, or if the exploitation of the labour no longer is needed for the yield that is extracted, then the city can be deemed useless, just as the islands once were.

In the midst of a White and Black middle-class flight, Mayor Richard Hatcher commented,

> There is much talk about Black control of the ghetto...What does that mean? I am mayor of a city of roughly 90,000 Black people, but we do not control the possibilities of jobs for them, of money for their schools, of state-funded social services. These things are in the hands of the United States Steel Corporation and the County Department of Welfare of the State of Indiana. Will the poor in Gary's worst slums be helped because the pawn-shop owner is Black not White? (Poinsett, 1970, p. 77)

The large concentration of a disposable racialised demographic within a city would only result in that city being isolated within a state and county, just as a neighbourhood of a disposable racialised demographic would only result in that part of the city being marginalised. From the botanical ordering of species grants the purveyor of State power the ability to name, define, and classify people as a taxonomy of dominion. Our ascribed identities identify our rank ("American", British, etc.) and identify our position within that rank (woman, Black, native). Our ascribed identities identify where we belong. But ultimately, our ascribed identities identify who we belong to, just like taxonomy exhibitions in an imperial museum.

Historical dates take on new meaning when we correspond them with slavery, colonialism, and debts: 1753 The British Museum is established; 1765 Champs de Mars begins construction; 1793 the National Museum of Natural History and the Louvre open; 1794 the Museum of French Monuments (Musee des Monuments Français) is founded; 1851 (the first) and 1862 the World Expo takes place in Britain; and 1867, 1878, 1889, 1900, and 1937 the Exposition Universelles takes place in France (Corbey, 1993; Merrill, 2012; Piketty et al., 2006). What role did slavery, colonialism, and debts have in the funding of their construction and production? Irony is beginning to take shape in modern history, as we see the British East India Company return after a 135-year absence under the ownership of an Indian entrepreneur (Doshi, 2017) – the revitalisation of a company that brought tea (a crop that is not grown anywhere on the islands of Great Britain) to England and has a 400-year brand of exploitation. How the State identifies populations becomes the way that we identify ourselves. We believe we take on identities based on interest, occupation, and geographic region, but all of those are social activities sponsored by the State. Self-determined identities are those that political challenge State-powered processes of identification. And self-determination first begins with an acknowledgement of the political history that resonates in ourselves. As Stuart Hall (1997) once remarked,

> People like me who came to England in the 1950s have been there for centuries; symbolically, we have been there for centuries. I was

coming home. I am the sugar at the bottom of the English cup of tea. I am the sweet tooth, the sugar plantations that rotted generations of English children's teeth. There are thousands of others beside me that are, you know, the cup of tea itself. Because they don't grow it in Lancashire, you know. Not a single tea plantation exists within the United Kingdom. This is the symbolization of English identity – I mean, what does anybody in the world know about an English person except that they can't get through the day without a cup of tea? Where does it come from? Ceylon – Sri Lanka, India. That is the outside history that is inside the history of the English. There is no English history without that other history. (p. 48).

A group of fifteen Caribbean nations have embarked on a mission for reparation justice from France, Britain, Spain, and the Netherlands for the independence debts that were levied against them alongside the centuries of profit from slavery. Within museums (in particular, the British Museum, Berlin Museum für Völkerkunde, and New York's Metropolitan Museum), a growing call for the return of indigenous remains and plundered artwork has been underway since the 1990s (The Economist, 1997).

In an effort to return Nemser's logic on concentration in the form of *congregation* (settler, direct, indirect, and hybrid colonialism); *enclosure* (location schema and system segmentation); *segregation* (city splitting and territory segmentation); and *collection* (the collection, identification, and order of things; botanical gardens -> botany -> Race science), I argue here that the colonial city project of various Empires and Republics modernised the old imperial cities, and the combination of those cities became the cities of the 20th century onward to the contemporary period. We have not inherited cities with the legacy of a colonial and imperial past; we are living within the colonial and imperial cities of the present that continue the aims and efforts of dispossession and extraction. It this chapter, I implore you, the reader, to see colonialism and imperialism. See it in the streets that you walk on, the streets that you drive down, the buildings that you enter and exit, and the conditions of the "Othered" bodies that you ignore. It is here in their combination that

extraction and dispossession remain fully in effect. It is here that the Geographies of Threat make their claim that this is the historical purpose and function of the city. The colony of exploration, settlement, and exploitation drives the State through city rule to constantly restrict for abandonment and austerity as well as expand for wealth accumulation and land acquisition. The State's desire to maintain power at all costs drives the city to carefully identify its population for labour and categorisation (**identification of populations**), to identify those populations as disposable or threatening (**identification of threats**), and then to identify those populations for acts of lawfare and warfare through violence work (**identification for violence**).

The *congregation* of the masses, the coloniser and colonised, both subjects of the Crown State in Seville, extends the works of *congregation* in New Spain and most profoundly in Ciudad de México. The city forced all to come to it, to be part of it, by force or by need. Extraction, dispossession, exploitation, and displacement are the very purpose of enclosure. With State power, displacement was inevitable: land theft through exchanges between unequals and through backdoor agreements, land theft with the protection rackets of the police or military. Space and land, people and populations become commodities of State power. Appropriation is a milder way to conceive of the dispossession that is an everyday occurrence in contemporary cities. Through organised abandonment and lawfare, legislation and legalities protect the State and private interest over what is considered the commons (public spaces, squares, community centres, and parks). New York City (specifically Manhattan) is instructive on Nemser's *enclosure*. Cities in Britain, most especially the imperial city of London, further formalise Nemser's idea of *segregation*. The colonial city project of the Spanish Empire in the planning of Ciudad de México, influenced by the cholera troubles of Kolkata, becomes the hallmark for the demographically informed city splitting of today. Nemser's idea of *collection* as a concentration in the infrastructure of Race, leads to Race's ordering in society and not just its identification. The collection of Boulevards, monuments, parks, and museums was also to collect populations and situate them in their place.

Concentration of conditioning for spatial control (gender) and spatial arrangements (Race) is the basis for racial and gender discrimination in social interactions and social arrangements. Discrimination is not racialisation or gendering and hence not the truest expression of White Supremacy or Patriarchy, or even the greater existence of the State. Discrimination is the stuff of social activities, the things that reflect the effects of generational spatial reinforcement, that were reinforced by the city and that then reinforce the need for future spatial rearrangements. Here, space is not a production for all; space as a commodity and the commodification of space are dual forms of activity under capitalism (Gregory, 1991). The space of the city is the truest, purest basis for Fields and Fields' (2012) *racecraft* to work its magic and not the media. The city, again, does not happen to become harmful to populations through system segmentation. The city did not abruptly come to employ city splitting and territory segmentation-based techniques. What is argued here is that this is the purpose of the city (returning to the three concepts of "Geographies of Threat"). And it is this spatiality in concentrating and identifiying populations in such a way that produces class, gender, Race, and the very fabricated society that allows that production to flourish. The immediacy of the ghetto does one type of work, but the maintenance of the ghetto across generations institutionalises that work (as was the case of Campo del Ghetto Nuovo in Venice, see Fig. 2.38).

What is the city about? What is the city's purpose? We do not experience our cities in their totalities. We experience them through our streets, parks, and public spaces. The city is about capital, and the city of capital, Clark (1984) argued,

> Did not need to have a representation of itself laid out upon the ground in bricks and mortar, or inscribed as a map in the minds of its city-dwellers. One might even say that capital preferred the city not to be an image – not to have form, not be accessible to the imagination, to readings and misreadings, to a conflict of claims on its space – in order that it might mass-produce an image of its own to put in place of those it destroyed. (p. 36)

The iconography of conquest within the maps, globes, and other visual retellings both celebrated past conquering achievements and proffered future realms to conquer. The iconography in these depictions was both influenced by and influenced ideologies of expansion, conquest, and occupation (Bucher, 1981). On the edges of maps and globes, "here be dragons" was not an empty note representing antiquated mythical fears; they were *legitime* and burdensome populational threats to the power of the realm. The fear did not prevent expansion; it just informed it and prepped it for conflict. The "dragons" were destroyed through conquest and occupation, displaced to outlining regions on new maps, or appropriated as new symbols and representations of State. Any present-day monsters on maps are in the form of reservations, refugee settlements, and prisons – the location schema for places and people that we will deal with later, at another time. They are what appears on the edges of the maps of the small towns and cities that exploit them for their own needs to fulfil the requirements of serving the State. With this understanding, the Congress of Vienna 1814 re-formed Europe into what we know it now. Held in Vienna, it balanced the various State powers and their controlling borders. It ushered a New Imperialism for the modern age with the rise of a new power in the United States after the American Revolution and the fall of the mighty Spanish Empire. In this context, the historical occurrence of the 1884–1885 Berlin Conference was freed from its mythical cabal-like machinations. The Berlin Conference assisted in defining what effective occupation was and what it henceforth should be. The Conference, held in an imperial city, was not to "carve up Africa" for colonisation and exploitation, as this was always well underway. The Conference simply came to terms with managing now "vacant land" and establishing better trade arrangements with competing Empires and Republics,

> Underpinning this constitutional vision for Central Africa, however, was a basic contradiction in the dynamics of late 19th-century capitalism. As early theorists of imperialism were to observe, various changes in the political economy of Europe... – had encouraged increased speculative interest in overseas investment (in trade, mining, ports, railways, telegraph systems, etc.). This, furthermore, seemed to encourage a competitive logic of acquisition: colonies and protectorates would have to be acquired in order to "protect" overseas

**Fig 2.38** 1516 Campo del Ghetto Nuovo (Plan of the Jewish Ghetto of Venice), Segregated and Held the Jewish Population for Nearly 300 Years Until 1797. (Public Domain)

trade and investment from the dangers posed by the monopolistic or protectionist policies of rival colonial powers. (Craven, 2015, p. 51)

The State had concerns about the maintenance of power. The unchartered corners of the map, if there were any, were no longer a concern. The State (these States) grew immensely powerful, and contraction from within was certain. Do they continue to grow with force? Or do they continue to grow through other means of governance? The lessons from the various colonial city projects as well as the strife in the imperial cities had to be managed. Territories had to be further extracted and excavated of resources. The removal of the easily answerable mystifications places us into the cold stare and logic of the State. The State is here for nothing less and nothing more than extraction and dispossession. "Fortress Europe" must be defended at all costs, not because of fears of migrants but because of the inability to manage their own surplus populations, much less the surplus populations from other States. The "Fortress" stands for a new conception of enclosure that is even more selective and extractive. "Europe" is loosely raised as a stand-in for a much smaller representation of "Europe" than what appears on maps. The re-invoking of this Nazi Germany era slogan for liberal policies on immigration and citizenship and conservative counter-efforts on perceived open borders (Van Avermaet, 2009). The concerns of the State become the fears of its citizenry that have become prepared in cities to protect it from the foreign horde, instead of hording the wealth of elites within the enclosure (Raspali, 1973). The collapse of cities began with Kolkata children flooding Belgium, a cascade of more and more from the East and Global South, the dispossessed and the disposable. London fell, and all was lost for the last camp of the saints of the old regime. And all "natives" need to be aware, while the State informs all citizenry to beware of them (see Fig. 2.39) (Craven, 2015).

"The colonial's sector is a sector built to last, all stone and steel. It's a sector of light and paved roads, where the trash cans constantly overflow with strange and wonderful garbage, undreamed-of leftovers. The colonist's feet can never be glimpsed, except perhaps in the sea, but then you can never get close enough. They are protected by solid shoes in a sector where the streets are clean and smooth, without a pothole, without a stone. The colonist's sector is a sated, sluggish sector, its belly is permanently full of good things. The colonist's sector is a

White folks' sector, a sector of foreigners. The colonized's sector, or at least the native quarters, the shanty town, the Medina, the reservation, is a disreputable place inhabited by a disreputable people...it's a world with no space, people are piled one on top of the other, squeezed tightly together...the colonized's sector is. Famished sector, hungry for bread, meat, shoes, coal, and light. The colonized's sector is a sector that crouches and cowers, a sector on its knees, a sector that is prostrate... this compartmentalized world, this world divided in two, is inhabited by different species... what divides this world is first and foremost what species, what race one belongs to".
– Frantz Fanon, 1961, in *The Wretched of the Earth*, pp. 4–5.

"Day by day, month by month, doubt by doubt, law and order became fascism; education, constraint; work, alienation; revolution, mere sport; leisure, a privilege of class; marijuana, a harmless weed; family, a stifling hothouse; affluence, oppression; success, a social disease; sex, an innocent pastime; youth, a permanent tribunal; maturity, the new senility; discipline, an attack on personality; Christianity... and the West... and white skin...."
– Jean Raspali, The Camp of Saints, pp. 92–93.

**Fig 2.39** A Common Sign in Johannesburg, South Africa. 1956. (Photo Credit: Three Lions/Getty Images)

# References

Anderson, B. R. O. (1983). *Imagined communities: Reflections on the origins and spread of nationalism.* Verso Books.

Arnold, D. (1986). Cholera and colonialism in British India. *Past & Present, 113*(1), 118–151. 10.1093/past/113.1.118

Van Avermaet, P. (2009). Fortress Europe? Language policy regimes for immigration and citizenship. In G. Hoban-Brun, C. Mar-Molinero, & P. Stevenson (Eds.), *Discourses on language and integration: Critical perspective on language* (pp. 15–44). John Benjamin Publishing Co.

Ballon, H. (Ed.). (2013). *The Greatest grid: The master plan of Manhattan 1811-2011.* Columbia University Press.

Beaven, B. (2005). *Leisure, citizenship and working-class men in Britain, 1850-1945.* Manchester University Press.

Beck, L. (2011). Illustrating the conquest in the long eighteenth century: Theodore de Bry and his legacy. In C. Ionescu (Ed.), *Book illustration in the long eighteenth century: Reconfiguring the visual periphery of the text* (pp. 501–540). Cambridge Scholars.

Bramham, P. & Wagg, S. (2014). Time, history, and leisure. In, *An introduction to leisure studies*(pp. 52–70). Sage Publications Ltd.

Bridges, W. (1811). *Map of the city of New York and island of Manhattan with explanatory remarks and references.* William Bridges.

Bucher, B. (1981). *Icon and conquest: A structural analysis of the illustrations of the de Bry's Great Voyages.* University of Chicago Press.

Campbell, C. (1989). *The Romantic ethic and the spirit of modern consumerism.* Basil Blackwell.

Carey, H. C. (1967). *The past, present, and the future.* Augutus M. Kelley.

Carroll, L. (1874). *The hunting of the snark: An agony in eight fits.* Macmillan and Co

Carr-Saunders, A. M. (1922). *The population problem: A study in human evolution.* Oxford University Press.

Chattopadhyay, S. (2000). Blurring boundaries: The limits of "White Town" in colonial Calcutta. *Journal of the Society of Architectural Historians 59*, 154–179. 10.2307/991588

Chattopadhyay, S. (2005). *Representing Calcutta: Modernity, nationalism, and the colonial uncanny.* Routledge.

Christian, J. (1945). Portuguese India and its historical records. *The Hispanic American Historical Review, 25*(1), 140–151. http://www.jstor.org/stable/2508413

Clark, T. J. (1984). *The painting of modern life: Paris in the art of Manet and his followers.* Alfred Knopf.

Coelho, P. R. P. (1973). The profitability of imperialism: The British experience in the West Indies 1768-1772.

*Explorations in Economic History, 10*(3), 253–280. 10.1016/0014-4983(73)90013-2.

Corbey, R. (1993). Ethnographic showcases, 1870-1930. *Anthropology, 8*(3), 338–369. http://www.jstor.org/stable/656317

Craven, M. (2015). Between law and history: The Berlin Conference of 1884-1885 and the logic of free trade. *London Review of International Law, 3*(1), 31–59. 10.1093/lril/lrv002

Crawfurd, J. (1968). *Journal of an embassy to the courts of Siam and Cochin China.* Oxford University Press.

Crouch, D., & Mundigo, A. (1977). The city planning ordinances of the Laws of the Indies revisited. Part II: Three American cities. *The Town Planning Review, 48*(4), 397–418. http://www.jstor.org/stable/40103295

Crump, J. (1986). Recreation in Coventry between the wars. In B. Lancatser and T. Mason (Eds.), *Life and labour in a 20ᵗʰ century city: The experience of a coventry.* Cryfield Press.

Davies, P. (1985). *Splendours of The Raj: British architecture in India, 1660 to 1947.* John Murray.

Dawson, A. (2006). Geography of fear: Crime and the transformation of public space in post-apartheid South Africa. In S. Low & N. Smith, *The politics of public space* (pp. 123–142). Routledge.

#Diffie, B. W. & Winius, G. D. (1977). *Foundations of the Portuguese Empire, 1415–1580.* University of Minnesota Press.

Doshi, V. (2017). How the East India Company became a weapon to challenge UK's colonial past. *The Guardian.* https://www.theguardian.com/world/2017/may/06/east-india-company-british-businessman

The Economist. (1997, May 8). Should plundered art go back? Bronzed off. *The Economist.* http://www.economist.com/node/149208

Emmanuel, A. (1972). White-settler colonialism and the myth of investment imperialism. *New Left Review, 73*, 35–57.

Engels, F. (1909). *The origin of the family private property and the state* (Trans. By E. Untermann. Charles H. Kerr & Company. https://archive.org/details/originoffamilypr00enge

Estes, N. (2019). *Our history is the future: Standing rock versus the Dakota Access Pipeline, and the long tradition of indigenous resistance.* Verso.

Evenson, N. (1989). *The Indian metropolis: A view towards the West.* Yale University Press.

Fanon, F. (1961). The wretched of the Earth. Francois Maspero.

Federici, S. (1994). *Caliban and the witch: Women, the body and primitive accumulation.* Autonomedia.

Fields, K. & Fields, B. J. (2012). *Racecraft: The soul of inequality in American life.* Verso.

Forbes, J. D. (1993). *Africans and Native Americans: The language of Race and the evolution of Red-Black peoples.* University of Illinois Press.

Foucault, M. (1980). Truth and power. In C. Gordon (Ed.), *Power/knowledge: Selected interviews and other writings, 1972-1977* (pp. 109–133). Random House.

Foucault, M. (1997). The birth of biopolitics. In P. Rabinow and J. D. Faubion (Eds.), *Ethics, Subjectivity, and Truth* (pp. 73–79). New Press.

Foucault, M. (2003). Lecture 11, 17 March 1976. In *Society must be defended: Lectures at the College de France* (pp. 239–264). Picador Press.

Foucault, M. (2004). *Abnormal: Lectures at the Collège de France, 1974-1975*. Picador.

Foucault, M. (2008). *The birth of biopolitics. Lectures at the Collège de France, 1978–1979*. Picador.

Frankema, E. (2010). Raising revenue in the British empire, 1870-1940: How 'extractive' were colonial taxes?. *Journal of Global History, 5*(3), 447–477. 10.1017/S1740022810000227

Georgetown University. (2017). *The Georgetown Slavery Archive*. Georgetown University Working Group on Slavery, Memory, and Reconciliation. http://slaveryarchive.georgetown.edu/

Giddens, A. (1985). *The nation-state and violence*. Polity Press.

Ginn, G. & Spearritt, P. (2016). Cities, imperial. In J. M. Mackenzie, N. Dalziel, N. Doumanis, & M. W. Charney, *The encyclopedia of Empire* (pp. 1–14). Chichester, UK: John Wiley & Sons. 10.1002/9781118455074.wbeoe306

Goldenberg, D. M. (2003). *The curse of Ham: Race and slavery in early Judaism, Christianity, and Islam*. Princeton University Press.

Goldsmith, O. (1774). *A history of the Earth and animated nature*, Volume 2. J. Nouse.

de Grazia, S. (1964). *Of time, work, and leisure*. Twentieth Century Books.

Gregory, D. (1991). Interventions in the historical geography of modernity: Social theory, spatiality and the politics of representation. *Geografiska Annaler. Series B, Human Geography, 73*(1), 17–44. 10.2307/490924

Hall, S. (1997). Old and new identities, old and new ethnicities. In A. D. King (Ed.), *Culture, globalization, and the world-system: Contemporary conditions for the representation of identity* (pp. 41–68). University of Minnesota Press. http://www.jstor.org.proxyiub.uits.iu.edu/stable/10.5749/j.ctttsqb3.7

Hamlin, C. (2009). *Cholera: The biography*. Oxford University of Press.

Harley, C. K. (2013). Slavery, the British Atlantic economy and the Industrial Revolution. *University of Oxford Discussion Papers in Economic and Social History, 2013*(113). http://www.economics.ox.ac.uk/materials/papers/12739/harley113.pdf

Harley, J. B. & Woodward, D. (Eds.). (1987). *The history of cartography*, vol. 1. The University of Chicago Press.

Harrison M. (1994). *Public health in British India: Anglo-Indian preventive medicine, 1859-1914*. Cambridge University Press.

Harvey, D. (2003). *Paris, capital of modernity*. London, UK: Routledge.

Hemingway, J. L. (1988). Leisure and civility: Reflections on a Greek ideal. *Leisure Sciences, 10*, 179–191.

Herrera Ángel, M. (2004). Spatial ordering of the Indian villages: Domination and resistance in colonial society. *Frontiers Magazine, 2*(2), 93–128.

Heuman, G. J. (1981). *Between Black and White: Race, politics and the free Coloreds of Jamaica 1792-1865*. Oxford University Press.

Hodkinson, S. (2012). The new urban enclosures. *City: Analysis of Urban Trends, Culture, Theory, Policy, Action, 16*(5), 500–518. 10.1080/13604813.2012.709403

Hume, A. (1858). *Condition of Liverpool, religious and social; including notices of the state of education, morals, pauperism, and crime*, (2nd ed). T. Brakell.

Hunnicutt, B. K. (2006). The history of western leisure. In C. Rojek, S. M. Shaw, & A. J. Veal (Eds.), *A handbook of leisure studies* (pp. 55–73). Palgrave Macmillan.

Isidore of Seville. (2006). *The etymologies of Isidore of Serville*. S. A. Barney, W. J. Lewis, J. A. Beach, & O. Berghof, Trans. Cambridge University Press.

King, T. L. (2019). *The black shoals: Offshore formations of Black and native studies*. Duke University Press.

Kittrie, O. F. (2016). *Lawfare: Law as weapon of war*. Oxford University Press.

Kipling, R. (1899). *The city of dreadful night*. A. Grosset & Co.

La Peyrère, I. (1655). *A theological systeme upon that presupposition, that men were before Adam*. London.

Lange, M., Mahoney, J., & Vom Hau, M. (2006). Colonialism and development: A comparative analysis of Spanish and British colonies. *American Journal of Sociology, 111*(5), 1412–1462. 10.1086/499510

Lankevich, G. J. (1999). *American metropolis: A history of New York City*. New York University Press.

Lauster, M. (2007). Walter Benjamin's myth of the "Flâneur". *The Modern Language Review, 102*(1), 139–156. http://www.jstor.org/stable/20467157

Law, J. (1984). On the methods of long-distance control: Vessels, navigation and the Portuguese route to India. *The Sociological Review, 32*, 234–263. 10.1111/j.1467-954X.1984.tb00114.x

Lederer, R. M. (1985). *Colonial American English: A glossary*. Verbatim.

Lefebvre, H. (1991). *The production of space*. Blackwell Publishing.

Livingstone, D. N. (2002). Race, space and moral climatology: Notes toward a genealogy. *Journal of Historical Geography, 28*, 159–180.

Lyman, T. S. (1980). *Spanish Laws concerning dis-coveries, pacifications, and settlements among the Indians: With an introduction and the first english translation of the New Ordinances of Philip II, July 1573, and of Book IV of the Recopilación de leyes de los reinos de las Indias, Relating to these Subjects*. American West Center, University of Utah.

Malthus, T. R. (1806). *An essay on the principle of po-pulations; Or, a view of its past and present effects on human happiness; With an inquiry into our pro-spects respecting the future removal or mitigation of the evils which it contains*, (vol. I 3rd ed). T. Bensley.

Marshall, P. (1990). The Whites of British India, 1780-1830: A failed colonial society? *The International History Review, 12*(1), 26–44. http://www.jstor.org/stable/40106131

Marx, K. (1976). *Capital*, Trans. by B. Fowkes and D. Fernbach. Vintage.

Mbembe, A. (2019). *Necropolitics*. Duke University Press.

McCabe, J. D. (1869). *Paris by sunlight and gaslight: A work descriptive of the mysteries and miseries, the virtues, the vices, the splendors, and the crimes of the city of Paris*. National Publishing Company.

McClellan, A. L. (1984). The politics and aesthetic of dis-play: Museums in Paris 1750-1800. *Art History, 7*(4), 438–464.

McNeill, W. H. (1982). *The pursuit of power: Technology, armed force and society since A.D. 1000*. Blackwell.

Merrill, L. (2012). Exhibiting Race 'under the World's huge glass case': William and Ellen Craft and William Wells Brown at the Great Exhibition in Crystal Palace, London, 1851. *Slavery & Abolition: A Journal of Slave and Post-Slave Studies, 33*(2), 321–326. \ 10.1080/0144039X.2012.669907

Metcalf, T. R. (1989). *An Imperial vision: Indian archi-tecture and Britain's Raj*. University of California Press.

Mizutani, S. (2013). *The meaning of White: Race, class, and the 'Domiciled Community' in British India 1858–1930*. Oxford University.

de Montesquieu, C. L. (1748). *De l'Esprit des lois*. Chez Barrillot & Fils.

Neill, A. (2002). *British discovery literature and the rise of global commerce*. Palgrave Macmillan.

Nemser, D. (2019). *Infrastructures of Race: Concentration and biopolitics in colonial*. University of Texas Press.

New York Life. (2017). Acknowledging our past: New York Life and slavery. *New York Life Insurance Company*. https://www.newyorklife.com/newsroom/acknowl-edging-our-past/

Nightingale, C. H. (2012). *Segregation: A global history of divided cities*. The University of Chicago Press.

Parry, J. H. (1963). *The age of reconnaissance*. Weidenfeld & Nicolson.

Pieper, J. (1952). *Leisure: The basis of culture* (Trans. By A. Dru). Pantheon Books, Inc.

Pike, R. (1967). Sevillian society in the sixteenth century: Slaves and freedmen. *The Hispanic American Historical Review, 47*(3), 344–359. 10.2307/2511025

Piketty, T., Postel-Vinay, G., & Rosenthal, J. (2006). Wealth concentration in a developing economy: Paris and France, 1807-1994. *The American Economic Review, 96*(1), 236–256.

Pinkney, D. H. (1955). Napoleon III's transformation of Paris: The origins and development of the idea. *The Journal of Modern History, 27*(2), 125–134. http://www.jstor.org/stable/1874987

Poinsett, A. (1970, November). Black takeover of U.S. ci-ties?. *Ebony, 1*, 76–84.

Porter, L. & Yiftachel, O. (2019). Urbanizing settler-colonial studies: Introduction to the special issue. *Settler Colonial Studies, 9*(2), 177–186. 10.1080/2201473X.2017.1409394

Rafael, V. L. (1993). *Contracting colonialism: Translation and Christian conversion in Tagalog society under early Spanish rule*. Duke University Press.

Raspali, R. (1973). *Le camp des Saints*. Éditions Robert Laffont.

Reeder, D. A. (1984). Introduction. In C. Booth, *Charles Booth's descriptive map of London poverty 1889*, Publication No. 130. London Topographical Society.

Rennell, J. (1790). Construction of the Map of Africa. In *Proceedings of the association for promoting the dis-covery of the interior parts of Africa* (pp. 211–236). C. Macrae.

Rojek, C. (1985). The structural characteristics of modern leisure. In *Capitalism and leisure Theory* (pp. 13–33). Tavistock Publications Ltd.

Rojek, C. (1997). 'Leisure' in the writings of Walter Benjamin. *Leisure Studies, 16*(3), 155–171. 10.1080/026143697375377

Rouse, J. (1987). *Knowledge and power: Toward a po-litical philosophy of science*. Cornell University Press.

Russell, R. V. (2017). Meanings from history. In *Pastimes* (6th ed., pp. 9–19). Sagamore Publishing.

Sanitary Commissioner. (1901). *The Thirty-Eight Annual Report of the Sanitary Commissioner. Judicial and Administration Statistics of British India, X111, Vital Statistics*. Government Press.

Schecter, B. (2005). *The devil's own work: The Civil War Draft Riots and the fight to reconstruct America*. Walker Publishing Company, Inc.

Schneer, J. (1999). *London 1900: The imperial me-tropolis*. Yale University Press.

Schuller, K. (2018). *The biopolitics of feeling: Race, sex, and science in the nineteenth century*. Duke University Press.

Scriver, P., & Prakash, V. (Eds.). (2007). *Colonial moder-nities: Building, dwelling and architecture in British India and Ceylon*. Routledge.

Seigel, M. (2018). *Violence work: State power and the limits of police*. Duke University Press.

Sen, S. (2017). *Colonizing, decolonizing, and globalizing Kolkata: From a colonial to a Post-Marxist City, Asian Cities*. Amsterdam University Press.

Serrano y Sanz, M. S. (Ed.). (1918). Ynstrucion para el Governador de Tierra Firme, la qual se le entrego 4 de Agosto DXIII. In *Origines de la Dominicion Espanola en America* (1 cclxxi). Madrid, ES.

Sierra Silva, P. M. (2018). *Urban slavery in Colonial Mexico: Puebla de losÁngeles, 1531-1706*. Cambridge University Press.

Small, S. (2011). Slavery, Colonialism and museums representations in Great Britain: Old and new circuits of migration. *Human Architecture: Journal of the Sociology of Self-Knowledge, 9*(4), 117–128. http://scholarworks.umb.edu/humanarchitecture/vol9/iss4/10

Stanislawski, D. (1946). The origin and spread of the grid pattern town. *Geographical Review, 36*(1), 105–120.

Stanton, W. (1960). *The leopard's spots: Scientific attitudes toward Race in America, 1815-59*. The University of Chicago Press.

Stevin, S. (1650). *Materiae politicae. Bvrgherlicke stoffen: Vervanghende ghedachtenissen der oeffeninghen des doorluchtichsten Prince Maurits van Orangie*. Justus Livius.

Stevin, S. (1955). *Principal Works*, 5 vols. Edited by E. Crone. Trans. by C. Dikshoorn. C. V. Swets & Zeitlinger.

Superintendent Government. (1902). *The Madras plague regulations and rules for district municipalities and other towns and villages*. Superintendent Government Press.

Swarns, R. L. (2016a, September 1). Georgetown University plans steps to atone for slave past. *The New York Times*. https://www.nytimes.com/2016/09/02/us/slaves-georgetown-university.html?smid=tw-share

Swarns, R. L. (2016b, December 18). Insurance policies on slaves: New York Life's complicated past. *The New York Times*. https://www.nytimes.com/2016/12/1 8/us/insurance-policies-on-slaves-new-york-lifes-complicated-past.html?_r=0

Swift, J. (1733). *On poetry A rhapsody*. J. Huggonson.

Tamayo, J. J. M. (2010). The doctrines of Indians and the construction of Catholic identity in the colonial indigenous of the New Kingdom of Granada (1556-1606). *Antitheses, 3*(5), 71–94.

Taylor, P. J. (1994). The state as container: Territoriality in the modern world-system. *Progress in Human Geography, 18*(2), 151–162. 10.1177/0309132594 01800202

Taylor, P. (1995). Beyond containers: Internationality, interstateness, interrrioriality *Progress in Human Geography, 19*(1), 1–15. 10.1177/030913259501900101

Tomich, D. (2003). The wealth of empire: Francisco Arango y Parreño, political economy, and the second slavery in Cuba. *Comparative Studies in Society and History, 45*(1), 4–28. http://www.jstor.org/stable/3 879480

Tooley, R. V. & Bricker, C. (1976). *Landmarks of mapmaking: An illustrated survey of maps and mapmakers*. Phaidon.

Trompf, G. W. (1979). *The idea of historical recurrence in Western thought: From antiquity to the Reformation*. University of California Press.

Turnbull, D. (2003). *Maps are territories: Science is an atlas*. The University of Chicago Press.

Vaughn, L. (2018). *Mapping society: The spatial dimensions of social cartography*. University College London Press.

Veblen, T. (1994). *The theory of the leisure class: An economic study of institutions*. Dover Publications, Inc.

Vink, M. (2003). "The world's oldest trade': Dutch slavery and slave trade in the Indian Ocean in the seventeenth century. *Journal of World History, 14*(2), 131–177. 10.1353/jwh.2003.0026

Violich, F. (1962). The evolution of the Spanish city: Issues basic to planning today. *Journal of the American Institute of Planners, 28*(3), 170–179.

Wall, D. D., Rothschild, N. A., & Copeland, C. (2008). Seneca Village and Little Africa: Two African American communities in Antebellum New York City *Historical Archeology, 42*, 97–107. 10.1007/BF03377066

Waring, E. J. (1868). *Pharmacopeia of India*. J.H. Allen & Co.

Werlen, B. (2005). Regions and everyday regionalizations: From a space-centred towards an action-centred human geoography. In H. Van Houtum, O. Kramsch, & W. Zierhofer (Eds.), *B/ordering space* (pp. 47–60). Ashgate Publishing.

Wilensky, H. L. (1961). The uneven distribution of leisure: The impact of economic growth on "free time". *Social Problems, 9*(1), 32–56. http://www.jstor.org/stable/ 799420

Williams, E. (1994). *Capitalism and slavery*. The University of North Carolina Press.

Zandvliet, K. (1998). *Mapping for money: Maps, plans and topographic paintings and their role in Dutch overseas expansion during the 16th and 17th centuries*. Batavian Lion International.

Zierhofer, W. (2005). State, power and space. *Social Geography, 1*, 29–36. www.social-geography.net/1/29

de Zuniga, D. O. (1677). *Anales Eclesiasticos y seculars... de Sevilla*. Imprenta Real.

# 3.
# THE DESIGN OF THE CITY: THE IDENTIFICATION OF THREATS

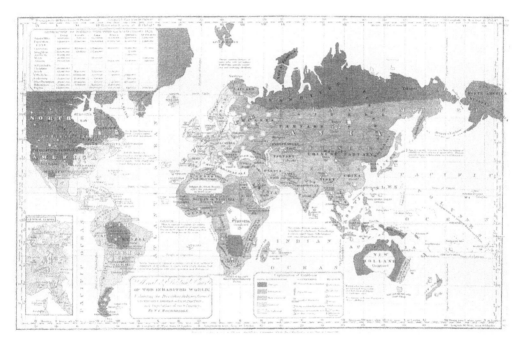

**Fig 3.1** C.W. Woodbridge Moral & Political Charts of the Inhabited World, Detailing Population Size, Racial Classification, Religious Affiliations, Types of Government, and State of Civilisation (Savage, Barbarous, Half Civilised, Civilised, and Enlightened), 1821. (Public Domain)

"Attention to aesthetic design and the provision of mass housing are to prevent social unrest. Society violently desires one thing that it will obtain or that it will not. Everything lies in that; everything will depend on the effort made and the attention paid to these alarming symptoms. [Return, Space then the last line] Architecture or revolution. Revolution can be avoided".

– Le Corbusier, 1923, in Vers une Archi-tecture, p. 243.

"Moses didn't want poor people, particularly poor people of color, to use Jones Beach, so they had legislation passed forbidding the use of buses on parkways. [Return, Space then the remaining part of the quote] Then he had this quote, and I can still [hear] him saying it to me.

DOI: 10.1201/9781003149545-3

'Legislation can always be changed. It's very hard to tear down a bridge once it's up'. So he built 180 or 170 bridges too low for buses. … We stood there with steno pads, and we have three columns: Whites, Blacks, Others. And I still remember that first column – There were a few Others, and almost no Blacks. The White would go on to the next page… this is how you can shape a metropolis for generations".

– According to Sidney M. Shapiro, in a Gothamist interview with Robert Caro, author of 1974's The Power Broker: Robert Moses and the Fall of New York (Robbins, 2016).

The palpable threat of dwindling resources in 2020, turned 2021, has only gotten worse throughout the world in the midst of a pandemic. This looming threat is the driving force behind the rampant extraction of natural resources since the Eugenics-inspired Conservation and Preservation movements of the 1870s (Mowatt, 2020). And like the 1800s, the threat was and is still not a naturally occurring phenomenon. Those rampant extractivist forces were fuelled by colonialism and expanded by imperialism. More and more lands became territories under the rule of European, British, and now "American" State powers (see Fig. 3.1). More and more peoples became subjects under rulership. And the threat is only generated by the greed inherent in the accumulation of capital and wealth as well as the fear that future generations of the State will not inherit the accumulated capital and wealth. At the 1909 National Conservation Commission, Gifford Pinchot, the "father" of ideals of conservation and chief delegate of the International Eugenics Congress, stated,

The problem of conservation of our natural resources…if our nation cares to make any provision for its grandchildren and its grandchildren's grandchildren, this provision must include conservation in all its branches – but above all, the conservation of the racial stock itself. (p. 126)

As the ideological and structural foundations of conservation and preservation took off in the United States, Germany was developing *Herrenvolk*, its own system of population and territorial control predicated along the same racially superior line (Vickery, 1974). Herrenvolk fostered the conceptualisations of *Lebensraum* (living room, living space), likely inspired by the U.S. continental expansion by way of the systematic elimination of anti-citizens (the indigenous populations, the formerly enslaved Black population, and the unfree labour of immigrants from Central America and Eastern Europe). The aims of this version of conservation and preservation was through the total decimation of indigenous populations through land removal, work camps, and the wholesale theft of food production. One population thrived at the expense of another (Smith, 1980).

As Germany was concerned with this threat domestically, the German State became the principal coordinating entity managing the concerns of other European States at the 1884–1885 Berlin Conference. The German phrase of *Torschlusspanik,* the "door-closing panic", described both anxieties of economies within the imperial cities of Germany, Britain, France, and Italy and the anxieties in watching the dispersal of wealth from conquest, enslavement, and extraction that other States were enjoying (Pakenham, 1991). The Conference initiated what is called the "Scramble for Africa" under the pretext that the resources to support the populations that resided in the seat of imperial power required new territories for extraction of resources. Those extraction efforts would also mitigate the growing surplus population under rule by dispersing them throughout the globe to serve as extraction agents, State emissaries, and security forces. Colonialism needed to be contrapuntally managed. Instead of each State developing their own version of the German Kaiser's *Weltpolitik* (world policy) that would lead to rivalling efforts to mine the continent to oblivion, a coordinated and agreed-upon partitioning would manage competition while opening the doorway for trade. The Belgian Crown quickly grabbed ahold of what would be called the Congo (see Fig. 3.2), as did all of the other attending States for the remaining territories. Each argued and bickered among themselves over what never belonged to them in the first place, other people's lives and other people's lands. All the while, indigenous populations in Africa awaited a second wave of fate after

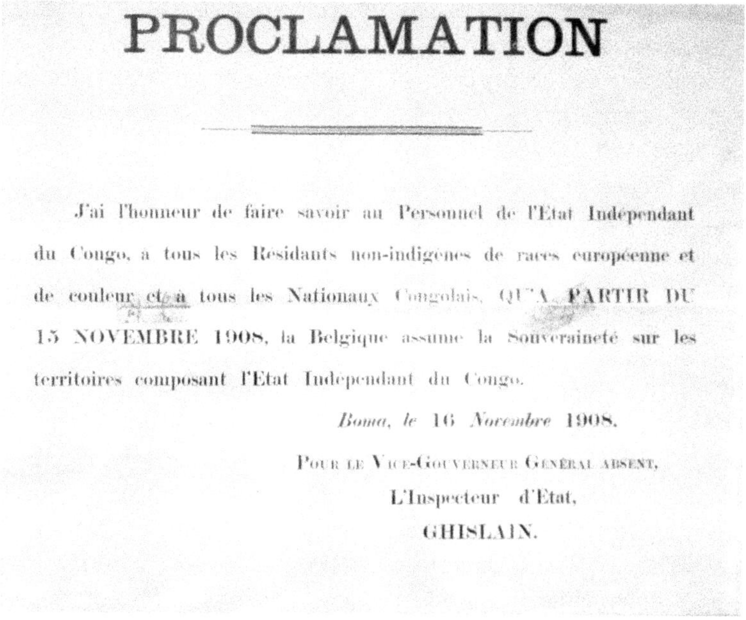

# PROCLAMATION

J'ai l'honneur de faire savoir au Personnel de l'Etat Indépendant du Congo, a tous les Résidants non-indigènes de races européenne et de couleur et a tous les Nationaux Congolais, QU'A PARTIR DU 15 NOVEMBRE 1908, la Belgique assume la Souveraineté sur les territoires composant l'Etat Indépendant du Congo.

Boma, le 16 Novembre 1908.

POUR LE VICE-GOUVERNEUR GÉNÉRAL ABSENT,

L'Inspecteur d'Etat,

GHISLAIN.

**Fig 3.2** "I have the honor to inform the staff of the Congo Independent State; to all non-indigenous Residents of European and colored races and to all Congolese Nationals, WHEREAS from November 15, 1908, Belgium assumes Sovereignty over the territories constituting the Independent State of Congo", Proclamation on the Founding of the Belgian Congo, November 16, 1908. (Public Domain)

centuries of enslavement. David Livingstone's three "C's" of commerce, Christianity, and civilisation were joined and driven by an added fourth of "C" of conquest. The members of the Conference also kept a keen eye on the growing influence of the settler colony of the United States as it had a strangle hold on North, Central, and South America; the Caribbean; as well as the colony of Liberia and what it would soon acquire from the Spanish-American War through its own version of *Weltpolitik*, the 1823 Monroe Doctrine. Where *Weltpolitik* was an internal State-guiding policy for expansion, the Doctrine of the 5th President was an external declaration of war to any and all powers of the world that crossed the Atlantic for the purposes of colonisation (Murphy, 2005). The Doctrine further forced the States of North, Central, and South America and the Caribbean into a confederacy that they could not oppose,

This power[ful] neighbor has never desired to incite them, nor has it exerted control over

them except to prevent their expansion, as in Panama; or to take possession of their territory, as in Mexico, Nicaragua, Santo Domingo, Haiti, and Cuba; or to cut off their trade with the rest of the world, as in Colombia; or to oblige them to buy what it cannot sell, as it is doing now, and to form a confederacy for the purposes of controlling. (José Martí as quoted by Foner, 1975, pp. 40–45)

A pseudo- "Pan-American Congress" was convened in Washington, D.C., in 1889, concurrent to the Berlin Conference, to create favourable commercial relationships with other States in North, Central, and South America and the Caribbean with the very real capability of hard power. All global trade possibilities had to consider the counsel of the settler colony of the United States, and all internal State resources had to be managed in some way by the various parts of the settler colonial and fiscal military power of the United States. The United States was swiftly becoming a world force with the territories of Cuba, Guam, the

Philippines, and Puerto Rico "gifted" to it soon after the 1898 end of the Spanish-American War, which only hastened the occupations and military interventions throughout South America and the Caribbean during the "Banana Wars" until 1934 (see Fig. 3.3). The 1823 Monroe Doctrine of the 5th President and the philosophical spirit of Manifest Destiny under the 7th President within the territories of the settler colony of the United States to expand its "area of freedom", ushered in a new era of the methods and tools for conquest, dispossession, governance, extraction, and the accumulation of wealth.

In the States of Europe and the settler colony of the United States, the perceived globalisation of economies was built upon the previous iterations of a globalised economy: feudalism, early colonialism, slavery, and racial capitalism. Resource extraction, dispossession through slavery and cheap labour, the exchange in geographical knowledge of regions, and the management of colonialism were the precursors to this emerging new globalisation. Much had changed between the years of the 1814–1815 Congress of Vienna and the 1876–1912 Berlin Conference such as the advent of the fiscal military State of the United States; yet, much had remained the same in terms of the maintenance of State power and the subjugation of indigenous and

working-class peoples of the world. The haphazard but still intentional occupation of and settler colonial apparatuses administered to the continents of North America, South America, and Asia were a thing of the past. On long tables during catered meals, the continent of Africa was carefully carved up and re-designed for the purposes of extraction; it still remains impacted by that design. Learning from the management of the "Congo Free State" held by Belgium, a new form of colonial governance, *laissez-faire*, arose where the raw capitalism of business could take place without extensive government intervention. The grid plan of the *Laws of the Indies,* the plaza of Ciudad de México, the "Black Town" of Chennai, the Boulevards of Paris, the poverty maps of London, the creation of premium space in New York, and lessons from many other enactments of State power emphasised the importance of city design for soft power governance. While the capabilities of hard power (force, coercion, and warfare) were always ready, the use of soft power (culture, values, and ideals) had become the preferred method of moving forward (Nye, 2004).

Through the spectacle of the city, there was now a way to foster a new image to erase the image from the hard power tactics of conquest, slavery, and early colonialism for the sake of capitalism. Thus, the

THE BIG STICK IN THE CARIBBEAN SEA

**Fig 3.3** The 26th President and His "Big Stick" in the Caribbean. The Political Artwork of William Allen Rogers, 1904. (Public Domain)

planning and design of cities were to become effective (and still are) tools for cultivating this soft power form of governance in which the spectacle of the city was "not a neutral form in which capitalism incidentally happened; it was a form of capital itself" (Clark, 1984, p. 36). Where maps were but the first foray in making the world legible to control, cities were to be the new way. Power over space corrupts people. And to long hold positions of power, prevents people from relinquishing that power. Maps are the communicative device of State power, of Empire, and cities were to become the new device. Only Empires make maps. Only States with exceptional power contain the ability to determine which maps are most official. But the map was now less important in staking claims of a territory; the maintenance of the city was the way forward in holding onto territories. If the city fell, so would the territory near, around, and in between cities. The threat is no longer beyond the border; it is within the gates of the city. As States no longer needed to fully administer hard power and warfare, the subtleties of the city were one way to segmentise and pacify the identified populations in the city, so "(architecture ou revolution) architecture or revolution. Revolution can be avoided" (Le Corbusier, 1923, p. 243).

## 3.1 Architecture or Revolution

Fascism was the primary technique administered through the modernist, particularly the high modernist, take on architecture. Brutalist architecture may have been a style conceived by modernist architects and city planners (Hanly & Meades, 2014; Phaidon Editors, 2018), but it was the regimes they served that demanded it, funded it, and utilised it for public housing of the disposable poor, the carceral facilities of the imprisoned, and the increasingly closed off government offices of so-called Democratic societies. The *béton brut* (raw, exposed, and unfinished concrete) of brutalism were the truths in lustre of the city of spectacle. While allusions of a shared (fabricated) society rule the populace's consciousness, the State remained the same in its lack of the commoner. These buildings (as all buildings do) are a direct response and outcome of the political powers at work. The social and natural world needed to be reordered, in some cases based on the mistakes in previous forms of autocracy and technocracy, but in most cases due to the rapid growth and expansion of the cities as settler colonial nation-states had yielded their authority to the new empires of the modern age (Taylor, 1999).

The great accumulation of capital that was achieved through racial capitalism and colonialism of the 19th century sponsored this process of modernisation through science and technology. The world needed to be legible in order to control it. Things and people needed to be in their right, accounted-for place. Ordered things and ordered people used science and technology to produce tools and strategies for measurement that aided in the taxation of land and property. And science and technology also advanced new methods in census data collection, fixing people to surnames that aided the taxation of people and neighbourhoods for the rationing of aid and resources, as well as for the Malthusian-recommended conscription into forms of service to the State (official labour for government projects or to the military for warfare). "The housing crisis will lead to the revolution. Worry about housing", so modern architecture leaned into the provision of mass housing in order to quell the rising potential of civil unrest (Le Corbusier, 1923, p. 243). But this proviso was not in earnest, not an effort to do right by its populace. In Le Corbusier's Paris, the poor and working classes were able to build strong coalitions and played a critical role in major revolutions. Low wages led to hunger and homelessness, and these were the galvanising experiences that prompted the 1789 women's march upon the capital in Versailles and then to the bloody Paris Commune of 1871 (see Fig. 3.4). The provision of housing, the ordering of housing, and the dependence on housing are but tools for the pacification of a population. This provision, ordering, and dependence on housing led to the concentration of the poor and working classes as a means of pacification through spatial conditioning. Fracturing of that concentration with city-splitting techniques prevented rebellion and also pacification through violence. The construction of buildings and other infrastructure were (and are) not passive indicators of the works of urban planners and real estate developers. These were active instruments in the wielding of State power.

**Fig 3.4** Illustration of the Women's March on Versailles on 5 October 1789. The March Was Against the High Prices of Bread and Scarcity of Bread for Common People. (Public Domain)

Within the architecture and design of space, a process of conditioning for those who utilise the philosophies, tools, implements, and constructs of the architect at the behest of a client are brought into subjugation and complicity. As Bataile (1997) stated,

> Architecture is the expression of the very being of societies in the same way that human physiognomy is the expression of the being of individuals…in practice, only the ideal being of society, that which orders and prohibits with authority, expresses itself in what we are architectural compositions in the strict sense of the term. (p. 21)

And within this conditioning was to be our connectedness to the architecture and to property. The body and the building become linked as if they are one and the same; "therefore an attack on architecture…grouping the servile multitudes under their shadow, imposing admiration and wonder, order and constraint, is necessarily, as it were, an attack on" humanity (Bataile, 1997, p. 21). To build buildings was (and still is) a political act, as was the demolition of them by the State, or the destruction of them by the rebelling populace (invoking Chicago's Daley the Elder's "Fire a Building"). But so too are the architectural designs and city plans that convey the political scripts and content that conceives of them before they are ever constructed.

The veneration of the past served as the maintenance of the established order, the old order. Le Corbusier (1923), in admiration for the Ancient Greeks, made note that "architecture is the masterly, correct and magnificent play of masses brought together in light" (p. 29). The planning map and the architectural rendering are processes in which architecture imbued the political onto the environmental landscape of the city. A census informed the makers and planners of who belonged where and how. A museum was the archive to past mistakes

**Fig 3.5** Description générale de l'Hostel Royal des Invalides établi par Louis le Grand dans la Plaine de Grenelle près Paris, avec les plans, Profils et élévations de ses faces, Coupes et Appartements. A Complex of Buildings Devoted to the Military Prominence of France (Museums, Monuments, Hospital for Veterans, and Residency for Veterans and Their FaMilies) Under Louis XIV, Authored by Le Jeune de Boulencourt, Paris, FR, 1683. (Institut National D'Histoire de L'Art)

and successes. Just as map making had become an industry sponsored by various aspects of the State to order things, and as the census was used as a form of knowledge and regulation, the physical construction of the museum served as a means to sustain the long historical dominance of the State. The lone museum, whether it was federally or privately constructed, was never of the public decree; it served the State as the greatest model for creation of entire museum districts for spectacle (see Fig. 3.5). Anderson's (1983) "the census, the map, and the museum" triumvirate of the imagined dominion of the State, corroborated the "semantic associations" that we had for/with buildings that retained their "historical memory" of and "collective imagination" from the official State (Leach, 1999, p. 118). Buildings, the

neighbourhoods, and the spaces they were situated within retained their purpose of racialised concentration and gendered control through a usage that was informed by this memory and imagination. A new usage, absent of this memory and imagination, would counter the original politics that were grafted into the architecture, subverted the status quo, and challenged the underpinnings of fabricated society. So, at all costs, the maintenance of buildings was an additional political dimension in pacification of the populace.

Buildings within the city continue to obscure our vision, as we only see part of reality that we are subjected to, and not all of it. What is occurring on this block, any given neighbourhood block, is all that we know, and this forecloses thinking about the city as a whole organism. It forecloses thinking about the city as a complete functioning entity, much less the State that the city serves. Our allegiances are to our respective blocks, and at best to our neighbourhood. The city is seen only as a sliver of its full brutal glory, so we ally ourselves with our city, too – when our "home team" wins a sports championship, in comparison with "lesser" cities during our travails, and as an identity to maintain when we find ourselves as new residents of those "lesser" city. Like a young Michael B. Jordan playing the character of Wallace on HBO's *The Wire* pronounced, "This is me, yo, right here", with his arms stretched and scanning his environment while he spoke with his peers, alluding to the location of the pit in the low-rise housing projects of fictional Baltimore.

But this allegiance, since it is linked to the infrastructure of the city that was created by the State, makes the allegiance in essence to the State and not to ourselves. Not what our true aspirations could be – free of the concrete that we have conscripted our lives to. Without a self-political wrestling and reckoning that can rips us away from pacification, the textual and spatial *heterotopia* of Foucault (1971, 1986) is simply a mirror of the greater world and not a disruptor of it. The heterotopia is yet another space, and not a different world. So, the possibilities of the heterotopia in the urban landscape are not quite realised. It is not an escape from being governed but just a different way to be governed and to manage our views of being governed. We can nickname our space endlessly to death ("Chi-Town", "The Windy City", "the South Side", "Bronzeville", "Back of the Yards", "Naptown", "Indiana Avenue", "Haughville", "Manhattantown", "Sugar Hill", "The Big Apple", "Bucktown", "Boogie Down", "Red Hook", "Five Points", "Hell's Kitchen", "Little Italy", "Chocolate City", "Pigtown", "The Motor City", "Paradise Valley", "Black Bottom", "Overtown", "Little Haiti", "Little Africa", "The Tenderloin", "Ghosttown", "Tremé", "Chinatown", "City of Angels", "Verdun", "The City of Spies", "Noord", "Nørrebro", "The Eternal City", "The City of Light", "Alvalade", "Gayexample", "Mitte", "The African Quarter", "East End", "Sur La Zone", "Bondi", "Hannam-Dong", "Thonglor", "Kabutocho", "The Forbidden City", "The Holy City", "Soho", "City of Kings", "Opebi", "Melville", "Bandra West", "The City of God", "Centro", "Navarte", "The Rez", "The 'Hood", "The Jects", and I could go on). We can name spaces to death and identify with them, but if their usage and function by the State is not challenged, then we merely fall victim to the order that is and has always been intended. We are far too dependent upon the constructed buildings with static purposes that reflect the legibility of the ruled and ordered world. The new city built upon or from the knowledge of the various settler-colonial city projects makes heterotopias dependent on the racialised visual grammar exercises on the map and the gendered textual grammar exercises on the official record of contracts. The map visualises the control that has been "established, in part, by exercising the power to represent the other" (King, 2019, p. 106).

The city as an articulation and function of State power exists to provide a means of circulation of law, resources, wealth, and the populace that serves it. Whether the city is the seat of governance (the capital) or the seat of commerce (the metropolis), the State resides on top of its function through subordinated cooperation and subjugated classification (Deleuze, 1997). The city capital could be built at any time and anywhere, as was the case for the creation of the federal capital city of Brasília in Brazil, but the metropolis cannot be easily made (Holston, 2009). Infrastructure and social activities of the fabricated Society do not automatically work that way. In the case of Brasília, the wishes of the Brazilian State to employ high modernism to the city led to hasty overreaches of State power in order to wield vast power over the land and space. A city was built, the capital was functioning, but the activity of a metropolis was never attained. The lesson learned was that the State, through the city, could not territorialise the expanse of land turned territory under any true, day-to-day governance. But the State, through at least effectively managing the city, could deterritorialise the notion of land so that the most accounted-for space within the consciousness of the populace was also within the city limits and city system. The city deterritorialises the expanse of territory that appears on the map and is made a consequence of geography. The city deterritorialises space by reducing all (social) activities in and through the cities. But this does not make cities capable of separating themselves from State rule. The State, in turn, deterritorialises the city from being autonomous of its rule by way of a dependency on economic systems like capitalism for the trade of goods, the production of materials, and the accumulation of wealth only achieved through the networked circulation between cities under its rule. There can be multiple autonomous States passively connected through exchanges, but there never can be autonomous cities (nor autonomous neighbourhoods in the city). Leadership of and within cities will be absorbed into the authoritative systems of the State. The village "headman" was no longer the native or local chief but was now employed as a census taker. The settlement village was no longer an independent community within the city limit but was now an absorbed neighbourhood. To deterritorialise is to move past the work of the State to only dispossess and extract, and this process is beyond just the replication of past forms of colonisation. To deterritorialise is to categorise, separate, and segment space into zones. The city, in its effort to maintain the effects of dispossession and extraction, must become a centre of industry. Garnier's (1918) *Une Cité Industrielle* (Industrial City) only functions via zones for the residential, commercial, and industrial (alongside the civic, health, and entertainment) (see Fig. 3.6). In contrast, a *Cité Chinoise or Cité Indigène* (Chinese City or Indigenous City) only functions as a space of separation with a *zone neutre*

**Fig 3.6** Garnier's Une Cité Industrielle, Centre, Vue Perspective. Garnier's Vision of the Ideal City From the Vantage Point of the City Centre With Clear Demarcated Areas for the Zones, 1952. (Public Domain)

(neutral zone) to operate as a buffer to the areas of commerce, business, and rule (see Fig. 3.7). But the ideal living arrangements in a fairly governed city, one governed by the people of the city as envisioned by Garnier, was immediately adopted and altered by many, including Le Corbusier (1923), to be used as a means of technocratic governance by the elite and ruling classes, through the "results of order. Where order reigns, well-being begins" (p. 52). Thus, the return and expansion of the grid ensured that social order was always imposed from above, not cultivated by the rumblings from below.

To build the modern, new city required the removal and displacement of people in the way, the "Othered". This is what stands in the way of the greatness of cities to become greater. But also, for cities to become modern and anew, the rehousing of the poor and working classes into colossal buildings could aid two efforts: proximity to work and control of disease. The business elites would benefit by bringing labourers in closer proximity to the city, the

site of production, and the ruling elites could monitor and curb the spread of disease through these controlled high-rise residencies. Le Corbusier, frustrated by the growing pains of Paris from Haussmann's 18th century renovation of the city, crafted the Plan Voisin (see Fig. 3.8). However, the plan was first proposed for the city of Moscow in Russia and simply retrofitted with Paris in mind. The Moscow plan began with the zealous removal of all citizens, especially the poor, and demolished all existing buildings to reconstruct the more favourable city. While the proposal was never adopted in Paris (it was later adopted in Chandigarh, India), the idea of it became a hallmark of both public housing projects and the tactic of slum clearance.

The space that we know, the space that appears before us today, is not a product of independent, naturally occurring innovation of a collection of great minds. The space that we inhabit is one of the totalities of the European, British, and "American" experience through domination. The old feudal

**Fig 3.7** *Cité Chinoise* With the Map of Shanghai, China, 1919. (Public Domain)

**Fig 3.8** Model of the Plan Voisin for Paris by Le Corbusier, as Displayed at the Nouveau Espirit Pavillion, 1925. (Siefkin/ Wiki Commons)

kingdoms and then settler colonial empires and republics accounted for all space as space of emplacement. Once "discovered" and occupied, the fixedness
of space provided an ease to rule over lands turned
into territories and peoples turned into populations. In
this defining conceptualisation of the "Geographies of
Threat", the **identification of populations** in
Chapter 2 was a fundamental aspect of spaces of
emplacement through the history of settlements and
cities, and it continues to be, as the living organism of
the city adapts over time. What now concerns us
here, in Chapter 3, is the production and management of space through the aforementioned means of
emplacement (concentration, circulation, demarcation, and classification of populations), the use of
**identification of threats**. Cities must be defended
from without and from within by fortification and
military force (see Fig. 3.9). The reclamation of the
land in imperial cities and the laissez-faire rule in
colonial cities were the two main purposes of the
State. The business of wealth extraction could not be
attacked or interrupted. Things and people must be
accounted for, not only for dispossession, extraction,
and exploitation, but also to maintain the order of the
State. Setting the basis of order is the **identification
of populations.** Maintaining the order is the **identification of threats**. And while reclamation of land
is the affair of lesser deemed States, laissez-faire is the
principal philosophy in the neoliberal governance of
the present-day austerity in administration and abandonment in management at all costs to save all
wealth. Discussing this dimension will allow us a
better vantage point in the discussion of the **identification for violence** to be levied at populations by
the State and State-sanctioned actors.

### 3.2 The Production of Space for Domination

The material reality of our lived experience in cities
under the authority of the State supports the
Lefebvrian critical view that space subsumes language, so authority is wielded by both the control of
space and the narrative articulation of space. In a
socio-historical understanding of space, there are
three dialectic spaces that helps us to explore
our spatial reality: *l'espace le perçu* (first space,
the space of everyday social practice); the

aforementioned *l'espace le conçu* (second space, the
conceived representations of space); and *l'espace le
vécu* (third space, the representational space of
imagination). The perceived first space is physically
mappable. Once space is within the grasp of rule,
then all things and people within that space can be
named through the discursive power of language.
While much is given to the additive phrase, "once
you name something, you then have power over it",
it is materially and experientially false or incomplete
as technically "once you fix something in a space,
you can name it and have power over it". Enslaved
natives were not held to the power of the settler
colonial power until they were captured, caged, and
concentrated. Space is fundamentally material, and
the State and the people under any form of rule
develop a codex in moving through this fixed space.
However, it is important to distinguish between the
occupation of space and the production of space. The
occupation of space precedes the language attributed
in space, but the language of space precedes the
production of space. The pursuit of dominion precedes dispossession and extraction of the native and
local, and dispossession and extraction precedes
subjugation and complicity of the worker and citizen. The State precedes the city, and the city precedes the society. Lefebvre's (1991) superstructures
of what I have been calling the fabricated society,
alongside the State, are "the forces of production and
their component elements (nature, labour, technology, knowledge); structures (property relations);
superstructures (institutions and the state itself)"
(p. 85). This superstructure of this fabricated society
is in service to the State and bears no marking uniquely specific to the space that it operates within.
This is why the mapping, design, and planning of
cities is one of the most shared elements across
warring and competing States. All cities have similar
types of infrastructure, routes of circulation, modes
of production, settings for leisure, and bureaucracies
to administer those trappings. The difference only
comes about in the level of capital that has been
accumulated and used to construct and expand the
city. Parks, plazas, squares, public transportation,
law enforcement, waste disposal, and other features
and services are fundamental aspects of cities
whereas fire management, libraries, schools, and

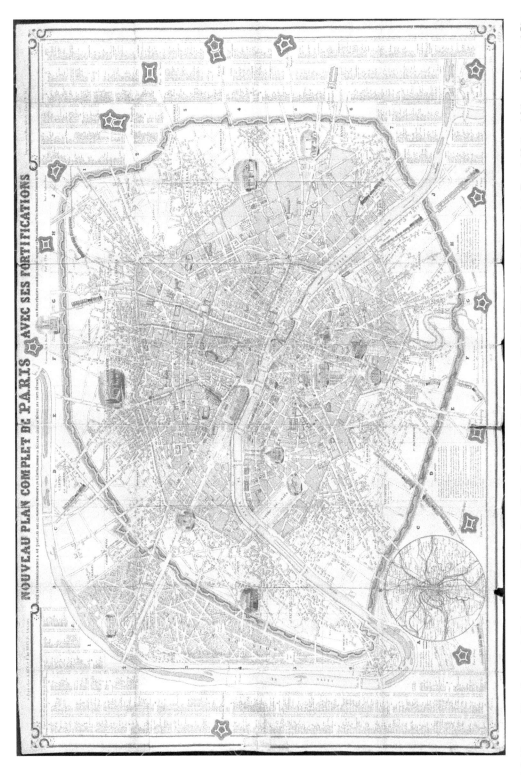

**Fig 3.9** Nouveau Plan Complet de Paris avec ses Fortifications ("New Complete Map of Paris with its fortifications"). J. N. Henriot, French National Library Maps and Plans Department, 1851. (Public Domain)

hospital are not. The superstructure of the fabricated society is the articulation of State power that becomes visible by the populace, not the State itself. The social space (Lefebvre's *l'espace le perçu*, the first space of *social practice*) in the fabricated society is built upon the "reproduction of production relations and property relations" that are equivalent, practically speaking, to a set of institutional and ideological superstructures that are not presented for what they are (and in this capacity social space comes complete with symbolisms and systems of meaning—sometimes an overload of meaning) (Lefebvre, 1991, p. 349).

The social space of families, communities, or neighbourhoods may be a product of our social relations and reflect the value usage of those relations in the space of a city, but they are still in context to the space that has been allocated by the State through the superstructures of fabricated society. Cheng et al. (2020) in the eventually recognised and seminal tome *Race and Modern Architecture,* remarked, "racial discourses have been deployed to organise and conceptualise the spaces of modernity, from the individual building to the city to the nation to the planet" (p. 19). There are boundaries to our social relations and the value usage of those relations. Racism must be looked at as being structurally constituted and articulated, as should the greater concept of White Supremacy, and not at the social "Race" relations level of behaviour and speech. The level of social relations is the location of the faint, the fake, and the intentionally allusive person-to-person interactions that muster beautiful slogans and protest signs of empty empathy against mistreatment rather than a re-ordered society. Gender discrimination and misogyny must also be looked at as being structural, as should the greater concept of patriarchy, and not at the social "fairness and equality" relations level. This, too, is the site of abstraction and of blurring the function of systems because the salience of individual experiences (of being shuttered, abused, and restrained) inflate the importance of the one other individual that has committed the harm rather than a re-ordered society. The State socially engineers the society that we see via public policy. Acknowledging a Black life matters and that more women are in leadership does not remove the

extractivism that has run amok and the capitalism that created it. The State regulates any superimposition onto another social relationship in some cases (the riot for food and housing) and allows the superimposition onto another social relationship in other cases (the riot for ethno-racial dominance), if it serves the interest of the State.

Arbitrary racial identities are given arbitrary and temporary authority over a space. The despised German or Irish immigrant would be grandfathered in as White if they embraced the settler way. The Southern Black resident would be admitted as an American citizen if they embraced the settler way. The White woman, ever tied to her domestic duties, would be admitted as a full partner if she embraced the settler way. It is no wonder that more expansive settlements of immigrants, inclusion and promotion of Black enlisted men, and Women's Suffrage occurred when expanding the Western part of the United States under Manifest Destiny and after than in the Eastern part of the United States. The arbitrariness continued when it involved the usefulness of the populace to occupy the space of the vast territory under rule. The State-regulated mobility and movement across borders and within restricted spaces (the United States' border with México and Apartheid South Africa's city and township entry points) allowed the mobility and movement across borders and beyond restricted spaces (the ships and their cargo hold for human trafficking, the shipping containers for the drug trade, the iron pipelines of arms dealing). Arbitrary forms of identification were given arbitrary and limited clearance through spaces. Space and boundaries were mere creations of the State through political conventions devised through the warfare of spatial conflicts and lawfare of trade agreements.

As previously noted by Lefebvre (1991),

> The very building of the towns thus embodied a plan which would determine the mode of occupation of the territory and define how it was to be reorganized under the political authority of urban power. The orders stipulate exactly how the chosen sites ought to be developed. The result is a strict hierarchical organization of space, a gradual progression

outward from the town centre, beginning with the *ciudad* and reaching out to the surrounding *pueblos.* The plan is followed with geometrical precision: from the inevitable Plaza Mayor a grid extends indefinitely in every direction. Each square or rectangular lot has its function assigned to it, while inversely every function is assigned its own place at a greater or lesser distance from the central square: church, administrative buildings, town gates, squares, streets, port installations, warehouses is superimposed upon a homogenous space...[it] is also an instrument of production: a superstructure foreign to the original space serves as a political means of introducing a social and economic structure in such a way it may gain foothold and indeed establish its "base" in a particular locality. (Lefebvre, 1991, p. 151)

Thus, Lefebvre established the conception of what we consider to be dominated space within the *spatial triad.* Dominated space is conceived space (the second space, *l'espace conçu,* "representations of space"). It is the political space of territory that has been brought under control through the market and through force, and it is also the space of control of the classes of the populace. Dominated space is also the economic space for the sites of production and labour and the sites of consumption and commerce. Dominated spaces are primarily the instrumental space for the execution of State power, and the experimentation of new ways to wield it. This articulation in the representations of space ensures that "the dominant form of space, that of the centres of wealth and power, endeavours to mould the spaces it dominates (i.e., peripheral spaces)" (Lefebvre, 1991, p. 49). And just as social space (first space) is granted by the State some measure of flexibility and leniency in its routine and practice, so too are some aspects of the dominated spaces in the representations of space (second space). Without some measure of experimentation and movement of the populace, capitalism cannot (and could not) expand and function. This abstraction in space allows for individualised accumulations of wealth that generate the desire of others to protect such space in the event that they are also afforded the luck of wealth accumulation. The individual becomes a "citizen of

this State [that] are private persons whose end is their own interest" (Hegel, 1952, para. 182), and this sets into motion the devolution of any meaningful community with others and isolates them through the embrace of the right of property as a marker of freedom given to them by the State. The "protection of property through the administration of justice", becomes the necessary action of the citizen (Hegel, 1952, para. 208). To be a free private property owner becomes the most noted marker in the society of wealth.

The appearance of wealth is the stuff of the social space, while the production of the wealth is the stuff of the second space. The exchanges that occur are the stuff of the abstract space that then creates a corridor or passageway between the first and second space, as exchanges elicit the use of State currency to acquire commodities that are consumed by the wealthy and the labouring earner, but solely produced by the earner. The wealthy may be able to traverse between these two spaces as their class and status enables this mobility; the labouring earner cannot do the same. The labouring earner has encounters within the second space as the subject. Labouring earners in the abstract space are held to or must use the complex web of street grids that they have no say over, within the schedules of their days that they have little or no say over, and for the fulfilment of plans of a greater authority that they have no say over. Self-determination is inconceivable because there is not even the remote chance of choice. This complex web brought to them and us by the capitalist system keeps us within the confines of something at every moment. The two essential elements of authority (a measure of freedom and the tying of will) grants the State the supreme authority over our lives (Marcuse, 2008). The only possibility of the labouring earner, the working class, is in the imagination fostered by representational spaces (third space). Since social space (first space) is merely the reproduction of relations of production as a fabricated society, and representations of space (second space) fix people within occupied geographic space serving the State, then representational spaces can inform us that,

> Spatiality is not only a product but also a producer and reproducer of the relations of

production and domination, an instrument of both allocative and authoritative power. Class struggle, as well as other social struggles are thus increasingly contained and defined in their spatiality and trapped in its "grid". Social struggle must then become consciously and politically spatial struggle to regain control over the social production of this "space". (Soja, 1985, p. 110)

The catch is that while the social production of space is authored by the State as a tool for both producing its dominance and reproducing its dominance, it is dependant upon the populace and chiefly the labouring earner, the working class, to do so. Imperialism, much like colonialism, is a thing of dependency for,

In the so-called underdeveloped countries, plundered, exploited, "protected" in a multitude of ways (economic, social, political, cultural, scientific), the obstacles in the way of growth and development become increasingly daunting. Meanwhile, the advanced countries use the more backward as a source of labour and as a resource for use values (energies, raw materials, qualitatively superior spaces for leisure activities). (Lefebvre, 1991, pp. 346–347)

## 3.3 Of Order and Ordinances

As Lefebvre articulated, these criticisms of space are questions as to the right to cities in relationship to space under capitalism. Capitalism gave way to the "total occupation of all pre-existing space and upon the production of new space" (p. 326). "Our" streets, parks, plazas, playgrounds, trails, residencies, and businesses are nothing more than sanitised expressions of the colonial that has long since settled upon the native and has erased their presence. The city is the settler colonial city as it has dispossessed original inhabitants of land on which it exists and concentrates them with others as a populace for the extraction of resources because it was created through the colonial city project. The erasure of the indigenous presence continuously occurs in our everyday practices within these streets and spaces. As

the historian David Wilson (2013) articulated, the utter elimination of indigenous peoples was done with such blunt force alongside such precision in measurement and instrumentation,

Actually, that the United States expanded from a handful of seacoast settlements into a single imperium nearly the size of Europe was a historical long shot and was made possible only by a mixture of random luck and an implacable desire to grasp. The Louisiana Purchase of 1803 ... and the wars on Mexico led to the annexation...

Fundamental to the US Imperial Expansion with North America – and thus to the Great European Migration – was the Land Ordinance of 1785... It did not deal with ethereal concepts such as the pursuit of happiness, but it declared in more practical terms how the land from the Appalachian Mountains up to the Mississippi river was to be conquered. This was to be done by surveyors' chains, each twenty-two yards in length. The measuring began at an arbitrary point in Ohio territory, and invisible lines were drawn on the land to form a grid of perfect rectangles marked by cairns, iron bars, and the occasional brass plate cemented into a masonry base. Each of the rectangles had its own map reference and as the US Imperium expanded the grid eventually reached the Pacific coast and stretched between Mexico and British North America. The lines on the land not only conquered natural topography and also made possible the liberated parcels of land from their previous occupants and their efficient allocation to newcomers. (p. 27)

Without this order, a fragile and new State had little chance of continuing forward. While the wealthy landowner came out of the American Revolution far more favourable than when he entered it, those who fought on the front lines, such as small-scale farmers and debtors, were facing increased cut wages and interest on loans. The removal of indigenous populations presented an opportunity to all. Those in debt swiftly moved in and claimed any land that they liked, while the federal government hastened a form of regulation of land and property that could unclog the courts and

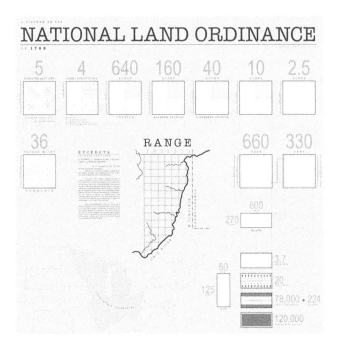

**Fig 3.10** A Diagram of the National Land Ordinance of 1785, Showing the Method of Subdivision Applied From the Scale of the United States Down to the Scale of a Single Lot. (Isomorphism3000/Wiki Commons)

settle the disputes. For you see, government needed the settler to further clear the territory. Settlement townships were formed by dividing six-mile squares that were then divided further into 36 sections of 640 acres within each (see Fig. 3.10). Some sections of the township were placed aside for churches, schooling, and other Society-fostering mechanisms. Massive territories were divided into smaller territories where a provisional governorship managed everyday affairs while reporting and filing taxation to the new State. Within the language of the Northwest Ordinance, 5,000 free White adults could elect their own law-making body, and if that population grew to 60,000, then an application for statehood could be filed to Congress. The continental imperialism of the United States was the first aim of this new State, and now a new understanding for all other States around the world to consider in their respective take on imperialism.

And from this territorial cordoning and division, the newer settlements sprung up, leading to the cities of what is now the Midwest, each with its version of the Philadelphia, French bastides/fortified town, and *Laws of the Indies* grid plans. The cordoning and division of space within the settlement-turned-city followed suit (see Fig. 3.11). The design of conquest was as much a fundamental aspect to its occurrence as the bloodshed of that conquest. Once removed from the land, the false territory of a new State could emerge through the systems of legislative backing, bureaucratic occupations, and marketing endeavours to entice the tepid but needy settlers of the newly formed United States. What was done to indigenous peoples was what was then done to other peoples and what was later done to the rest of the world. But it is now what will be done to anyone as seen through the experiences of State actions during a contemporary pandemic. At the time of working on aspects of this chapter, the absence of people halted the workday bustle during the initial phases of quarantine for COVID-19 in Canada and the United States. The threat of unrest throughout cities in Brazil, the Democratic Republic of the Congo, Guatemala, Hong Kong, Nigeria, the United States, and the United Kingdom, among other cities, due to state-sanctioned violence negated the effects of the

**Fig 3.11** The Great American Grid, Comparison of Twenty Grids, 2011. (isomorphism3000/Wiki Commons)

illusions of benign normalcy and made the occupation of indigenous land and the production of occupation more apparent. What was a city without its busy-ness? It was plainly an administrative centre whose ongoing service is the dispossession of the unhoused, unemployed, and untreatable, and extraction of labour of the essential worker. The capital, the metropolis, the Gotham, and "the big city" were all openly settler cities that continue their ways of dispossession and extraction in secluded board rooms, alleyways, and side streets. The absence of the "busy" during quarantine was an important revelation of the possibilities of what else could be built upon this emptiness, this canvas of Whiteness, this new form of the colonial power. For Whiteness in all its awesome power was only the blank space where a theft had occurred (Fig. 3.11).

Cities were the sites for the articulation of State power, but they were also the sites of a fabricated society. What is the society? Society, the socius, is the location in which power is experienced as a dominating force – neoliberalism, austerity, repression, extraction, and abandonment. We pursue our perceived individual and groups enactments and living togetherness, as a location for negotiated exercises of living with oppression (James' *captive maternal*). We also extend the re-ordering practices by the State in aspects of negotiating the use of space by not changing the reality in which we live. It is a space for us to think and enact new and counter ideations. It is also a location for the waging of resistance against State power and conceiving of a new reality. But while cities do learn from each other as States do, the urban function and processes of cities may differ. Hugill (2017) made note on such a difference by indicating the settler colonial city and the colonial city differ,

> fundamentally... because (a) ...accumulation strategies are primarily oriented around the enrichment of settler constituencies, rather than far-flung metropolitan sponsors, (b) the colonial relation remains a central and enduring element of its contemporary life, albeit in dynamic and frequently recomposed forms, (c) and Indigenous peoples themselves have more often been excluded from, rather than exploited in, its core economic activities. (pp. 6–7)

Cities during this time of the coronavirus pandemic, as this chapter and book is being drafted, show the ruptures in the management of cities and the weaknesses of the State at an even clearer visibility. The pandemic denies the State's ability to fully control a thing. The pandemic was (and still is) un-mappable. And the perceived first space (space of social practice) of Lefebvre is supposedly physically mappable. Sure, the coronavirus can be traced as in where it was, maybe where it originated, but even this is not with the level of precision and resolute certainty that the science and technology of high modernism has espoused with other examples of mastery over the living world. The conceived second space is known – both the conceived space of the imagined and governed – and is officially mapped through the institutions of the State. But even then, with this body of knowledge, level of expertise, and even administrative bureaucracy, we have no idea where the coronavirus is going and how it will get there. It is a thing that cannot be ordered, and it is most assuredly rupturing all systems, all orders, and all status quos. The people infected with the cor-onavirus are even unknown until they come forward or display signs visible enough and physically dis-abling enough that a revelation of surprise is no longer possible. However, the lived third space is the disruptor of the real and the imagined, used, prac-ticed, experienced, and contested unpredictable ways. What comes after the pandemic, a new strain or a new disease, is uncertain, even though at the time of this chapter we have now moved into a stage of the advancement of a vaccine. The State and its populace are both displaying modes of confidence with a ting of lunacy as the affirmation of mastery of nature and unknown is yet again on the cusp. It is of little concern that the coronavirus-induced cracks and ruptures may have worsened the social levee system of the State, which has not only been fortified by a wall of the rule of law but also the wall of the very bodies of the populace that it now buries in the thousands.

In the mid-20th century, the British Crown, through a series of acts, made legal claims to the processes of conversion of indigenous lands in Kenya into lands of the British Crown, thereby making the

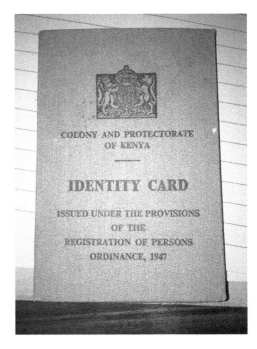

**Fig 3.12** Identity Card Within the British Colony and Protectorate of Kenya, 1947. (Raphael.langart/Wiki Commons)

indigenous peoples of Kenya subjects to the Crown, whether they knew it or not. Unlike Madras in Indian, Nairobi did not have an industrialisation premise; there was no nearby extraction of natural resources as the basis for the creation of the city. Nairobi was a city for the occupation of territory in the event another competing State would lay claim to its land and hold an advantage on the entire continent. The land of Kenya and elsewhere was to be taken command of, as a great deal of the land on the continent of Africa was under the banner of British Imperialism. Through a sleight of hand, land turned territory was converted further into property, and as a result turned natives into subjects. (see Fig. 3.12). Subjugation positioned these peoples as landless, which turned them into homeless law-breakers unless they conceded to became complicit labourers of the colony and Crown. A so-called benevolent policy of villagisation was a form of concentration of a population through removal and reorganisation.

In new spatial contexts, villagers were to be no longer *Gĩkũyũ, but Bantu at best and British subjects of the Crown at worst.* And this complicity extended itself to the greater State of a later independent Kenya. Cities such as Nairobi became the means to inflict laws on those that broke them, even if they were engaging in practices that pre-dated this colonial rule. To become the colonial subject remade the African indigenous "body" into an instrument that further advanced land acquisition claims and property valuations for extraction. Unlike the North American indigenous "body", the African indigenous "body" was no longer even remembered as indigenous. The colonial settlement built an empire in the immediate and for the long-term. In the immediate, Black subjugation defined the settler and the settlement, less dispossession through removal from lands and more dispossession through centralisation within the cities. The city aided in the fostering of order in territories that the settler could be easily outnumbered by the native. Settler colonialism was the great "come up" that happened for settlers, the thing that removed them from downward mobility in the imperial city. Crinson (2020) contextualised the creation of the "colonial mind" as the intentional spatial planning of the Kenyan landscape and the construction of colonial infrastructure as the understood, "context of the empire as a continuing structure of consciousness… through the means of state planning, the organisation of space and facilities, the fantasy of the managed compartmentalized world" (p. 276).

Nairobi, founded in 1899, was to be the capital city for the colony; yet, it was mainly filled with gendered male British colonialists and migrants from the Empire without their families. This planned city of Nairobi was a gendered city to ensure that the labour of the indigenous African population was relegated to farming, construction, service, housekeeping, and sex work, with the latter two mainly held by the indigenous gendered female population. Laws that governed social activity were modified to inflict damage onto the native, and not the settler (Berman, 1990). The prison, nearly 30 such facilities constructed within a 10-year period, were among the first buildings in Nairobi, Mombasa, and other cities in Kenya to be built. The gendered male indigenous population was disproportionately sentenced, and the gendered female indigenous population became a pseudo-middle management class of property owners and farm subsidisers, but regardless of the class position, both were in service to the whims of the State. However, the very function of the prison for this colonial city was to reify all things White as non-criminal and all things native and African as "criminal", in both the spatial location of the prison in the hinterlands and the disparities in sentencing (Marshall, 2017). The laws of the colony were only enforced on the native, not the settler. The court and the prison were respectively the institutions of privileges and compliancy, but both also created mechanisms to create forced labour for the extraction of wealth creamed from the top of agricultural work and for the needs of the State in building roads and railways as well as for the taxation of property and land. As Kenya's British Colonial Defence Minister commented, "we are slave traders and the employment of our slaves are, in this instance, by the Public Works Department" (Elkins, 2005, p. 130). Police records, tax records, and census records maintained different socio-political takes on the population in the city, where the infractions of one class of Bantu would have led to further penalties, and the other class would have led to greater taxation and social restriction. One became tied to the false city due to the presence of incarceration and the presence and reliance of steady work and income.

The laws of the colony were created to bend the wills of some, and to bend for the wills of others. The courts of the State were interwoven into the infrastructure of society. The court presided over the infractions of the rule of law. The court was against the social actions on display in the fabricated society. Within the codified legalese, the State determined which of their own laws they would recognise and which laws would be applied to which populations. Without most subjects to the Crown fully recognising it, these were what established the social boundaries of who was ruled and who were the rulers in any given social activity of the State. But the law in cities like Nairobi had to entertain a balance of harsh discipline and leniency onto the native, lest they become unruly and lawless (Bushe & Great Britain Colonial Office, 1934). As well, they could not fully allow the imperial city transplanted settler a sense of autonomy or full reign of the land in the territory because after all they, too, were subjects of the Crown. The people, the settler and the native, could not become challenges to the State at all costs as that would disrupt the purpose of the creation of the city.

While law subjugated one population over the other, Crown rule subjugated them both. And the ways that settler colonialism happened to indigenous populations of the African continent imparted lasting technologies in dispossession and extraction onto the native/indigenous person that have endured into the present. The city became the bedrock for the alienation from land in exchange for the illusion of sanctity in State law: rights were given, all must be governed, property can be owned, and the rule of law must be upheld, because only the settler and citizen were granted these wonderful rights and "opportunities". The eventual unravelling and dismantling of settlerdom was the result of the Mau Mau rebellion in the 1950s and the broader independence movement. But in many insidious ways, the dismantling of settlerdom (worldwide) was due to the tottery maintenance of the role and position of settlers by the State. The settler class had become more a burden and expense than a benefit for the former colonial and now Imperial State. And the lasting vestige of the colonial State of Kenya and the colonial city projects of Nairobi that have seemingly escaped the calls and demands for decolonisation in the present day have been the prisons and their incarcerated populations.

This is why the design of the city is presented here as less about the physical structure, the aesthetics, and the functioning of buildings and city infrastructure, but instead about the regulation of the population of cities through the splendour of the city that attracts complicity and provides harsh restriction for the maintenance of order. With the spectacle of infrastructure, Brown (2020) remarked that skyscrapers as architectural marvels, "from its distancing apex – reduces bodies to specks…the skyscraper called attention to the malleable nature of perception" (p. 205). While on the matter of the restrictive order of building property, Hirt (2015) questioned the sensibilities and pride of citizens of the United States with, "reputation[s] for being independent and freedom-loving and respecting

private property was worldwide put up with such tedious laws governing the building of their everyday environments and way of life?" (p. ix). To do so highlights the intended usefulness in the **identification of populations** by Race, gender, and class (as well as other related and distinct categorisations like religion, ethnicity, national origin, sexual orientation, and disability) as a necessary operation in governance, not a happenstance survey of identities. To engage in massive evictions in Bombay (now Mumbai), the British colonial system had to,

> Shift a large number of Indians outside the Fort walls [which] required government to be in possession of detailed land use and information. Once again, the need for a comprehensive and revenue survey was greatly felt. Only when the government's claims of all of Bombay's lands were assured, could revenue rates be increased, and assertion of political hegemony have meaning. (Dossal, 2010, pp. 57–58)

While the colonial government was not initially successful in evicting nearly 1,800 Indian businessmen of a total population of 10,801, of which 4,061 were Hindus, the shared relationship with census data and property control was evident. When businessmen were not rallying against the Crown during the 1800s, they were coalescing with other Crown officials, British businessmen, and merchants to create elite neighbourhoods through the relocation of the lower classes and lower castes of different sections of town to areas in the distant north, and even beyond the city limits. It wasn't so much that power was shared between the new indigenous business and the Crow officials, but power simply showed that a proto-post racialisation State was possible. If the culture of rule was adopted, then so would a portion of a population be adopted into the ruling class,

> the emergence of this cosmopolitan and eclectic political culture in Bombay owed something to the degree of autonomy from colonial domination that the city's elites had been able to assert since the earliest days of the East India Company settlement… The Company's political weakness and the relative poverty of its merchants increased its dependence on Indian

merchants and dubashes. As a result, Bombay's elites had been able to appropriate considerable influence and wealth. Commercial partnership lent itself to political collaboration. Bombay's mercantile elites acquired a grip on important and lucrative areas of the city's economy, including and indeed especially the cotton textile industry... From the 1830s onwards, they were firmly entrenched in local government. They were...consulted by colonial officials. They gained ready access to...the Governor's court...they focused their attention on the city, where political power and influence was open to them, and ignored the hinterlands over which they had little control...As they battled for power within the Municipal Corporation where they gained, by the 1880s, greater representation on a relatively wide franchise, they took particular pride in public standards in the city. (Chandavarkar, 2004, pp. 16–17)

And with this new class of business elites, wealth dominance in the city of Bombay expanded its reach, borders, and even its population (Chandavarkar, 2009). It was this business elite class's tastes that marked the physical space of the city, not only socially but also structurally. The indigenous elite were sponsors for public works and capital projects as well as principal consultants on roadway construction. Initially, the British Government in India unilaterally employed planning practices established in England, as intended by the Land Acquisition Act of 1894, to,

sub-divide land into plots for houses, open spaces, schools, hospitals, other public facilities and roads, and sell the plots for private owner ship and development in accordance with the rules prescribed. Carrying out of development works such as construction of roads with streetlights, drains, sewers, water supply and provision of electricity within the area covered by Town Planning Schemes [instituted after 1915] were considered as the responsibilities of Improvement Trusts. At some places, Improvement Trusts were mainly involved in road widening works and development of adjacent areas. Some of the

activities which the Trusts were engaged in, were those of improving extremely congested areas by slum clearance and undertaking housing projects for the low-income groups. (Ansari, 1977, p. 9)

The system in the Improvement Trust overstepped municipal governance and side-skirted local laws in favour of greater State interests. The space of early- and mid-20th century Bombay became less the design of the British and more,

Buildings designed for India...were not simply copies of British buildings. Central to their production was the issue of finding the appropriate Anglo-Indian style for India, a style that calibrated the correct distance between colonising elite[s] and those they ruled. (Chandavarkar, 2004, p. 71)

Eventually, the designation of "slums" and treatment of such spaces were also British practices that were appropriated. This was especially the case under the Maharashtra Slum Areas (Improvement, Clearance and Redevelopment) Act in 1971,

a. any area is or may be a source of danger to the health, safety or convenience of the public of that area or of its neighbourhood, by reason of the area having inadequate or no basic amenities, or being insanitary, squalid, overcrowded or otherwise; or

b. the buildings in any area, used or intended to be used for human habitation are
   i. in any respect, unfit for human habitation; or
   ii. by reasons of dilapidation, overcrowding, faulty arrangement and design of such buildings, narrowness or faulty arrangement of streets, lack of ventilation, light or sanitation facilities or any combination of these factors, detrimental to the health, safety or convenience of the public of that area, the Competent Authority may, by notification in the *Official Gazette*, declare such area to be a slum area. (Section 4(1) as cited by Thatra, 2020, p. 20)

**Fig 3.13** Slums and Corporate Buildings in the Financial Capital of India, Mumbai, Also Known as "Maya Nagari" for Its Money, Fashion, Luxury, and Films, Despite 60% of Its Residents Residing in These Areas, 2011. (Nishantid85/Wiki Commons)

Instead of viewing these "slums" as areas that cropped up and littered across the city due to the false promises of labour and housing, they should be seen as designed spaces of isolation, abandonment, and occupation in response to the failures of a city that continued to attract populations for labour opportunity that no longer existed. As wealth accumulation around these areas increased, the extraction of labour at exploitative wages resulted in perpetual destitution (see Fig. 3.13). Living in these spaces, in proximity to wealth, appeared to be far better than living in the hinterlands. But the lustre of a Bollywood only glossed over the realities of a shuttering mill industry (Adarkar & Menon, 2004). The land that the mills once sat on eventually became shopping malls for a small business elite class. In 100 years, from 1875 to 1975, and with independence, those in power changed hands, but the work of power never changed hands. The creation of a cosmopolitan city that defied cultural norms of caste in favour of a breadth of religious, linguistic, and other ethnic identifying characteristics was rendered into present-day Detroit, 1970s Pittsburgh

in the United States, or 1950s Manchester in the United Kingdom. The spatial inequalities of this particular socio-history accounted for the complexities of Dalits in present-day Mumbai, and not the notions of a long history of caste exclusion. The society of Bombay was tenuous because the new actors in the State were still in service to that State (and the State in the present day). Poverty was ever present in Bombay but deepened with job loss in the eventual Mumbai. Slums emerged as real spaces where a neighbourhood once sat. What sits in its place are the waning fantasies of a corrupt system still driving extraction where there is little to squeeze.

Primitive accumulation was always violent, never benign. The social means of production that would become capital was only achieved through varying forms of dispossession. Spatially, dispossession took the forms of forced removal from lands, banishment to outer regions, forced centralisation within cities, neighbourhood marginalisation within cities, slum poverty concentration, removal from home dwelling through eviction, and organised city service abandonment. But dispossession could also be thought of as what occurred to the dispossessed, such as confinement and incarceration, restrictions on celebrating and practicing cultural customs, inability to redress grievances, theft of loved ones, State-sanctioned violence that produced trauma, and State-sanctioned violence that produced death. This dispossession was all due to the basic desire to accumulate wealth. For this violence of dispossession and accumulation to occur, an enclosure must be created to manage the processes of both with the might of the greater State at the behest of the landowners that comprise a role within the State to privatise public land and public space and to erect the industries of extraction. Differentiating populations of people aided the process by creating false class experiences that pitted worker against worker under equally false banners of some dominant ethnic solidarity. A process of differentiation, racialisation, relegated considerable percentages of those populations into lower wage, wage dependent, and precarious lifestyle-tied positions of employment.

All the while, a process of extracting labour from the rest of the population occurred at vary degrees of dispossession, extraction, and exploitation. Within those differentiated populations, additional forms of differentiation gendered populations to ensure that even childbearing could be regulated and harnessed for the means of future labour and service to the State. The age of globalisation ushered in the neo-liberal State through which the wealth and capital gained from land and property formed the foundational mode of capital accumulation (Lefebvre, 2003). The city, the pinnacle achievement of the State and the principal example of the process of urbanisation, was also the chief organising tool of society. With the city, the State was able to sell off bits and pieces of the public to privatised bodies in order to accumulate greater volumes of wealth, as "accumulation by dispossession" (Harvey, 2003). Unlike other States, the United States fashioned a series of laws, procedures, and areas of academic study to harness and maintain local zoning control. And, unlike other States, "in none of them is local-level land-use control as strong as it is in the United States and in none does the single-family home hold such a legally privileged position" (Hirt, 2015, p. 62).

Cities were (and are) growing machines: growth in populations looking for better employment and housing, growth in services rendered and needed, growth in investments and assets. As needed, housing and streets can be constructed for a secured workforce. As desired, parks and buildings can always be built for additional revenue. But also, and as needed, those same housing, streets, parks, and buildings can be demolished for revenue. Yet, even still, those homes, streets, parks, and buildings could just be forgotten, abandoned, and left alone for revenue. The wind of neo-liberalism can blow in any direction under any political party banner and campaign promise. In this zenith of globalisation and neo-liberalism, in the height of a devastating pandemic that has caused 1.4 million deaths, with the United States leading all of the nation-states with 260,000 deaths (60 million cases), the State's illusion of serving the fabricated society has been all but eviscerated.

Some post-pandemic predictions have leaned toward the political right, toward greater austerity measures in the city, not just from State measures to hoard wealth but from the combined actions of those with wealth responding to likely increased taxations that will drive them and their amenities out of the city. Austerity and an evaporation of revenue from a wealthier tax base will usher in a period of "suicide by city" for the State. This is the fear of the rising immigrant, Black/Brown/Red agitation and the socialist order that allegedly took over the city with a violent wave of crime and riot. Some other post-pandemic predictions have leaned toward the political left, toward greater urbanisation as cities provide the greatest chance of protection for when the next pandemic arises but also a range of higher paid managerial jobs at lower costs due to massive investment in public services. This is the assurance of the protective State, responsible corporate partners, and a "kinder" community that will deepen pacification through the return to the city with an onslaught of festivals, concerts, and sporting events. Meanwhile, in both predictions fair housing, increased minimum wage, tolerance for collective action, and affordable health care are never the provisions to curb the tide or properly correct the wrongs. With the current environment and this likely future, it is evident that the State candidly exploits its fabricated Society. And, in many ways, design and planning are tools to maximise this exploitation under other guises. As Lefebvre (2003) posited that the analysis of the urban phenomenon,

> Only makes sense if it is able to distinguish organization and institutions, to the extent that they control the exterior and interior functions of the city and can therefore combine them. Structures are also twofold: they are *morphological* (sites and situations, buildings, streets and squares, monuments, neighbourhoods) and *sociological* (distribution of the population, ages and sexes, households, active or passive population, socioprofessional categories, managers and the managed). As for its form in the conventional sense of the word, that is to say geometric or plastic, there is a spatial element that must be accounted for – grid or radial-concentric. However, such an arrangement does not become obvious unless we turn our attention to circulation, unless we restrict the urban problematic to the problems of circulation. The invention of new forms (X-shaped, spiral, helical, concave, etc.) is merely a simplistic solution to the urban problematic. (p. 116)

### 3.4 The *Laws of the Indies*

Legacies of knowledge transference are vital to developing a larger conceptual lens and articulation of their possible impacts. The shared map, the shared technique, the shared governance documents, and the shared schools of training are the means for this knowledge transference. To simply say that the past settlements turned colonial city projects are what birthed the modern city in more than just design but in their very functionality of oppressing populations has to be evidenced. Whether this book does its job will be the evaluation of the reader, but there is no denying that at best what is presented in this chapter and throughout this book is either the skeleton to such an argument or a meatier indictment of the claim. Situating the Spanish Empire as the initial internationalised State, moving past ruling neighbouring regions, to dominating distant and remote lands after the Roman Empire. What they undertook

was more than raiding, pillaging, slaving, and extracting expeditions. The aim of the Spanish Crown was to create a permanent means and vehicle to sustain those pursuits. As it has been previously discussed, the Spanish Empire's 1573 *Laws of the Indies* are infinitely more impactful to our present day than the use of terms like *Indios* and *Negros*. The ways that the city grid sought to subjugate and the *conquistadores* that they sought to maintain in subservience reveal such a need to focus on the infrastructure,

> … let it be known: That in order that the discoveries and new settlements and pacification of the land and provinces which are to be discovered, settled, and pacified in the Indies… and for the welfare the natives, among other things, we have prepared the following ordinances:
>
> 1. No person, regardless of state or condition, should, on his own authority make a new discovery by sea or land, or enter a settlement or hamlet in areas already discovered…
> 2. Those who are in charge of governing the Indies, whether spiritually or temporally, should inform themselves diligently whether within their districts, including lands and provinces bordering them, there is something to be discovered and pacified of the wealth and quality, [and] of the peoples and nations who inhabit there; but do this within sending to them war personnel nor persons who can cause scandal…
> 3. Having made, within the confines of the province, a discovery by land, pacified it, [and] subjected it to our obedience, find an appropriate site to be settled by Spaniards – and if not, [arrange] for the vassal Indians so they be secure…
> 4. If the boundaries of the settlement are populated, utilizing commerce and ransom, go with vassal Indians and interpreters to discover those lands and with churchmen and Spaniards, carrying offerings and ransoms and peace, try to learn about the place, the contents and quality of the land, the nation(s) to which the people there

belong, who governs them, and carefully take note of all you can learn and understand, and always send these narratives to the Governor so that they reach the Council [Consejo de Indias].

5. Look carefully at the places and ports where it might be possible to build Spanish settlements without damage to the Indian populations.... (Mundigo & Crouch, 1977, pp. 249–250)

It cannot be understated how the *Laws of the Indies* unapologetically began with its philosophy in mind, the pacification of the land. And despite its perceived banality, pacification was clearance with coercive force. Pacification came before occupation, and with occupation a way was made for settlement. And so, the *Laws of the Indies* continued:

33 Having populated and settled the newly discovered area, pacified it, and subjected it to our mandate, efforts should be made to discover and populate adjacent areas that are being discovered for the first time...

34 In order to populate those areas that are already discovered, pacified, and under our mandate, as well as areas that might be discovered and pacified in the course of time, the following sequence should be adhered to: choose the province, county, and place that will be settled taking into consideration the health of the area...

38. Once the region, province county and land are decided upon by the experts discoverers, select the site to build a town and capital of the province and its subjects, without damage to the Indians for having occupied the area or because they agree to it of good will.

39. The site and position of the towns should be selected in places where water is nearby and where it would be possible to demolish neighbouring towns and properties in order to take advantage of the materials which are essential for building; and, [there should be] land also for farming, cultivation, and pasturation, so as to avoid excessive work and cost, since any of the above would be costly if they were far...

However, a settlement was far from being a "tent city". Local governance must be created in order for

the distant State, in this case the Spanish Crown, to dictate and rule. The level of detail and expanse of the local government depended on the intention of what the settlement was to become or remain:

42 Having selected the site for capital towns in each country, determine the areas which could be subjected and incorporated within the jurisdiction of the head town [county seat] as farms, granges and gardens, without detriment to Indians or natives.

43 Having selected the area, province, and site where the new settlement is to be built, and, having established the existing opportunities for development, the governor in whose district [the site] is or borders upon, should decide whether the site that is to be populated should become a city, town or village settlement. In compliance with his decision, it should form a Council, commonwealth [*república*] and name corresponding officials and members in accordance with stipulations in the Book of the Republic of Spaniards [*Libro de la Republica de Españoles*]. Thus in case it were to become a metropolitan city it should have a judge with title and name of *adelantado* [title often given to the governor of a province, probably interim governor, or governor, or principal mayor; a *corregidor* or ordinary mayor who would have *insolidum* jurisdiction and who jointly with the regiment would carry on the administration of the commonwealth [with the help also of]: three officers of the Royal Exchequer [*Hacienda Real*], twelve magistrates [*regidores*], two executors, two jurors for each parish, one general procurer, one scribe for the Council, two public scribes – one for mines, another for registers, one main town crier, one broker for commercial transactions, two ushers to diocesan or suffragan bishops, eight [lower] magistrates and other such essential officials. For the towns and villages, an ordinary mayor, four magistrates, one constable, one scribe for the Council and public scribe, and a majordomo. (Mundigo & Crouch, 1977, p. 252)

Government was the means for the State to function. Government also established the confines of justice on the ground. Without and through government, the rights to land, the registration of the land and of the different peoples, the distribution of land with their appropriate designations (zoning), measurement and method of taxation, and the accounting of the population (census) could not come into existence. With settlement, and after creating forms of governance, came the need for structure and design of the physical environment. The settlement needed to meet a threshold of persons, too, in order that this physical environment could be commandeered from the previous "open" space. The occupants of the initially constructed settlement should give some classification of distinction above all others that would soon occupy more spaces within the growing settlement. An order of things must be followed that was based on the ideas of the State:

89 The persons who were placed in charge of populating a town with Spaniards should see to it that within a specified terms, assigned for its establishment, it should have at least thirty neighbours, each one with his own house...if this is not accomplished he should lose everything already built or formed and he will incur a fine of a thousand gold pesos...

90 The aforesaid stipulations and territory should be divided as follows: Separate first the land which is needed for the house plots [solares] of the town, then allocate sufficient public land and grounds for pasturation where the cattle the neighbours are expected to bring with them can obtain abundant feed, plus another portion for the natives of the area. The rest of the grounds and territory should be divided into four parts: one for the person in charge of building the town, the other three should be subdivided into thirty lots for the thirty neighbours of the town...

99 Those who have made a commitment to build the said new town, who after having succeeded in carrying out its settlement, as an honour to them and to their descendants [and in] their laudable memory as founders, we pronounce them: *hijosdalgo* illustrious men of known ancestry. To them and to their legitimate heirs, in whatever place they might reside or in any part of the Indies, they will be *hijosdalgo*, that is persons of noble ascendancy and known ancestry...

100 Those who should want to make a commitment to building a new settlement in the form and manner already prescribed, be it of more or less than 30 neighbours, it should be of no less than twelve persons and be awarded the authorization and territory in accordance with the prescribed conditions. (Mundigo & Crouch, 1977, p. 253)

The inspiration for the Northwest Ordinance of 1787 of the newly formed United States and its preciseness in measurement, among many other plans for occupied territories and city plans, were seen through the continued pages of the document. The ordering of things continued:

110 Having made the discovery, selected the province, county and area that is to be settled, and the site in the location, where the new town is to be built and having taken possession of it, those placed in charge of its execution are to do it in the following manner: On arriving at the place where the new settlement is to be founded – which according to our will and disposition shall be one which is vacant and which can be occupied without doing harm to the Indians and natives or with their free consent – a plan for the site is to be made, dividing it into squares, streets building lots, using cord and ruler, beginning with the main square from the streets are to run to the gates and principal roads and leaving sufficient open space so that even if the town grows it can always spread in the same manner. Having thus agreed upon the site and place to be selected to be populated, a layout should be made in the following way:...

112 The main plaza is to be the starting point for the town; if the town is situated on the sea coast it should be placed at the landing plan of the port, but inland it should be at the centre of the town. The plaza should be square or rectangular, in which case it should have at least one and half its width for length in as much as this shape is best for fiestas in which horses are used and for any other fiestas should be held.

113 The size of the plaza shall be proportioned to the number of inhabitants taking into consideration the fact that in Indian towns, in as much as they are new, the intention is that they

will increase and thus the plaza should be decided upon taking into consideration the growth the town may experience. [The plaza] shall be not less than two hundred feet wide and three hundred feet long, nor larger than eight hundred feet long and five hundred and thirty-two feet wide. A good proportion is six hundred feet long and four hundred wide.

From the plaza shall begin four principal streets: One from the middle of each side and two streets from each corner of the plaza; the four corners of the plaza shall face the four principal winds, because in this manner, the streets running from the plaza will not be exposed to the four principal winds which would cause much inconvenience...

117 The streets shall run from the main plaza in such a manner that even if the town increases considerably in size, it shall not result in some inconvenience that will make ugly what needed to be rebuilt, or endanger its defense or comfort.

118 Here and there in the town, smaller plazas of good proportion shall be laid out, where the temples associated with the principal church, the parish churches, and the monasteries can be built.... (Mundigo & Crouch, 1977, pp. 254–255)

121 Next, a site and lot shall be assigned for the royal council and cabildo house and for the custom house and arsenal, near the temple, located in such a manner that in times of need the one may aid the other; the hospital for the poor and those sick of noncontagious diseases shall be built near the temple and its cloister...

126 In the plaza, no lots shall be assigned to private individuals; instead they shall be used for the building of the church and royal houses and for city use, but shops and houses for the merchants should be built first, to which all the settlers of the town shall contribute and a moderate tax shall be imposed on goods so that these buildings may be built.

127 The other building lots shall be distributed by lottery to the settlers, continuing with the lots closer to the main plaza, and the lots that are left shall be held by us for assignment to those who shall late become settlers, or for the use that we may wish to make of them, and so that this may be ascertained better, the town shall maintain a plan of what is being built.

128 Having made the plan of the town and having distributed building lots, each of the settlers shall set up his tent on his plot if he should have one....

129 Within the town, a common shall be delimited, large enough that although the population may experience a rapid expansion, there will always be sufficient space where the people may go to for recreation and take their cattle to pasture without them making any damage.... (Mundigo & Crouch, 1977, p. 256)

Through governance, a society was constructed with a clear spatial reasoning. While the presence of religion and the engagement in commerce formed much of the activities of the day to day, the usefulness of fiestas was important. Similar to Roman rule, the usefulness of these events was to occupy the time and space, as well as the minds of the city's occupants. No month was spared of an event of some sort and some degree of magnitude. Each event needed existing space or the carving out of new space to enact its function. The fiesta, the park, and most importantly, the plaza were the necessary humanising endeavours to also engage in while working through the brutal regime of colonialism through coercion or domination. And through that spatial reasoning, notions of taste and aesthetic were adjoined to the construction of settlement, now town:

134 They shall try as far as possible to have the buildings all of one type for the sake of the beauty of the town.

135 The faithful executors and architects as well as persons who may deputed for this purpose by the governor shall be most careful in overseeing that the above [ordinances] be executed; and they shall hurry in their labor and building so that the town may be completed in a short time...

To hasten the erection of the town was important; public works was not something to "dilly and dally" with. The quickened pace of construction suggested that any delay in such construction opened the doorway to the indefensibility of the town, both in its physical features but also in the minds of those being conquered and doing the conquering:

> 136 If natives should resolve to take defensive position toward the [new] settlement, they should be made aware of how we intend to settle, not to do damage to them nor take away their lands, but instead to gain their friendship and teach them how to live civilly, and also to teach them to know our God so they learn His law through which they will be saved. This will be done by religious, clerics, and other persons designated for the purpose by the governor and through good interpreters, taking care by the best means available that the town settlement is carried out peacefully and with their consent, but if they [the natives] still do not want to concur after having been summoned repeatedly by various means, the settlers should build their own town without taking what belongs to the Indians and without doing them more harm that it were necessary for the protection of the town in order that the settlers are not disturbed.
>
> 137 While the town is being completed, the settlers should try, in as much as this is possible, to avoid communication and traffic with the Indians, or going to their towns, or amusing themselves or spilling themselves on the ground; nor [should the settlers] allow the Indians to enter within the confines of the town until it is built and its defenses ready and houses built so that when the Indians see them they will be struck with admiration and will understand that the Spaniards are there to settle permanently and not temporarily…
>
> 138 Having completed the erection of the town and the buildings within it, and not before this is done, the governor and settlers, with great care and holy zeal, should try to bring peace into the fraternity of the Holy Church and bring on to our obedience all the natives of the province and its counties, by the best means they know or can understand, and in the following manner…
>
> 139 Obtain information of the diversity of nations, languages, sects, and prejudices of the natives within the province, and about the lords they may pledge allegiance to, and by means of commerce and exchange, [the Spaniards] should try to establish friendship with them [the Indians],

> showing great love and caressing them and also giving them things in barter that will attract their interest, and not showing greediness for their things. [The Spaniards] should establish friendship and alliances with the principal lords and other influential persons who would be most useful in the pacification of the land…
>
> 140 Having made peace and alliance with [the Indian lords] and with their republics, make careful efforts so that they get together and then [our] preachers, with utmost solemnity, should communicate and begin to persuade them that they should desire to understand matters pertaining to the Holy Catholic faith…Then shall begin our teaching [efforts] with great providence and discretion…Thus you will not start by reprimanding their vices or their idolatry, nor taking away their women nor their idols, because they should not be scandalized or develop an enmity against the Christian doctrine. Instead, they should be taught first, and after they have been instructed, they should be persuaded that on their own will they should abandon all that runs contrary…
> (Mundigo & Crouch, 1977, pp. 257–258)

If the swift movement from tents to towns were not done, all that the State intended with this strike in this new territory would be lost. With this construction, additional populating of the town becomes key:

> 148 The Spaniards to whom the Indians are entrusted [*encomendados*], should seek with great care that these Indians be settled into towns, and that, within these, churches be built so that the Indians can be instructed into Christian doctrine and live in good order. Because we order you to see to it that these Ordinances, as presented above, be incorporated, complied with, and executed, and that you make what in them is contained be complied with and executed, and never take action or move against them, nor consent that others take action or move against either their content or form, under penalty of our Lord.
> (Mundigo & Crouch, 1977, p. 258)

While the intent of these body of *Laws* were issued as governance for the Spanish Empire's possessions

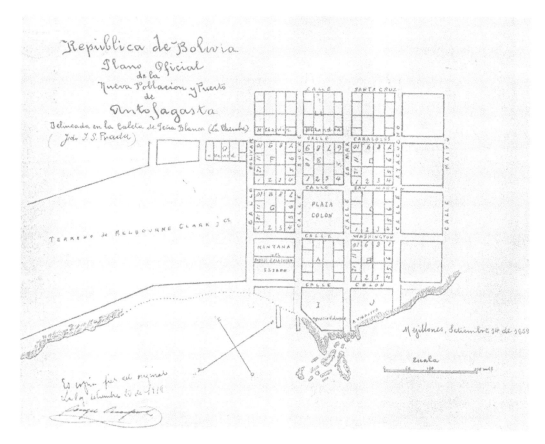

**Fig 3.14** Plano oficial de la nueva población y puerto de Antofagasta (Chile), por José Santos Prada, 1869. (Public Domain)

in the Americas (most pronouncedly in México, then New Spain, but also with the port city of Antofagasta in Chile; see 'Fig. 3.14) and South East Asia (specifically, the Philippines and the city Manila; see Fig. 3.15–3.17), they represented a sophisticated compilation of previous laws that influenced the constant refinement in its execution.

Through forced city design, now populations could be more intensely made into subjects and be taxed based on their property of residence or ownership. As James C. Scott (1999) remarked in *Seeing Like A State* about the level of detail that the decree to order of people went to,

Nowhere is this better illustrated than in the Philippines under the Spanish. Filipinos were instructed by the decree of November 21, 1849 to take on permanent Hispanic surnames...He had observed, as his decree states, that Filipinos generally lacked individual surnames, which might "distinguish them by families" and that their practice of adopting baptismal names drawn from a small group of saints' names resulted in great "confusion." The remedy was the *catalogo*, a compendium not only of personal names but also of nouns and adjectives drawn from flora, fauna, minerals, geography, and the arts and intended to be used by authorities in assigning permanent, inherited surnames. Each local official was to be given a supply of surnames sufficient for his jurisdiction, "taking care that the distribution be made by letters of the alphabet." In practice, each town was given a number of pages from the alphabetized *catalogo*, producing whole towns with surnames beginning with the same letter. In situations where there has been little in-migration in the past 150 years, the traces of this administrative exercise are still perfectly visible across the landscape. For

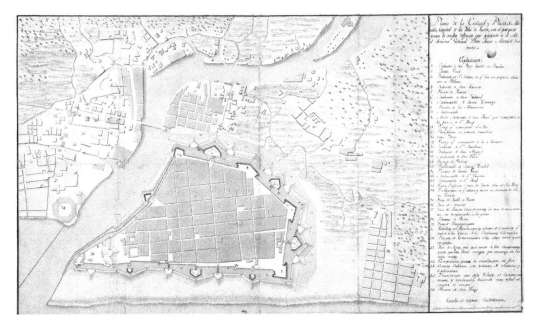

**Fig 3.15** Plano de la ciudad y plaza de Manila (the Philippines), capital de la isla de Luzón, con el proyecto para la mejor defensa que propuso. 1766. (Public Domain)

example, in the Bikol region, the entire alphabet is laid out like a garland over the provinces of Albay, Sorsogon, and Catanduanes which in 1849 belonged to the single jurisdiction of Albay. Beginning with A at the provincial capital, the letters *B* and *C* mark the towns along the cost beyond Tabaco to Wiki. We return and trace along the coast of Sorosgon the letters *E* to *L*, then starting down the Iraya Valley at Daraga with M, we stop with S to Polangui and Libon, and finish the alphabet with a quick tour around the island of Catanduanes.

The confusion for which the decree is the antidote is largely that of the administrator and the tax collector. Universal last names, they believe, will facilitate the administration of justice, finance, and public order as well as make it simpler for prospective marriage partners to calculate their degree of consanguinity. For a utilitarian state builder of [Governor] Claveria's temper, however, the ultimate goal was a complete and legible list of subjects and taxpayers. (p. 69)

The 148 regulations served both as community-building documents and town design plans, but the *Laws of the Indies* was a stark change in the operation of the State in its conquest. These were the orders for constructing an entirely new city as opposed to constructing a city built on top of the ruins of a former city of a former Empire (Aztecan, Incan, or Mayan). The foundation of a city, both symbolically and literally, employed the checkerboard system of square blocks that formed grids. With a grid as the basis for the layout of a city, the intent of the city in executing State interests could be achieved and implemented into every corner and detail of the city. There was no room for another thought, logic, or intent. The city would create unity socially, but first by creating unity through planning. Every detail was based on the centralised control of the State through its executors, and every property built upon a plot of land had its purpose to the whole. What the Spanish Empire did to the notion of the city was to modernise the logic in Roman planning for order with greater intent in function and with adaptability in any geographical location under their control. The *Laws of the Indies* modified itself depending on the geographic area, the climate and topography of a region, and the population of its settlement turned city occupants. As Mundigo and Crouch (1977), in their

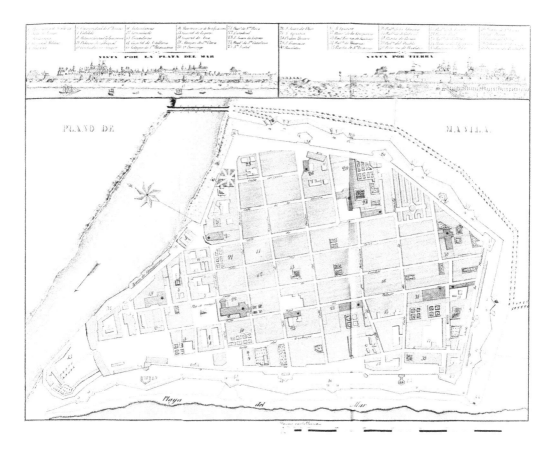

**Fig 3.16** Plano de Manila, 1851. (Public Domain)

seminal first English translation of the full *Laws of the Indies*, explained,

> Gradually the indications of the Laws of the Indies were layered over with the new arrangements of urban fabric. William Carr Lane, Mayor of St. Louis, which had been founded by the French in 1764, conquered and subject to Spanish control (including modifications to its planned development according to the Laws of the Indies) from 1796 to 1804, before being transferred to the United State as part of the Louisiana Purchase, commented in 1825 that "the Regulations adopted in the first stage did not suit the second, and those of the second, are in their turn out of date". (p. 267)

## 3.5 Planned, Zoned, and Cleared

The problem in cities is that people are scattered about in their pseudo ethnic and classed neighbourhood pockets. Planning commissions serve the wishes of the greater government to rectify past problems, to address current problems, and to pre-empt future problems. As it was previously discussed, Ciudad de México, Chicago, and Rio de Janeiro used both the allure of major events to systematically "correct" their city structures based on previously held planning commission recommendations and the moral panic of the crisis. Areas of the cities were re-zoned and cleared with force. Within the schema of this articulation of the "Geographies of Threat", to conceptualise a logic of the function of cities in service to a greater State goal of population dominance, the administration of cities is the primary tool that accomplishes this goal. The 1968 Olympic Games, the 2016 Olympic bid, and the 2016 Olympic Games were but the means that made us aware of the intention and machinations that reside behind the false transparencies in city governance. For the games, a city would divert funds away from neighbourhoods

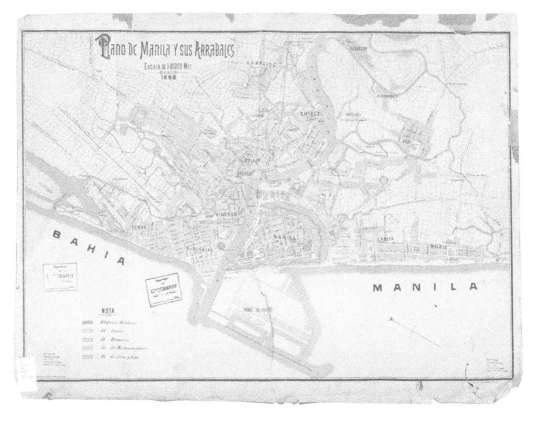

**Fig 3.17** Plano de Manila y sus arrabales (Map of Manila and Its Suburbs), 1898. (Public Domain)

because the city would decide whether the games occurred or not. The games and the crisis were two effective tools that provided the most ideal public face to engage in the diversion.

With Chicago's bid for the 2016 Games, as discussed in Chapter 1, one could see the geographic shifts in the landscape of the city to gear up for a success International Olympic Committee (IOC) visit and bid submission. The sites for the construction of stadia and the Olympic Village for athletes were in two working-class and low-income communities Bus lines were altered in such a way that made work commutes difficult. Utility costs increased dramatically. A historical park was forevermore altered to accommodate the locations for athletic performance. Again, on the surface this construction would have clearly served the Olympics within a bustling city while further dispossessing neighbourhoods and communities that had been abandoned but had mitigated their decay with communal independence. But quick searches and archived records of maps

revealed how there was a plan for a Chicago New South Coast and a new Magnificent Mile South (Magnificent Mile North is the city of upscale shopping, events, and living arrangements within the city). Without current residents' input and vote, these plans represented a way to occupy occupied territory within the city for a perceived growing managerial class. Appeals to energy efficiency, carbon footprint reduction, and reduced travel times to downtown occupations were provided as rationales for a transformed environment – an environment that already had thousands of occupants in it. The Chicago 2016 Bid Book, the final 60-page bid proposal to the IOC, was entitled "Reaching for a Better World". The bid team and legions of celebrity endorsements all circled around this geographical area like vultures, hoping to swoop in and claim the victory for putting on a splendid show, but no one thought to engage residents of the areas of the city most impacted, most devastatingly impacted. And none of those bid team members or endorsers thought to divert their energies and the resources they had accumulated to do right by those they left out, to lobby for open and renovated schools and for bus lines that went south or west to the types of occupations that many in those neighbourhoods worked within. Those neighbourhoods returned to abandonment. Maps and agendas could be provided to anyone upon request at townhall meetings, but the real planning maps and agendas were hardly ever made available, made public once they were conceived, or generated from large-scale public meetings. However, the map functions as an "inventory, spatialization, and fetishization of possession" that does not contextualise "the White human figure can appear as a body" (King, 2019, p. 89). And those alleged tangential documents, the documents that only "showed ideas and not final decisions", were unfiled and re-filed under different and hard-to-locate categories that ultimately revealed the hidden hands in suggesting who belonged in the city and where (Baade & Sanderson, 2012; Bennett et al., 2013; Mowatt & Travis, 2015; Rundio & Heere, 2016).

The bid failed for a multitude of reasons other than the proposal itself, and there has been a lack of learning or understanding the correct lessons from the loss on the part of city planners, bid enthusiasts from elite and aspiring classes, and academicians (Chicago has an image problem due to violence in the city; van Dijk & Weitkamp, 2014). Persuasive powers in marketing go only so far in covering up decades of abandonment, and to use the skills of planning to correct that abandonment with dispossession cannot be overstated here enough as both troubling and also the contemporary recurrence of power maintaining itself for itself. Planning is at the heart of Class Conflict, White Supremacy, and Patriarchy into the structural realities that we actually experience and are impacted by. However, planning is not the ideological philosophy that creates, drives, or cultivates those constructs, but it is the way in which the governing ideological philosophy can be given a tangible full life in the real world. The Games were soft power directed at the residents of the prime real estate and property that was in the way of city plans for a new Chicago. Improved and diversified workspaces of city planning and administration have not altered the intentions

and machinations that have continued to rage on. While the racialised and gendered representations in the executors of city plans have changed, the processes of dehumanisation in a city have not.

Through the court ruling of the *Village of Euclid v. Ambler Co.* (1926), Euclidean planning and zoning had become the much-embraced default approach of city planning in the United States. In the Supreme Court decision, cities now had the full authority to regulate and segregate land usage. This legal decision went along with the social elite sentiments of the American Planning Association to plan, design, and build with "health, safety, morals, convenience, prosperity and the general welfare" as their primary public concern (Hirt, 2015, p. 47). Zoning legally, socially, and eventually legislatively through local ordinances, assisted a governance structure of (planned) exclusion, (zoned) concentration, and ("slum" clearance) removal in cities. City planning ordinances of yesterday and today dictate style norms for the type of building, the aesthetic boundaries on appearance, the determination of the type of use and occupancy, the responsibilities of land/property/building owners, and the general order and condition the residents have to meet. "Beautifying the city" was a planned programme of a new viceroy to New Spain in the late 1800s, a programme that alleviated sanitation concerns and addressed public intoxications of the lower classes while building new plazas, streets, and marketplaces (Glasco, 2010). The aim and scope of the *Laws of the Indies* settlement continued to guide the expanded city. But city planning ordinances also allowed for a form of governing rule without public representation and with fewer officers and executors than the form of governance in outright conquest and occupation in the *Laws of the Indies*.

In both antiquated and contemporary cases, city planning ordinances make for quick work in dividing and ordering the lands and peoples under which an administration of rule over the territory and populace would otherwise be met with insurgent opposition. There is no sufficient counter claim, counter plan, or counter order. The onslaught that is the historical recurrence of the articulation of power maintenance is weaved into the landscape of the city. Once again as Mundigo and Crouch (1977) noted, "the

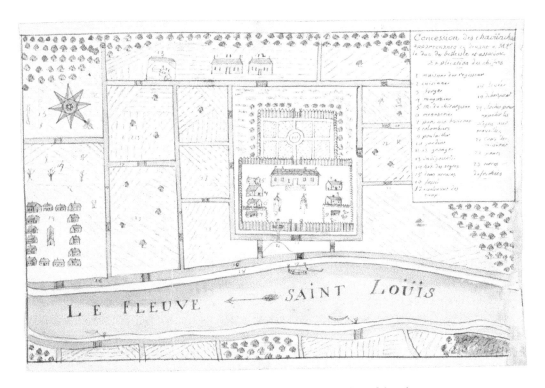

**Fig 3.18** Map of the Chaouachas Concession (Saint Louis), 1747. (The Newberry Library)

indications of the Laws of the Indies were layered over with the new arrangements of urban fabric" that was any city, and most especially in St. Louis (p. 267). Crouch and Mundigo (1977) continued that seminal work on the *Laws of the Indies* by highlighting how "the three layers of the city building [French outpost, Spanish city, and a United States midwestern city]" was one of the primary examples of the legacy of city plans across empires (p. 406). For the French outpost, the city followed a plan that was also implemented in "Montréal [in Canada], New Orleans, and Mobile [in the state of Alabama in the United States]". The French and later British approach to settlement development was built along the fortification model, an erected fort and pattern of housing within and beyond its defensible walls. In the previously presented 1747 map, we can see the designated dwellings for "negros" at #14 built at a distance from the main city and not considered part of any known defensive strategy against the indigenous peoples of the Kaskaskia tribe (see Figs. 3.18 and 3.19). The maps of French colonial officer Jean-François-Benjamin

Dumont de Montigny, and then twenty-years later of Captain Guy Dufossat, show the trading post well before the work of Pierre Laclède Liquest and René-Auguste Chouteau (who would expand the economic base of the post with the opening of a mill).

The map of 1780 St. Louis displayed the Laclède plan of the city and the rapid growth of the city. In just under forty years removed from the 1747 de Montigny map, the 1780 map of St. Louis situated the settlement in French-controlled Illinois with greatly expanded fortifications for defence. The French settlement and garrison were now under the control of the Spanish government and had successfully defended itself from the warring British and the various indigenous groups that had to be coercively rallied, included hundreds of Chippewa, Menominee, Sioux, and Winnebago nations that were depicted as forces in the northern portion of the map (see Fig. 3.20). While some semblance of the *Laws of the Indies* grid plan can be seen in the map of 1780, little changed under forty-year Spanish rule through a secret treaty between the French and

**Fig 3.19** #14 Habitat des Negres.

Spanish Empires (expanded grid with a semblance of a plaza; see Fig. 3.21). As Crouch and Mundigo (1977) indicated,

> both the French and the Spanish [city] plans of St. Louis called for a 300 foot wide public space running along the river, possibly in response to Ordinance 129 [of the Laws of the Indies]...the block thus formed were 240 by 300 feet, except that the three central units of the French plan were 3000 feet square. The Spanish city seems to be smaller – about 13 blocks wide rather than 19...but shows a central square plaza developed as focus of the community. (p. 407)

Once under the rule of the United States in 1804, St. Louis swiftly turned from an outpost to a settlement to a brief Spanish colonial city project to finally a far-flung city of a new but quickly forming settler co-lonial imperial power (see Fig. 3.22). The public space, the promenade along the river, was removed first for defensive purposes and later for the purposes of land revenue generation. Crouch and Mundigo (1977) further explained that the new five-person board for the city seized the opportunity to open the land and property for sale to more established wealthy families. Land speculation turned public space and publicly seized space as a commodity, with prices rising from "$30 per acre in 1815 to $2000 per acre in 1819", and with that newfound money streets were paved between the 1820s to 1830s (Crouch & Mundigo, 1977, p. 408).

By the time St. Louis fell into the hands of the "nation's first full-time city planner" Harland Bartholomew in 1916, leadership of the city was incredibly entrenched with "dreams" and machina-tions of dealing with its population of Black and working-class White citizens. An issue that in-tensified these aspirations in 1917 was the influx of Black "refugees" from East St. Louis, Illinois, just across the Mississippi River that was between the two cities. Hundreds of Black Illinoisans were mas-sacred, and hundreds more fled in make-shift boats, canoes, and drifting platforms to St. Louis across the dangerous river and greatly swelled its already sig-nificant Black population. During the same year as Bartholomew's initial arrival, city officials had al-ready rashly passed their own version of the same racial restrictive covenants initiated by the afore-mentioned Baltimore covenants (Gordon, 2008). The Supreme Court made covenants illegal but did not recommend any enforcement strategies in their deconstruction. The zoning push was a response to more effectively and legally curb the "Negro inva-sion" (see Fig. 3.23), a refrain that was repeated in several papers of the early to mid-20th century United States (see Figs. 3.24 and 3.25).

With the 1915 U.S. Supreme Court ruling, Hadacheck v. Sebastian, a city was sanctioned with the authority to exercise "police power over land use". Black citizens in St. Louis (and other cities) were first deemed to be noise nuisances, but the enforcement of such complaints was only effective in implementing case-by-case, individualised removal. What was (and is always) needed were mass

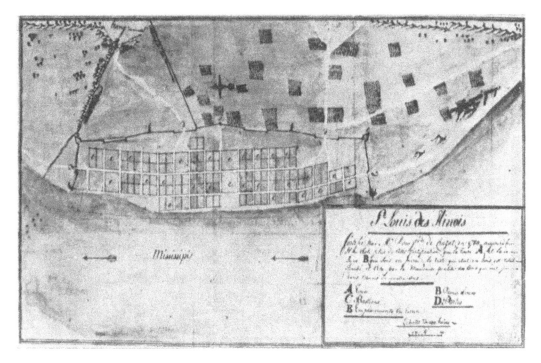

**Fig 3.20** Map of St. Louis des Ilinois, 1780. (Public Domain)

dispossession and extraction strategies. With the advent of Baltimore Mayor Mahool's 1910 covenants, public health was used as a far more effective tool in wholesale neighbourhood removal. An 1892 *Baltimore News* opined,

> Open drains, great lots filled with high weeds, ashes and garbage accumulated in the alleyways, cellars filled with filthy black water, houses that are total strangers to the touch of whitewash or scrubbing brush, human bodies that have been strangers for months to soap and water, villainous looking negroes who loiter and sleep around the street corners and never work; vile and vicious women, with but a smock to cover their Black nakedness, lounging in the doorways or squatting upon the steps, hurling foul epithets at every passerby; foul streets, foul people, in foul tenements filled with foul air; that's "Pigtown". (Crooks, 1968, p. 20)

The *Baltimore Sun* on December 20, 1910, published a summary of the final public reading of the new and first racially restrictive residential ordinance in the United States,

> That no Negro can move into a block in which more than half of the residents are White.
>
> That no White person can move into a block in which more than half of the residents are colored.
>
> That a violator of the law is punishable by a fine of not more than $100 or imprisonment of from 30 days to 1 year, or both.
>
> .
>
> That no section of the city is exempted from the conditions of the ordinance. It applies to every house. (*Baltimore Sun*, p. 16. col. 4; as cited by Power, 1983, pp. 299–300)

And just like that, racially restrictive covenants became another quiver to inform the State through its administration of cities with methods of cordoning, concentrating, and eventually removing large swaths of people and their property. Once Baltimore instituted covenants in 1910, Minneapolis, MN,

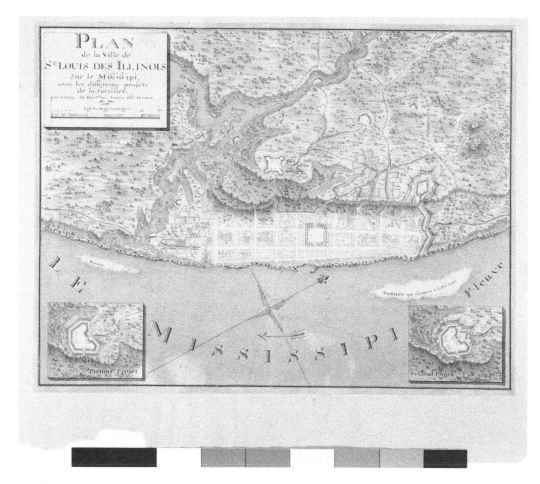

**Fig 3.21** Map of St. Louis des Illinois, 1796. (*St. Louis Post-Dispatch*/Public Domain)

became one of the first to follow suit by inserting into the language of property deeds their own twist on exclusionary coverages, as "premises shall not at any time be conveyed, mortgaged or leased to any person or persons of Chinese, Japanese, Moorish, Turkish, Negro, Mongolian or African blood or descent" ("Scott, Henry, and Lenora", 1914). The ramifications of these covenants have rippled into the present in both the creation and permanence of certain neighbourhood compositions, the maintenance of a certain city planning ethos, and the production of culture that could find yourself over-policed and dead within eight minutes and thirty-six seconds (Delegard & Ehrman-Solberg, 2017). And while covenants were deemed illegal, the principles of them found their way into the zoning laws that followed. The threat to profit, person, and property

could be responded to by racially demarcating populations on maps and records. By further associating accounts and concerns of "crime" and disease associated with those racialised locations, a city was enabled to segregate those populations more easily but now with the deployment of broader public support.

While the old colonial cities concentrated these populations in their founding, the imperial cities initially had not. Just as the settler colonial city was founded with the function of dispossessing inhabitants of land, the city was also the imperial city that was able to develop tools for concentrating and reconcentrating populations for the purpose of extracting perpetual labour from the populations that were simultaneously made unstable and penniless due to the generational loss of wealth tied to

**Fig 3.22** A Plan of the City of St. Louis, Mo., as Incorporated Under the Amending Act of the General Assembly of Missouri, 1842. (The Missouri History Museum/Public Domain)

**Fig 3.23** "Negro Invasion of White residence districts in St. Louis already has caused a damage to property of about 25 million". *St. Louis Globe-Democrat*, February 27, 1916. (*St. Louis Post-Dispatch*)

property theft. As discussed in Chapter 2, the city of Seville, as an imperial city, harboured the largest community of enslaved people in Spain. Spaniards of considerable economic means could acquire this population or hire this population for all manner of work. The surplus of labour truly blossomed the leisured lifestyle of property owners that owned or hired a few or many. However, concerns about this growing population created perceived serious security problems for local municipal government:

> The city fathers feared that the urban slaves, led by the Moriscos, might band together and seize the town, and the official uneasiness on the score found expression in a series of municipal

ordinances restricting the movements of slaves. Slaves were prohibited, for example, from carrying arms except in the company of their masters or in the performance of their regular duties. The government also placed severe limitations on the number of slaves permitted to assemble at any given time in public places such as taverns, inns, and cheap restaurants. City officials expressed concern about gangs of slaves who frequented the Sevillian taverns both day and night, and who often became intoxicated and disorderly. (Pike, 1967, p. 351)

What is being connected here is that the management of this enslaved population led to their segregation and restriction in mobility and housing in

**Fig 3.24** "Where the Blight of Negro Invasion has Depreciated Property Values Greatly". *Baltimore Sun*, September 14, 1909. (*The Baltimore Sun*)

Imperial Seville and contributed to the development of a philosophy of city governance that weaved its way into the early segregated residences for the "Negros" that were also enslaved in French colonial St. Louis. And what is being connected further is the historical recurrence of this perspective of certain populations in a cityscape, as in *City of Chicago v Morales* (1999), where the city ordinance targeted individuals in public space "areas in which the presence of gang members had a demonstrable effect on the activities of law-abiding persons in the surrounding community", thereby determining that loitering was a criminal act – a shared State knowledge base on population management through the protection of property and zoning. The ordinances of their respective times partially informed the ways that cities began to respond to both populations that had been identified in some way and the concerns that those populations posed to the general welfare of the rest of a city. Thus, what St. Louis came to note of racialised migrancy as an issue in the late-19th century and major area of "Negro invasion" concern in the early 20th century was directly an outgrowth of this practice and plan execution that harkens to Seville. St. Louis of 1916 and 1917 was just the latest city to engage in such plans.

RER, CINCINNATI, SUNDAY, JANUARY 4, 1931

## CITY DWELLING

### Analyzed By Varsity.

**Professor Tells Sociological Society Of Progress**

In Gathering Data On Population, Institutions And Changes In Community Life.

SPECIAL DISPATCH TO THE ENQUIRER.

Cleveland, January 3—Describing the scope of community studies undertaken in Cincinnati by the University of Cincinnati Department of Sociology and the uses to which the findings are being put, James A Quinn, Assistant Professor of Sociology in the College of Liberal Arts of Cincinnati University, addressed members of the Social Research Division of the American Sociological Society, which held its annual meeting here this week.

"We have organized a program of community studies in Cincinnati for the purpose of learning more about the urban community as a type of phenomenon of human association," Professor Quinn said.

"The first major project was the preparation of a research tract map which districted the city in close conformity with the natural areas and which afforded small, permanent units for the collection and comparison of data. This project was reported to the association last year by Dr. E. E. Eubank.

**Files Held Treasure.**

"The tract map, while fundamental, was not the only necessary aid to research. Most of the social data for the city reposed in the files of private citizens, governmental bureaus, social welfare agencies, business firms, religious and educational institutions. This data was relatively useless for ecological studies until it could be distributed in terms of the research tracts. The need for some effective means of distributing this data led to the preparation of a research directory by which any street address in the city could be easily and speedily located in the proper tract without use of a map.

"The research tracts are now the basic units of population data for Cincinnati. They were used by the United States Bureau of the Census for the 1930 decennial enumeration. They also have been adopted by the Cincinnati Board of Education for the collection of the annual school census.

"These latter materials are particularly significant in that they furnish annually comparable data concerning an important population group classified by age, sex, color, nationality, and grade.

**School Enumeration Aided.**

"Incidentally, the director of the school census used our research directory for the purpose of checking the work of his enumerators. He distributed among the various research tracts the Cincinnati children who at the time of the school census were enrolled in the public, parochial and private schools and found that in the more mobile districts the enumerators had missed more than 50 per cent of the children.

"If these field enumerators were as careful as those who took the Federal census, considerable doubt is raised concerning the accuracy of the census population data.

"We have completed several studies of the distribution of institutions including schools, churches and missions, hospital, clinics and dispensaries, social service centers, commercial recreation resources, hotels and rooming houses.

"The distribution of transportation systems and of industrial, commercial and residential sites was carefully surveyed in 1924-1925 by the United City Planning Committee. We recently made a limited number of studies of local areas which showed changes in the type of land utilization since that time but have not extended these investigations to the city as a whole.

**Traffic Zones Plotted.**

"We have studied trolley, bus and automobile transportation and have plotted time-cost zones, measuring out from the central business area. These zones need careful checking and refining. 'Topographic' time-cost maps of this sort are necessary to make Cincinnati comparable with cities of less rugged topography.

"We have plotted on spot maps many types of social data which have helped to characterize the local areas and to locate problems for intensive research. These data include dependency, boy and girl juvenile delinquency, major crime, divorce, insanity, infant mortality, certain communicable diseases, unemployment and mobility.

"Most of these data are being collected annually or biannually for the purpose of studying trends. We are gradually accumulating historical facts which help to portray the growth and changes of the city as a whole and of the various areas. Areas of foreign-born and Negro population have been roughly marked out and some of them subjected to careful study.

"A study of Negro invasions into white residential areas affords one approach to the study of social conflict here because social conflict is the general topic for these Christmas meetings. It must be remembered, however, that the center of interest in this representative project was not 'social conflict,' but the 'nature' of the city.

**Negro-White Divisions Studied.**

"In this study we obtained the exact location of Negro and white residence by house-to-house visitation. The color of the residents and the number of families were recorded for each address. Detailed maps were prepared for each block. From these we constructed a summary cross-hatch map, which showed the areas of solid Negro and solid white residence, and the transitional areas by per cent of Negro population.

"Interviews with tradesmen and old residents gave some indication of the history, speed and direction of the invasions. Social data relative to divorce, delinquency and dependency were examined on spot maps to discover possible relations between them and the margins of invasions.

"The study is projected to extend over several years. Data like the above will be collected at two or three year intervals in order to discover precisely how fast and in what directions the invasions are proceeding and what changes in the culture of the areas, the altitude of invaders and invaded and the types of special problems seem to be associated with the phenomenon of Negro invasion.

"Case studies of persons and groups and ethnological surveys of areas will also be needed. The findings must, of course, be interpreted in light of related community studies.

**Three Conclusions Reached.**

"Three items arising from the study of invasions may be offered tentatively. (1) Invaders unconsciously use the tactics which army generals use in the field, i. e., they thrust into a new area along lines of least resistance. The sector between lines of thrust is then subjected to pressure from three sides and gradually pinched out. (2) Barriers to Negro invasion vary significantly with the type of area being invaded. (3) There is no conclusive evidence that social disorganization increases along the margin of invasion.

"Due to its rugged topography, Cincinnati presents an interesting but perplexing problem of organization as a natural urban area. The scheme of concentric circles which fits Chicago so nicely is sadly disarranged among Cincinnati's hills. Good residence areas are sometimes closer to the central business section than are areas of working-men's homes. Adjacent communities, separated by precipitous bluffs, are frequently of the most sharply contrasting types.

"May 1, in closing, stress again the fact tha the projects which we have mentioned are merely units in the development of a continuous, systematic program of study of the phenomenon, the urban community, particularly as represented by Cincinnati.

"The program covers both for the city as a whole and for its various areas, the ecological distribution and trends of (a) population and its elements, (b) institutions, (c) land values and types of land utilization, (d) indices of social life and (e) personality types. Detailed sociological researches are being and will be conducted within this ecological frame of reference."

**CLUB TO GIVE DANCE.**

Frat dance sponsored by the SamaPara Club, an organization composed of several societies of the Eighth Ward, will be held at Columbian Hall, Woodburn Avenue and McMillan Street, Wednesday night. Jerome Overbrook is Chairman of Arrangements. Proceeds of the dance are to be added to a fund to benefit charitable enterprises.

**Fig 3.25** A Sociological Study on City Dwelling Discusses Among City Planning Points, "the Negro invasion" That Is Likened to an Invading Army in The Enquirer. Cincinnati, Ohio, 4 January 1931. (The Cincinnati Enquirer)

The city is both a combination of the settler colonial city and the imperial city.

And similar to Baltimore, St Louis enacted full-fledged zoning practices that resulted in racial restriction as well as "gentleman agreements" for Black and any other non-White populations in the city (Jewish populations in Baltimore were relegated to western suburban areas, away from both Black and "Gentiles"; Power, 1996). The St. Louis Real Estate Exchange initiated a series of campaigns in 1915 to influence voting in the city-wide ballot in 1916 (see Fig. 3.26). With a 75% majority, the ordinance was passed. And even with a Supreme Court ruling against such zoning ordinances in 1917, 1940, and 1948, "gentleman agreements" persisted and influenced new strategies. For Osterweil (2020), "law develops to codify Whiteness…Whiteness became the meta-property from which all other private property flows and is derived" (p. 26). The legalese in the lawfare to back up this period in St. Louis was only as poignant as the racialised legalese was palpable,

The preamble to most of the St. Louis restrictions read, "to preserve the character of said neighborhood as a desirable place of residence for persons of the Caucasian Race and to maintain the values of their respective properties."

The restrictive covenant at the heart of the landmark U.S. Supreme Court decision originating in St. Louis that eventually outlawed them, bound "the signatories, their heirs, assigns, legal representatives, and successors in

**Fig 3.26** White Homeowners and Real Estate Companies Foresaw Social Decay and Economic Decline With the "invasion" of Black Families. In 1915, They Banded Together to Form the United Welfare Association and Dedicated Themselves to Fight for a Segregation Ordinance. (The Missouri Historical Society/Public Domain)

title to restrict the property against sale to or occupancy by people but wholly of the Caucasian race" – specified late in the same document as "people of the Negro or Mongolian Race."

The boilerplate covenant drafted by the St. Louis Real Estate Exchange included "a restriction against selling, conveying, leasing, or renting to a negro or negroes, or the delivery of possession, to or permitting to be occupied by negro or negroes of said property and properties in the said City blocks...." (Gordon, 2008, p. 73) This resulted in the creation of the Delmar Boulevard divide, and the neighbourhood area of The Ville becoming one of the main designated areas for Black middle-class residents to reside within. By 1954, The Ville would get an increase of Black residents with the redevelopment of the Mill Creek Valley area in order to build an addition to St. Louis University and Highway 40. Public housing also increased north of Delmar.

But there are two criticisms to previous planning work that are being made here. The first is that the assumption that this was urban planning used for bad purposes misses the long persistent history. Is it that urban planning keeps attracting "bad" actors and doing "bad" things or is it that urban planning is fundamentally about these very actions?

The ease in the execution of neighbourhood demolition and the legacies of Haussmann, Le

Corbusier, etc., illustrate just the refinements to the intent of the wielders of planning techniques. And while there are architects and planners of note who have devised more elaborate ways to dispossess, it is not those architects and urban planners who represent the ultimate intent in planning but instead the State that dictated the need for such plans. And the second criticism is less an assumption and more an implied notion that there is a specific bias in planning toward Black and any other racialised populations. But when we see the full picture across multiple groups across multiple cities, the arbitrariness in the application planning techniques on cities gives us another picture – one in which the planning methods for dispossession and extraction are engaged in endless dispossession and extraction. Once the indigenous have been removed, the European immigrant will be concentrated and then removed. Once the European immigrant has been removed, the Black resident will be concentrated and then removed. Once the Black resident has been removed, the Brown or Queer resident will be concentrated and then removed. Once the Brown or Queer resident has been removed, the working-class resident will be been removed. Once the working-class, then the middle-class, and it continues. In many cases, the real estate industry as a whole has played a pernicious role in devaluing the homes and property of Black owners in particular (Baradaran,

2017; Satter, 2009; Taylor, 2019); this only tells one crucial side of the complicated story. While voting represents for some one facet of a response (voting on political representatives who decide on zoning laws), the degree in which business and real estate developers have opposed these zoning practices as well highlights how even aspiring classes have been impacted as these practices cut into their ability to make profits. The State will employ public support if it garners it through marketing schemes (Rothstein, 2017). The State will employ State representatives in city councils and city administration through lifestyle luxuries (Johnson, 2020). The State will employ banks and real estate developers through brokered opportunities for subsidises (Taylor, 2019). But in reality, if the State cycles through all of these levels of support, and loses that support, it will not stop the military dispossession machine of the State from finding another means to enact its mission. This further illustrates that the call and desire for such spatial practices come from the logic of the State to design an entire city for the purposes of extraction for the sake of extraction.

The city of St. Louis was designing itself, and the State was designing St. Louis as "the crossroads to America". The work of the Home Owner's Loan Corporation of 1933 as part of the New Deal worked to stabilise the housing market with the restructuring of mortgages. However, the housing market is not an abstraction, it is people. The housing market is is. So, the assistance of new methods of home financing not only favoured White homeowners but also established an assessment tool that overlapped with the racially restricted neighbourhoods of most cities (such as Detroit; see Fig. 3.27). As Gordon (2008) noted,

> the key to the rating system – was [current] racial occupancy. The standard local area survey form prefaced its narrative description with required entries for local population, the "class and occupation" of residents, the percentage of foreign born and Negro residents, and the degree of "shifting or infiltration". The most commonly noted unfavorable factors in C areas [shaded yellow, definitely declining in

investment] were "expiring restrictions or lack of them" and "infiltration of a lower grade population". D areas [shaded red, determined as hazardous] were almost invariably marked by "infiltration" or the presence of a "colored settlement" or "Negro colony" – and the summary judgment that "the only hope is for the demolition of these buildings and transition of the area into a business district". (p. 92)

With the New Deal plan, real estate brokers began to develop their own internal "ranking of races and nationalities with respect to their beneficial effect on land values", as studied by Rose Helper (1969) in the seemingly forgotten yet profoundly significant study of 121 interviews in the three different sections of Chicago between 1955 and 1956, and a follow up in 1964–1965. Helper backed up the respondents' information with content in Chicago Real Estate Board documents, proceedings of the National Association of Real Estate Boards, and city-business partnership communications. Alongside Black populations, Greek, Italian, Jewish, Mexican, and Russian populations were particularly deemed the least desirable due to their perceived socio-spatial effect on housing values ("crime", vice, and disease). This explained the basis for the appearance of the shaded red areas of concern where there were no Black residents present to concentrate and then remove. As Rothstein (2017) noted about the areas shaded red that "not a single foreigner or Negro" was accounted for nor justified the actions based on the prevailing notion of concern "due to the colored element controlling the district" (p. 30).

Similar to racially restrictive covenants, other populations may have been added due to local sentiments, but these racialised ethnicities were the most consistently least deemed populations nationally. The Federal Housing Administration from its onset created the 1936 *Underwriting Manual* to legalise this process, thus making redlining the new process of the land [emphasis added by author],

> 228 Deed restrictions are apt to prove more effective than a zoning ordinance in providing protection from adverse influences. Where the

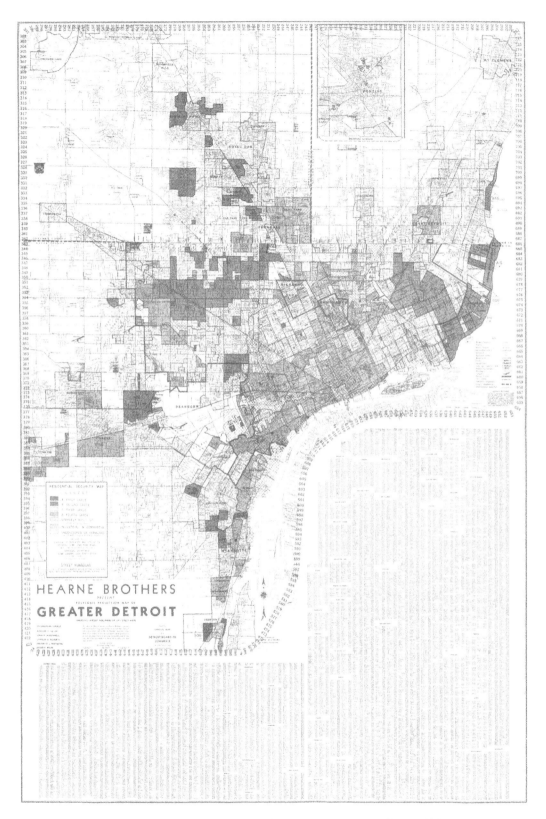

**Fig 3.27** Residential Security Map of Detroit. Green Areas Are "Best" for Mortgage Lenders and Offering of Maximum Financial Assistance and Blue are "Desirable" With Older Homes That Maintain Neighbourhood Stability, 1939. (National Archives/Public Domain)

same deed restrictions apply over a broad area and where these restrictions relate to types of structures, use to which improvements may be put, and *racial occupancy*, a favorable condition is apt to exist. Where adjacent lots or blocks possess altogether different restrictions, especially for type and use of structures and *racial occupancy*, the effect of such restrictions is minimized and adequate protection cannot be considered to be present.... It must be realized that deed restrictions, to be effective, must be enforced. In this respect they are like zoning ordinances...

229 The geographical position of a location may afford in certain instances reliable protection against adverse influences. The Valuator should consider carefully the immunity or lack of immunity offered to the location because of its geographical position within the city. Natural or artificially established barriers will prove effective in protecting a neighborhood and the locations within it from adverse influences. *Usually the protection against adverse influences afforded by these means include prevention of the infiltration of business and industrial uses, lower-class occupancy, and inharmonious racial groups.*

233 The Valuator should investigate areas surrounding the location to determine whether or not incompatible *racial* and *social* groups are present, to the end that an intelligent prediction may be made regarding the possibility or probability of the location being invaded by such groups. If a neighborhood is to retain stability it is necessary that properties shall continue to be occupied by the same *social* and *racial* classes. A change in *social* or *racial* occupancy generally leads to instability and a reduction in values... Once the character of a neighborhood has been established it is usually impossible to induce a higher social class than those already in the neighborhood to purchase and occupy properties in its various locations.

The social class of the parents of children at the school will in many instances have a vital bearing. Thus, although physical surrounds of a neighborhood area may be favorable and conducive to enjoyable, pleasant living in its locations, if the children of people living in such an area are compelled to attend school where the majority or a goodly number of the pupils represent a far lower level of society or

an *incompatible racial element*, the neighborhood under consideration will prove far less stable and desirable than if this condition did not exist. In many instances where a school has earned a prestige through the class of pupils attending, it will be found that such prestige will be a vital element in maintaining the desirability of the entire area comprising the school district.

284. (3). Recorded deed restrictions should strengthen and supplement zoning ordinances and to be really effective should include the provisions listed below. The restrictions should be recorded with the deed and should run for a period of at least twenty years. Recommended restrictions include the following:

a. Allocation of definite areas for specific uses such as single or double-family houses, apartments, and business structures.

b. The placement of buildings so that they will have adequate light and air with assurance of a space of at least ten feet between buildings.

c. Prohibition of the resubdivision of lots.

d. Prohibition of the erection of more than one dwelling per lot.

e. Control of the design of all buildings through requiring their approval by a qualified committee and by appropriate cost limitations.

f. Prohibition of nuisances or undesirable buildings such as stables, pig pens, temporary dwellings, and high fences.

g. *Prohibition of the occupancy of properties except by the race for which they were intended.*

h. Appropriate provisions for enforcement.

289. (1). Adequacy of Civic, Social, and Commercial Centers – These elements of comfortable living usually follow rather than precede development. Those centers serving the city or section in which the development is situated should be readily available to its occupants. *Schools should be appropriate to the needs of the new community and they should not be attended in large numbers by inharmonious racial groups.* Employment centers, preferably diversified in nature, should be

at a convenient distance. (Federal Housing Administration, 1936)

Racial covenants, redlining, and zoning were intelligibly front-facing efforts for residence restriction and insurance, city-based tactics for dispossession of potential and current renter and home ownership opportunities and extraction of homeowners' money. The practices of poverty production and maintenance for later spatial isolation and removal had become noted tactics in Britain. The State took advantage of Reverend Albert Hume's colour-coded maps of 1850s London and Liverpool that informed them about the demography of those cities and used them to their advantage. The practices of 1850s London and Liverpool were the same as were employed in 1930s Baltimore and St. Louis. The concerns around public health as the most galvanising approach to make policy and practices possible in those British cities were only fuelled by the concerns of disease exposure in the city of Chennai in India (then Madras). And the epidemic turned pandemic only grew in scale because of the extraction activities in the Indian Hinterlands, the forced concentration of infected Indian labourers in a racially designated population areas, followed by spatial abandonment of any aid or service to that population, and exacerbated by police actions in those areas that increased exposure to a temporary population that returned to their cities of origin for hospitalisation. For the newly infected Londoner, cholera was an Indian disease (the Asiatic Cholera). Zoned concentration, residential segregation, and architectural manipulation produced the salient myths that governed perceptions that would be transferred to new locales throughout the world for fear of new diseases from the same old dirty racial "Other". As Akcan (2020) opined,

> *Der Spiegel* referred to Berlin's immigrant borough Kreuzberg as the Harlem of Germany. The federal housing minister Hans-Jochen Vogel had called the area, "a small Harlem" and politicians often warned about the "Turkish ghetto"... Ghettos are developing, and sociologists are prophesying the downfall of the cities, increased criminality, and social misery like those found in Harlem... The first Harlem symptoms are already visible. In the eroding sectors of German cities, "a new subproletariat is growing in which the seed of social diseases is sown"...How did a New York neighborhood known for racism against its African American population become a metaphor to describe a district renowned for its Turkish guest workers in Berlin? (p. 324)

The myth was made reality through the social engineering of the discourse. But it was the back-facing effort that was most telling, this was lawfare that held and wielded the power of warfare at bay; this was the early targeting of a neighbourhood, and not the targeting of individuals, with policing force for public health and public safety management. Just as the allusions of moral panic in "crime" and the allure of mega-events in the present day achieve the ends in cultivating perceptions of threats, public health is an age-old allusion of shifting standards for social inclusion and social exclusion that marshal those forces for city management (Molina, 2005; Shah, 2001). Residential segregation was/is just the residue behaviour in imperial cities to manage their burgeoning cosmopolitan populace, while the in-city dispossession and extraction were/are the articulated legacies of the settler colonial cities. In the present day, both city approaches operate in tandem in virtually every city in the world. And this is the "natural" and built environment in which we live, because the home is our point of defensible action and control as a private property owner of our lived experience within the State. We have accepted the myths of cities as being spaces for social life that comprise the fabricated society because it cognitively works for us at the micro-level. At the micro-level resides our fears and need for protection of ourselves and those that we love who reside within the properties of our ownership, the properties that are assigned to us with the adjoining amenities (we think) that are owed to us with our taxation.

Cities are gendered as they are racialised, because patriarchy (and not sexism) has gendered them. They are also not composed of self-gendering social arrangements, due to the conscriptions and whims of sexist real estate brokers and bank lenders.

Cities are gendered through design because they also work through gender norms and fears to restrict and afford the ways in which a city may operate for the idealised "Other". Historically, this could be read in speeches of one the leading suffragettes of the 19th century, Francis Willard. While campaigning for women's suffrage, Willard began to call for "home protection" and social purity that affirmed the moral superiority of women (Ware, 1992). This had an appeal amongst Southerners in the United States and the Victorian middle class in Britain, as motherhood was a duty of upholding the nation-state and manhood required an avoidance to vice. Lady Henry Somerset, ally in England, was enamoured by the position, and this led to her two-year stay to influence the mind-set of the British Women's Temperance Association. Willard was given extensive speaking engagements. In one such speech, "The Race Problem: Francis Willard on the Political Puzzle of the South", Willard's response [to rival Ida B. Wells] could be linked to various issues on Race and African emigration,

> If I were black and young, no steamer could revolve its wheels fast enough to convey me to the dark continent. I should go where my color was the correct thing, and leave these pale faces to work out their own. (p. 8)

On immigration and "racial diversity" in cities within the United States,

> Alien illiterates...rule our cities today...the saloon is their palace...the Anglo-Saxon race will never submit to be dominated by the Negro so long as his altitude reaches no higher than the personal liberty of the saloon, and the power of appreciating the amount of liquor that dollar will buy. (p. 8)

And that, "the problem on [the Southerners'] hands is immeasurable. The coloured race multiplies like the locusts of Egypt. The grog-shop is its centre of power" as "lurid vengeance has devoured the devourers of women and children" (p. 8). For Willard, as mentioned in Chapter 1, Southern White populations and the safety of the White home needed to be protected from the drunken, uneducated Black

male beast. This same beast now had voting rights over White women in the United States at the time, and this was the Race problem. According to Willard (1890), she was without "an atom of race prejudice" (p. 8).

Nearly 60–70 years later, the bus riots in Boston continued this defence of home, but now extended it to the defence of sites of education, defence against the mobility and transit across neighbourhoods for the racial "Other", and defence in the use of tax funds across districts to enable White families to relocate their children to new school while retaining their homes (Formisano, 2012; McRae, 2018). By the late 20th century, schooling was not an effective tool in teaching complicity among the racial "Other", but a burden that the State was proudly willing to take (see Fig. 3.28). It was no longer the one that the fabricated society had the patience to wait for. What had been incorrectly labelled as an anti-busing protest was in fact the reification of what was White in Boston because they, too, had an "investment in property rights and parental rights expressed by northern White women", who had much in common with White southern women's work to support and preserve segregation (McRae, 2018, p. 232). The White women of Boston put their bodies on the line to stop the busses, as they were fully aware that "the bodies of white women functioned as repositories of Jim Crow's rules" (McRae, 2018, p. 115). They formed organisations like ROAR (Retore Our Alienated Rights) and engaged in a variety demonstrations and tactics to block the desegregation measure (see Figs. 3.29 and 3.30). And both the actions during lynching and the actions during desegregation, racialised "womanhood, [as] White women embodied a political system that elevated Whiteness and imbued women with political power based on their exclusions of African Americans" (McRae, 2018, p. 115). School systems that produce our social realities and could impact our future realities are tied to housing, and this is why the caveat on schools was indicated in the Federal Housing Administration's *Underwriting Manual.*

Housing and school integration would not lead to revolt, but it would upset and unsettle the order. However, in the converse, the segregation of schools,

THE WHITE MAN'S BURDEN.— *The Journal, Detroit.*

**Fig 3.28** "The White Man's Burden", Contained in an Article on the Philippine-American War. The Journal, Detroit, 1898. (Public Domain)

**Fig 3.29** Protesters March Down Day Boulevard in South Boston in an Anti-busing Demonstration, 29 September 1974. (Photo Credit: David L. Ryan/The Boston Globe via Getty Images)

the defunding of schools, and the eventual closing of schools could be a useful line of weaponry to force undesirable populations to also move (Ewing, 2018). And this was the reality that Elizabeth McRae's *Mothers of Massive Resistance* (2018) fully conveyed in the United States. To activate more foot soldiers for

the State order, former restrictions on education, voting, employment, and home ownership will be loosened if not outright eliminated. Gender discrimination can be rectified if patriarchy is maintained, thereby making some women only experience discrimination and others fully oppressed. Through Citizens' Councils,

**Fig 3.30** The Lynching of an Effigy of Judge W. Arthur Garrity Hangs on L Street in South Boston, 18 June 1976. (Photo Credit: Ted Dully/The Boston Globe via Getty Images)

Mothers' League, Parent Teacher Associations, United Daughters of the Confederacy, or Women for Constitutional Government, and within cities like Boston, Jackson (Mississippi), New Orleans, Richmond (Virginia), or Topeka (Kansas), these women are the principal enforcers of "customary segregation" and with that "the cooperation of grassroots women and the state, morphed into legal, long-lasting, local segregation" (p. 37). The tactics used to solidify the oppression of the racial "Other" that were employed by these women were some of the very same tactics used to create and maintain barriers to women in voting and labour. The (once) oppressed make for good soldiers for oppression. Power was maintained, and if we could just look for the underlying reality, we could see the con and the intent. If power was not altered, uprooted, or changed, then actions of reform were deemed permissible by the State. And this is why space, and the infrastructure in it through the ideation of the city, is both an example of Henri Lefebvre's dominated space and a Amilcar Cabral's contested zone of struggle as the city continuously dispossesses, selectively colonises, breeds dependence, and intensifies marginalisation of its populace (Agbude et al., 2015; Fuchs, 2019).

In addition to schools, employment affects the spatial arrangement of cities as labour extraction in all sectors is the engine of the city's functionality. The classification of labourers is achieved through the **identification of populations** that suit this extractivist need. Housing of those identified populations is based on their occupation type and extractive role and value, and failures to meet those housing demands and needs form the basis for Le Corbusier's warnings of architecture or revolution. The promise of employment is one of the key drivers of a new influx of residents to migrate to a city. This is as true in Mumbai and Nairobi of yesterday as it is in St. Louis and Ciudad de México of today. With the collapse of the economies, market interest, and capital accumulation, jobs become scarce, and populations become stuck in a city that no longer wants them. They become surplus populations to the extraction purpose of the city that once wanted their labour. In some cases, industries also move away or become forced to move away from cities due to the regulatory power of the State through its bureaucracies. Additionally, the warfare practices in one city that has been backed by the lawfare of that same city in many ways also instigates dispossession and departure to elsewhere. This was as true in East St. Louis in 1917 (population shift across river to St. Louis) as it is today in Caracas, Venezuela (population shift to São Paulo and Bogotá in neighbouring Brazil and Columbia), or Aleppo, Syria (population shift to Gaziantep and Istanbul in Turkey). In the case of the present, it will be seen what the experiences of these new refugees in these cities will become. If they arrive in the city, will they become residentially restricted to designated areas? If they earn some degree of living and eventually wealth, will they remain residentially segregated? Will policing them turn to a greater emphasis on curbing their presence in their new city and restricting their mobility? And will the effects of any of these outcomes highlight yet another example of how a city works toward those outcomes?

Opportunity and terror are two illusive tools that States can wield, condone, or sanction within their borders to move populations around as needed. But quite possibly, opportunity and terror are two illusive tools that States can wield, condone, or sanction to shift populations between their respective borders and cities as needed. Low-cost migrant labour can be moved around globally through the use of these tools. Private prejudices and individual actors can aid either of these realities, but they cannot make this reality come to pass. *De jure segregation* (by law) may support these individual actors and may produce new actors, but the existence of a such a law effectively mass produces agents for those ends. De jure segregation then fosters *de facto segregation* (by social reality) that spreads throughout an already conditioned and fabricated society. However, both de jure and de facto segregation then generate sufficient public demand and support for wholesale abandonment that provides protections from progressive overreach that inhibits the actions of mass produced actors. This is what leads to *totalitarian resegregation,* the affirmed rule of concentrated mass dispossession, a unique feature to the structure and function of a city that was never quite present to this degree during the times of imperial and colonial cities. A "just society" under this rule is then not the protection of collective rights but the comport of what the State has deemed as the image of a "just society", infringed individual private property owners that have been pooled together. While it can be argued that media influences our line of thinking, and educational systems instruct our conduct and complicity, our spatial arrangements ultimately socially engineer the populace. This is the plan, the work of the plan in its design of the city. Le Corbusier was a willing architect and designer who conveyed his own philosophies on this take in the *The Radiant City* (1964),

> The despot is not a man. It is the Plan. The correct, realistic, exact plan, the one that will provide your solution once the problem has been posited clearly, in its entirety, in its indispensable harmony. This plan has been drawn up well away from the frenzy in the mayor's office or the town hall, from the cries of the electorate or the laments of society's victims. It has been drawn up by serene and lucid minds. It has taken account of nothing but human truths. It has ignored all current regulations, all existing usages, and channels. It has not considered whether or not it could be carried out with the constitution now in force. It is a biological creation destined for human beings and capable of realization by modern techniques. (p. 154)

In returning to St. Louis, three city plans have impacted the landscape of the city: 1) "A City Plan for St. Louis" in 1907; 2) the Bartholomew lead *Comprehensive Plan* of 1947; and 3) the 1975 Community Development Commission. But the three city plans also showed the undeniable intent of the city to construct itself at the exclusion of some of its occupants. The 1907 plan articulated the practice of reserving and cordoning off the best parts of the city for privileged elites (and the aspiring classes). As an independent and non-partisan reform collective, The Civic League of Saint Louis (1907) was organised to bring the energies of social reform to bear upon the city. This initial plan concerned itself with class (protect and privilege the wealthy) and the question of what do about the poor, "masses of human beings ignorant of the simplest laws of sanitation, the evils of child labour, the corruption in political life, and above all, the weakening of the ties which bind together the home" (p. 37). For the league, a city's proper development was most concerned with the "health and morals of its citizens" (p. 41). One district in particularly was noted for its "larger portion of" immigrant "Bohemians, with the Germans next in number and a few Slavs and Hungarians. The people of this district are, as a whole, poor, self-respecting, law-abiding, and ambitious for their children and thrifty" (p. 49). Inferring that some populations were concerning, yet redeemable was worth noting in subsequent plans, but the 1907 plan set the standard for the use of land in the city. By 1915, the United Welfare Association made the protection of property values and the assurance of racial restrictions. Inspired by the 1909 Burnham plan for Chicago, the City Planning Commission of St. Louis hired a young Harland Bartholomew from Newark, New Jersey, to become the city's chief engineer and secretary. The previously mentioned Civil League was the primary motivator for the creation of such a commission to regulate city land use. To use zoning regulations for land use heralds back to Frankfurt, Germany, in the 1800s. Legislation determined the height and overall projection of buildings for a variety of uses (industrial, residential, and mixed zones). But the more generalised use of zoning for social engineering through spatial Social Darwinism quickly became the standard in most of its applications. King (2019) remarked on these institutionalised discourses as a "recursive feedback loop" legitimised by "hiding the ways that humans are both produced by (written by) and produce these codes" (p. 76). Los Angeles and San Francisco in California were two of the cities that first experimented with its application on restricting Chinese and Japanese populations and their uses of certain businesses and establishments outside of residential areas that they resided in at greater numbers (Molina, 2005; Shah, 2001).

Yet, despite this already present reality in urban planning, the design of a city could be thought to be impartial and objective. After all, "zoning is not a completely new practice. It involves establishing restrictions to regulate the height, occupation and lot area covered by buildings" (St. Louis City Plan Commission, 1917, pp. 66–67). The protection of property values overrode the narrative that was articulated in the 1907 plan of "poverty upliftment". Areas that had higher rates of tax collection due to higher incomes were more favoured in talks and studies developing the eventual 1947 plan (St. Louis City Plan Commission, 1947). By 1918, the city of St. Louis adopted the comprehensive system of zoning based on use: 1) first residential – single family homes; 2) second residential (rental properties, shared housing facilities, offices, churches,

hotels, social clubs, and other institutions); 3) commercial development; 4) industrial use; and 5) unrestricted use; that territorialised the city (City of St. Louis, 1918). As Hirt (2015) queried, "in the United States, many believe that single-family, two-family, and multi-family housing somehow represent principally different types of human environment" (p. 163). The plan, by nature of its emphasis, favoured the areas and housing standards that were predominantly White as the Black population of St. Louis was predominantly in the central area of the city with fewer single-family units and nearer industrialised areas. Fearing protections to their properties, landowners in industrial areas increased rent, causing a number of terminations of rental agreements. Rent increases in the areas broke apart this centralisation. This only worsened with multifamily units falling into least-protected zoned areas, which made into the 1947 Plan as the least favourable of residential properties. The aim or goal of the 1947 Plan was forward thinking, envisioning the city of St. Louis in the year 1970. With a predicted population of 1 million, how could the city accommodate this population without major disruptions (like the *Laws of the Indies* argued). Ease of traffic, preparedness for greater density in transit, improved single-family use in line with core principles of the family, and greater diversity in economic development beyond industry, these were the things the plan accounted for. The city was divided into eleven districts with specific regulations to the density of populations, height limits in areas zoned as commercial and residential, larger streets for travel and off-street parking for all dwellings, hotel development, and the seat of city government would receive its own special designated district (in hopes of the unification of city and county government).

Further, demarcations of "obsolete" and "blighted" were now official districts in the city that targeted neighbourhood areas with higher concentrations of Black residents for their removal, as the Plan drew the Mayor's attention to "new slum clearance and rehabilitation powers granted the city under the 1945 Constitution" (p. 4). Under Section Four "General Powers and Duties",

> It shall be the function and duty of the commission to make and adopt a comprehensive plan for the physical development of the

city. Such plan, with the accompanying maps, plats, charts and descriptive matter, shall show the commission's recommendations for the development of said area, including, among other things, the general location, character and extent of streets, viaducts, subways, bridges, water-ways, water fronts, boulevards, highways, parkways, playgrounds, squares, parks, air fields, and other public ways, grounds and open spaces, the general location of public buildings and other public property, and the general location and extent of public utilities and terminals, whether publicly or privately owned, or operated, for water, light, sanitation, transportation, communication, power and other purposes; also the removal relocation, widening, narrowing, vacating, abandonment, change of use or extension of any of the foregoing ways, grounds, open spaces, buildings, property, utilities or terminals; as well as a zoning plan for the control of the height, area, bulk, location and use of buildings and premises and of population density; the general location, character, layout, and extent of community centers and neighborhood units; and the general character, extent and layout of the replanning of blighted districts and slum areas. (p. 75)

The 1947 Plan became the gold standard to use throughout the United States as it instituted a legal way to enact racialised actions of in-city dispossession without the rhetoric of the former racial covenants. But the use of "obsolete" and "blighted" were the basis for immediate and subsequent proposal for slum clearance and urban renewal. Following the 1947 Plan, the Housing Authority and Land Clearance for Redevelopment Authority of the state of Missouri was the most instrumental unit in city government for large-scale slum clearance. The Plaza Square Urban Renewal Area in the 1950s was the first major project. Declared obsolete, St. Louis' Mill Creek Valley and Desoto-Carr neighbourhoods were completely demolished as the second and third projects. In Mill Creek Valley alone, across 454 acres, 20,000 people and thousands of homes were gone and were deemed one of the two demarcations notations of "obsolete" or "blighted". Quantitatively, according to technical studies, 99% of the structures were in need of major repairs with additional issues of poor roofing, lack of running water, sinking foundations, and no private bathrooms. Qualitatively, according to reports from non-Mill Creek Valley residents and visitors,

> people going and coming from work through this district are offended by the State of decay they witness on all sides. Unfortunately, too, every visitor who arrives in our city by train is given a poor impression of St. Louis as he or she is transported immediately through such dismal districts. (Taylor, 2014, p. 254)

This was not a demolition of abandoned buildings; this was an annihilation of a neighbourhood for nothing more than a beautification project of city leaders in order to remove the "ugly" from their sights (Fig. 3.31; Sandweiss, 2001). "Now progress has won again" (Rice, 1959), and 93% or the neighbourhood was gone, 95% of those residents were also Black. In total, throughout the city of St. Louis, Bartholomew unhoused 70,000 residents of predominantly Black neighbourhoods. For most, no cash was offered for homes, and no relocation plan was provided. Once the U.S. Congress passed the National Housing Act of 1949, an abundance of resources went to cities through the United States for more clearance initiatives. From 1951 to 1955, many of the displaced residents eventually were relocated into the massive segregated Pruitt-Igoe Public Housing complex, some from Mill Creek Valley and many from Desoto-Carr neighbourhood (see Fig. 3.32), that resembled many of Le Corbuiser's towers for the working class in his failed 1925 Plan Voisin (see Fig. 3.8), until it too was demolished in the 1970s. St. Louis was a beacon of the possibilities of what a city could do to refashion itself at the sake of populations **identified as threats**.

In what will likely be a seminal text on the history of cities, Walter Johnson in *The Broken Heat of America*, links what occurred here in Mill Creek with what has and always seems to happen in St. Louis. Unlike many others who insist that Harland Bartholomew was not racist because he never uttered any such slurs or integrated them explicitly in his writings, proposals, or speeches, Johnson (2020) clearly and cleanly indicates, Bartholomew's vision and 1947 *Comprehensive Plan* was a "beginner's guide to building a racist city – incising and

# Mill Creek—The Past Comes Tumbling Down

## Tour of Mansions Now Being Razed Reveals Ghostly Grandeur of Late Victorian Era

By Jack Rice
*Of the Post-Dispatch Staff*

MILL CREEK VALLEY is a ghost town where the wreckers work by day and the scavengers by night. Neither the wreckers nor the scavengers are sociable with the ghosts, but the ghosts are there, right on the top of the heap with the broken marble fireplaces and the broken wine bottles in the Victorian houses.

Mill Creek has old mansions, and romantic fingers in mansions gone wrong. Progress played its usual tricks on Mill Creek. Wealth came, built up a stately front, and then wealth moved west to new outskirts of town and renewed privacy as the population crowded in, the force of numbers defeating the force of money.

The city's first park and its first industry and its first big show of residential grandeur were in Mill Creek Valley. The boundaries of Mill Creek are Twentieth street to Grand, going east to west, and from the railroad tracks to Olive, going south to north.

Measured in time, Mill Creek's boundaries sprawl from here to Joseph Taillon. Pierre Laclede gave the Mill Creek area to Taillon in the 1760s and Taillon went into the milling business. He had a natural starter in a clear, strong spring. The spring beat a path to the Mississippi river from a starting point that doesn't look s p r i n g - f e d now. The spring's source, by current labels, was at the corner of Vandeventer and Market.

Taillon dammed the spring and a pond formed. Auguste Chouteau bought the property and figured if a pond was good, a lake would be better. So Chouteau had a lake, and then he had a mansion by the lake.

Wreckers demolishing buildings in the Mill Creek district. The picture was taken from the rear of 3500 block on Laclede avenue.

**Fig 3.31** Mill Creek—The Past Comes Tumbling Down, Jack Rice, October 18, 1959, p 95. (©) (2021), St. Louis Post Dispatch.

intensifying existing differences of [R]ace and class in the physical form of the built environment" (p. 297). Johnson goes further on the very next page,

> As tragic as the destruction of these neighbourhoods has seemed to many subsequent observers, for Bartholomew it was an acceptable cost than a fortunate happenstance. For at the very heart of his plan was a proposal to demolish most of Black St. Louis. Of course, Bartholomew did not say that. He did not need to. There was not a single explicit reference to "Negroes" or "segregation" in the *Comprehensive Plan*. Instead, there were maps and tables that outlined the deplorable conditions of the slumlord rentier-owned neighbourhoods east of Grand: the density of habitation, the number of outdoor toilets, the usage of buildings built before 1900, the proportion of "sub-standard"

(a term undefined) accommodations. Rather than seeing the poor conditions as an index of racist exploitation in a segregated housing market and trying to do something to build the neighbourhood up, Bartholomew simply proposed tearing them down...an area of almost three thousand acres – three times the size of Central Park in New York City, seven times the size of the French Quarter in New Orleans, almost ten times the size of the National Mall in Washington, D.C., and thirty times the size of Disneyland in Los Angeles...All told, Bartholomew was recommending the renovation by destruction of over twenty square miles. (pp. 298–299)

Bartholomew died at the age of 100 in 1989, ironically in Clayton, Missouri, a wealthier suburb than the city he eviscerated. The proclaimed "Dean

**Fig 3.32** Brutalist Architecture of the Pruitt-Igoe Housing Complex - United States Geological Survey in St. Louis, MO, 1956. (Public Domain)

of City Planners" and father of modern slum clearance rightfully served on the National Slum Clearance Advisory Committee. I know what some of you may be thinking: here was a person and not a system that caused so much damage. Here is the culprit of so much misery, so much Black misery. Bartholomew was employed by cities throughout the United States to do their city-splitting bidding that also included the Transportation Plan in the 1950s for Washington, D.C., that zoned the city for transit and spatial exclusion. His fingerprints on cities in the United States as well as urban planning impressions in the city of São Paulo, Brazil, in the 1920s draw additional comparisons with Le Corbusier and his influence on the Brazilian planned city and capital of Brasília (Luiz Ignácio de Anhaia Mello looking to Bartholomew, Mello, 1927; and Lúcio Costa as a student of Le Corbusier, and Oscar Neimeyer influenced by him, Beal, 2010; Niemeyer, 2000). He repeated his technique in all cases – strict zoning laws, slum demarcation, slum clearance, wider streets, and highway construction around the major parts of a downtown area – and like a completed dispossession checklist, done.

Through zoning and slum clearance, Bartholomew's legendary contemporary Robert Moses in New York City exploited the leeway given by the Housing Act of 1949 and demolished the predominantly Black "Manhattantown" and created the Park West Village (Brown, 2005) – once again through official means, another individual within a bureaucratic operation, this time as chairman of the New York City Slum Clearance Committee. The Brooklyn-Queens Expressway divided "Red Hook" in Brooklyn from the wealthy Cobble Hill and Brooklyn Heights. The Long Island Expressway overpass and the Van Wyck and Henry Hudson Expressways point of access prevented public transportation that would have brought an influx of Blacks, Puerto Ricans, and Italians to desirable locations for recreation and employment opportunities. Moses over his long and unofficial 44-year planning reign of terror was responsible for nearly 32 expressways and parkways and displacing just over 250,000 people in total overall (Caro, 1974). Moses' massive goal for the LOMAX, the Lower Manhattan Expressway, to link New York City with New Jersey, would have turned Little

Italy into rubble and was only halted by a strong and persistent collective of local organisers who exerted weight on the political and economic classes of the city (Dory, 2018; Jacobs, 1961).

Much of this Rothstein (2017) covered in the aforementioned *The Color of Law*, as well as Avila (2014) in *The Folklore of the Freeway*. Interstate 35, while servicing Austin, Texas, and serving as a route from the Mexican Border to Duluth, Minnesota, fractured the historically Black community of Wheatvale through the City Plan of 1928. The forced removal of 10,000 people in "Overtown" occurred to build Interstate 95 in Miami. The Riverfront Expressway and the Interstate 10 Bridge in New Orleans reduced the "Tremé" to a quarter of its former glory. The demolition of 600 or more homes in Nashville, Tennessee, was needed to construct Interstate 40. Interstate 75 levelled the thriving areas of the "Paradise Valley" and "Black Bottom" in Detroit. Interstate 65 flattened the historic "Indiana Avenue" in Indianapolis through millions of dollars pumped in through the new Unigov system of governance (consolidated city-county government), while Interstate 70 displaced 17,000 people by splicing the Black, German, Greek, Jewish, Irish, and Italian community of Southside and demolishing 8,000 buildings. Interstate 75 would bulldoze the West End and create a new neighbourhood in Queensgate with new residents in Cincinnati. The Embarcadero Freeway split San Francisco. Respectively, the Golden State Freeway ran roughshod through Boyle Heights, and the Santa Monica Freeway destroyed the non-slum "Sugar Hill" in Los Angeles. Through the execution and benefits gain from Bartholomew's plan, backed by the 1949 Public Housing Act and strengthened by the 1956 Interstate Highway Act, cities lined up to utilise the construction of highways and interstates to devastate and separate Black populations in the North and South, Black and Latinx populations in the West, and Black and poor White populations in the Midwest of the United States. The Dan Ryan Expressway in Chicago also built during this time used the same methods and displaced some 50,000 residents, and then relocated many of them in public housing units that would eventually be destroyed as well. Where it was the Mill Creek Valley in St. Louis among others, it was Bronzeville, also known as the Black Metropolis, in Chicago. Where it was the Pruitt-Igoe in St. Louis as the

alternative offer, it was the Robert Taylor Homes and Stateway Gardens in Chicago. People who moved to these cities were moved over and over and over again. This is in-city dispossession, and the extraction is the tax funds received, the monetary benefits levied from the new aesthetically pleasing order, and the marketing that attracts entertainment and city investment. Any concentration of "Negroes" in a geographical area is only begging for "crime", and any proximity to that concentration of "Negro" neighbourhoods is only begging for vandalism (Fullilove, 2016). "Negro" removal is a necessity to property ownership. While many see urban renewal as "Negro removal", the long and interlocked history presented here places it within an international scope and a very indigenous lens of Native removal.

## 3.6 A Third Conclusion

What can we conclude of this through an international scope? The use of interstates, highways, and expressway construction to rupture communities in the United States from the 1920s to the 1970s was soon adopted in plans by other countries from the 1970s onward: the South Eastern Freeway and its likely splitting of Gardiners Creek in Melbourne, Australia; the 2$^{nd}$ Ring Road and a line for the subway decimated parts of old Beijing in China; the Spadina Expressway project in Toronto, Canada; the A2 Motorway in Amsterdam, Netherlands; the East London River Crossing that would have cut the Oxleas Wood community in two in London; the United Kingdom and Trans-Amazonian Highway's wanton destruction of the rain forest and indigenous land were just overseas versions of "White roads through Black bedrooms" (Ayres, 1967, p. 97). The aforementioned use of events was used for not only major capital construction campaigns but also the destruction of neighbourhoods (Greene, 2003): Rio and various other cities in Brazil for the 2014 World Cup and 260,000 households with the 2016 Olympics; the theft in public funds for the East End in London that went instead to the 2012 Olympics; the Apartheid-like removals for the 2010 Word Cup in Cape Town, South Africa; the expansive use and re-occupation of First Nation's Territories for the 2010 Winter Olympics; Beijing and additional parts of Old Beijing for the 2008 Olympics; the "cleaning

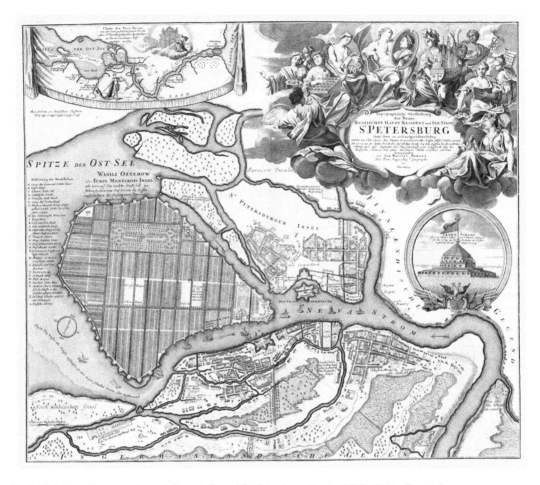

**Fig 3.33** Johann Homann Map and General Plan of St. Petersburg, Russia, 1717. (Public Domain)

operations" of Albanian Roma and the greater forced evictions and relocations of the 2004 Olympics in Athens; the false promises that turned into removals for the 1992 Olympics in Barcelona, Spain; the eviction of 720,000 people in Seoul, Korea, for the 1988 Olympics; the aforementioned massacre in Ciudad de México for the 1968 Olympics; for as the activist and Moses' rival, Jane Jacobs (1961), proffered, "somehow, when the fair became part of the city, it did not work like the fair" (p. 6).

The beautification project, highway, and mega-event were and still are small excuses for grander visions. The re-ordered city by way of the grid re-spatialised the old cities of Saint Petersburg and Edinburgh, moving beyond the walls of the old fortified town (see Figs. 3.33 and 3.34). The Howard of 1900s London; the Burnham of 1909 Chicago;

the Le Corbusier of 1925 Paris; Spence-Sales of 1940s–1960s; various cities throughout Canada; the Bartholomew of 1947 St. Louis; and the Moses of 20th century New York, each served as developers of modern city planning that resulted in removal and displacement under the pretences of urban renewal. Each could be singled out, but each administration, council, and government that hired them and legions of others to do their bidding competently, with zeal or not, was obscured by history. Even the city planning of dictators, despots, and ruthless leadership in Nazi Germany, Il Duce's Italy, and Apartheid South Africa can be obscured if we analyze State power through the lens of the individual experience – the narratives of "We cannot have a really healthy city until the slum dwellers are moved out of their hatcheries of contagion and decently

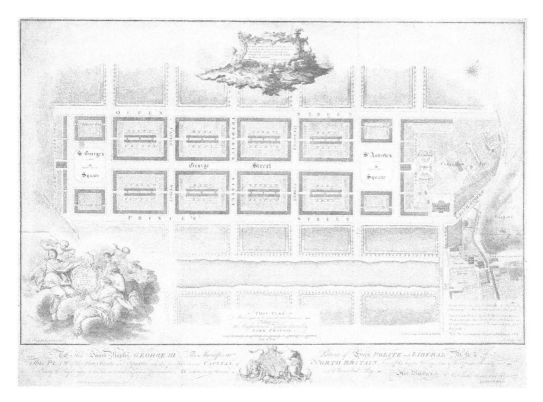

**Fig 3.34** James Craig Plan of the New Streets and Squares for the First Plan of the New Town, Edinburgh, Scotland, 1768. (Geographicus/Public Domain)

housed" (Slums vs. Health, 1946, B4) and there could be hope for improved conditions "if it were not to revert again to a blighted or slum area, as though possessed of a congenital disease", resulting in the need for such areas to "be planned as a whole" (Berman v. Parker, 1954).

To slum clear is to rally the powers and minds of the State and its people against the horror of blight. As Herscher (2020) poignantly commented that blight removal had thus come,

> to be an important component of a "reverse welfare state" in which public resources are dedicated to the advancement of corporate welfare, in this case with a rhetoric that masked private interest as public good. (p. 297)

To slum clear is the opportunity to involve all of the forces of governance and control to "partici-pate in the integrated transformation of a ghetto"

(Meyer, 1965, p. 109). Even Black radical con-ceptions of spatial arrangements cannot evade the influence of years of infrastructural conditioning. The William Penn and Thomas Holme's 1682 plan for Philadelphia gave way to the conditions Du Bois (1899) studied in the 1890s (see Figs. 3.35 and 3.36). Complete with denotations of criminal classes, *The Philadelphia Negro* perpe-tuated temporally fixed spatial concepts while arguing against the biological basis for Race. Citizen criminality replaced enslaved inhumanity, and the police replaced the patrol. In response to the state-violence in policing and city adminis-trative abandonment of Harlem in New York City, writer June Meyer (nee June Jordan) and architect R. Buckminster Fuller conceived of the "Skyrise for Harlem", a plan to redevelop public housing. The plan was not to displace but to actually in-tensify concentration. And while this plan was never formally published in *Esquire* due to

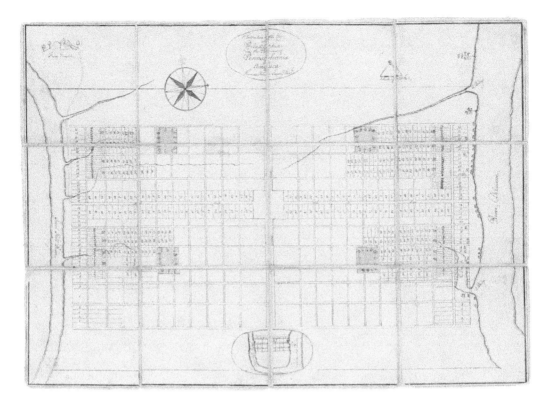

**Fig 3.35** William Penn Appointed Thomas Holme Map of the Original City of Philadelphia in A Portraiture of the City of Philadelphia, 1682. (Public Domain)

political differences between the author and publisher (they wanted to publish it as "Instant Slum Clearance" and not "Skyrise for Harlem"), the plan still seemed to situate the people of Harlem in derelict need – a plan without input from the very people who it would impact.

The people in rags, the working class, the poor, the Lumpenproletariat, are the revolting masses in their unsightliness. But their usefulness for labour keeps them at varying levels of proximity to and within cities rather than at a distance or banished to the hinterlands. Proximity that is a Qatari stadium construction worker-near, which means that once they are flown in, they are only flown out in a casket once they are dead from work hazards in constructing a stadium or hotel. Proximity that is South African *Bantustáns*-near, a demarcated and abandoned space beyond the city, in the hinterlands of the governed territory. Proximity that South East Asian-near,

confined to constant migrating from home village to palace city for hospitality work, day in and day out. Proximity that is also settler colonial United States' Jim Crow era-near, living on the other side of the train tracks or being bussed from across town. Proximity that may also be "Downton Abbey"-near, living in the servant quarters just next door to change linens and clean out bedpans. And lastly, proxmity that is Native-near, being kept in someone's bedroom or closet after being abducted and now service the desires of someone's abductor.

This forms the basis for why the Lumpenproletariat are the other type of revolting masses in their wretchedness that may cease to tolerate the conditions of the city. In the long historical list of planners, Haussmann of 18th century France may take the extra credit for initiating and coupling city planning with large-scale "slum clearance". The social control of the poor of *La Zone* went alongside

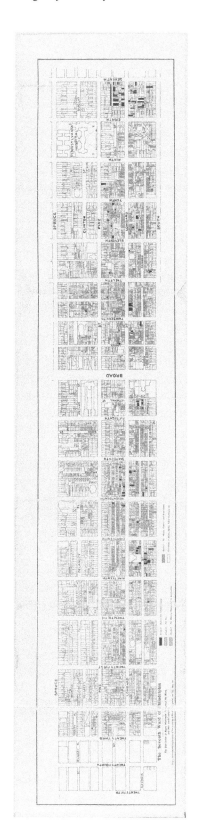

**Fig 3.36** "Map of the Distribution of Black Inhabitants of the 7th Ward of Philadelphia in The Philadelphia Negro, 1899. (Public Domain)

the elevation of the already elevated. They had to be criminalised with an added dose of being deemed disease ridden in order for any plan to be endorsed and to work. But the results were clear in reflection on the work of Haussmann in cleaving the city of Paris, Émile Zola (2004) remarked,

> Paris sliced by strokes of a saber: the veins opened, nourishing one hundred thousand earth movers and stone masons; criss-crossed by admirable strategic routes, placing forts in the heart of the old neighborhoods.

Robert Moses, the heralded planner of New York, was a staunch student of Haussmann (Moses, 1942). As yet another example of the historical recurrence of the maintenance of State power, Moses "modelled his activities in the reshaping of New York on what he saw as Haussmann's virtues", the elevation of the elite, the increased routes of circulation for capital extraction and wealth accumulation, the confinement of the poor, and the cordoning of the rebellious working class (Harvey, 2006, p. 18).

But whether the State finds willing and competent executors or not, their plans are the plans that are always carried out. "Geographies of threat" is ultimately a spatial conceptualisation of the art of statecraft through the functional management of the city. To rule is to produce space through dispossession and occupation. To rule is to also make that which is within it legible through dispossession and concentration, and once it is legible, it can be controlled for the purposes of extraction. The reach of the State from its capital city is only as strong as the settler colonial and imperial cities that the State constructs to govern the entirety of its population of a given territory. As Hirt (2015) reminded readers, "to this day, there is no federal law on urban land use" (p. 35), so the role of cities in administering the desires of the cities is the principal site of governance and not the national or federal legislative body. At the level of the city, populations are managed through zoning through either order-construction (land use focus through distinctive, single-use property and areas) or disorder-suppression (order-maintenance through loitering, nuisance, no knock warrants, and raids) functions that give property and not people primacy in governance (Garnett, 2010). This is the greater lesson on zoning that is gleaned from looking at examples retrospectively. Zoning is about the State's power to shape the socially constructed ideals of home, family, and country as the imposition of a moral geography into the infrastructure of the city. Once in the infrastructure of a city, and not the so-called social fabric of a society, the State has its hold and power on generations of the populace. It becomes the planned way of life.

City planning turned capital building/mega-event planning is a useful absence of city governing and social responsibility. Thus, liberal fantasies of bringing an "end to municipal corruption, [fostering] urban renewal, and [ensuring] the protection of civil right" miss the underlying point that the city and its changing regimes are functioning properly (Countryman, 2006, p. 13). In returning to Jane Jacobs (1961),

> Cities are an immense laboratory of trial and error, failure and success, in city building and city design. This is the laboratory in which city planning should have been learning and forming and testing its theories. Instead the practitioners and teachers of this discipline (if it can be called) have ignored the study of success and failure in real life, have been incurious about the reasons for unexpected success, and are guided instead by principles derived from the behavior and appearance of towns, suburbs, tuberculosis sanatoria, fairs, and imaginary dream cities – from anything but cities themselves. (p. 6)

For the city is the laboratory of the State, in its tragically awkward inability to do anything other than repress and oppress,

> ...and by analogy, [enacting] the principles of sorting out – and of bringing order by repression of all plans but the planners' – have been extended to all manner of city functions... from beginning to end, from Howard and Burnham to the latest amendment on urban-renewal law, the entire concoction is irrelevant to the workings of cities. Unstudied,

unrespected, cities have served as sacrificial victims. (Jacobs, 1961, p. 25)

And, of course, many of us may take offence to this argument. Who is repressed? Where is the oppression? The evidence of what a city does once it identifies a certain population has been made clear by legions of scholars who have agreed with this reality and have challenged this position. Our lack of acceptance is trivial and amounts to nothing more than coinage in someone's cup on our walk to work. The conceptualisation of "Geographies of Threat" through the **identification of populations** first, and then the **identification of threats** second, is choosing an intellectual path or route to "overname" rather than "undername" this reality and long history. To "overname" allows for some degree of accuracy in identifying the severity of what has been done and what will likely keep being done. There is a needed power behind conceptualising the creation and dehumanisation of surplus populations in the cities of the world. Surplus populations do not add value and, in fact, take away value from a city. They do not make cities economically thrive. They provide the lowest form of service. Surplus populations take up space. Surplus populations (can) take my place if I must be replaced. Surplus population (can) take your space as will ultimately destroy your property. They are threats. They are threats to property (value). They are threats to (my) money. They are threats to us, if we are not them. Surplus populations need to be gone. Surplus populations need to be ran out of town (see Fig. 3.37).

> "Any settlement is an inscription in space of the social relations in the society that built it...our cities are patriarchy written in stone, brick, glass and concrete".
> –Jane Darke, 1996, in "The Man-Shaped City", p. 88.

> "Somehow, when the fair became part of the city, it did not work like the fair".
> –Jane Jacobs The Death and Life Of Great American Cities (1961), p. 6.

**Fig 3.37** Unidentified Photographer, "Running the Negro out of Tulsa". The 1921 Tulsa Massacre and the Destruction of Greenwood, OK, 1 June 1921. (International Center of Photography/Gift of Brian Wallis - The Oklahoma Historical Society)

## References

Adarkar, N. & Menon, M. (Eds.). (2004). *One hundred years one hundred voices: The millworkers of Girangaon: An oral history.* Seagull Press.

Agbude, G. A., Lukman, L. A., & Ovia, E. (2015). Amilcar Cabral and the development paradigms in Africa: Revisiting the earlier strategies for the African Union. *Journal of African Union Studies*, *4*(1), 5–24. 10.23 07/26893842

Akcan, E. (2020). Open architecture, rightlessness, and citizens-to-come. In I. Cheng, C. L. Dais, & M. O. Wilson, *Race and modern architecture: A critical history from the Enlightenment to the present* (pp. 324–338). University of Pittsburgh Press.

Anderson, B. R. O. (1983). *Imagined communities: Reflections on the origins and spread of nationalism.* Verso Books.

Ansari, J. H. (1977). Evolution of town planning practice and system of urban government in India. *Urban and Rural Planning Thought*, *20*(1), 9–23.

Avila, E. (2014). *The folklore of the freeway: Race and revolt in the modernist city.* University of Minnesota Press.

Ayres, B. D. (1967, December 31). White roads through Black bedrooms. *The New York Times*, 97. https://timesmach ine.nytimes.com/timesmachine/1967/12/31/9698145 9.html?pageNumber=97

Baade, R. A. & Sanderson, A. R. (2012). An analysis of the political economy for bidding for the Sumer Olympic Games: Lessons from the Chicago 2016 bid. In W. Meannig & A. Zimbalist, *International handbook on the economics of mega sporting events* (pp. 85 –107). Edward Elgar.

Baradaran, M. (2017). *The color of money: The Black banks and the racial wealth gap.* Belknap Press.

Bataile, G. (1997). Architecture. In N. Leach (Ed.), *Rethinking architecture: A reader in cultural theory* (pp. 20–21). Routledge.

Beal, S. (2010). The real and promised Brasília: An asymmetrical symbol in 1960s Brazilian iterature. *Hispania*, *93*(1), 1–10. http://www.jstor.org.proxy.library.emory. edu/stable/25703388

Bennett, L., Bennett, M., Alexander, S., & Persky, J. (2013). The political and civic implications of Chicago's unsuccessful bid to host the 2016 Olympic Games. *Journal of Sport and Social Issues*, *37*(4), 364–383. 10.1177/0193723513499921

Berman v. Parker, 348 US 26 (United States Supreme Court, 1954).

Berman, B. (1990). *Control and crisis in colonial Kenya: The dialectic of domination.* Ohio University Press

Brown, J. (2005). A tale of two visions: Harland Bartholomew, Robert Moses, and the development of the American freeway. *Journal of Planning History*, *4*(1), 3–32. 10.1177/1538513204272856

Brown, A. (2020). Erecting the skyscraper, erasing Race. In I. Cheng, C. L. Dais, & M. O. Wilson, *Race and modern architecture: A critical history from the Enlightenment to the present* (pp. 203–217). University of Pittsburgh Press.

Bushe, H. G. & Great Britain Colonial Office. (1934). *Report of the Commission of Inquiry into the Administration of Justice in Kenya, Uganda and the Tanganyika Territory in Criminal Matters May, 1933 and Correspondence arising out of the Report*. HMSO.

Caro, R. (1974). *The power broker*. Vintage Books.

Chandavarkar, R. (2004). Introduction: From neighbour-hood to nation: The rise and fall of the left in Bombay's Girangaon in the Twentieth Century. In N. Adarkar & M. Menon (Eds.), *One hundred years one hundred voices: The millworkers of Girangaon: An oral history*. Seagull Press.

Chandavarkar, R. (2009). *History, culture and the Indian city*. Cambridge University Press.

Cheng, I., Dais, C. L. & Wilson, M. O. (2020). *Race and modern architecture: A critical history from the Enlightenment to the present*. University of Pittsburgh Press.

*City of Chicago v. Jesus Morales*, 527 US 41 (United States Supreme Court, 1999).

City of St. Louis. (1918, July 15). *Ordinance no. 30.199*.

City Plan Commission. (1917). *Problems of St. Louis*. St. Louis, MO: City Plan Commission.

City Plan Commission. (1947). *Comprehensive city plan*. St. Louis, MO: City Plan Commission.

Clark, T. J. (1984). *The painting of modern life: Paris in the art of Manet and his followers*. Alfred Knopf.

Le Corbusier. (1923). *Vers une architecture* ("Towards a new architecture). Georges Crès.

Le Corbusier. (1964/1933). *The radiant city: Elements of a doctrine of urbanism to be used as the basis of machine-age civilization* [Trans. by P. Knight]. Orion Press.

Countryman, M. J. (2006). *Up south: Civil rights and Black power in Philadelphia*. University of Pennsylvania Press.

Crinson, M. (2020). "Compartmentalized world": Race, architecture, and colonial crisis in Kenya and London. In I. Cheng, C. L. Dais, & M. O. Wilson, *Race and modern architecture: A critical history from the Enlightenment to the present* (pp. 259–276). University of Pittsburgh Press.

Crooks, J. B. (1968). *Politics & progress: The rise of urban progressivism in Baltimore, 1895 to 1911*. Louisiana State University Press.

Crouch, D., & Mundigo, A. (1977). The city planning or-dinances of the Laws of the Indies revisited. Part II:

Three American cities. *The Town Planning Review*, *48*(4), 397–418. http://www.jstor.org/stable/401 03295

Delegard, K. & Ehrman-Solberg, K. (2017). "Playground of the people"? Mapping racial covenants in twentieth-century Minneapolis. *Open Rivers: Rethinking The Mississippi* (6). 10.24926/2471190X.2820

Deleuze, G. (1997). City/State (with Félix Guattari). In N. Leach (Ed.), *Rethinking architecture: A reader in cultural theory* (pp. 313–318). Routledge.

van Dijk, T. & Weitkamp, G. (2014). Power in dreams? The spatial effects of Chicago's failed Olympic Bid. *International Planning Studies*, *19*(2), 111–131. 10.1080/13563475.2013.830681

Dory, J. (2018). Clash of urban philosophies: Moses versus Jacobs. Journal of Planning History, 17(1), 20–41. 10.1177/1538513217691999

Dossal, M. (2010). *Theatre of conflict, city of hope: Mumbai 1660 to present times*. Oxford University Press.

Du Bois, W. E. B. (1899). *The Philadelphia Negro: A social study*. University of Pennsylvania Press.

Elkins, C. (2005). *Britain's gulag: The brutal end of empire in Kenya*. Pimlico.

Ewing, E. (2018). *Ghosts in the schoolyard: Racism and school closings on Chicago's South Side*. University of Chicago Press.

Federal Housing Administration (1936, April 1). *Underwriting manual: Underwriting and valuation procedure under Title II of the National Housing Act with revisions to April 1, 1936*. Part II, Section 2, United States Federal Housing Administration. Washington, D.C.

Foner, P. (1975). Introduction to *"Inside the monster" by José Martí: Writings on the United States and American Imperialism* [Edited by P. Foner].Monthly Review Press.

Formisano, R. P. (2012). *Boston against busing: Race, class, and ethnicity in the 1960s and 1970s*. University of North Carolina Press.

Foucault, M. (1971). *The order of things*. Vintage Books.

Foucault, M. (1986). *Of other spaces* [Trans. by J. Miskowiec]. *Diacritics*, *16*(1), 22–27. 10.2307/464 648

Fuchs, C. (2019). Henri Lefebvre's theory of the produc-tion of space and the critical theory of communica-tion. *Communication Theory*, *29*(2)129–150. 10.1 093/ct/qty025

Fullilove, M. T. (2016). *Root shock: How teaching up city neighborhoods hurts America, and what we can do about it*. New Village Press.

Garnett, N. S. (2010). *Ordering the city: Land use, poli-cing, and the restoration of urban America*. Yale University Press.

Garnier, T. (1918). *Une cité industrielle: Étude pour la construction des villes*, volume 1. A. Vincent.

Glasco, S. B. (2010). *Constructing Mexico City: Colonial conflicts over culture, space, and authority.* Palgrave MacMillan.

Gordon, C. (2008). *Mapping decline: St. Louis and the fate of the American city.* University of Pennsylvania Press.

Greene, S. J. (2003). Staged cities: Mega-events, slum clearance, and global capital. *Yale Human Rights and Development Law Journal,* 6(1), 161–187. https://digitalcommons.law.yale.edu/yhrdlj/vol6/iss1/6

Hadacheck v. Sebastia, 239 U.S. 394, 36 S. Ct. 143, 60 L. Ed. 348 (United States Supreme Court 1915).

Hanly, F. (Producer) & Meades, J. (Director) (2014, February 16). *Bunkers, brutalism and bloodymindedness: Concrete poetry with Jonathan Meades* [Documentary]. BBC Four.

Harvey, D. (2003). *The new imperialism.* Oxford University Press.

Harvey, D. (2006). The political economy of public space. In S. Low & N. Smith (Eds.), *The politics of public space* (pp. 17–34). Routledge.

Hegel, G. W. F. (1952). *The philosophy of right* [Trans. T. M. Knox]. Oxford University Press.

Helper, R. (1969). *Racial policies and practices of real estate brokers.* University of Minneapolis Press.

Herscher, A. (2020). Black and blight. In I. Cheng, C. L. Dais, & M. O. Wilson, *Race and modern architecture: A critical history from the Enlightenment to the present* (pp. 291–307). University of Pittsburgh Press.

Hirt, S. A. (2015). *Zoned in the USA: The origins and implications of American land-use regulations.* Cornell University Press.

Holston, J. (2009). The spirit of Brasília: Modernity as experiment and risk. In R. E. Biron (Ed.), *City/Art: The urban scene in Latin America* (pp. 85–112). Duke University Press.

Hugill, D. (2017). What is a settler-colonial city?. *Geography Compass, 11*(5), 1–11. 10.1111/gec3.12315

Jacobs, J. (1961). *The death and life of great American cities.* Random House and Vintage Books.

Johnson, W. (2020). *The broken heart of America: St. Louis and the violent history of the United States.* Basic Books.

King, T. L. (2019). *The black shoals: Offshore formations of Black and native studies.* Duke University Press.

Leach, N. (1999). Architecture or revolution?. In N. Leach (Ed.), *Architecture and revolution: Contemporary perspectives on Central and Eastern Europe* (pp. 112–126). Routledge.

Lefebvre, H. (1991). *The production of space.* Blackwell.

Lefebvre, H. (2003). *The urban revolution.* University of Minnesota Press.

Marcuse, H. (2008). *A study on authority.* Verso.

Marshall, Y. (2017). *The bleaching carceral: Police, native and location in Nairobi, 1844-1906* [Unpublished dissertation]. Columbia University.

McRae, E. G. (2018). *Mothers of massive resistance: White women and the politics of White Supremacy.* Oxford University Press.

Mello, L. I. R. A. (1927, June 19). Problemas de urbanismo: Mais uma contribuição para o calçamento. *Revista Politécnica, 83,* 343–365.

Meyer, J. (1965, April 1). Instant slum clearance. *Esquire.* https://classic.esquire.com/article/1965/4/1/instant-slum-clearance

Molina, N. (2005). *Fit to be citizens?: Public health and Race in Los Angeles, 1879-1939.* University of North Carolina Press.

Moses, R. (1942). What happened to Haussmann. *Architectural Forum, 77*(1), 57–66.

Mowatt, R. A., & Travis, J. (2015). Event planning, public participation & failure: A 2016 Olympic bid case study. *Revue Loisir et Societe · Leisure and Society, 38*(2), 249–267.

Mowatt, R. A. (2020). A people's history of leisure studies: *The Great Race,* the National Park Service, and the U.S. Forest Service. *Journal of Parks and Recreation Administration, 38*(3), 152–172. 10.18666/JPRA-2019-9674

Mundigo, A. I. & Crouch, D. P. (1977). The city planning ordinances of the Laws of the Indies revisited. Part I: Their philosophy and implications. *The Town Planning Review, 48*(3), 247–268. https://www.jstor.org/stable/40103542

Murphy, G. (2005). *Geographic morality and the new world.* Duke University Press.

Niemeyer, O. (2000). *The curves of time: The memoirs of Oscar Niemeyer.* Phaidon.

Nye, J. S. (2004). *Soft power: The means to success in world politics.* Public Affairs.

Osterweil, V. (2020). *In defense of looting: A riotous history of uncivil action.* Bold Type Books.

Pakenham, T. (1991). *The scramble for Africa: The White man's conquest of the dark continent from 1876-1912.* Random House.

Phaidon Editors. (2018). *Atlas of brutalist architecture.* Phaidon Press.

Pike, R. (1967). Sevillian society in the sixteenth century: Slaves and freedmen. *The Hispanic American Historical Review, 47*(3), 344–359.

Power, G. (1983). Apartheid Baltimore style: The residential segregation ordinances of 1910-1913. *Maryland Law Review, 42*(4), 289–328. http://digitalcommons.law.umaryland.edu/mlr/vol42/iss2/4

Power, G. (1996). The residential segregation of Baltimore's Jews: Restrictive covenants or gentlemen's agreement. *Generations,* 5–7.

Rice, J. (1959, October 18). Editorial: Mill Creek – The past comes tumbling down. *The St. Louis Post-Dispatch*. 3H.

Robbins, C. (2016, February 17). Robert Caro wonders what New York is going to become. *Gothamist*. https://gothamist.com/news/robert-caro-wonders-what-new-york-is-going-to-become

Rothstein, R. (2017). *The color of law: A forgotten history of how our government segregated America*. Liveright Publishing Corporation.

Rundio, A. & Heere, B. (2016). The battle for the bid: Chicago 2016, No Games Chicago, and the lessons to be learned. *Sport Management Review*, *19*(5), 587–598. 10.1016/j.smr.2016.06.001

Sandweiss, E. (2001). *St. Louis: The evolution of an American urban landscape*. Temple University Press.

Satter, B. (2009). *Family properties: How the struggle over Race and real estate transformed Chicago and urban America*. MacMillan Press.

(1914, April 23). Scott, Henry, and Leonora Scott to Nels Anderson. Transaction on May 26, 1910. *Hennepin County Deeds Book* 759, p. 538, Document 712111.

Scott, J. C. (1999). *Seeing like a state: How certain schemes to improve the human condition have failed*. Yale University Press.

Shah, N. (2001). *Contagious divides: Epidemics and Race in San Francisco's Chinatown*. University of California Press.

Slums vs. health. (1946). *The Washington Post*, *5*(12), B4.

Smith, W. (1980). Friedrich Ratzel and the origins of Lebensraum. *German Studies Review*, *3*(1), 51–68. 10.2307/1429483

Soja, E. (1985). The spatiality of social life: Towards a transformative retheorization. In D. Gregory and J. Urry (Eds.), *Social relations and spatial structures* (pp. 90–127). Macmillan.

Taylor, D. (2014). *Toxic communities: Environmental racism, industrial pollution, and residential mobility*. New York University Press.

Taylor, K. (2019). *Race for profit: How banks and the real estate industry undermined Black homeownership*. University of North Carolina Press.

Taylor, P. J. (1999). *Modernities: A geohistorical interpretation*. University of Minnesota Press.

Thatra, G. (2020). Dalit Chembur: Spatializing the caste question in Bombay, c. 1920s-1970s. *Journal of Urban History*, 1–35. 10.1177/0096144220923631

The Civic League. (1907). *A city plan for Saint Louis: Reports of the several committees appointed by the executive board of the Civic League to draft a city plan*. The Civic League of Saint Louis. St. Louis, MO.

The National Conservation Commission. (1909). *Report of the National Conservation Commission*. The National Conservation Commission.

Vickery, K. P. (1974). Herrenvolk democracy and egalitarianism in South Africa and the U.S. South. *Comparative Studies in Society and History*, *16*(13), 309–328. 10.1017/s0010417500012469

Village of Euclid v. Ambler Realty Co., 272 US 365 (United States Supreme Court, 1926).

Ware, V. (1992). *Beyond the pale: White women, racism and history*. Verso.

Willard, F. E. (1890, October 23). The Race problem: Miss Willard on the political puzzle of the South. *The Voice*, 8.

Wilson, D. A. (2013). The great European migration and indigenous populations. In G. Morton & D. A. Wilson (Eds.), *Irish and Scottish encounters with Indigenous peoples: Canada, the United States, New Zeland, and Australia* (pp. 22–48). McGill-Queen's University Press.

Zola, E. (2004/1872). *The rush for the spoil* (*La Curée*) [Trans. by B. Nelson]. Oxford Word's Classic.

# 4.
# THE SOCIETY OF THE CITY: THE IDENTIFICATION FOR VIOLENCE

**Fig 4.1** "The American Way of Life", Black Residents of Louisville (KY) Displaced by the Great Ohio River Flood in Line to Receive Aid From a Relief Station Around the Corner, 1937. (Photo Credit: Margaret Bourke-White/Public Domain)

"La Guerra dura haze la paz segura"/"Cruel war makes peace secure"
– Jack D. Forbes, retelling of Spanish Colonial Military Officer, Juan Fernandez de la Fuente's philosophy, in Columbus and Other Cannibals: The Wetiko Disease of Exploitation, Imperialism, and Terrorism (1979), P. 124

"Violence directed systematically against non-combatants through irregular means, from the state, has been a central part of Americans' way of war".
– John Grenier, in The First Way of War: American War Making on the Frontier (2005), p. 224

There is something that is vitally important in conceiving of the State in its spatial formation and spatial dominance. While the State can be, and has been, skilfully interrogated in its political manifestation through various apparatuses and institutions as well as in its historical-philosophical foundations through key actors of the Empire, it is in the geography and in the conception of space that deliberations are implemented and schools of thought are given structural form. But it is not just in some vague notion of space that this social construction is made into reality. It is upon the land turned territory that the State exercises itself and ascribes onto others the necessary identifications in service to itself. This position is less a critique of the past work of a range of scholars, thinkers,

DOI: 10.1201/9781003149545-4

organisers, and activists, and more a specific way to give those ideas a locus and a congress convened to discuss the particular subject of the violence of the State through its cities. Variously appointed occupations of State actors carry out violence through processes within institutions that then bolster the ordinances and policies that have been approved by the will of the State. Colonialism is "violence in its natural state" (Fanon, 1963, p. 61). So, it becomes quite natural for violence to be deployed as a method to rule over a populace. Violence is the currency of colonialism and capitalism that is spent on maintaining the social order of daily life. And with that precarious daily life, the subjects of colonial and capitalist rule lives in "systematic negation" of their humanity. But that work of violence is often implemented in a location, in a space, and that work of violence is often tied to property. Property is one of the primary ways to extract labour within a facility that concentrates and encloses populations, and it is one of the primary ways that people who have been turned into subjects and populations, who then have been turned into citizens of the city, become private property owners. Private property owners lay claims to the sites of the labour extraction but are also dismembered individuals from their fellow labourers and community members.

The methods in administering and managing governance by way of councils, boards, committees, and task forces usually apply the logics of a noted thinker in antiquity or of the contemporary period. With the backing of that noted thinker, those governing bodies must make those methods and logics manifest somewhere, in a space or on a plot of land: Filippo Brunelleschi, with the vision to bring the prominence of a structural Renaissance financed by the ruling elites of Florence of 1402–1461; Baron Georges-Eugène Haussmann, with the work of fortifying from revolting classes and the remaking of Paris from 1853 to 1870; Daniel Burnham, with the designed reconstruction of a city to create model citizenry in Chicago from 1893 to 1913; Adolf Loos, with the notions of educating the masses of people with architecture under the philosophy of cultural superiority in Vienna and Prague from 1899 to 1932; Le Corbusier, with the founding of modern architecture on behalf of assisting State functionality

in Paris (and later Geneva and Chandigarh), most notably from 1922 to 1940, and in a range of cities thereafter; Harland Bartholomew, who most prominently developed slum clearance and reconcentration in St. Louis and Louisville from 1911 to 1962; Robert Moses' utter domination of the landscape, neighbourhoods, and direction of New York City from 1924 to 1968; and Philip Johnson's use of a range of styles that seductively drew people into the fabricated Society, most notably in the East Coast of the United States from 1949 to 1979.

As the *Laws of the Indies* articulated, those responsible for such tasks "shall hurry in their labor and building so that the town may be completed in a short time" (Mundigo & Crouch, 1977, p. 257). There is something vitally important in not just getting ideas on the map, articulated in the text of a plan, or even passed as a law, but also having those ideas, articulations, and laws structurally erected, existing in space, and made into reality. This imprint on space is necessary for the State to begin, continue, and have any chance at becoming "eternal" in the minds of the populace. The fabricated society depends on a space in order for it to do its part in creating and maintaining the collective imaginations of citizens – "World's Highest Standard of Living" in the midst of disaster on top of squalor and residential segregation (see Fig. 4.1). The space and the cities, the neighbourhoods and the communities, and the buildings and fortifications within those cities give the State credibility and legitimacy in its reign. And the work of these noted planners, designers, and architects have been, and still remain, key to how cities are conceived and how cities function.

But this rulership and governance is not fixed from a one-time use of force onto its populace to secure the colonial territory in antiquity or to slum-clear the neighbourhood in the contemporary era. State power must constantly re-ascribe itself over and over and over and over and over and over... forever. Sovereignty may be awesome and awe-inspiring to those who do not wield it, but it is a tenuously constant position to maintain with drastic actions that must be instituted over the State's populace and against that State's rival States. Because sovereignty is not fixed, it is also a tactic that must engage in drastic actions over that which it governs:

space, people, and things. The populace of a State knows its spatial boundaries all too well due to the harsh beatings that come from crossing those boundaries that leads to misery and horror of lost loved ones or more pleasantly from the allure of property ownership that encourages defence of those boundaries that secure their individual property when they mark their ownership holding a sign that reads "sold". While the populace knows its space and place, the State has no true spatial demarcation. It goes where the resources are, where the extraction is favourable, and where the next population to conquer (or re-conquer out of forgetfulness that it has already conquered them before) lives. The State goes where it needs to, allowing itself to grow so that it can avoid attrition and decay.

Territorial jurisdiction is the stuff for our minds, the populace's fantasies and concerns – the country and its countryside, the nation and its borders, and the city and its limits. Domestic affairs and international affairs are just the everyday affairs in extraction and dispossession anywhere, everywhere, and nowhere. The site and space for this extraction and dispossession are respectively Lefebvre's *le terroir et le terroire* (soil and territory). For "land-as-soil" is the conception of space that enables extraction for the purposes of the accumulation of wealth, and "land-as-territory" is the conception of space that presents the imagined notion of territory, boundary, and demarcation (Lefebvre, 1991, p. 242). Above all other forms and intents of political manipulation, statecraft most especially conjures forth *l'espace étatique* (state space) as the very notion of space as a false reality. What is made in that space is the fiction written within it: the country and its countryside, the nation and its borders, and the city and its limits.

The *politique de l'espace* (spatial policy), crafted by various State institutions, are the principal ways that State power can be leveraged and mobilised in order to consolidate the governance of an approved regime. But it is within a regional boundary, a territorial area, and a city limit that those State institutions can confidently manage any populace. In these borders, State institutions can erect and maintain "large scale, long-term productive capacities" (Brenner & Elden, 2009, p. 369). Monuments to the State (stadia, housing developments, skyscrapers, highways, and bridges) are

the ways that the populace fantasises the State in their mind. The fantasies stoke the flames of nationalistic fervour, in support of the present State or the creation of the idealised State, but both conceptions fixate on and are fixed to the territoriality of the State: "*For theLove of God and Country*", "*Dues, Patria, e Familia* / 'God, Nation, and Country'", "*Éirinn go Brách* / 'Ireland Forever'", "*The Sun Never Sets On The British Empire*", "*Heim ins Reich* / 'Back Home into the Reich'", "*Proud American*", "*Blut und Bodern* / 'Blood and Soil'", "*Ein Volk, eih Reich, ein Führer* / 'One People, One Empire, One Leader'", "*Hakkō ichiu* / 'Eight Corners of the World Under One Roof'", "*Kosovo je Srbija* / 'Kosovo is Serbia'", "*Glory to Ukraine! Glory to Heroes!*", "*Patria o Muerte* / 'Homeland or Death'", "*Naya Pakistan/* 'New Pakistan'", "*With you, For you, For Singapore*", "*Make America Great Again*", "*Remember the Alamo!*", "*Don't Mess With Texas*", and "*Tutto Nello Stato, Niente Al Di Fuori Dello Stato, Nulla Contro Lo Stato* / 'Everything in the State, Nothing Outside the State, Nothing Against the State'".

This is especially troubling when slogans, phrases, and campaigns are "political pieties about overpopulation" that court anxieties with policies for forced male sterilisation and female infanticide that also grow the practise of postcolonial femicide in the national public sphere with nationalist slogans of "*Chhota Parvivaar Sukgi Parivaar* / "A Small Family is a Happy Family'" in India (Bhatnagar et al., 2005, p. 14). Boundaries (borders, walls, lines, fences, and checkpoints) are the immeasurably important infrastructures the State uses to impart harsh realities onto its populace. Boundary making aids in the containment of a populace by creating citizenship that is associated with the space within the demarcated region, that then invokes a collective imagination of a false shared interest against those beyond that demarcation. Boundary making creates,

> Territory [that] is always being produced and reproduced by the actions of the state and through political struggles over the latter; yet at the same time, in the modern world, territory also conditions state operations and ongoing efforts to contest them. States make their own territories, not under circumstances they have

chosen, but under the given and inherited circumstances with which they are confronted. (Brenner & Elden, 2009, p. 367)

## 4.1 Traps of Territory, Traps of Structure

The tenuous existence of the State makes boundary making a necessary endeavour as opposed to a useful option. The State then territorialises, deterritorialises, and reterritorialises over and over and over and over and over...forever. It must locate, remove, and occupy space to make itself known and to make itself be. Territorialisation must dispossess those who are present through force (the hard power of warfare, police actions, coercion), inertia (the socio-spatial power of spread and sprawl in and of cities, patterns and modes of mobility), or co-optation (the soft power of religion, social life, and lawfare). The settlement becomes the town, that becomes the city. At the locus of the city, the State deterritorialises indigenous and independent-constructed settlements of people to remind the populace of its might and to maintain stability (its own fragile stability as the sole stabilising force). Populations are redistributed within the city limits as needed for its production of material that generates the necessary wealth that subsidises the entire operation. Populations can be shuffled, reshuffled, and even pushed into another city limit based on the needs of the city to manage its affairs for the sake of the everyday affairs of the State. And lastly, the State reterritorialises when new lands are engulfed into its schemes and stratagem and when old States succumb to their own early decay, leaving space, people, and things left for remaining States to quarrel or come to terms over. Boundary making is,

> The production of a space, the national territory, a physical space, mapped, modified, transformed by the networks, circuits and flows that are established within it—roads, canals, railroads, commercial and financial circuits, motorways and air routes, etc. Thus, this space is a material – natural – space in which the actions of human generations, of classes and of political forces have left their mark, as producers of durable objects and realities (rather than only of isolated things and products, of tools and of

goods destined for consumption). (Lefebvre, 2009, p. 224)

Agnew (1994) critiqued the geographic assumptions that are intellectually conceived by scholars as a "territorial trap". This trap holds steady that the State has sovereignty over a jurisdiction and that jurisdiction comprises the "real" function of the social, political, and economic activities of that State. Scholarship falls within the trap when it utters the phrase "international relations", "bordering nations", and "countries with ties" as if the State truly functions within geographic boundaries – as if when we travel to those locations in real life, set foot or wheel on the ground that somehow a nation, a country is visible. While the trap can be an intellectual exercise that prevents a clearer analysis, the "territorial trap" is the intended trap for us as a populace to fall within. The territory is where the realities of being a subject, being subjected, and being subjugated all take place. Our ideas and identities are intertwined with the spaces that we have been placed in and restricted to. The **identification of populations** is a large-scale operation to segmentise the population for a class, caste, Race, or ethnic group depending upon the most effective mode of extraction and dispossession that needs to take place within any given territory and against any given territory. Race, in particular, is organised through territorialisation, deterritorialisation, and reterritorialisation within the boundaries that a State creates. Race restricts movement on the street, quarantines within the block, marginalises the neighbourhood, and aids in controlling the city.

The populations that are then placed into systems of **identification of threats** are both a way to marshal State forces to control and subdue the "Othered" population, but to also rally support from the remaining populace, who see support of controlling the "Othered" is the foremost way to avoid being "Othered". An identity that is ascribed onto me of African American invokes both a necessary citizenship affiliation to an illusion of country/region, a *tierra natal*, and a linkage to a continent that has no power in its formation and formal arrangement as a continent. The identity can give me a sense of personal pride with little to be prideful about but the vestiges of stories and experiences of social life (family get togethers, artistic creation, T-shirts, and personal exploits of persons of note – "I went to the Motherland"). No access to governance over the affairs of those experiences is given due to the limits of that social identity, and no political identity. No resources are mustered and managed to offer alternative socio-economic conditions than the ones that I experience where I reside. State-sanctioned violence, the reign of capitalism, and the colonial mentality would still be my reality in the "Motherland". And even if I counter the labelling of African American with that of Jamaican due to a lineage in my father's family, very little is still gained. This would just be an association with another land of dispossessed people being extracted in some similar and some different ways, in this case with an independent nation that has still chosen to function within the Commonwealth of an old Crown that once colonised it. An assumed identity of African American may attract particular discrimination to a (socio-politically) confined mobility while Jamaican may tempt me to embrace particular exertions to a (politico-economically) prevented full independence. I can be a colonised subject in the State that I was born within, or I can be a coloniser in a State that is struggling to wrestle itself from post-colonial realities, but both identities serve as extensions of the "territorial trap" of the geo-spatial arrangement of boundaries if the celebration of identity trumps the organising from my locus of identity, the place where my feet stand. The site of the city may be the locus of State power, but the site of the city (and by extension the nation) is not the State. The full State is never residing in one city; it is dispersed throughout a network of cities. And this network of cities is the true State, nation, or country.

The socio-politically constructive process of identification gets lost or is masked in our own social maintenance of identity. This is the spatiality, the lasting effect, of the production of space in the city. Where the identity of African "breaks form" and ignores the mental and spatial aspects of American (here, limited to meaning of the United States), the identity of African American re-engenders it to a border (United States) that is now cut off from the imagination (of Africa as a continental home of descent). The imagination of an African American community forecloses the political analysis that the neighbourhood functions like a South African *bantustán*, a territorialised residential area outside of the city of Pretoria that dispossess its population while extracting their labour. We fail to disentangle community (a group of shared interests) with a neighbourhood, as if where we reside in properties of ownership and control automatically links us. And much like those Black homelands of Apartheid South Africa, the myth of the self-rule of land within the bounded territory of another State may run so deep that the realities of the State's true rules can be forgotten. The identity of Jamaican re-asserts me within another border working toward similar ends, just with racially diverse actors of the Spanish conception of *patria* (State as fatherland, homeland), but both situate me within territories forged by blood and maintained through more of it.

But I argue here is that there is also a "structural trap", a trap that is also about geographical assumptions that are made. Society is that "structural trap" because society is an aberration, a fabrication. As it has been teased and mentioned before, society is a false reality made possible by the State. The history of the city, of cities, lies within the historical origins of the colonial city and the revision of the social and geo-spatial arrangements of the imperial city that both form the basis for the creation of Society. The newly fashioned or conceived city built upon "old tech" is the principal method for the articulation of State power. Thus, notions of the public park and plaza (social spaces) are situated as extensions of enclosures and not truly as the commons. At least under capitalism, as it was under feudalism, the shared ownership of the cultural and natural world was aspirational. Either the State or its fabricated society was (and would always be) in the way of any full actualised common ownership of resources, property, and land. The commons were (and is) a site of struggle and resistance. But until that struggle is embraced, the tragedy is less in the State power that seizes and extracts from space and more the tragedy of overuse by the commoners (Hardin, 1968; Ostrom, 1990). Aspects of tourism and events are used for organised congregation and displacement, and not as patterns of social travel and mobility. Disability and prowess are but practises of the right to maim or the right to adorn in the administration of affordances for health. Disability is intentionally situated here in connection to class, as the modification of the city and fabricated society are only accommodated by one's function as a labourer (American Disabilities Act workplace accommodation and improvements) or altered based on family income and wealth (for treatments, counselling, equipment upgrades).

So-called "natural" landscapes and public lands are spaces of dispossession and extraction, forces that bear upon space. Space, structurally, is the production of space for the explicit purpose of serving the forces that created it and for those who forcibly occupy it. *Rule by law*, rather than *rule of law*, is the instrument in which we can see the power of the State working to oppress. As an example, through the neighbourhood, the State can go after Black women (eviction). While through the streets, the State can go after Black men (policing). Race and gender are tools for subjugation, but where Race works ideally at the spatial level of territory, gender works most effectively at the spatial level of structure. Both can function at either level; however, it is within society that gender is made a cogent reality. How gender is spatially organised in society offers the State another division to manage the ownership and association with property and the accumulation of wealth through the extraction of resources. Here, too, is a view that sexual orientation is situated as an extension of gender by the State, in its expectation of roles and the enforcement of those roles when considering it in the broader schema of "Geographies of Threat" examination of the colonial and imperial city. In the European and United Kingdom world and throughout its history, women have had limited to no rights to property ownership, with the exception of the empowerment of widows to own the lands of their deceased husbands and to use that property to leverage further accumulations of wealth through the Magna Carta of 1215 (Scutt, 2016). But beyond this, even in this act of empowerment, women in the historic document and the historical period were never conceived of beyond their relationship with men, their ability to

produce a child, or their sexual status (with rare exceptions; Leyser, 1995).

This is theft of land set the stage for the series of Inclosure Acts over the span of centuries that reduced farmers into renters, that then became debtors, that then became conscripts of military forces to brutalise the racialised populations of the world (Shrubsole, 2019). These 5,200 acts from 1604 to 1914 established and formalised a new form of class dependent on the provision of labour for sufficiency on the State. But unlike Race being used to limit and restrict movement, gender limits and restricts both literal and broader notions of ownership and possession, for "[gendered] women still experience the city through a set of barriers – physical, social, economic, and symbolic – that shape their daily lives in ways that are deeply (although not only) gendered" (Kern, 2020, p. 5). The bodies of gendered women are both public and State property. The street, the hallway, the alley, and the stairwell are not the spaces for the right of gendered women's mobility, and "no amount of lighting is going to abolish the patriarchy" (Kern, 2020, p. 289). Boswell and Spade (1996) have suggested that sexual assault is supported not only by "a generic culture surrounding and promoting rape," but also by the characteristics of the "specific settings" in which gendered women and men interact (p. 133). Women are not in possession of themselves or their bodies in the movement. As James (2007) articulated, Black women and women of colour provide "the reproductive and productive labor to stabilize cultural and wealth" (p. 256). Society is the "structural trap" that situates property in relationship to other property and in relationship to a market value. Some property is superior or subordinate to another in its use and value; thus, the possession of it becomes of the utmost importance or grave concern whether through birth, inheritance, or acquisition. The need to control individual property on a plot of privatised "land" within the bounds of a city is the affair of State institutions (city zoning commissions, real estate developers, property owners, banks). This was the basis, in this opinion, for "the overthrow of mother right", the once understood authority of lineage of disposing of property by the mother (the right to inheritance) in European States of antiquity.

And this was what would become, through imperialism and colonialism, "the world historical defeat of the female sex...man took command in the home...woman was degraded and reduced to servitude...a mere instrument for the production of children" (Engels, 1972, pp. 120–121). But that antiquity makes its way to the present through the global domination that was colonialism and the ongoing domination of imperialism – as the Spanish Civil Code of 1889 governed the affairs of the former colony of the Philippines and remained a feature in the present-day Philippine Family Code and Muslim Personal Laws, pertaining to parental authority, social access, and property rights along gendered lines (Ezer et al., 2011). Or in Lima, Peru and the control of dissent led by women against the privatisation of public services, the closure of employment opportunities, and reinforcing class divisions managed by then-Mayor Andrade under the ten-year reign of the Fujimori regime (Gandolfo, 2009). In Lima, only the State has sovereignty of any form of transgression.

Our perceptions of structural gender and territorialised Race become naturally occurring aspects of the fabricated society, although their conceptions are both dependent upon the politico-economic classification system of labour (education, wages, income, and lifestyle). The State utilises city-splitting techniques in order to create distance, separation, instability, and the lack of cohesion for organising within/on properties (structures – gender) and between/across neighbourhoods (territories - Race). The rule by law violently dictates the mobility of the racial "Other", and the rule by law violently socialises the mobility of the gendered "Other".

Worldwide, the year 2020 gave us a window into the ways that the State invokes the work of violence onto a populace for social control, and that same populace responded with articulation of Clover's (2016) ordering of the riot, the blockade, the barricade, the occupation, and the commune that defy the intent of preventing independent cohesion. The only cohesion is State manufactured or permissible cohesion. This cohesion is an "abstract homogeneity" that is tied to city pride, home teams, school spirit, country loving, and cosmopolitanism. But there "is not [a real] homogeneous [society]; it simply has homogeneity as its goal, its sense, its

'objective'... in itself it is multiform" (Lefebvre, 1991, p. 287). The city is the site for the State to create society, the only social life that is allowable through State approval. Gentrification in vagueness of a titled phenomenon is a mask for urban renewal that works as a form of spatial eugenics, and "can't detach the social world from the built environment" (Kern, 2020, p. 288). Gentrification is a designed and planned phenomenon, not a happenstance occurrence from seemingly independent shifts in population. As if 5,000 college students, hipsters, or managerial class members convened and decided to move into the inner city. As if 15,000 nurses' aides, mechanics, or warehouse inventory crew members convened and decided to move out to the suburbs. And especially in terms of class, gender, and Race, we fail to note the fears of "crime" are often most articulated by White women and other members of the managerial class who aid the city's plans to redevelop through dispossession. And we fail to note that the impact of the responses or solutions of those fears of "crime" are most felt by the numbers of Black and Brown men held in the dead cities of prisons and the Black and Brown women held in stasis in abandoned neighbourhoods that will eventually be gentrified.

Thus, social life in public space is of the making of the State, despite our (mis)perceptions of independence and freedom. So, in pursuing an emancipatory direction in an understanding of space, it is of the utmost importance to adopt a moral and political imagination of what we conceive of as public space and the social life that occurs in it. But while the city is the site for State power to function, the State itself is a site that operates for "contested processes, projects, and strategies" as it is also "a social relation that is produced and transformed through continual struggle" (Brenner & Elden, 2009, p. 364). Where the city is the site and means for the "territorial trap" to ensnare us, and the State is the site and ways that the "structural trap" hides from us its intent, both structures fabricate notions of a nation and society that obscures our perception of reality. As Kern (2020) noted about "female fear",

> Surveys on the fear of crime and fear of violence were popular with social scientists in the 1980s

and 1990s for gathering data about where, when, and with whom women experience fear. Study after study produced the similar patterns: women identified cities, night-time, and strangers as primary sources of threat. […] By this time, enough data had been gathered on domestic violence and crimes against women in general for social scientists to know that women are much more likely to experience violence at the hands of people known to them, in private spaces such as home and workplaces. Men were more likely to be victims of (reported) crimes in public spaces…of course these studies didn't ask if people felt safe in their homes. (p. 145)

And while there were some gendered assumptions in the line of questions or focus of the studies, little has been considered "intersectionally". For certain gendered and racialised women, this paradox is a reality (both the fear and actual), but for others being disappeared from and murdered in your home in the city, a city like Los Angeles, is quite real and quite confirmed. As of drafting this chapter, there has yet to be any published extensive academic articulation of the long career of the Grim Sleeper Killer of Los Angeles, Lonnie Frankin, Jr., who operated in South Central for nearly 20 years and killed more than 25 women in their homes (arrested and charged for 10 in 2010) (Pelisek, 2017; Zupello, 2016). The rape and murder of Black women just does not matter (Mowatt, 2018). Or it matters when we are directed in a way to consider it as a point to matter. Our national perception of the Montgomery Bus Boycott of 1955 is associated with the tiredness of one woman, Rosa Parks, who refused to give up her seat – not the work of Rosa Parks and other members of The Committee for Equal Justice for Mrs. Recy Taylor of 1944, the Citizens Committee for Gertrude Perkins of 1949, and the Women's Political Council of 1954 for the sexual assault of Black women by the bus drivers and members of the police department that held and humiliated them at the end of a bus route (Buirski et al., 2017; McGuire, 2010; Tyner, 2012). Yes, Recy Taylor's name in recent times has been brought up in the public sphere at awards shows and social media platforms, but mainly to invoke the need to remember the name alongside the name of Parks.

Little to any change has occurred in the public memory of the city of Montgomery; Alabama's bus boycott was a boycott over the assault on Black women and not "tired feet". The rapist, sexual assaulter, and the serial killer are what Tyner (2012) labelled "urban redevelopers" in the ways that they alter the landscape of mobility that thereby forecloses opportunity. And by necessary extension, the disappearance, rape, and murder of indigenous women just does not register into our consciousness (Hargreaves, 2017). Or that the widespread rape of gendered girls and women in India just does not count in our understanding of mobilities in the fabricated society (Sharpe, 1993). Gender violence in the city is part of the mission of dispossession, as the "extreme fear serial killing generates" alongside other acts of intimate and physical terror that are expanded through film and other aspects of popular culture (Lewis, 2009). The city, in a disposable neighbourhood, that was filled with disposable people was where the Grim Sleeper was allowed to flourish by the State. Through the city, Race and gender are inextricably entangled to produce a persistent condition of violence – whether it is focusing on the survivor in life or the victim in death and the visceral nature of State and structural violence of their being, a corporeality, or it is focusing on the perpetrator, and more in particular, the laws that grant perpetration to flourish. Race and gender cannot be separated as their "violences" cannot. No *Law & Order SVU* is assigned a detail to the 'Hood, the Rez, or the barrio.

The places we work, the neighbourhood relations we have, the locations for education and religiosity, and the spaces we shop and play foster an "illusion of transparency" and authenticity in our experiences with the spectacle of the city. A Latin conception of *socios* (Society) is for us to engage in varying levels of bounded freedom and foster an embrace in ascribed and associated identities. This is the reason why it is so painstakingly fabricated for us. The bike trail is for us to become fit (as if there is no other place to do so), the park fountain is for us to take our wedding photos (like every single other couple), and the coffee shop is for us to be seen (since the creation of them in the 1800s). Model cities and Levittowns are built just to asway racial anxieties of "crime" and disease of the city and produce model citizens, bought off by Levitt and Sons designs, Department of Housing and Urban Development Manuals, and the desire for a "Cult of Domesticity" conforming to a gender order and affirming a 100% White racial order (see Fig. 4.2; Rothstein, 2017). The Latin conception of *natio* (Nation) is for us to hold allegiance to and defend as it grants rights and privileges, as it is in the "production of the nation by the State, dominating a territory" that governance of a State colonises lands and minds (Lefebvre, 1991, p. 281). This is the reason why it must be defended as opposed to the neighbourhoods of children and elders who merit our care. The flag standing in front of our homes is for us to not forget the territory where we reside (as if it changed overnight, every night), the strutting pride through Global entry when returning from international travel (and the expectation of it in another country, because…'*Merica*), and the every-four-year concern for the plight of democracy (in the voting booth).

Nationalism is for us to revel in and create "an imagined political community… [that is] imagined as both limited and sovereign" because we never know each other, much less care about each other, just the State that created it for us (Anderson, 1983, p. 6). Only the image of our false "communion" with each other is in our minds and then takes the form of strident nationalism that is enough for us to dispossess, restrict, and kill for through other conjured imaginations of political feelings given physical form as fences, walls, and barrages of bullets (Denvir, 2020). And that image is enough to satisfy through "backlash governance" instead of actual governance that addresses the schools, hospitals, and roads that have long been and are increasing their respective abandonments (Metzl, 2019). The *agora* (the Greek proto-public space, the collective space that was free of privatisation) has been subsumed into the *polis* (the Greek proto-public sphere, the physical and thought space that is heavily restricted, regulated, and selective) to the space of the public in the city yet under social rule of the fabricated society and the actual rule of the State (Habermas, 2001, p. xi).

The Nation and the idea of nationalism that comes with it, is a concept was born in an age in which Enlightenment and Revolution were destroying the legitimacy of the divinely-ordained, hierarchical dynastic realm… The

**Fig 4.2** An Aerial View of Levittown, Pennsylvania, Comprised of 72,000 People in 17,300 Homes Over 22 Square Miles. Built off the Premise of Social Equality (Same House, Equal Status). One of Seven Such Levittowns, 1947. (Public Domain)

gauge and emblem of this freedom is the sovereign state. (Anderson, 1983, p. 7)

Comradery and community are built upon this fiction that creates deep bonds that the populace is "willing to die for such limited imaginings" (Anderson, 1983, p. 6). Just like Society, the Nation is,

> the product, the child, of a space, the so-called national territory, the State turns back toward its own historical conditions and antecedents, and transforms them. Subsequently, the State engenders social relations in space; it reaches still further as it unfurls; it produces a support, its own space, which is itself complex. This space regulates and organizes a disintegrating national space at the heart of a consolidating worldwide space (*l'espace mondial*). (Lefebvre, 2009, p. 225, emphasis added by author)

And it is through,

> Nation states, attached to a territory, managers of this space, arbitrate and act as dominant power from and by…space. They manage it as eminent owners, almost in the way this word meant under the ancient regime, whereby the written rights and powers of the nobles and the king were superimposed upon the common rights of the peasants, "commoners", holders of perpetual usufruct. An analogous superimposition governs the modern State and its relationship to its space (territory). Methods (sometimes compelling and sometimes violent)…give concrete expression to this eminent right which we know extends itself to under the ground and to air space, forests and water sources, rivers and coasts, maritime territories and to recently extended territorial waters. (Lefebvre, 2009, p 275)

## 4.2 The Instrumental and Complicit Lawfare of Cities

Behind the veil that hides the State, the false transparency of State institutions, the ubiquity of cities, the hyper-visibility of Society, and the conjured notions of a Nation or country is the machinery of domination and the brutal savagery of primitive

accumulation. Capitalism and the imperialism that drives it (and the colonialism that grew it) requires organised mass dispossession and mass extraction. To occupy vast amounts of territory ushers in military resources that are sustained over a period of time in order to exert presence and land claim. To generate immeasurable sums of wealth necessitates legalised extraction of resources and of the labour of the dispossessed. The production of capital that is demanded of the State makes good use of Society and Nation to dispel the adverse realities of living as an underclass and working class while a ruling and elite class thrive. And the production of capital at the site of a city makes good use of the limits of the city as an enclosure to organise this process of exploitation. To turn the indigenous peoples of the world into forced or wage labourers in the lands of their indigeneity or to take those turned indigenous people elsewhere and place them in another location as a forced or wage labourer reveals the primary purpose of a State. "Slavery, colonialism, and forced labor, among other forms of violence, were not aberrations in the history of capitalism, but were at" the core of the history of the production of capital through the production of labor by way of the production of space (Beckert, 2015, p. 441). Production is the acquisition of the objects of nature within the limits of and by means of a certain social form that has been created by the State. Products of material production are in turn material goods that are given a value. But this production also calls forth a means of production that encourages productive consumption. The State and the city both centralise the site of production as a socio-politically produced space, because

> wealth, unduly centralized, endangers the efficient workings of the machinery of government. Land monopoly – in the hands of individuals, corporations or syndicates – is at bottom the prime cause of the inequalities which obtain; which desolate fertile acres turned over to vast ranches and into bonanza farms of a thousand acres, where not one family finds a habitation, where muscle and brain are supplanted by machinery, and the small farmer is swallowed up and turned into a tenant or slave. While in

large cities thousands upon thousands of human beings are crowded into narrow quarters where vice festers, where crime flourishes undeterred, and where death is the most welcome of all visitors. (Fortune, 1884, pp. iii–iv)

This emphasis on mass production within the production of space gives production a primacy above all other facets of social life. The need to extend this production evolves the primitive accumulation of capital into a modern capitalist mode of production. The Crown (various Crowns of the Spanish, French, and British empires) grew dependent on the accumulation of wealth that was extracted from mass exploitation of labour. The Crown had to evolve into the State by the revolting interests of nobility or elite aspiring lower classes. But this need to extend this production also requires an evolution of violence to protect the interest of the extracting and dispossessing State. What brings about such violence? The State has grown dependent on this accumulation of capital. If capital is threatened, the State serves to forcibly intervene to ensure that the wealth continues to flow. Capital needs the force of the State to protect it, and the State needs capital to continue to exist. This dependency creates a new mutual/shared conception of State that is more than the parts of elected representatives and bureaucratic actors in State institutions. The State envelopes the owners of large swaths of land and corporate engines that extract. Extraction at this point is for extraction's sake, as the accumulation from extraction and dispossession do not net the costs. This shared rulership,

> presents itself as the result of a victorious struggle both against seigniorial power, with its revolting prerogatives, and against the regime of the guilds, with the fetters it placed on the free development of production and the free exploitation of man by man. But the knights of industry only supplanted the knights of the sword by exploiting events not of their own making. They have succeeded by means as vile as those that served the Roman freedman to become the master of his *patronus*. (Marx, 1976, p. 875)

The State brings forth "the accumulation of dispossession" for the sake of this process and

protection racket (Harvey, 2004a, p. 64). This extends (or appropriately over-extends),

> Marx's general theory of capital accumulation [which] is constructed under certain crucial initial assumptions which broadly match those of classical political economy and which exclude primitive accumulation processes... "Primitive" or "original" accumulation has already occurred and accumulation now proceeds as expanded reproduction (albeit through the exploitation of living labour in production) within a closed economy working under conditions of "peace, property and equality". [...] The disadvantage of these assumptions is that they relegate accumulation based upon predation, fraud, and violence to an "original stage" that is considered no longer relevant or...as being somehow "outside of" the capitalist system". (Harvey, 2004b, pp. 73–74)

Capital is merely the agent of capitalism while the State is the agent of modern imperialism. Lawfare and warfare are distinctly different methods of wielding violence and force in the processes of the State and in service of capital and resource extraction.

The deployment of lawfare uses the law and legal and legislative authority as a substitute for armed force of warfare (Kittrie, 2016). Warfare is too abrupt, too disrupting, and now too expansive when we consider the mechanisms and schemas that are required to impact and destroy,

> The lives and narratives of those imprisoned in the household or its formal detention centers: Immigration Customs Enforcement – the former Immigration and Naturalization Service – holding cells, psychiatric wards, jails, police precincts, maximum security, death row, closets, or basements, hiding places from domestic batterers or the predation of aggressively 'affectionate' adult kin. (James, 2007, p. 5).

The household becomes (and always has been) the most crucial site for the rupture of violence to take effect on the individuals of the populace, particularly women (re: the legal protections around mass forced evictions and the legal abandonment of protection in commonality of domestic violence; Brickell, 2020). For queer communities, as an extension of the gender (expected and resisted) roles, the "queer home can be a site of oppression, exploitation, and abuse" (Tyner, 2012, p. 57). Home, households, and housing become the principal political entity to violate targeted portions of the populace whether it is in the capital city of Phnom Penh in Cambodia, the state of Tamil Nadu and the city of Chennai in India, or New York City in the United States.

As warfare is an exceptionally costly endeavour to enact and to sustain, lawfare is conceived of as a cost-saving measure that increases the wealth generated by the accumulation of capital after the initial phase in the dispossession of a people has ended (the cost-cutting focus of the State of Michigan and city council of Flint, Michigan, during the Flint Water Crisis in 2014 after decades of neglect; see Fig. 4.3). Lawfare can then be returned to repeated trials and experiments in further extraction ("urban renewal" and slum clearance through the zoning laws and ordinances of various cities in the United States). Instrumental lawfare uses the power of courts and armies of lawyers in the same mode of military strategists and their armies in order to achieve the same results. Instrumental lawfare is not the rule of law, because at least that rule is guided by actual law, executive order, and legislation that was created to govern and is then construed into domination. Instrumental lawfare is more the manipulation of law, the circumventing of law through legal means in order to dominate and extricate (The *Laws of the Indies* that was used to guide city planning throughout the 1500s but also to extermine indigenous populations; the Indian Removal Act of 1830 that would "resettle" indigenous populations after most had been exterminated; the 1910 Racial Restrictive Covenants in Baltimore and Minneapolis, Minnesota, that supposedly addressed public health concerns but actually dispossessed populations of their homes and social mobility; the 1947 Bartholomew Plan of St. Louis that beautified the city by devastating a Black neighbourhood). What makes lawfare unique in the United States is that it is,

hard for U.S. Society – with its relatively shared values, vibrant democratic institutions, and

**Fig 4.3** The Flint River in Flint, Michigan, USA, in the Late 1970s During a U.S. Army Corps of Engineers Flood Control Project. (Photo Credit: U.S. Army Corps of Engineers/Public Domain)

powerful law enforcement institutions – to agree on what laws were "given or predetermined" and thus should not be subject to instrumental tinkering or manipulation, either in their content or their enforcement. (Kittrie, 2016, p. 36)

As described in a reading of Kittrie (2016) through the lens of this book, the compliance-leverage disparity in lawfare then employs techniques and tactics to dominate law-abiding support and opposition. Lawfare in this regard calls for and provides restraint and legal strategy to armed forces and law enforcement agents (no total war of Sherman's 1864 march and decimation of Atlanta, Georgia, during the U.S. Civil War; the police and military pullback during the Los Angeles Riot turned Rebellion in 1991 and Tottenham Riot of 2011 in London, U.K.). "Strategic incapacitation" is a legally developed procedure turned technique by law enforcement when engaging the riot. In order to restore a modicum of order in the short-term of a protest, strike, or riot, the suppression of civil liberties is allowable (Noakes et al., 2005; Gillham & Noakes, 2007). As a counter to the lawsuits filed by protestors in the 1970s due to the rapid escalation of force during most protests and demonstrations of the era, law enforcement began to use

(and are still using) techniques that include "the establishment of extensive no-protest zones, the increased use of less-lethal weapons, the strategic use of arrests, and a reinvigoration of surveillance and infiltration of movement organizations" (Gillham & Noakes, 2007, p. 343; see Fig. 4.4). While strategic incapacitation does emphasise the importance of risk management (reducing injury to law enforcement) and does provide some legal protection to actions (lawsuit), the strategy can be considered an offensive that, if employed well, can control the riot as the psychology behind riots often points to protest increasing in fervour based on the action of law enforcement that is present (Oliver & Myers, 2003). The concerns of Constitutionality are lessened as "transgressive activists are not seen as legitimate by the mainstream media and public" in the broader fabricated society (Gillham & Noakes, 2007, p. 341). Lawfare additionally fosters a higher degree of complicity among the citizenry of the State to accept the actions of the State and its actors. Such as the Dakota Wars of 1862 and the mass hanging of 38 Sioux leaders in Mankato, Minnesota; Chinese immigrants during the Rock Springs Massacre in 1885 in Sweetwater County, Wyoming, see Figs. 4.5 and 4.6; the unrelentless bombing of Bagdad, Iraq during

Fig 4.4 The March of Millions on Sunday, December 8, in Kyiv, Ukraine, December 8, 2013. (Photo Credit: Ivan Bandura/Wiki Commons)

**Fig 4.5** Federal Troops on South Front Street in Rock Springs, Wyoming, September 1885. (The National Archives Photo/ Public Domain)

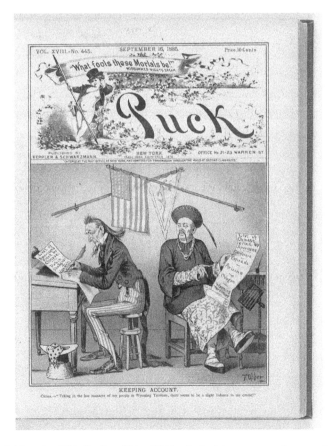

**Fig 4.6** Picture of Puck Magazine With Caption: China "Taking in the late massacre of my people in Wyoming Territory, there seems to be a slight balance to my credit!", 16 September 1885. (The Library of Congress/Public Domain)

Desert Storm, Desert Shield, and Operation Iraqi Freedom and beyond in 1991, 2001, and 2003. Additionally, lawfare in this respect exceptionally works against an opposition that would most astoundingly respond lawfully (Black Chicagoans during the Chicago Race Riot of 1919; the Black residents of the Greenwood District of Tulsa, Oklahoma, during the Tulsa Race Massacre in 1921; Kristallnacht or November Pogrom in various cities in Germany, Austria, and Sudetenland [parts of which are in modern-day Czech Republic]; the Hindus of Noakhali, Bengal [modern-day Bangladesh], in the Noakhali Riots of 1946; Armenians during the Sumgait Pogrom of 1988 in Azerbaijan; and Serbs during the March Pogrom of 2004 in Kosovo).

It should be clear that lawfare is the crowning achievement in Statecraft, to use legal methods, legal argumentation, and the use of law to accomplish military aims that are directed by the State. Governance and rule over processes of dispossession and extraction make force necessary. Extermination, submission, repulsion, repression, displacement, and even coercion require the use and potential use of force operators. Lawfare either is the enabling of force to be performed legally or the provision of alternative non-force methods. As a former U.S. Department of Defence Attorney, Kittrie (2016) articulated lawfare in benign ways in analysing U.S. engagement in conflicts in other States as well as in critical ways against terror-based groups, primarily in the Middle East. However, the knowledge of such a tool begs for its theoretical framework to be used to view the actions of the settler colony of the United States and other States to its own population as well as viewing the actions of States to expand their capital accumulating mission. The argument and proclamation for national security that justifies and rallies resources for international conflicts can be likened to the justification and rallying in "urban renewal", the "War on Drugs", and fighting against crime in cities. The ultimate aim of lawfare is to move farther away from kinetic warfare, the use of lethal force on an active battlefield, and more toward non-kinetic warfare, the use of legal, media, and psychological assaults.

The most concerning articulation and implementation of lawfare is the imposition of martial law that involves suspension of *habeas corpus* (the right to a hearing and trial for imprisonment), particularly in the city (Wallace & Kreisel, 2003). Internationally, numerous cases of martial law have been instituted on colonial subjects, imperial citizenry, and subjugated populaces of: British-controlled India in 1817 Cuttack, 1832 Palakonda, 1844 Savantwadi, and 1870 Calcutta; as well as British-controlled Ireland in the 1916 Easter Rebellion, particularly in Dublin, the 1919 Irish War of Independence, the 1922 Irish Civil War, and The Troubles of 1960s–1990s; Communist Poland imposition of martial law from December 1981 to July 1983, particularly in Warsaw; the 12-year U.S.-backed Uruguayan Dictatorship (1973–1985), in Montevideo most prominently; the detention and mass curfew of 2019 *Ley de Seguridad del Estado* within Santiago de Chile throughout *El Estallido Social* (The Social Outbreak); the enforcement actions by Israeli Defence Forces on Arab citizens in 1950s Jaffa, Lod, and Ramla; in Taiwan during the 38 years of martial law known as the White Terror that imprisoned more than 140,000 Taiwanese citizens, especially in Taipei, with conflicting accounts of nearly 5,000 having been executed by the Chinese Nationalist Party; and most infamously during the Black War from 1824 to 1832 in Australia, when legal immunity was extended to all White Australians for killing Aboriginal Australians, and remained in force for three years to clear space for the emerging and growing settlements, in addition to the 48-year martial law (1963–2011) in Syria by the Ba'ath Party. In the 68 times that it has been enacted at the local and federal level within the United States, the ungovernable racialised "Other" (in 1961, within the city of Montgomery by the Governor of Alabama against the "outside" agitation of civil rights activists and organisers, the Freedom Riders); the native "savage" (in 1862, just prior to the hanging of 38 Dakota men in Mankato); the racialised religious "Other" (in 1857, when the 15th President and Utah Governor called for the annihilation of Mormons in Salt Lake City and the rest of the State); and the strike labourer (in 1934, the Minneapolis General Strike after the police's killing of strikers during Bloody Friday) compose 47 of those 68 instances. The frequency and duration of martial law imposition, both in the United States and world-wide, display a "metastasisation" of martial law (Vidal, 2002): the uncritical unquestioning of the law, the garnering of public support through the obscuring of facts, and the nullification of the senses that overlook the morally wrong actions or irresponsibility of the State. While there are a host of examples that can be drawn into the discussion or that have been teased, such as the Flint Water Crisis of 2014 or the Grenfell Tower Blaze of London in 2017, in particular, the near meltdown of the nuclear power plant just outside of Detroit provides an example of the legal, media, and psychological assaults of early domestic lawfare and its lasting manipulation of perceptions in society.

### 4.3 The Violent Disposability of Cities

Power is a central concept in our understanding of society. As a concept, it occupies our social and cultural analysis of and between the peoples in a given society. For Foucault, power is "the name that one attributes to a complex strategical situation in a particular society; power is not an institution, and not a structure; neither is it a certain strength we are endowed with..." (Foucault, 1978a, p. 93). It is "omnipresent" for Foucault because it is continuously produced from everywhere. Power is intentionally exercised by the people, the State, and State actors in a variety of ways between, to, and within each facet of a society, and it is not solely held within any. Through this exercise, power creates apparatuses of knowledge that inform what to make of the world through the practise of social construction as a social activity. Human knowledge is inexplicably interlocked with power, for "there is no power relation without the correlative constitution of a field of knowledge, nor any knowledge that does not presuppose and constitute at the same time power relations" (Foucault, 1991a, p. 27). Meaning making is constructed through the interactions of the people, the State, and State actors as they engage in

the exercise of power. The point of analysis for scholars to explain what is occurring in society is the site where power produces an effect, an impact, or a change. But power as a function and not a concept guides our critique of the role that it plays upon a people through a State regime and its representative, as well as the manner that a people respond and react to that State regime and its representatives (Gibson, 2007). The point of analysis for scholars in examining the functionary role of power is how it is cultivated and wielded, in particular and germane to this essay related to nuclear power, a power that is conceptual, functional, and symbolic.

The State, for Gramsci, is "the entire complex of practical and theoretical activities with which the ruling class not only justifies and maintains its dominance but manages to win the active consent of those over whom it rules" (Carnoy, 1986, p. 65). Dominance is power as a function, but for Gramsci, dominance can solely be enacted by the State and its functionaries (political authorities like legislative officials; political representatives like bureaucratic executives; political subordinates like the legion of officers, staffers, and aides; and, at nuclear energy production plants, engineers and technicians). Further, hegemony is a cultivated form of dominance of both political and military might over its populace that impacts and controls society. While Foucault rejects concentrating power within the State, he still does not negate the influence the State has, because "nothing in society will be changed if the mechanisms of power that function outside, below and alongside the State apparatuses, on a much more minute and everyday level are not also changed" (Foucault, 1978b, p. 60). And one principal practise of the State apparatus is the creation of laws and the civil institutions that comprise society (industry, education, health care, religion, and media). As we make note of Foucault, "if we speak of the power of laws, institutions, and ideologies, if we speak of structures or mechanisms of power, it is only insofar as we suppose that certain persons exercise power over others. The term 'power' designates relationships between 'partners'" (Foucault, 2000, p. 337). The State apparatus in this practise intentionally creates the classes and categorisations of its populace to maintain its role of dominance. For Gramsci, "they operate without sanctions or compulsory obligations but still exerts a collective pressure…and obtains objective results in the evolution of customs, ways of thinking, morality etc." (Gramsci, 1980, p. 242). The State is an undeniable apparatus for knowledge production. Whether as a concept or a function, power is productive and reproductive in its hegemonic ability to govern and structure. And in this Gramscian productive and reproductive role, power is also an ideology, establishing both a system of belief and a relational force that can impact the manner in which people think and move. Power can be cultivated as a symbol by a State regime to influence the ideas and ideals of its citizenry, and power can literally be harnessed as an energy source to engage the very function of a society (and in turn, broaden or enliven the symbol of power even further).

It is in this symbolic power (not power as a concept or function) that the State can influence its populace via consent. Ideology informs and educates the populace because dominance has been obtained by consent through cultural texts, stories, and images that are made. Gramsci's notion of power as ideology is further expanded upon by Stuart Hall (1997). Hall's articulation of culture is not something to remain in the realm of study or to be enamoured, but as a critically crucial site for social action and for intervention. This intervention is informed by such an intellectual critique because it is the site where the populace is then fashioned into consensual citizens, negotiated actors, or agents of resistance and subversion (Hall, 1993; Proctor, 2004). Where hegemony controls its populace via physical exertion, it also controls through cultural domination. This cultural domination presents the position of the wealthy that embeds itself in society in such a way that the State uses or partners with this class to legitimise and extend its dominance. Where there is disagreement between Gramsci and Foucault, in that Foucauldian understanding of power is "productive as well as coercive, situational as well as pervasive", and for Gramsci, power functions as both educative and formative, both see the State apparatus as a site of power exertion and power articulation (McCoy, 2009, p. 71). But while

the State exerts and articulates itself onto the populace, the populace either consents to be coerced and go along with what has been dictated or engages in agency and decides for itself what it will do in response. In particular, Foucault saw media as one of the avenues for cultural forms of power to be broadcasted and projected onto a society on a susceptible populace. Knowledge is then contingent and contextual to a specific moment of time. This specific moment of time, a history, has then a corresponding *épistémè* that is "something like a worldview, a slice of history common to all branches of knowledge, which imposes on each one [branch of knowledge] the same norms and postulates, a general stage of reason, a certain structure of thought" that cannot be escaped by all, but in particular those within the "business" of knowledge production (Foucault, 1972, p. 191). Those within and from the halls of knowledge production influence the way society thinks and either assists in enabling or limiting the way the rest of society will function (often on behalf of the State). Books, articles, reports, and other documents are artifacts of the épistémè that can be analysed to identify the effects of society's power relationship.

Hall reconciled Foucault's lack of full acknowledgement of the State and critiqued Gramsci's overriding role of ideology: "the moment of power is not in ideology or culture as an instance. The moment of power is in the historically situated intervention of ideology in practices of signification" that are in media and discourse ("what is said and what is done"; Hall, 1997, pp. 30–31). And with this, Hall identified these moments as Gramscian conjunctures, moments when history and culture shift gears in response to clear contradictions in differences in ideology in society, and the most pressing moment for intellectuals to take notice and to question. Because culture "is now as integral to how these societies work, how the global society works, as the economic itself" (Hall & Schwarz, 2007, p. 156). Culture, by way of the cultural industries of media and discourse, plays a crucial social, political, and economic role in the production of ideas. The exercise of power, both social and cultural power, must use discourse to do so since the use of might is typically held within the realms of the military and law. The production of "ideas, cultures and histories cannot be understood or studied without their force or more precisely their configurations of power, also being studied" (Said, 1978, p. 12). Power is configured in these moments or conjunctures. But the West did not just define the East, but also itself through cultural products and associations as well as the manner it wields its might. Hall sees the West and East as fabricated notions of "Othering" instead of any geographical fact, and it enables a greater reach for the influence of dominant ideas throughout the world in every society (Hall, 1993). There is no irony that the Atomic age commenced as a conjuncture with the bombing devastation of Japanese imperial cities, Hiroshima and Nagasaki, and their populace. With that act of violence, it became known worldwide that "Nuclear energy was conceived in secrecy, born in war, and first revealed to the world in horror. No matter how much proponents try to separate the peaceful from the weapons atom, the connection is firmly embedded in the minds of the public" (Smith, 1988, p. 62). The bombing of those non-White imperial cities of a known military enemy of the State articulated an ideological power to the world that was immediately conceptual (as the "ultimate weapon"), functional (physical production of the bomb), and symbolic (the potential and actual devastation that could be unleashed).

Language in the artifacts of épistémè, as identified by Foucault, are evidence of support or subversion of the hegemonic ideal that dictates the conditions in a society. But "the conditions of existence [are] cultural, political and economic. All three things had to be articulated to make sense of any situation, event or conjuncture" (Hall & Schwarz, 2007, p. 56) Alongside this language, or making use of this language, is the media and, more specifically, the press. As Gramsci (1996) opined,

> the press is the most dynamic part of the ideological structure but not the only one. Everything that directly or indirectly influences or could influence public opinion belongs to it: libraries, schools, associations and clubs of various kinds, even architecture, the layout of streets and their names. (p. 53)

The State receives its power in its association of "'person, places, and activities' which take place across and between specific local sites and in interaction with particular global settings" (McCarthy & Dimitriadis, 2000, p. 171). The condition of violence, the conditioning of the populace to be victimised by violence, and the belief that certain populations must experience violence more than others makes it possible for schools in particular to be violent for students of colour and queer students. In these spaces, the survivor in life or the victim in death is part of the rationale for the violence, if not the main culprit for what was reaped. In conceding, we give the State its control of "person, place, and activities". For the nuclear power plant is the new factory that a new hegemony (or an evolved old one) has now been borne within, and places like Detroit (or near it) were ideal (see Fig. 4.7). So, power, as a conception and function, can be derived from this new condition of existence, the living with the bomb and the capacity to "harness its energy." Power instigates the conjunctures, as much as power is a product of the conjuncture.

Power as a function, as a source of energy related to nuclear power (the response to), has had several conjunctures. "Our power is the perception of our power" said *Mikhail Gorbachev, as played by David Dencik* in the fictionalisation of the Chernobyl Disaster, HBO's *Chernobyl* (Mazin & Renck, 2019). Nuclear power represents that symbolic power far more than it actually (safely) powers through energy. Nuclear power simultaneously showcases the cultivated intelligence, the economic ability, the social responsibility, and the military might of a State to its citizenry, its enemies, and the world at large (Patterson, 1983). To engage in nuclear energy conversion into nuclear power, at all costs, is to indulge in these areas as a full player at the table of a new type of civilisation in the mind of the State. But the conversion of nuclear energy is one of three things: it is nuclear weaponry, nuclear power production, or nuclear waste containment in our conceptual map of meaning making that has been cultivated in media discourse and public opinion of what the nuclear is to a populace (Gamson & Modigliani, 1989). But public opinion is often a response, in support or subversion, to the discourse in media and its cultural texts like televised news coverage, journalistic reporting, and popular culture

**Fig 4.7** Enrico Fermi Atomic Plant in Monroe, Michigan Located at Lagoona Beach on Lake Erie (35 Miles From Detroit). c. 1967. (The U.S. Army Corps of Engineers/Public Domain)

forms of entertainment. Media discourse and public opinion alert us of certain conjunctures, and another conjuncture that is germane to nuclear power was the partial meltdown at Three Mile Island, near Middletown, Pennsylvania, on March 28, 1979. Unlike the atomic bombing of Japan or the hydrogen bombing of some remote Pacific island or western desert, Three Mile Island served as a conjuncture through a dualistic discourse to contrast the potentiality of destruction and the possibility of endless energy production.

A combination of structural failures (secondary system and primary systems valves not closing) and human error (lack of recognition of nuclear reactor coolant due to the structural failure) resulted in the release of radioactive gas and iodine into the environment. The clean-up of the surrounding area took nearly 14 years (from August 1979 to December 1993; Walker, 2004). Nuclear power, or at least the threat of the risk was firmly on the "American" mind. And while the U.S. Government Accountability Office reported more than 150 incidents from 2001 to 2006 (Sovacool, 2009), the partial meltdown in 1966 in Detroit did not greatly impact nor linger in the "American" mind. Detroit has been and still is the largest majority Black city in America, with 80% of the population, and 10%

Latinx, and only 10% White (U.S. Census Bureau, 1970). Detroit is a the city that in contemporary times people have predicted will be vacant in 2040 based on Census trends that estimate that 1 person leaves the city every 22 minutes (Chaison, 2014). Detroit is also the city that people have written and speculated, "would the last person out of Detroit turn out the lights?" (Gurney, 2012). So, why wasn't the partial meltdown at Fermi 1 that was only 30 miles from Detroit, Michigan, and 27 miles to Toledo, Ohio, not a conjuncture?

Maybe it is due to the polemics in discourse. Fuller's (1975) important book, *We Almost Lost Detroit,* momentarily reignited attention on the partial meltdown nearly ten years later in 1975, challenging the épistémè that was growing around support for nuclear power. A year later, Kikuchi of the nearby University of Michigan published "We Didn't Almost Lose Detroit," a rebuttal to Fuller's calculations of 133,000 deaths in the Detroit area following a Class 1 emergency, indicating that it was a discrepancy of 133,000 vs. 23 deaths (Kikuchi, 1976). More officially, the Detroit Edison Company (now DTE Electric Company) operated Fermi 1 and published its own 1976 response to Fuller, *We Did Not Almost Lose Detroit* (Detroit Edison & Page, 1976). Detroit Edison criticised Fuller for being a nuclear critic and the book for not being technically sound, and because the "treatment of much the source information is distorted such that the average reader without technical background could easily be misled to agree with the anti-nuclear stance of the author", as explained in the abstract (Detroit Edison & Page, 1976, p. 2). Detroit Edition accused Fuller of setting "a mood of impending disaster [that] is created by the simple use of well-chosen modifiers and phrases sprinkled throughout the book" (Detroit Edison & Page, 1976, p. 2). Then, in 1977, on their album *Bridges,* Gil Scott-Heron and Brian Jackson (Gil's ninth album and the duos fifth album) featured the track, "We Almost Lost Detroit" (Scott-Heron & Jackson, 1977). Gil proclaimed over Brian's keys,

"Just thirty miles from Detroit...
It ticks each night as the city sleeps
Seconds from annihilation
But no one stopped to think about the people..."

Detroit was disposable because it had been planned to be abandoned. And Detroit was (and still is) an ideal location to experiment with such a dangerous energy source because of its planned abandonment – an abandonment that only opens up possibilities in the present day to new adventurous property reclaimers that have been officially recognised by new formal local policies rather than the old formal local policies designated residents of colour (Herbert, 2021). Detroit was out of the national, "imagined community" line of sight, unlike Chicago, Dallas, Los Angeles, New York, and Washington D.C., which never would have been considered locations for a plant. But Detroit was also not Niagara Falls, New York, the now-obscure Love Canal neighbourhood area and toxic waste disaster where homes were built upon and near buried dioxin and other chemicals (Blum, 2008). And Detroit was not Afton, North Carolina in Warren County, where a decade of toxic dumping along the road had poisoned thousands of people through ground water and soil contamination (Bullard, 1983). What distinguished Detroit from these two locations was that Detroit was a known "slum" in the eyes of the State.

As Mike Davis (2006) in *Planet of the Slums* cautioned,

Urban segregation is not a frozen status quo, but rather a ceaseless social war in which the state intervenes regularly in the name of "progress," "beautification" and even "social justice for the poor" to redraw spatial boundaries to the advantage of landowners, foreign investors, elite home-owners, and middle-class commuter. (p. 98)

The labour to resist may only assist the value in being disposable, as those who engaged in rebellions in 1967 and 1968, as well as the Race riots of 1863, 1943, and 1975, discovered (Fine, 2007; Schneider, 1980; Sugrue, 1996). As Hall astutely noted, "Race and crime were [and are] at the very centre of what" any political regime that becomes the leader of the State operates "on to try to roll back [any] social democratic feelings" of any conjuncture in history that has begun to lean in that direction (Hall & Schwarz, 2007, p. 148). The people of the State-fabricated society had little choice but to embrace racialised narratives, support the racial lawfare, and even become volunteers or vigilantes for its cause (see Fig. 4.8). The State has primacy on our conception of reality by the infrastructure it regulates and in turn regulates us (see Fig. 4.9). The forces of the State are overwhelming because the State always intends to overwhelm and nothing else. Hall once again reminded us that,

culture is now as integral to how these societies work, how the global society works, as the economic itself. All economics these days are cultural, as all culture is economic. In that sense, I am not talking about having a politics, and then being interested in the cinema, I'm talking about a redefinition of the political itself, an expansion of the notion of the political to include the cultural. (Hall & Schwarz, 2007, p. 156)

Detroit, the city, is not essential, not the populace at least. Detroit has been hollowed to serve a purpose, but the purpose of that husk does not equate with value of importance. Interestingly, Three Mile Island near Middletown, Pennsylvania; Chernobyl near Prypiat, Ukraine; and Fukushima

**Fig 4.8** Sign With American Flag "We want White tenants in our white community", Directly Opposite the Sojourner Truth Homes, a New U.S. Federal Housing Project in Detroit, Michigan. A Riot Was Caused by White Neighbours' Attempts to Prevent "Negro" Tenants From Moving in, February 1942. (the Library of Congress/Public Domain)

**Fig 4.9** The Detroit Wall, a Concrete Wall, One Half Mile Long, Detroit, Michigan. This Wall Was Erected in August 1941 to Separate the "Negro" Section From a New Suburban Housing Development for Whites. It Should Be Noted the Wall Was Built a Year Before the Sign in Fig. 4.8. (The Library of Congress/Public Domain)

Daiichi near Ōkuma of the Fukushima Prefecture were labour towns. They either were created specifically for servicing the nuclear plant (in the case of Prypiat, in then Soviet-controlled Ukraine and Belarus) or were company towns for other energy-producing or energy-using industries (Middletown and Ōkuma) (Alexievich, 2006; Koerner, 2014; Nadesan, 2013; Walker, 2004). Further, most if not all of the nuclear power plants in the United States are near the racial or economic "Other", thus making the sprawling lists of accidents at them more than troubling (Bodansky, 2004). The same is the case for Richland, Washington, and Ozersk in the Ural Mountains of Russia; the two towns in Kate Brown's (2015) *Plutopia*, are hidden away from the public eye and are selected for the task of production in the nuclear industry for the maintenance of State power. The waste produced is even carted off to "reservations [that] have been targeted as sites for 16 proposed nuclear waste dumps. Over 100 proposals have been floated in recent years to dump toxic waste in Indiana communities" (see Fig. 4.10; LaDuke, 1999, p. 2). While the promise of money and employment has lured as many as

> The sixteen tribes lined up for $100,000 grants from DOE to study the prospect of "temporarily" storing nuclear waste for a half century under its "monitored retrievable storage" ("MRS") program...although most have pulled such proposals when independent studies have been conducted on the effects of such waste on the environment and health of residents on reservations, going as far as declaring "nuclear free zones". (Bullard, 1994, p. 455).

In addition to the public health implications and confirmed indices for cancer and other illnesses of those who live proximate to sites for nuclear testing, nuclear waste dumping, and nuclear power plants (Kyne & Bolin, 2016; Taylor, 2007), Race along with gender, class, occupation, and exposure to environmental toxins related to nuclear waste or nuclear testing have been shown to be significant in studies of health but are often overlooked for more specific focus on the diseases that result from exposure (Makhijani et al., 2006). Brown found that women from the communities nearby were often selected to work as technicians despite not having any formal background in a field tied to their assigned work or training for the tasks that would be performed at these facilities. Many of these women were often exposed enough to instigate miscarriages, deformities of babies, and cancer (Brown, 2015). Gil's vocals on "We Almost Lost Detroit" ring true, "when it comes to people's safety/Money wins out every time" (Scott-Heron & Jackson, 1977). This begs us to ask similar questions that noted environmental scholar Robert

Bullard has asked, "Why do some communities get 'dumped on' while others escape? Why are environmental regulations vigorously enforced in some communities and not in others?…What institutional changes would enable the United States to become a just and sustainable society" (Bullard, 1983, p. 15)?

"The West" and "the East", now jointly operating under a global regime of nuclear power extraction and other resource extraction, have also jointly adopted an approach of who could most likely be harmed by such a risky energy solution for the sake of those who would benefit, and they are not the same (Belletto, 2009). Old enemies became partners, as breeder plants like Fermi produce far more waste than energy, and that access waste can be used for weaponry but can also be sold. This supports past criticisms of the myth of national security related to nuclear strategic development, production, and threatened deployment (Belletto, 2009). In fact, the United States has purchased and received from Russia tons of excess weapons-grade uranium over the years, and Russia has also been served by the United States. Thus, this partnership reveals a sleight of hand that serves some greater purpose of deterrent or ultimate weapon, a sleight of hand that extends to the very notion of human sacrifice zones, a term from the Soviet Union that denoted cities and towns made unhabitable due to nuclear testing and production and now a fitting term for a range of neighbourhood areas long since devastated by environmental hazards (Bullard, 1983). However, unlike the old Soviet Union nomenclature, the use of the term is applied to areas where people remain, disposable people (Lerner, 2010). For the West and the East truly support Hall's unmasking of "Our ideas of 'East' and 'West' have never been free of myth and fantasy, and even to this day they are not primarily ideas about place and geography" (Hall, 1996, p. 185). This is at the crux of Robert Bullard's (2004) seminal articulation of environmental racism for the United Nations and what is needed in response, environmental justice:

> Environmental racism reinforces the stratification of *people* (by race, ethnicity, status and power), *place* (in central cities, suburbs, rural areas, unincorporated areas or Native American

# Native American Reservations and Trust Lands within a 50-Mile Radius of a Nuclear Power Plant

**ARIZONA**
**Palo Verde**
Ak-Chin Indian Community
Tohono O'odham
Trust Land
Gila River Reservation

**CONNECTICUT**
**Millstone**
Mohegan Reservation
Mashantucket Pequot
Reservation
Narragansett
Reservation
Shinnecock Indian Nation

**FLORIDA**
**St. Lucie**
Brighton Reservation
(Seminole Tribes
of Florida)
Fort Pierce Reservation

**Turkey Point**
Hollywood Reservation
(Seminole Tribes
of Florida)
Miccosukee Reservation
Miccosukee Trust Land

**IOWA**
**Duane Arnold**
Sac & Fox Trust Land
Sac & Fox Reservation

**KANSAS**
Iowa Reservation
Iowa Trust Land

**LOUISIANA**
**River Bend**
Tunica-Biloxi Reservation

**MASSACHUSETTS**
**Pilgrim**
Wampanoag
Tribe of Gay Head
(Aquinnah)
Trust Land

**MICHIGAN**
**Palisades**
Pottawatomi Reservation
Matchebenashshewish
Band
Pokagon Reservation
Pokagon Trust Land*

**DC Cook**
Pokagon Reservation
Pokagon Trust Land

**MINNESOTA**
**Monticello**
Shakopee Community
Shakopee Trust Land
Mille Lacs Reservation

**Prairie Island**
Prairie Island Community*
Prairie Island Trust Land*
Shakopee Community
Shakopee Trust Land

**NEBRASKA**
**Cooper**
Sac & Fox Trust Land
Sac & Fox Reservation
Iowa Reservation
Iowa Trust Land
Kickapoo

**NEW YORK**
**FitzPatrick**
Onondaga Reservation
Oneida Reservation

**Nine Mile Point**
Onondaga Reservation
Oneida Reservation

**NORTH CAROLINA**
**McGuire**
Catawba Reservation

**SOUTH CAROLINA**
**Catawba**
Catawba Reservation

**Oconee**
Eastern Cherokee
Reservation

**Summer**
Catawba Reservation

**VIRGINIA**
**Surry**
Pamunkey Reservation

**WASHINGTON**
**Columbia**
Yakama Reservation
Yakama Trust Land

**WISCONSIN**
**Point Beach**
Oneida Trust Land
Oneida Reservation

* Tribe is located within the 10-mile emergency preparedness zone of operating reactors.
Notes: This table uses NRC-abbreviated reactor names and Native American Reservation and Trust land names.
There are no reservations or Trust lands within 50 miles of a reactor in Alaska or Hawaii. For more information on other Tribal concerns, go to the NRC Web site at *https://www.nrc.gov*.
NRC-abbreviated reactor names listed. Data are current as of August 2017, and the next printed update will be August 2019.

**U.S.NRC**
United States Nuclear Regulatory Commission
*Protecting People and the Environment*

**Fig 4.10** Infographics of the Native American Reservations and Trust Lands Within a 50-Mile Radius of Nuclear Power Plant from the 2017–2018 Information Digest, NUREG 1350, Volume 29. August 2017 (The U.S. National Regulatory Commission/Public Domain)

reservations) and *work* (in that office workers, for example, are afforded greater protections than farm workers). It institutionalizes unequal enforcement, trades human health for profit, places the burden of proof on the "victims" rather than the polluters, legitimizes human exposure to harmful chemicals, pesticides and hazardous substances, promotes "risky" technologies, exploits the vulnerability of economically and politically disenfranchised communities, subsidizes ecological destruction, creates an industry around risk assessment, delays cleanup actions and fails to develop pollution prevention and precaution processes as the overarching and dominant strategy. (p. iii)

The forces that rally around extraction always threaten the welfare of the indigenous, non-White, and disposable population to the near act of utter elimination. And so, within a listing of 17 principles, they very specifically articulated, "environmental justice calls for universal protection from nuclear testing and the extraction, production and disposal of toxic/hazardous wastes and poisons that threaten the fundamental right to clean air, land, water, and food" (Lee, 1992). This summit and subsequent gatherings have only been successful due to the local and grassroots work of many environmental organisations led by or concerned with environmental racism, including those specific to nuclear power, such as Citizens Against Nuclear Trash Coalition, Eastern Navajo Nation, "Mohave tribe in California, the Skull Valley Goshutes in Idaho and the Western Shoshone in Yucca Mountain, Nevada", Citizens for a Better Tomorrow, and Union of Concerned Scientists. But the focus study and attention in many cases has often left many groups out of representation in the artifacts about nuclear power. African Americans have rarely registered on metres of attention, and much of their involvement in the antinuclear movement has been ignored, despite protests during the Presidency of Truman and his decision to drop the bomb on the cities of Hiroshima and Nagasaki in Japan (Intondi, 2015). But even acts of resistance born with the intent of marginalisation can still serve the interests of the State, whether in the political or cultural realm.

With Spivak (1988), we see that the result of 'the West' representing and defining 'the East' (or 'non-West') on its behalf was "to constitute the colonial subject as other", because to be a subject is to be ruled and to be ruled is to serve at the pleasure (p. 24). The subjects of Detroit and the smaller surrounding cities will always serve the "Fermis", in some way or another, as an engineer, a technician, security guard, or food truck vendor. Cities will always serve their masters. Where Detroit was offered up as a potential sacrifice to the State's continued extractivism, Kyiv and the greater territory of Ukraine has been sacrificed many times beyond the more recent city of Pripyat, now a ghost city after the Chernobyl blast. The Ukraine as a whole, and Kyiv as a city, faced the full might of the Soviet regime through a mass starvation programme over the span of 3 years. A famine that would claim the lives of 5–10 million people began with the "Soviet Union's disastrous decision to force peasants to give up their land and join collective farms; the eviction of 'kulaks,' the wealthier peasants, from their homes" (Applebaum, 2017, p. xxvi). The *Holodomor,* the extent of the famine in then Ukrainian Soviet Socialist Republic, has to be viewed as part of a "Five-Year Plan" that gathered all smalls and congealed them into a single large farm structure in order to grow grain production for domestic needs and for export revenue generation, the Kyiv oblast (administrative region) leading all others in food delivery quotas. Grain was collected by official State representatives. The ethnitised "kulaks" under greater scrutiny were targeted by these representatives at an increased level, a dekulakisation of property, farmland, and their personhood with the city of Kyiv and the greater Kyiv oblast that was hardest hit with 1.1 million lives lost (see Figs. 4.11 and 4.12).

If any city (like people) fails at their job, a replacement (city) is assured. And if their failure is sufficient enough to cost the functioning of, let's say, a nuclear power plant, a replacement is also still assured. Inevitability is a schema in which the State wields power. And inevitability in its continuous onslaught – whether you consent or counter that power – can lead to resignation. A cognitive resignation is

**Fig 4.11** *The Daily Express* With the Headline Featuring the Forced Starvations in the Ukraine, August 6, 1934. (Public Domain)

what is displayed in the dramatisation of HBO's *Chernobyl*, in the real-life Soviet Union among surviving interviewees, and it is likely the case with Detroit. It was only a blip and the cautions of Fuller on what could have occurred in Detroit that have grown ever fainter as the years have gone on, despite incidents like Three Mile Island and disasters like Chernobyl or Fukushima. In similar respects, outside of the Ukraine, the memory of the Holodomor is non-existent despite the presence of memorials and the recognition of it as an act of genocide by nearly 20 States around the world. Merely another blip.

Even the prospects of disaster tourism only represent even more the seeming inability to resist State apparatuses and the actions of institutions in civil society to succumb to lack of concern for the most impacted populace related to nuclear activity.

The prospects of disaster tourism also demonstrated the full embrace of consent to the master narrative of the State rather than a critical eye to question the realities of the uneven burden of risk. Because the épistémè of media, entertainment, and even video games have re-written the conceptual codes of Chernobyl and the evacuation zone between the Ukraine and Belarus, there has been a spike in tourists wishing to visit, explore, and play, and not activists or concerned citizens wishing to challenge nuclear activity (Stone, 2013;Yankovska & Hannam, 2014Stone, 2013). For Lefebvre, this represents the dual process of fetishism (mystification of spatial practices that is induced into Society by political forces), and occultation (the systematic obscuring of State-based spatial interventions) is what lies at the heart of the modern form of the State form

**Fig 4.12** A Sign in Russian Reads, "The burying of people is strictly prohibited" During the Holodomor. Photo taken in Kharkiv, Ukraine, 1933 by Alexander Wienerberge. (The Innitzer Collection/National Museum of the Holodomor-Genocide in Kyiv-Ukraine)

(Lefebvre, 1976–1978). So, where Fermi 1 failed with the "faint" possibility to destroying an American city, Fermi 2 and Fermi 3 was built to replace it proximate to the location of Fermi and still proximate to Detroit.

Almost losing Detroit created no significant or lasting conjuncture in questioning or querying nuclear power. Fuller's cautionary tale, *We Almost Lost Detroit*, was followed up by Gil Scott-Heron and Brian Jackson's song of the same name. These two Foucauldian épistémès alerted us to a near-violent crisis, but without any fame or attention. The near-violent crisis that occurred did not illuminate a process of the failures of government oversight, corporate greed, or an apathetic public, although there are claims and realities of each. The racial bias in site selection is simply not apparent because of the invisibility of the communities that live near or around the site. These communities are stuck bearing the burdens of harmful waste dumping

alongside the looming threat with the high-risk operation of nuclear power plants (Reese, 2006; Taliman, 1992). Detroit, and what occurs in or around the city, cannot produce a Gramscian conjuncture in the "American" mind. In that brief moment, we can see why Hall (1997) said that "hegemony is never for ever" (p. 30). Thus, it remains the same. We could still lose a Detroit, lose another Prypiat, or lose New Orleans again, and no official discourse has been able to absolutely guarantee it from not happening. But maybe it is because certain cities become disposable cities when their surplus value is far below its accumulation yield. Regardless of this lack of guarantee of safety, there will be nuclear power and other risky and environmentally damaging extraction projects. "A just world is a sane word...[And] there was nothing sane about Chernobyl", posits a reflective Valery Legasov, as played by Jared Harris in HBO's *Chernobyl*, as he is making a set of recorded tapes to tell the "truth" someday. The violent disposability of a city and its populace are a culmination of an even more violent spatial ordering, where cities themselves and not just people can die. What is sanity, when the real and possible loss of a city with a populace could occur, but the skilfully use of lawfare has reverted this history to a forgotten footnote?

## 4.4 The Condoned Violence of the State-Fabricated Society

Disposable cities are dominated by disposable people, surplus populations to the economic interest of the State. The countless people who lived and died during the Great Depression – whether it was by job loss or the opportunistic use of a natural disaster, a critical lens can capture the evidence that suggests such a disposability. Margaret Bourke-White's 1937 picture of Black residents of Louisville, Kentucky, depicted them huddled in line and clustered together in the shot underneath a promotional billboard bearing a beaming wholesome "American" White family with a dog (see Fig. 4.1). The slogan, "World's Highest Standard of Living", in prominent lettering provides irony not only due to the racialised opposing capture of Black residents standing in line seeking aid after the Great Ohio Flood of 1937, but also as it reflects an unattainable mode of life for most in the United States due to the economic cataclysm of the late 1920s and 1930s. The unattainable lifestyle during the period was as much in opposition to the attainable downward mobility in the United States then as it is today. Debt and rising health care costs in the midst of a pandemic have only provided more lines of people seeking aid in various cities. The Great Ohio Flood of 1937 claimed nearly 400 lives and left over one million people homeless across five states during the wintertime of 1937. The great scourge of coronavirus has claimed nearly 3 million worldwide and 650,000 lives at the time of this publishing. Bourke-White's image was the lead feature in the February 15, 1937, issue of *LIFE* magazine. The issue focused on how severely the flood ravaged Louisville, in particular. In the issue, *LIFE* wrote, that Louisville "will henceforth rank with Johnstown in 1889 and Dayton in 1913 among the worst-flooded cities in American history"…until Hurricane Katrina hit New Orleans in 2005. And while the published feature and image in *LIFE* reflected a journalistic intent of what was then one of the most popular periodicals, it did and continues to reflect a society's ability to still move forward, to look away after looking deeply within. This is the actual advertised "American Way" on the billboard, the épistémè of fabricated society of the United States that is cultivated by acts of lawfare and warfare onto its populace while engaging in lawfare and warfare onto other populations in other States with the blessing of the submissive fabricated society.

Violence then is not something that is committed onto an environment or territory, but onto the population of an environment or territory.

> Curiously, space is a stranger to customary political reflection. Political thought and the representations which it elaborates remain "up in the air", with only an abstract relation with the soil [terroirs] and even the national territory… Space belongs to the geographers in the academic division of labor. But then it reintroduces itself subversively through the effects of peripheries, the margins, the regions, the villages and local communities long abandoned, neglected, even abased through centralizing state power.
>   sovereignty is
>   exercised over people, rather than over things… The State is conceived in itself and by itself, as a real abstraction, without spatial body, without concrete support other than "subjects" or "humans"…This requires a spatialization of political theory, not without a critique of its deterritorialized abstraction, which, at the same time, takes into account localities and regions, differences and multiple (conflictual) associations, attached to the soil [sol], to dwelling, the circulation of people and things, in the practical functioning of space. This similarly entails a reconsideration of the economy in terms of space, of the flux of stocks, of mobile elements and stable elements, in short, of the production and reproduction of (social) space. (Lefebvre 1976–1978, pp. 164–165)

The city of Louisville had already evicted and displaced the Black population from all downtown locations with a comprehensive plan that was also conceived by Harland Bartholomew and his team in the late 1920s, finalised in 1931, and published in 1932. Besides the aforementioned Comprehensive Plan for St. Louis in 1947, the 1932 "The Negro Housing Problem in Louisville" would find him outright articulating what he did not in the text of the St. Louis plan:

> There are a number of obstacles that are fundamental to any scheme for improving housing conditions among Negroes. [These in-clude] A lack of desire among a large portion of the population for something better than they are accustomed to … if it were possible to create among the Negro masses a real desire for decent accommodations, the slums would auto-matically eliminate themselves as it would be impossible for the owner of rundown property to obtain tenants unless he made such improve-ments that would attract them. (p. 7)

And just like what would eventually be done in St. Louis, displacement/deterritorialisation was swiftly followed by reterritorialisation into public housing complexes that could be more conceived of as prison campuses for the unclean criminals of the city.

Bartholomew would return to Louisville to continue his machine of harm in 1957 with the second plan for Louisville. And just like in St. Louis, both designated areas for public housing were razed in the 1960s and 1970s. Displacement upon dis-placement upon displacement. And this displace-ment took place behind an ideological wall (from the City Council, business leaders, and Harland Bartholomew & Associates), a physical wall (of ex-pressways that make it difficult for pedestrians to cross), and a psychological wall (that results in present-day society seeing the order as natural) (Throgmoton, 2004). Constructed by the lawfare of city plans and the racial ordinances that preceded them, and: the racial segregation empowering *Plessy v. Ferguson* of 1896; the police empowering *Hadacheck v. Sebastian* (1915); the covenant em-powering *Hopkins v. City of Richmond* of 1915; the redlining empowering by nature of making racialised zoning illegal, *Buchanan v. Warley* of 1917; the

zoning empowering *Village of Euclid v. Ambler Realty Corporation* of 1926, among so many others (Silver, 1997; U.S. Supreme Court, 1895). The economic health and the lure of tourist dollars were the drivers of this lawfare-conceived work, and it was backed by the warfare of law enforcement now empowered to remove and evict throughout the United States, especially in relationship to public housing.

The *Laws of the Indies* and its strict design of the city is the great grandparent of modern day (and still used) Euclidean zoning, named after the ruling from the 1926 *Village of Euclid* case. To reduce this zoning approach to how any locality and munici-pality, town and city in the United States has divided its territory by permitted and prohibited land use (residential, commercial, and industrial) misses the ways that it has consistently split the populace as an intent and not as a happenstance action. This re-duction in understanding the Euclidean zoning ap-proach results in our inability to see it as a governing philosophy. A philosophy that falsely lures new re-sidents to a city or suburb under the pretext of jobs and safety, and then displaces them once those re-sidents have fulfilled their purpose. A philosophy that builds housing that is either public or private, and then demolishes it for the next planned develop-ment. A philosophy that constructs public and pri-vate spaces for communal events, and then manufactures divisions among a populace through the construction of walls and other physical dividers. The "Race" walls of Miami or the 1836 constructed "neutral ground" street medians of New Orleans to divide Creole French and the Anglo New Orleans, division were laws *and* infrastructure (Thomas, 2018; Travieso, 2020). The Euclidean zoning phi-losophy, if willed into existence by State actors and wielded correctly by masterful architects, designers, and planners, does not exacerbate segregation; it segregates. The Euclidean zoning philosophy does not create urban sprawl; it plans for sprawl, pushing the undesirables to the outer reaches of the realm. The Euclidean zoning philosophy does not lead to limited housing options; it is the limiter. In the 90+ years of its existence, the Euclidean zoning philosophy has made class, gender, and Race ingrained in the State-fabricated society.

A zoning philosophy and empowered police force that is backed by the legal protections of law-fare are the forces that directed a SWAT team to kill Breonna Taylor in Louisville in 2020. The philosophy and force were what created and then utilised gentrification to designate Breonna's apartment complex and apartment at 3003 Springfield Drive as a location to use selective State-sanctioned violence by way of police tactics on March 13, 2020 (tactics that would not be tolerated in suburbs or areas of wealth). A warrant for a drug arrest with no actual drug search resulted in a shooting death. Slum clearance in 2020 no longer needs comprehensive plans, so city blocks and neighbourhoods can be cleared through departmental tactical operations. Gentrification no longer needs to be piecemealed, as an entire block can be made anew through "Place-Based Investigations". This work can be excused by the place-making efforts of a nearly $1 billion set of capital projects that includes the complicity of the Beecher Terrace Initiative and the $10 million grant for a Sports and Learning Complex to the Louisville Urban League. The "Vision Russell" initiative of the Louisville Metro Housing Authority project will retain the memory of a former neighbourhood (Beecher Terrace, named after the brother of the Harriet Beecher Stowe of Uncle Tom's Cabin fame) but potentially not all of the former residents who "temporarily" relocated during the revitalisation project; 220,000 square feet of long-abandoned warehouses in a predominantly Black Russell neighbourhood area are the results of the two aforementioned Bartholomew city plans.

Erased from memory are the policies that made this present-day reality possible, and in its place are dreams and hopes from segments of the populace in Louisville that comprise a manufactured society. The entrenchment of inequity in living space in the cities of the United States are repressed from public memory and discursive language (Mullins, 2021), and this gives the State's ability to continuously perpetuate these realities into the geography of a city. "Russell: A Place of Promise" enlisted residents to embrace the plan that may lead to even stronger housing enforcement and higher rents that will drive this population to move for a fourth time. While "Russell: A Place of Promise" is branded as a justice-based initiative that has been financially incubated by the Louisville Metro Government and the city violence-eliminating Cities United effort, it ignores the underlining myth of Black wealth generation that conveys a possibility the money and wealth can be positively segregated like people and space. The near $52 million and 24-acre sports complex is expected to draw 17 major events per year and will provide services to more affluent families in the growing privatised sports market (with a track floor that will be made by the same company that was to build the track floor for the cancelled 2020 Olympics in Tokyo). An opportunistic windfall of $15.9 million annually for the city will never result in a windfall for a neighbourhood as it is presently demographically configured. The once-called Harlem of the South will go the same way that Harlem of New York has been heading. (Bailey & Duvall, 2020)

In Harlem,

> There used to be a corner where Puerto Ricans and Dominicans hung out and played the bongos and drank beer. Now they can't do that. But you can do that in Washington Heights. So, there's this double standard. That's wrong. How can neighborhoods under the same mayor be treated so differently? Now you can't even stand in front of your own building without being harassed. Or if you sit on the benches the police will come along and point to the no loitering sign and say you can't stay here…[This is] because of new people moving in and putting pressure on the police to make things orderly. (Freeman, 2006, p. 105)

With desires for city expansion and revenue generation at the city level, and concerns of real estate tax assessment, these are the drivers of gentrification. Plans for demolition and rent increases is one way to rebuild anew, while developer–law enforcement partnerships are another whether it is in: Atlanta (Thompson, 2020); Baltimore (Covington & Taylor, 1989); Boston (Anguelovski et al., 2020); Chicago (Hwang & Sampson, 2014; Papachristos 2011); Denver (Cardona, 2007); Houston (Wright & Herman, 2018); Los Angeles (Davis, 2006); Miami (Samara & Chang, 2008); New Orleans (Parekh, 2015); New York City (Beck, 2020; Laniyonu, 2018;

Vitale, 2008); Oakland (Ramírez, 2020); Portland (Sullivan, 2006); San Francisco (Herring, 2019); Seattle (Gibson, 2004); Topeka (Van Dyke, 2013); Washington, D.C. (Saunders & Kirby, 2010); or Wichita (Billingham, 2017).

*Geographies of Threat* attempts to conceptually articulate that these ideas, approaches, and philosophies are shared between cities and across State regimes. The coercive benevolence in city policing is just the local version of the "benevolent assimilation" across State policing at the global level. The occupation and administration of the processes of subjugating of an entire population in the Philippine islands in the late 1800s (Miller, 1982), bares direct similarities to the occupation and administering of the processes of coercive repression in the neighbourhoods of the United States at the same time. The soft power lawfare of the Benevolent Assimilation Proclamation could not mask the warfare that came before, during, and after it. The transference of ideas and techniques inside dominions of control of a State and between States are a hallmark of State rule. And so there should be little surprise to discover that similar strategies have been adopted from the United States' use and have been implemented in Barcelona, Spain (Anguelovski et al., 2020); Rotterdam, the Netherlands (Uitermark et al., 2007); and Vancouver, Canada (Ley & Dobson, 2008). Under the banner, slogan, or call for urban renewal that has been re-phrased as urban development and revitalisation, the deployment of "Safe and Clean Neighborhoods Program", "quality-of-life" policing, zero tolerance policies, complaint-oriented policing, and "safe streets" initiatives, Place-based Investigations, and, therapeutic policing,

> [that] tells residents [of skid row] to "get a real job," even as stable and decently paying employment continues to dwindle. It tells them to "get off the streets," despite the declining availability of affordable housing. It tells them to "get clean and sober," despite the continued defunding and privatization of health and rehabilitative services. (Stuart, 2016, pp. 19–20)

The new and improved order maintenance within the coercive benevolence of lawfare in cities supports the disinvestment of neighbourhood areas. Order maintenance through lawfare supports city administration/services' organised abandonment and the corporate feudalism inherent in housing and the very living in a city. The coffee shops, bike repair shop, craft beer tavern, and Pilates and yoga studios are not the markings of a functioning society; they are the markings of a completed phase in gentrification, precipitated by gender-appropriate appeals to the protection and support of "particular product brands, styles, and kinds of activities" (Kern, 2020, p. 40). This phase ushers in the legion of aspiring elites to clean up the streets, crime, and people of yesteryear, the disposable people. They assist in the clean-up by wagging and pointing fingers, making 911 calls, and making 311 calls. The 311 call to save them from the rat infestation and their senior neighbours who are breeding them, because,

> a deeper analysis that also looked at a month's worth of rat-related 311 calls [that]… incorporated demographic and socioeconomic data. It became clear that mapping 311 calls isn't a good way to tell where rats are; it's a way to tell where the wealthy White people live. (Lipstein, 2019)

While those senior (long-standing and -residing) neighbours were significantly represented in the

> controlling for significant demographic and neighborhood variables, [and among] those reporting frequent rat exposure were less likely to believe their neighbors cared about or worked hard to get rid of rats, were less likely to know how to report rats to the city, and were less likely to believe the city would act if notified. (German & Latkin, 2016, p. 258)

Disposable, yet long-standing residents bring on abandonment. Lucrative, yet newer residents marshal already ready city services and assistance. But it is not the gentrifiers or even developers that control the violent force of gentrification; it is the State through the dusty plans conceived decades before that dreamed corridors to newly decorated downtown areas once inhabited by the disposable. Through abandonment, conditions worsen neighbourhoods to the point of no-return. Rats are just the next infestation that may also include roaches, stray dogs, feral cats, chipped lead paint, inoperable fire hydrants, fallen trees, drooping power lines, broken streetlights, vacant lots with overgrown plant life, unmanaged parks, rusty playground apparatus, labelled failing or closed schools, boarded-up businesses, and blighted houses. Abandonment is argued here not as a response to these conditions, to these people, but as an intent. Just like Kelling and Wilson's (1982) "Broken Windows" policing was a philosophically proactive approach to "crime" and policing, Drucker's (1999) *organized abandonment* was articulated as a proactive approach to cut costs from underperforming aspects of one's organisation or area of leadership. To disavow, to end provisions will most assuredly free up the wasted resources for future growth opportunities. With the

> first policy, and the foundation for all others is to abandon yesterday. The first need is to free resources from being committed to maintaining what no longer contributes to performance, and no longer produces results. In fact, it is not possible to create tomorrow unless one first sloughs off yesterday. To maintain yesterday is always extremely difficult and time consuming. To maintain yesterday always commits the institution's scarcest and most valuable resources, and above all its ablest people, to non-results. Yet, to do anything different, let alone to innovate, always runs into unexpected difficulties. It therefore always demands leadership by people of high and proven ability. And if these people are committed to maintaining yesterday, they are simply not available to create tomorrow. The first change policy, therefore, throughout the entire institution, has to be Organized Abandonment. (Drucker, 1999, p. 74)

Methodically effective for corporate entities, for non-profit management, for school districts, for city councils and administrations, and for representatives of the State. Organized abandonment calls for comprehensive assessment and future planning based on current assets (The Civil League of St. Louis in 1906). Organized abandonment calls for facing the reality that,

> neither studies nor market research nor computer modelling are a substitute for the test of reality. Everything improved or new needs therefore first to be tested on a small scale, that is, it needs to be piloted. (Drucker, 1999, p. 87)

The piloting of the abandonment can take the form in a city of a neighbourhood area (Paris's Sur la Zone in the 1930s and 1940s, see Fig. 4.13; St. Louis' Mill Creek Valley in the 1940s; Louisville's Beecher Terrace in the 1950s; Chicago's "Bronzeville" in the 1950s and 1960s; Miami's "Little Haiti" in the 1970s; New York's borough of the Bronx in the 1970s and 1980s, see Fig. 4.14; London's Brixton in the 1980s; Toronto's Parksdale in the 1990s; and Berlin's Neukölln in the 2000s, etc.). But the piloting of the abandonment can take the form in a State of an undesirable city (Cleveland, Ohio, post-1950s; Detroit post-1960s rebellion; Gary, Indiana, and Youngstown, Ohio, post-1970s steel-industry decline, see Fig. 4.15; Rio de Janeiro post-1980s political scandal and corruption; Baltimore post-1990s crack era; Flint, Michigan, post-2000s auto-industry downsizing; New Orleans post-2005 Hurricane Katrina; Cape Town, South Africa, post-2010s; and pre-COVID-19 Wuhan, China). But abandonment is always intentional once the extraction resources and accumulation of access value has reached its final phase. And abandonment is also not new. The 400-year Dutch rule of Batavia (now Jakarta, Indonesia) secluded Chinese, enslaved populations brought in from elsewhere, and indigenous Indonesians were relegated to areas with limited or inadequate clean water. The modern-day sinking of Jakarta and eventual forced abandonment of this capital city is built upon the Dutch's abandonment of the settlement that was built upon an indigenous city in 1619, the old city that was left for better service southern "suburb" of Weltevreden in 1808, and a colonial city left for failure after independence in 1945 (see Fig. 4.16).

Organized abandonment calls for the shaping and re-shaping of culture, and the symbolic message

**Fig 4.13** Saint-Ouen Vue des Fortifications of La Zone. Saint-Ouen in the Distance, and the Shanty-Town in the Foreground, c. 1930. (Public Domain)

and action of abandonment aids reinvestment in a reverse-engineering way. It addresses heightened concerns over populations and areas by no longer "feeding" the ill, dirty, and disregarded that then signals that the "bottom" is coming. Early investors jump at the opportunity to acquire abandoned assets and hold on to them until the time is right to sell or develop. The fire-sale of neighbourhoods is built

**Fig 4.14** Urban Decay. Falsa Promesas/ "False Promises", 1980. (Photo Credit: John Fekner of Charlotte Street Studios/ Wiki Commons)

**Fig 4.15** The Interstate Inn. An Abandoned Motel Next to the Junction of Interstate 65, Interstate 90, U.S. 12, and U.S. 20 in Eastern Gary, Indiana. Due to Technicalities in Federal Government Guidelines, Gary Is Unable to Receive Funding for Demolition of Much of Its Blighted Infrastructure, June 11, 2011. (Public Domain)

upon the disposable disposed peoples over generations. And once sold, immediate deployment of resources needs to be placed into the old area in order to make this "new" management technique of organized abandonment a success. The success is the reverse engineering of this organized abandonment by concentrating the disposed into undesirable corners of the city, then displacing when that property or land is now useful and reconcentrating them into new neighbourhoods or new structures like public and restricted housing, the success of reacting to a problem that was caused or created for the fire-sale of neighbourhoods. The literal fire of infrastructure, like the 2017 Grenfell Tower blaze, was built with combustible cladding to cut costs that later cut lives (see Fig. 4.17). The cruel disregard of life was either planned or was less important than the calculation of capital that could be reaped. Lawfare granted deregulations of fire and building codes for developers, and lawfare allowed for overlooking other regulations and operating violations. Death and life are in the way of property and profits,

while Grenfell Tower was still slow-burning, an exclusive, government-backed group of senior high-profile grandees from the world of politics and business, has arranged a meeting of experts to discuss the subject of "cladding." The group was known as RTI – or the "Red Tape Initiative". They had convened a few months earlier in April 2017. The group's objectives were clear: to dismantle EU regulations that were considered a hindrance to profit-making... Such was the thinking of the dominant power brokers, during the dying embers of Grenfell Tower. In this atmosphere, safety regulation was sneered at as "red tape folly"; and dismissed as "expensive" and "burdensome". (Bhandar, 2018)

The violent extractivism of resources from neighbourhoods inside cities is a long-standing practise that simply received an appropriate name in the late 1990s. While the Elizabeth Povinelli's (2011) "economies of abandonment" and Ruth Wilson Gilmore's (2015) "organized state abandonment" are signals of retreat by the State within its city

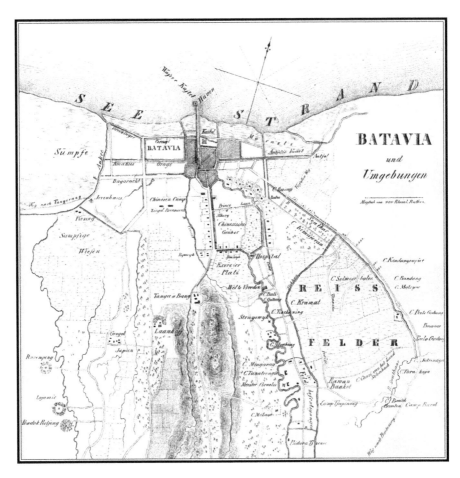

**Fig 4.16** The Oud (Old) Batavia With the Newly Developed Weltevreden Area South of the City, The Chinese Campong in the Middle, 1846. (Eduard Selberg/Wiki Commons/Public Domain)

territories and structures, long forgotten spaces re-enliven the colonial dreams of discovery. But it takes time for spaces to be forgotten. Planned and strategised decay is a slow process that requires those in power to tolerate the mundane speed, that delays the gratification. Violence is a consequence of disinvestment. Gun violence, rape, domestic violence, arson, and robbery are not immediate enough to cleanse an area, but they are effective in the long run if allowed to take their toll. The State tested one pilot after another that then eventually achieved a mastery of State actors of "making live, making die, and letting die" techniques (Povinelli, 2011, p. 29). It is no wonder that the councils and residents of dying cities and towns have turned to pleading for the construction of prisons in or

nearby, which as Gilmore (2008) described as a "dead city...built and staffed for the singularly unproductive purpose of keeping civilly dead women and men in cages for part or all of their lives" (p. 45). Just as neighbourhood areas were test-piloted spaces for greater usage throughout the city, designated cities were the test-piloted spaces for greater usage throughout its network of cities of rule. *Urbicide*, the death of the city, happens within cities because they are also being killed by the State (the aforementioned attempt at killing Detroit, the death of Prypiat, and the near-allowed death of New Orleans). Death and life are distributed and redistributed to achieve the maximum desired accumulation of capital with fewer costs. So, to focus on gentrifiers in gentrification is wrong, just as even

**Fig 4.17** Grenfell Tower in West London, After the Tragic Fire, June 18, 2017. (Photo Credit: ChiralJon/Wiki Commons)

focusing on gentrification is wrong. Gentrifiers are ingeniously merchant-classes that are deployed in the middle of a "battle", while the police are the shock troops. Gentrification converts a devasting political philosophy into a social phenomenon that is up for debate and discussion rather condemnation and halting. Abandonment is the "imperial arts of paternalist civilizational governance" (Povinelli, 2011, p. 2). Abandonment is the military dispossession machine that consumes all and then converts that which it consumed within its fiery stoking furnace into abominations of (social) life. This is society, the State-fabricated Society that condones the violence of the State in the city.

### 4.5 The Public Square, The Park, The Plaza

Cresswell (1996) explained,

> the meaning of a place is subject of particular discourses of power, which express themselves as discourses of normality...the meaning of a place, then, is (in part) created through a discourse that sets up a process of differentiation (between us and them). (p. 60)

The myth of Society is propped up by the State through the creation of communal connections and the social fostering of emotional connections to spaces: home, neighbourhood, city, and the State as a country or Nation. The ancient Greek and the Roman agora, the Italian piazza of the Renaissance, the *Laws'* plaza, the science in the German quadrate of the Enlightenment, the British town squares, the Philadelphian public square, and the city centre of the modern era all coalesce the city with a geographic central focus and less obvious centralised governance focus (see Fig. 4.18). Society is organised around or from the central point outward. Going as far back as the aforementioned *Laws of the Indies,* ordinance no. 129 read as follows,

> Within the town, a common shall be delimited, large enough that although the population may experience a rapid expansion, there will always be sufficient space where the people may go to for recreation and take their cattle to pasture without them making any damage.... (Mundigo & Crouch, 1977, p. 256)

St. Augustine, Florida, in the United States, was the first settlement in North America and was under the

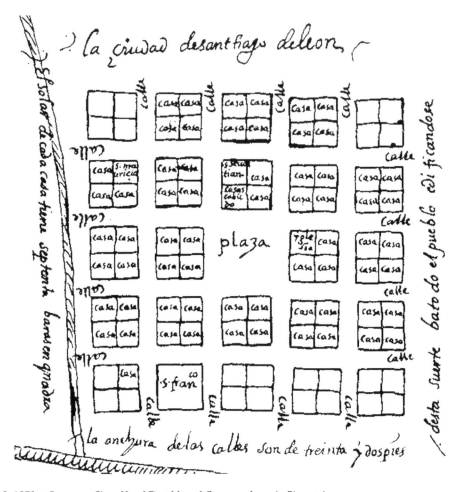

**Fig 4.18** 1578 – Caracas – Close Up of First Map of Governor Juan de Pimental.

Spanish Empire in 1565. This required the settlement to be laid out in the specifics of the *Laws of the Indies*. Throughout the 200-year rule of the Spanish Empire, St. Augustine was developed with the grid plan, as were all cities and towns under Spanish rule. In the plan, the rectangularly squared Plaza de la Constitución also had a market area constructed. As *Geographies of Threat* has worked to emphasise, the philosophy of *Laws* most influences the governance of cities by the State and not just city design and planning. Within such plazas with a market, enslaved populations would be sold with other goods (see Figs. 4.19 and 4.20). This practise in this location continued when the city came into the possession of the British Crown and later the United States: "the sale of a negro woman Sally at public auction in the market

'house' to settle the Mary Hanford estate; and the auction of twenty-eight-year-old Tamaha, for $180" in 1836 (Lawson, 1939). And within the market, slave patrols would gather, plan, and share their strategies for apprehension of, "all slaves or free persons of colour, who may be found in the streets thirty minutes after the ringing of the Bell without having a proper pass from their masters or guardians" (Nolan, 2009).

And it continued to be a common reframe in plans, Haussmann was commissioned by Emperor Napoléon II to make 1853 Paris *aérer, unifier, et embellir* ("more air, more connected, and more space") with larger boulevards, parks, and public space. As Delagard and Ehrman-Solberg (2017) noted for 1883 plans,

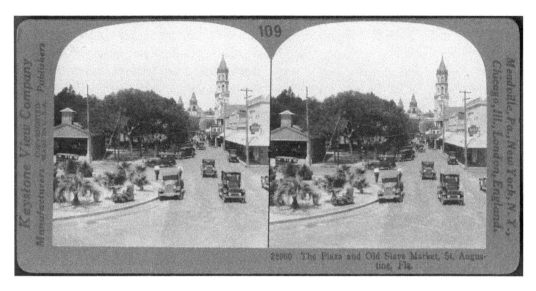

**Fig 4.19** The Plaza and the Old Slave Market at St. Augustine, Florida. (Boston Library)

Minneapolitans love their parks, which have been named the nation's best by the Trust for Public Land for several years in a row. From its beginning in 1883, the Minneapolis Park Board sought to acquire all the land bordering streams, lakes, and rivers. This strategy created the nationally renowned Grand Rounds, the 60 miles of public trails and parkways that meander along Minnehaha Creek to link the Mississippi River gorge to the Chain of Lakes. This carefully planned green space transformed Mill City into the City of Lakes in the early twentieth century. Residents like to brag that their waterfront is the playground of the people. But the initial visualizations generated by Mapping Prejudice show that some of the most desirable green spaces in the city were ringed by residential districts that barred

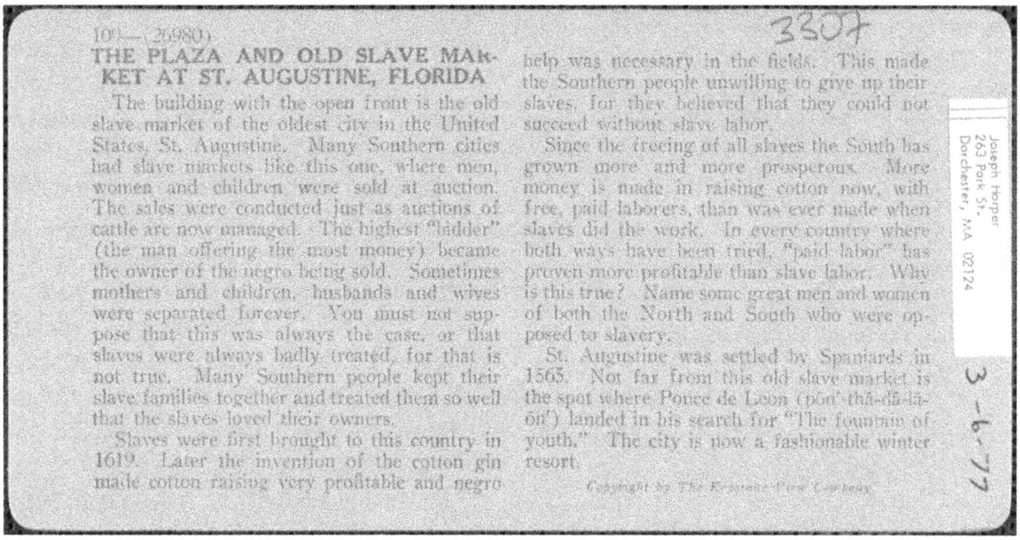
109—(26980)

THE PLAZA AND OLD SLAVE MARKET AT ST. AUGUSTINE, FLORIDA

The building with the open front is the old slave market of the oldest city in the United States, St. Augustine. Many Southern cities had slave markets like this one, where men, women and children were sold at auction. The sales were conducted just as auctions of cattle are now managed. The highest "bidder" (the man offering the most money) became the owner of the negro being sold. Sometimes mothers and children, husbands and wives were separated forever. You must not suppose that this was always the case, or that slaves were always badly treated, for that is not true. Many Southern people kept their slave families together and treated them so well that the slaves loved their owners.

Slaves were first brought to this country in 1619. Later the invention of the cotton gin made cotton raising very profitable and negro help was necessary in the fields. This made the Southern people unwilling to give up their slaves, for they believed that they could not succeed without slave labor.

Since the freeing of all slaves the South has grown more and more prosperous. More money is made in raising cotton now, with free, paid laborers, than was ever made when slaves did the work. In every country where both ways have been tried, "paid labor" has proven more profitable than slave labor. Why is this true? Name some great men and women of both the North and South who were opposed to slavery.

St. Augustine was settled by Spaniards in 1565. Not far from this old slave market is the spot where Ponce de Leon (pōn'-thā-dā-lā-ōn') landed in his search for "The fountain of youth." The city is now a fashionable winter resort.

Copyright by The Keystone View Company

3307

Joseph Harper
263 Park St.
Dorchester, MA 02124

3-6-77

**Fig 4.20** The Plaza and the Old Slave Market at St. Augustine, Florida Newspaper Clipping. March 6, 1977 (Boston Library)

people of color from taking up residence. The result was an invisible racial cordon around the city's urban commons.

It is then no wonder in returning back to Louisville that Bartholomew's Plan of 1931,

> envisioned 35 miles of riverfront drives linking recreational areas, keystoned by an open plaza between Third and Seventh. The Illinois Central tracks were to run beneath an elevated highway and to be protected by a floodwall. The government center was to be built south of Main between Fourth and Sixth overlooking the landscaped plaza. Parking for 4,000 cars was planned under the plaza. The fountain shown on the wharf was at the foot of Fifth St. The cost of the development was estimated at $10 million by Harland Bartholomew and Associates, St. Louis.
> (Thomas, 1978, pp. 220–221)

With a riverfront plaza as the centrepiece of the project and the crucial feature that fostered the populace of the city complicit to the displacing deeds that ensued, and then again in 1957, Bartholomew was pushing for such features in order to "allow for more breathing space for downtown". Bartholomew would go on to create the aforementioned public square in place of St. Louis's Mill Creek Valley neighbourhood area of 20,000 people. And Bartholomew would be employed by the City of Los Angeles to conceive of the Parks, Playgrounds and Beaches Plan of 1927 with the Olmstead brothers just prior to Louisville's project. With an emphasis on private power over public space a

> "citizens' committee" composed primarily of Chamber of Commerce members and their associates, a diverse group of movers and shakers with representatives from a cross-section of local manufacturing and industry, the financial sector, real estate, and commerce.
> (Hise & Deverell, 2000, p. 2)

While the plan was never executed, it does maintain the focus on the play area, the space for recreation as a mask to control the population (or at least who should be restricted from such spaces). If Rio De

Janeiro was to become a city of the future, it had to be environmentally friendly (create open spaces) through Mayor Paes' plan for the 2016 Olympics (Paes, 2012). Urban removal, or slum clearance, is the violent dispossession of people. From the public square, central park, or plaza the city can manage all spatial arrangements of neighbourhoods and spatial uses of people.

As the centre of activity, the public space was the location for gathering and city breathing, for exchange and deliberation. The public square, either as a park or plaza, was benevolently bestowed by the State as *Patria* (father) upon the city's citizenry and residents, whether master or slave. Neighbourhoods and commerce were organised from it, and social and business life sprang from it. The square was the crucial intersection between capitalism and capital punishment, not only for the arrest and punishment of laws but also the exacting of justice by the Crown of England in the 1700s. London, a city vast in size, needed multiple sites to conduct the deeds in the most public and common of spaces. The aim was to discipline the plebian and proletarian in a very public manner, to grow the crowd and the spectacle, and to grow the power of the Crown in the imagination of the ruled (Wilf, 1993). So commonplace was the public square hanging that rulership and governance was in every way a *thanatocracy* that rested on the criminalisation of a class of people. Through this public display of capital punishment, the execution accompanied the transition from feudalism to the emergent capitalist State structure (Lincbaugh, 1991). Whether it was in the Haymarket Square over wages and quality of life or some other violation of labour position in society, the public-facing spectacle, even when moved to enclosed spaces, had a chilling effect if dissent was performed in the square (see Fig. 4.21 and 4.22). The capitalist State required the labourer to be disciplined and cajoled into accepting their status, their lower wages, and their fewer material gains from their labour. The sovereignty of the State not only governed the land, but it also governed the body of its subjects in defence of the accumulation of wealth, property, and capital. In the public square, the State (the new State) could renew its claims of sovereignty over and over again with each hanging death (see Fig. 4.22).

THE HAYMARKET RIOT. The Explosion and the Conflict.

**Fig 4.21** Explosion That Set Off the Haymarket Riot in 1886, 1889. (Michael J. Schaack/Public Domain)

**Fig 4.22** Four of the Chicago "anarchists" Being Hanged in Cook County Jail. (Public Domain)

**Fig 4.23** Congo Square, Now Louis Armstrong Park, and Formerly the Gathering Space of the Houmas. New Orleans, LA (the Author)

The square, like New Orleans' Congo Square (now Louis Armstrong Park), a square in a place of dispossession of the indigenous Houmas that was once their site for harvest celebrations (see Fig. 4.23). A space that was then occupied by colonising forces. A square that was the space for compliance and order of those disposed during enslavement (Donaldson, 1984), predicated by the *Le Code Noir* decree of 1724 that restricted general movement of the enslaved (especially in relationship to congregation, unlike in Spanish-controlled colonial and Imperial cities), and the removal of all Jews from colonies (Stovall, 2006). But as an aftereffect of the Haitian Revolution from 1791 to 1904, a *Place des Nègres* in 1817 New Orleans was resolved to be a logical approach to quelling further insurrections due to the sheer brutality of enslavement by allotting time *and* space for rest, respite, and recreation. The functionality of Congo Square inspired the British architect and planner Benjamin Latrobe to conceive of public squares beyond their aesthetic amenities, although his attention was buildings of the State.

The square, like in 1916 Waco, Texas, was the ideal location for exacting the vengeance of the White Society onto the 17-year-old Jesse Washington, a Black labourer with a disability, for the alleged murder of Lucy Fryer. Waco, the county seat and not the site of the murder, was the most appropriate site to exact the vengeance. The public square that was across from the courthouse was the most appropriate space to do the exacting. And in that public square, Jesse Washington burned for hours, to the delight or dismay of over 15,000 attendees (Mowatt, 2012; see Fig. 4.24). The public square or park was the ideal location for communities to gather as a Society to exact justice onto indigenous population over sovereignty and fealty through mass hangings and to later memorialise the act (Lybeck, 2015), or to place trophies from the act of lynching for all to see, as was also the case in the lynching of Will James by placing his head on a stake in a park in 1909 Cairo, Illinois (Mowatt, 2012). In the public square, the State no longer had to get its hands dirty as the populace would act on its behalf to discipline and exact

**Fig 4.24** Crowd of People Gathered in Street and Square to Watch the Lynching of Jesse Washington, May 15, 2016. (The Library of Congress, Public Domain)

punishment to violating the "natural" constructed order of individual rights and privileges. Violence unleashed onto vulnerable populations has been a useful tool to set the tone for legal apparatus to make that violence allowable and the perceptions of those populations actionable.

The public square, park, or plaza is an effective space to coalesce Society into a mindset that is sub-servient and at the command of the State. The public square cultivates and coerces *governmentality* among the populace. It is ultimately how the populace has governed itself with government by the State often in absentia, based on those State-established policies and practises. Governmentality is also not straightforwardly the seats of traditionally conceived authority as the responsibility to rule the network of cities is untenable. But it is only through the network of cities that actual territory is ruled over. The network of cities is all that exists of the State's power and dominance. Anything and anywhere outside of the city limit remains virtually stateless, and left scrambling for its life by managing its own affairs and by appealing from distant capitols. The State is the promise that is given, and governmentality is the embrace and belief of that promise.

Disorder, dissent, and rebellion are the responses when the State can't follow through on its promise of stateliness (i.e., jobs, education, and opportunity). And anything and anywhere abandoned by the State within the city limits are rife with the possibilities of rebellions because many cities have acquired too much land to properly coercively govern . The State disappears most of the time from the lives of the ci-tizenry but remains foremost in the mind through governmentality (Foucault, 1991b). Governmentality are the schools, health centres, and public spaces that direct our movement and thinking under an imposed social control by a revolving regime (McCarthy & Dimitriadis, 2000). Governmentality is the mentality of rule that exists in three axes: power, hierarchy, and reciprocity (Marwick, 2012). While self-expression is evident in the spaces of the city, so too is the social control and the norming of power relationships and differentials tied to class, gender, and Race that are sustained and expanded. They exacerbate some of the worst examples of how we see each other and pro-vide the way to legitimate a cruelty on communities of the "Other" in a city, supporting the socio-political philosophies and values that have shaped neigh-bourhoods. In 2020, we are in the midst of the re-awakening of the State(s), through the coercive enterprise of surveillance and mediated social control (Harvey, 2004), as they are fighting their decline that was only magnified by COVID-19. The public square, park, or plaza is the ideal location to erect monuments to former grandeur of rule and violence, to erect prominent monuments of lost causes and civil wars 30 years after such ways as in 1891 Atlanta, Georgia with the Henry O. Grady Statue (see Fig. 4.31) Henry Grad, a fierce proponent and creator of the narrative of a new South to rise from the ashes of the Civil War.

The racial resentment in Society is forged by the State through its production of space that is then reinforced through systems of education and media (McCarthy & Dimitriadis, 2000). Power has been a contested tool and socio-political expression not just in contemporary politics but also within the long history of European and British civilisation. The location of its contestation is embedded in the halls of major social institutions of various European, British, and U.S. societies. Judicial systems are just one institution or venue for power to express itself upon those deemed powerless. Additionally, the location of its contestation can also be found in the physical space of European, British, and U.S. society, in the public and private-public space. Public parks, public malls, streetscapes, stadia, and arena all exert a power over the less powerful to restrict bodies and regulate behaviours.

## 4.6 The Animation of Public Space by the Forces of Ethno-Nationalism

But in the vein of Stuart Hall conceptions of power, power does not only subside in grips of the dominant elites and governments of the European, British, and U.S. world, but also in the act of resistance and within the location of contestations of those less powerful (Osborne & Segal, 1997). It is within this context that on one hand, we view ethno-nationalist populism as the struggle for power by the disenfranchised labourers and economically impoverished of the fabricated society. They seek to violently usurp power from the elite classes that in their view have capitulated to "Browning" of the State, despite sharing an underscored similarity with those majority in the elite class, Whiteness (Denvir, 2020; Metzl, 2019). But therein lies the tolerated State sanctioning of their existence, the exploiting of an

ethnic consciousness for the sanctioned violence to likely come from it.

"It's like writing history with lightening. My only regret is that is so terribly true", was said by the 28th President after a personal viewing of D. W. Griffith's *The Birth of a Nation* in the White House in 1915 (Benbow, 2010, p. 509). And with that statement and the popularity of the movie, the second Ku Klux Klan (the Klan) was formed. The second Klan maintained its anti-Black stance but broadened its views to include anti-immigrant (Jews and Italians), anti-Catholic, and anti-Communist ideals (Gordon, 2017). Its membership swelled and eventually resulted in a 30,000 march on Washington on August 8, 1925. *The Washington Post* placed the march on the front page with a picture entitled "Pennsylvania Avenue Mass of White During Klansmen's Parade". The Post's account described the "parade" in somewhat majestic fashion, as "phantom-like hosts of the Klan spread their white robe over the most historic thoroughfare yesterday in one of the greatest demonstrations this city has ever known" ("White Robbed Klan", 1925, p. 1). The banal labelling of the march, and of such an organisation with the legacy like the Klan, as a simple parade spoke to the perceived mainstream nature of their presence, even in their second re-grouping of the organisation.

Quite startling, the Klan was so mainstream that in various parts of the United States the Klan outright "sponsored, in public, baseball teams, father-son outings, beautiful baby contests, weddings, baby christenings, junior leagues, road rallies, festivals" according to Kathleen Blee (Weeks, 2015). A familial culture within the Klan was key, as they established youth groups, a Tri-K Klub for young girls, and a Klan University for older youth. According to Blee (1991), the Klan,

> As early as 1921…presented Lanier University in Atlanta with a substantial endowment, citing its full agreement with principles of the university…Lanier University advertised itself as an institution dedicated to the teachings of "pure Americanism"…two years later, The Ku Klux Klan tried to purchase Valparaiso University in

northern Indiana to become a Klan University but failed. (p. 160)

The second Klan made an increased effort to be gender inclusive in membership and leadership (Blee, 2002). According to McWhirter (2011), the second Klan had far more strident directive and purpose. The Klan, although reflecting a populist tinge, also embraced all sectors and classes of American society under the purpose,

> To shield the sanctity of the home and the chastity of womanhood; to maintain White supremacy; to teach and faithfully inculcate a high spiritual philosophy through an exalted ritualism; and by a practical devotedness to conserve, protect and maintain the distinctive institutions, rights, privileges, principles and ideals of a pure Americanism. (McWhirter, 2011, p. 65)

The day after the August 1925 march, a smaller contingency of the Klan travelled to Arlington to place wreaths on the Tomb of the Unknown Soldier and the grave of William Jennings Bryan, famed American populist orator and alleged supporter of the Klan who died that year. Later in the evening an initiation ceremony of 200 new members was conducted ("200 Join", 1925). With nearly 75,000 people present, all witnessed the burning of an electrically lit 80-foot cross at the Arlington Park horse grounds, in the spirit of what was depicted in *The Birth of Nation* and was not a tradition of the Klan until its depiction. On September 13, 1926, the Klan returned to march on Washington once more; however, this time only 15,000 attended and participated (see Fig. 4.25).

> What is the cause of all this [rise of the second Klan]? There can be little doubt but that in its present form is a legacy of the World War...The

**Fig 4.25** Ku Klux Klan, Women Marching Down Pennsylvania Ave. With the U.S. Congress in the Background. Harris & Ewing Photographers, Washington, D.C., 1926 (The Library of Congress/ Public Domain)

wages of War is Hate...Hate is Fear...The shape of fear looms over them. Germany fears the Jew, England fears the Indian; America fears the Negro, the Christian fears the Moslem, Europe fears Asia, Protestants fears Catholic, Religion fears Science. Above all, Wealth fears Democracy. (p. 293)

In an effort to preserve history, facilitate awareness, and provide educational leisure opportunities, the 65,000 square foot Illinois Holocaust Museum and Education Center opened in 2009 in the Chicago suburb of Skokie. Schools from around the Midwest of the United States have brought students on field trips to learn from the numerous displays, exhibits on geno-cide (the Jewish Holocaust and other genocides), 21,000 video/audio testimonials, and 8,000 artefacts attesting to the atrocities inflicted on those of the Jewish faith both in Nazi-controlled Germany and through hate crimes in contemporary times (Levine, 2009). Some 2,100 video-taped testimonials from Holocaust survivors are kept and shown to visitors to ensure that this chapter of history is not forgotten but also to be learned from so that it does not occur again. Also, programming staff utilise the space and re-sources of the Museum and Center to raise awareness of all forms of injustice and violence by holding forums and workshops (Regencia, 2010).

The grand opening of the Illinois Holocaust Museum and the ensuing protest was not the first time that an issue of anger toward Jewish identity arose in Skokie, Illinois. Similar to many cities across the United States with other cultural or racial groups, Skokie uniquely became a suburb that at-tracted a high percentage of Jewish immigrants, specifically a high number of Jewish death camp survivors. At one point it was believed that this small northern suburb of Chicago had the largest per ca-pita concentration of Jewish survivors outside of Israel/Occupied Palestine. The population of the suburb was nearly 50% Jewish. As a consequence, Skokie developed a distinct Jewish flare due to this migration as restaurants, social clubs, and synago-gues sprung up and around the suburb with the clear and apparent influences of European Jewish popu-lations. This highly visible Jewish identity garnered the attention of the resurgent American Neo-Nazi movement, the National Socialist Party of America

(NSPA) under the leadership of Frank Collin (Levine, 2009).

In 1977, the NSPA chose a little-known public park in Skokie as the second site for their planned demonstration primarily to show their growing strength against other racial and cultural groups. In Skokie, much of their rhetoric centred on Jews, Israel, Zionism, and the Holocaust. The NSPA initially chose Marquette Park in Chicago, based on the negative response that Martin Luther King, Jr., received in 1966 (when he was struck by a rock) as the site for the demonstration. George Lincoln Rockwell, leader of the American Nazi Party (the National Socialist White People's Party – NSWPP, a precursor to Frank Collin and the NSPA that Collin was a member of), organised a "White People's March" in neighbouring Gage Park to recruit members (see Fig. 4.26 and 4.27). NSPA continued the efforts of the American Nazi Party in Marquette Park, purchasing a building as an office years after a former member of the American Nazi Party murdered Rockwell.

However, the city of Chicago and the Chicago Park District officials required the NSPA to take out a large sum public-safety insurance bond and approved a policy banning political demonstrations. Skokie, near to Chicago, was then selected by the NSPA, a permit was requested, but was turned down by the Village government because of their concern and sensitivity to the numerous Jewish residents of the Village (Skokie Park District, 1976a). Specifically, in two meetings of the Board of Commissioners of the Skokie Park District, the Board first directed Daniel Brown, Director of the Skokie Park District at the time, to inform Frank Collin that the district did not have a "Birch Park," and second, passed an ordi-nance on public assemblies and parades that re-quired at least 30 days of notice and an insurance bond over $300,000 (Skokie Park District, 1976b). However, after this second refusal, the NSPA sub-sequently chose to take the Village of Skokie to court for violating their basic rights to demonstrate on public property. Over the span of three years and with the American Civil Liberties Union (ACLU) providing defence, the NSPA won the Supreme Court ruling that overturned the Village's decision (Dubey, 1977). The Village of Skokie granted the

**Fig 4.26** Front of Flyer for a White Peoples Rally in Gage Park, Chicago Featuring George Lincoln Rockwell. (Chicago Historical Society)

NSPA permission to use the space in front of the Village Hall with the restriction that swastikas (symbols that affirm neo-Nazi identity) could not be worn or present. The legal battle became a landmark case on Freedom of Speech in the United States (National Socialist Party of America v. the Village of Skokie, 1977). The site of the planned march ultimately became the modern site for the Museum and Centre, linking the past issues against Jewish identity with the continued awareness against acts of hatred and violence (Levine, 2009).

NSPA organisers chose to hold three demonstrations in Chicago's Marquette Park, whose officials chose to eliminate the insurance requirement and political demonstration ban out of fear of legal liability (Berlet, 2001). The first rally of 25 members

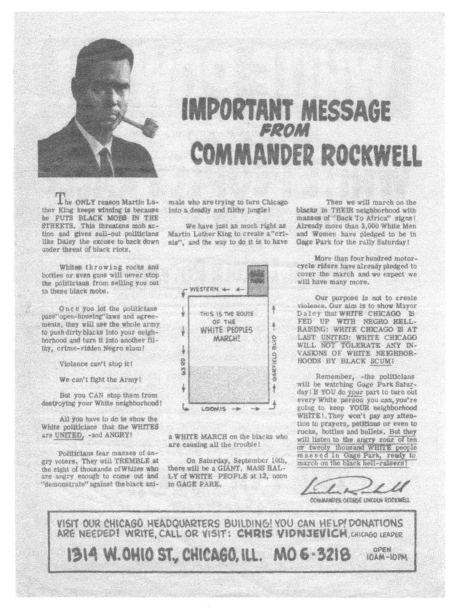

**Fig 4.27** Back of Flyer for a White Peoples Rally in Gage Park, Chicago Featuring George Lincoln Rockwell. (Chicago Historical Society)

was on July 9, 1978 and was organised as an anti-integration rally (Black families were moving into the "White ethnic" neighbourhood) with roughly 2,000 counter protestors (Kneeland, 1978). The second on June 28, 1986, was a joint rally with the American First Committee of 30 of their combined members, 75 counter protestors, and thousands of White residents, and was spurred on by the second term of

Mayor Harold Washington, Chicago's first Black mayor (Gibson & Zambrano, 1986). The last rally on August 28, 1988, attracted 500 White Nationalists of various organisations, another 300 counter protestors, and hundreds of resident onlookers ("Mob Attacks", 1988). Frank Collin in 1979 was also convicted for child molestation and sentenced to seven years in prison, which resulted in the NSPA moving from Illinois to North Carolina under new leadership (Kaplan, 2000). Furthermore, the attempts of the NSPA and "White Ethnic" residents of the Marquette Park were not successful to preventing housing integration as Census trends in 2000 showed Black and Latinx populations at 53% and 35%, respectively (in the 1980 Census, Black and Latinx were at 5.3% and 11%) (U.S. Census 1981; 2001).

Yet, in Emanuel African Methodist Episcopal Church on the evening of June 17, 2015, Dylann Roof proceeded to kill nine people (Cynthia Hurd, Susie Jackson, Ethel Lee Lance, Depayne Middleton-Doctor, Clementa Pinckney, Tywanza Sanders, Daniel Simmons, Sharonda Coleman-Singleton, and Myra Thompson) as they attended a prayer service. Roof hoped that his attack would be a call to arms, "worsen race relations, increase racial tensions that would lead to a Race war" (Cobb, 2017). His biggest complaint as he planned his act was that he could not find any like-minded "patriots" to take up the cause, because as it seemed "other White Nationalists" were all talk. The Charleston shooting became a touch point for the question of White Nationalism and its symbolism. The presence of Confederate Monuments began to be in question, and their removal was the answer for some. Ironically, many of those monuments were featured (and still are) featured in public parks throughout the United States.

Prior to the major rally in August, there were preceding activities that the diligence and persistence of White nationalist organising abilities to respond to the removal of the statue. Richard Spencer and the National Policy Institute was the earliest to respond to the city council vote to remove the statue and to rename Lee Park "Emancipation Park" in May 2017 (another park named after another Confederate General Thomas "Stonewall" Jackson was also up for renaming) (Griggs, 2017). This smaller rally was followed by another Klan-led rally after a permit was secured by members but was moved by the City to another park (McKenzie, 2017). Similar to NSPA Rally planned for Skokie, IL, the City was sued by the lead organiser Jason Kessler with support by the ACLU that resulted in an injunction, and Kessler and the groups were able to hold the rally at the intended location. Other

similarities to past gatherings of White Nationalism were as follows: the chanting and use of the slogan "blut und boden" at the 1939 Bund Rally in Madison Square Garden in New York City; the aforementioned invocation of anti-Jewish sentiments at the Klan March in Washington; and the invocation of conciliatory free speech from an outside actor (this case, Virginia Senator, Tim Kaine) at the first rally on the evening of August 11 on the University of Virginia's campus in Charlottesville.

However, the disruption and ultimate tragedy of the rally on August 12 provides further cautionary commentary. Neither law enforcement officers nor counter protestors were prepared for the number of White Nationalist representatives who attended the second day, nor their readiness for direct action and provocation. The White Nationalists that appeared initiated agitation with counter protestors while armed, as Virginia is an open carry state. Additionally, in virtual spaces, several digital platforms and social media sites were utilised to enable White Nationalists to attend and gather resources for their actions, such as Google and GoDaddy (for general searching of information for event logistics) ("Google Cancels", 2017), AirBnB (for lodging needs of visiting White Nationalists from other states) (Bromwich, 2017), and PayPal (for raising money for travel and the purchase of supplies) (Berr, 2017). The ACLU also faced criticism for once again protecting White Nationalists' use of free speech and assembly; however, they did issue a statement indicating that they will no longer engage in cases where free speech is coupled with the presence or use of guns and ammunition.

The public outrage of both rallies and the subsequent vehicular killing of Heather D. Hayer, a counter protestor, may be perceived as a detriment to the White Nationalist organisation that was involved, but this is far from the case. Nathan Domigo, founder of Identity Evropa, indicated, "this is a huge victory for us...we are going to get national attention" (Stapley, 2017). And the words of David Duke, long-standing White Nationalist political candidate and party member, provide a further emphasis of such a caution in understanding the outcomes of the rally, "a turning point for the people of this country. We are determined to take our country back"

(Cohen, 2017). And while they never lost it, the sloganeering does serve continued purpose to re-cultivate a variety of sanctioned violence that the United States has not seen since the era of racial massacres from 1890 to 1930.

Duke's words are only lessons taught by George Lincoln Rockwell, leader of the NSWPP and the American Nazi Party until his murder (see Figs. 4.26 and 4.29). Rockwell in *White Power* (1966) de-manded of all believers in White Nationalism and White Supremacy that,

> We must have an all-White America, an America which our children and our grand-children will play and go to school with other White children...We must have an America without swarming Black filth...an America... free of alien, Jewish influence; and America in which White people are the sole masters of our own destiny. (p. 345)

The 49 listed and active White Nationalist groups by the Southern Poverty Law Center within the United States all reflect a different interpretation and ar-ticulation of Rockwell's points.

If examined in isolation they appear as mo-mentary points of concern that easily disperse into forgotten history. Within each case, White Nationalism grew and adapted by becoming more mainstream than fringe; more savvy in its use of the protections of free speech than exclaiming a rhetoric of violence; more concerned with claiming and occupying space than being reclusive; and more organised in activities than aggressively hap-hazard. White Nationalists of the Democratic party through their surrogates, the Red Shirts, not only broke up a coalition between North Carolina Populist, the Famer's Alliance, and the Black Republicans but also orchestrated the Wilmington Race Riot of 1898 and the 2,000-person White mob that burned homes, destroyed the only Black press of the entire state, and ousted Black elected officials (Kirshenbaum, 1998). Nearly three dec-ades later, William Joseph Simmons, Imperial Wizard of the first Klan, invoked these sentiments as well as the populist agrarian cause in *Klan Unmasked* (1924),

> We Americans are barely reproducing our numbers on our own soil. In comparison with the colored and foreign elements our percentage is every year being reduced. In full view, within a few decades at most, lies the new America... the new America, if the present tendencies continue, will be a nation composed of a majority of American white farmers only in the middle western and plains states. Black farmers...the coastal regions of the South and the Mississippi Delta, and Japanese farmers will rapidly multiply their numbers on the Pacific coast. (Simmons, 1923, p. 104)

While Silk (2007) posited in a discussion on the re-constitution of urban space that,

> Somewhat butting against Martin Luther King Boulevard, semantically, ideologically, if not physically, "Confederate Park" (which com-memorates the Confederate soldiers who died in the 1st Battle of Memphis in the Civil War) and "Nathan Bedford Forrest Park" (named after, and indeed the burial site of, the General who led the Confederacy during the second battle of Memphis and was the first "Grand Wizard" of the Ku Klux Klan after the war) create a topographic web of glorification and memorialization of an "Old South" based on slave labor,
> White supremacy, the Confederate "cause". Indeed, these two names, along with Jefferson Davis Park (commemorating the only President of the Confederate States in America), are sites of local contestation. (p. 262)

At the time of drafting this chapter, members of militia groups, Three Percenters and other con-glomerations that have been allowed to roam free and grow over the past 12 years, have stormed the U.S. Capitol as Congress is engaged the electoral hearing to confirm the presidency of the 46th President. It is less that this is a defining moment and more a signalling that power once again will use whatever means to maintain itself, and those methods have occurred and re-occurred throughout history. The social construction of racialised iden-tities is at the very heart of societies' production of ethno-nationalist populism (McKean, 2016). Identity is confusingly exacerbated by its meiosis into social identity, cultural identity, and ethnic identity. Monuments of historic figures of the Confederacy and of nativist, populist, and eugenic histories are being protected by the "flawed" human beings myth; yet, these human beings were enemies to humanity in their ideology and actions (Gilbert, 2017). There is a tension between White Nationalists as populists and any non-White "Other" organisation, institution, business, or residence regardless of geography or the level of socioeconomic attainment of either group. Although American White Nationalists in each state are independent of each other, they each have a dubious relationship with either anti-government, White purity, or neo-Fascist sentiment. Thus, it is troubling when a member of a Missouri militia stated, "…some of the places we train are public parks where you can find all sorts of people frequenting the area" (Donovan, 2010).

These individuals are fully aware of their connection with the group and continuously receive and provide information from/to the group, the "imagined community". This was the case when David Copeland, a Neo-Nazi, on April 17–30 placed nail bombs in three distinct public locations in London, one of which was the Admiral Duncan Pub in "SoHo", which is in the centre of gay community of London ("Profile: Copeland the Killer", 2000). This was the case of Anders Behring Breivik on July 22, 2011, in Norway, detonating a van bomb killing eight people, and then opening fire on 65 children at a nearby youth summer camp of the Workers' Youth League (Hartman, 2011). Or, the case of Amanda and Jerad Miller, avid cosplayers, on June 8, 2014, who posted on Facebook that "the dawn of a new day. May all our coming sacrifices be worth it" as they killed two police officers eating at a pizzeria in Las Vegas and then proceeded to drape "Don't Tread On Me" and Swastika flags on their bodies (Warren, 2014). It is not surprising that the Klan marched on Washington; the NSPA chose to demonstrate in a public park; or the various White Nationalist organisations chose a campus, city streets, and a public park. The political act of protesting is highlighted in its violation of the sanctum of these public and private-public spaces. To protest where children

may play and find entertainment, families may eat and choose to vacation, and adults may engage in sports, changes the personalised simplicity of these settings with the complications of political, cultural, and ideological difference. But for now, signs and shouts consistently proclaim, "THE FUTURE OF AMERICA, RED NECKS AND WHITE SKINS" (Horton, 2004, p. 25).

As ethno-nationalist populism in the United States continues to turn to calls of fascism, it is far more important to see the relevance of public spaces in obscuring those calls with either benign displays of free speech rallies or violent protections of the first amendment. The true magnitude of White Supremacy is still elusive in many of our discussions that favour a focus on White privilege. Rowan (1996) warned while tuning into early interview-styled radio shows, hearing about summer training cops, and witnessing gatherings in public spaces such as parks that,

> The sprouting up of highly armed militias and paramilitary groups across America, all of them expressing some degree of racial paranoia and hatred…But those pressing to create a constitutional crisis by promoting a ghastly race war are going underground. (p. 8)

This turn to fascism by perceived White Nationalist populism underscores a tension with the fundamentals of populism, anti-elitism in individuals or government. If populism can be seen as resistance to elitism, then this persistent embracing of White Nationalism could be seen as a form co-option of the fundamentals of populism, a co-option of resistance that is being further commodified in the present day with coloured baseball hats and green avatars. But in reality, there is no turn, no uptick, no betrayal as White Nationalism (and by extension, White Separatism) has always been an organised mechanism to maintain the desired order in cities and within the greater State. The animation of public space is a form of street warfare, condoned by the State. The public square, park, or plaza is the site for either making "America" great again or for just violently making and remaking the State over and over again. And once again, it is

War that binds geographies and produces temporal conjunctures. The White Power Movement has only expanded as an after effect of wartime (Belew, 2018). The techniques of State violence abroad are brought home to the streets and societies. The various types of equipment of State violence abroad are modified for domestic use. The personnel of State violence abroad are left to fend for themselves upon their return. The appetites of the populace for State violence abroad are satisfied on the streets of the city. The only issue that the State did not consider in cultivating a culture of war is that has produced a movement that no longer wishes to prop up the current State, it wishes to replace it.

## 4.7 The Violence in Cities

Once the land has been measured, the buildings have been designed, the rooms have been quartered, and all space has been given its order, the fabricated society can now commence. As a fabrication, the society we live in defends the infrastructures that give us a social life and social meaning. As actors servicing the State, we work to uphold the perceived order of the defence of person, property, profits. The criminal is the threat to both, but only at the personal level. The criminal is only another citizen of the populace that has been excommunicated of their citizenship. The criminal is only some "Other" that never will be a citizen, just a vagrant and squatter on the land. Criminality then begs and calls for lethality. Criminality and lethality are the ways Orlando Patterson' "Social Death" functions. If "slavery was a substitute for death in war" (Patterson, 1982, p. 5), what substitutes slavery? The excommunicated citizen and the "Other" are not fully human and cannot be accepted into the full functioning of the fabricated society. The control over the fabricated society gives the State its sovereignty that consists of,

> the power to manufacture an entire crowd of people who specifically live at the edge of life, or even on its outer edge – people for whom living means continually standing up to death, and doing so under conditions in which death itself

increasingly tends to become spectral …. This life is a superfluous one, therefore, whose price is so meager that it has no equivalence, whether market or – even less – human; this is a species of life whose value is extra-economic…As a rule, such death is something to which nobody feels any obligation to respond. Nobody even bears the slightest feelings of responsibility or justice towards this sort of life or, rather, death. Necropolitical power proceeds by a sort of inversion between life and death, as if life was merely death's medium. It ever seeks to abolish the distinction between means and ends. (Mbembe, 2019, pp. 37–38)

Where the public execution by the State and the lynching by the fabricated society provided order and proper ordering for the criminal to know their place, the decline of the performance and spectacle left a void. The popular sovereignty in the act of lynching only strengthens the connection and allegiance to the State that maintains its sovereignty over the populace by performing those executions as forms of pedagogy to society of who should die, and how bad should their death be (see Fig. 4.28). Patterson (1982) continues to enlighten,

> the death commuted was punishment for some capital offense, or death from exposure or starvation. The condition of slavery did not absolve or erase the prospect of death; it was, peculiarly, a conditional commutation. The execution was suspended only as long as the slave acquiesced in his powerlessness… Because the slave had no socially recognized existence outside of his master, he became a social nonperson. (p. 5)

So, again I ask here, if, "slavery was a substitute for death in war" (Patterson, 1982, p. 5), what is the substitute for slavery? I argue here it is criminality as that is the most unifying mechanism for the State to remain legitimate and the fabricated society to be most effectively coerced. The production of space in the city produces the racialised and gendered ways that order is achieved. The space of the city was designed for the work patterns of those gendered men

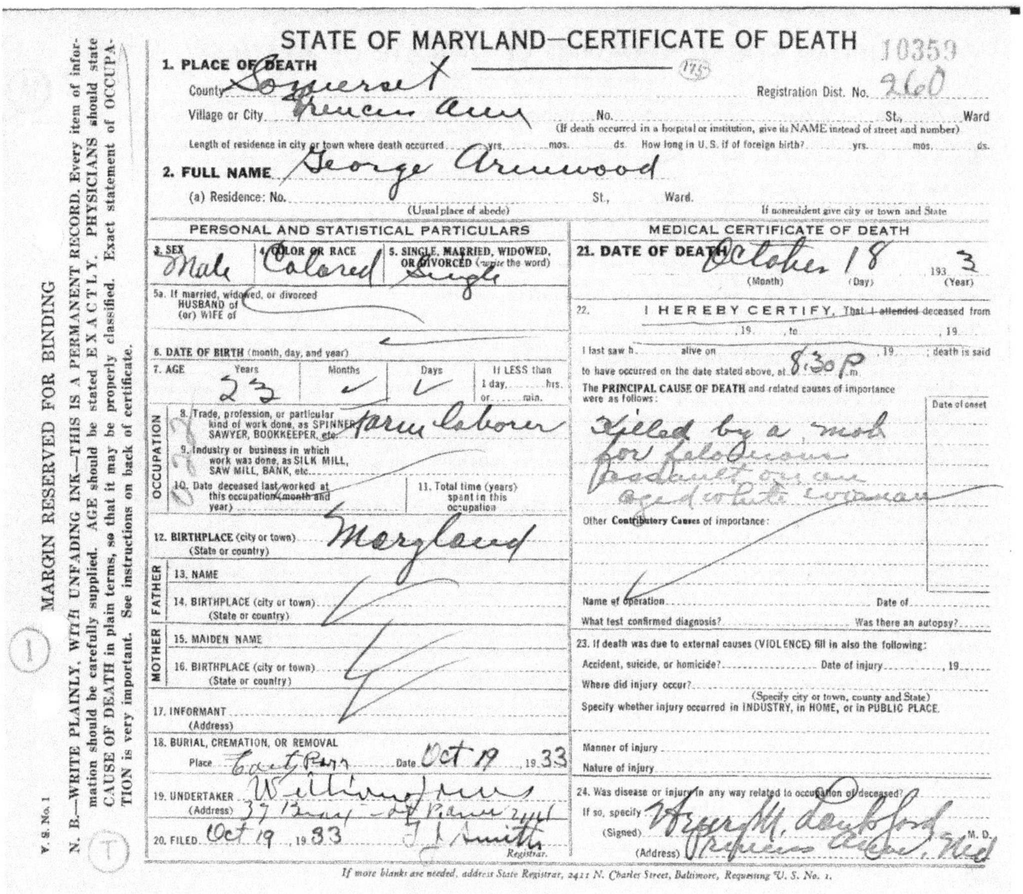

STATE OF MARYLAND—CERTIFICATE OF DEATH 10359

MARGIN RESERVED FOR BINDING

N. B.—WRITE PLAINLY, WITH UNFADING INK—THIS IS A PERMANENT RECORD. Every item of information should be carefully supplied. AGE should be stated EXACTLY. PHYSICIANS should state CAUSE OF DEATH in plain terms, so that it may be properly classified. Exact statement of OCCUPATION is very important. See instructions on back of certificate.

1. PLACE OF DEATH
County Somerset Registration Dist. No. 260
Village or City Princess Anne No. St., Ward
(If death occurred in a hospital or institution, give its NAME instead of street and number)
Length of residence in city or town where death occurred yrs. mos. ds. How long in U.S. if of foreign birth? yrs. mos. ds.

2. FULL NAME George Armwood
(a) Residence: No. St., Ward. (Usual place of abode) If nonresident give city or town and State

| PERSONAL AND STATISTICAL PARTICULARS | MEDICAL CERTIFICATE OF DEATH |
|---|---|
| 3. SEX Male; 4. COLOR OR RACE Colored; 5. SINGLE, MARRIED, WIDOWED, OR DIVORCED (write the word) Single | 21. DATE OF DEATH October 18 1933 (Month) (Day) (Year) |
| 5a. If married, widowed, or divorced HUSBAND of (or) WIFE of | 22. I HEREBY CERTIFY, That I attended deceased from 19 , to 19 |
| 6. DATE OF BIRTH (month, day, and year) | I last saw h alive on 19 ; death is said to have occurred on the date stated above, at 8:30 P.m. |
| 7. AGE Years 23 Months Days If LESS than 1 day, hrs. or min. | The PRINCIPAL CAUSE OF DEATH and related causes of importance were as follows: Killed by a mob for felonious assault on an aged white woman. Date of onset |
| OCCUPATION 8. Trade, profession, or particular kind of work done, as SPINNER, SAWYER, BOOKKEEPER, etc. farm laborer; 9. Industry or business in which work was done, as SILK MILL, SAW MILL, BANK, etc.; 10. Date deceased last worked at this occupation (month and year); 11. Total time (years) spent in this occupation | Other Contributory Causes of importance: |
| 12. BIRTHPLACE (city or town) (State or country) Maryland | Name of operation Date of |
| FATHER 13. NAME; 14. BIRTHPLACE (city or town) (State or country) | What test confirmed diagnosis? Was there an autopsy? |
| MOTHER 15. MAIDEN NAME; 16. BIRTHPLACE (city or town) (State or country) | 23. If death was due to external causes (VIOLENCE) fill in also the following: Accident, suicide, or homicide? Date of injury , 19 Where did injury occur? (Specify city or town, county and State) Specify whether injury occurred in INDUSTRY, in HOME, or in PUBLIC PLACE. |
| 17. INFORMANT (Address) | Manner of injury |
| 18. BURIAL, CREMATION, OR REMOVAL Place [illegible] Date Oct 19 1933 | Nature of injury |
| 19. UNDERTAKER [illegible] (Address) [illegible] | 24. Was disease or injury in any way related to occupation of deceased? If so, specify |
| 20. FILED Oct 19 1933 [illegible] Registrar. | (Signed) [illegible] M. D. (Address) Princess Anne, Md |

If more blanks are needed, address State Registrar, 2411 N. Charles Street, Baltimore, Requesting V. S. No. 1.

V. S. No. 1

**Fig 4.28** The death certificate of George Armwood, lynched "by mob for felonious assault on an aged White woman" on 18 October 1933 in Somerset County, MD. 1,000 laid siege on to the Princess Anne jail, beat and abducted him, hung him from a tree until his death, then dragged body to the courthouse, displayed the body with hung from a telephone pole, burned the body, and then dragged the remains to a lumberyard. (Maryland State Archives/Department of Health Bureau of Vital Statistics)

and those gendered women. The day and night, the home and the street. Through a feminist geographical lens, the directional and functional map of the city likely "shifts from day to night, weekday to weekend, season to season" because of how the State creates mutability in gender oppression (Kern, 2020, p. 169). Through a Black geographical lens, the directional and functional map of the city is fixed, as "the power of transparent space works to hierarchically position individuals, communities, regions, and nations" because of how the State policies space for control (McKittrick, 2006, p. 6). Through a Marxist geographical lens, the directional and functional map of the city is absolute, because of "property relationship…within which [the] monopoly control can operate" thereby classifying the labourer, the elite, and the rulers (Harvey, 2009, p. 14). For the map serves as a device that hides the violence committed by way of "the textual representation of Whiteness as order, civilization, and logos" (King, 2019, p. 89).

A violation of the time of day or location results in harm, but different notions of harm based on class, gender, and Race. This distinction is exploited by the State in engineering and conjuring the criminal. The criminal engages in those "specific activities that are only transparently recognized as 'criminal' when they are attached to statuses that invoke race (gang member), ethnicity ('illegal alien'), and/or national origin (suspected terrorist)" (Cacho, 2012, p. 43). The criminal is never the activity of the State in evicting people from homes, providing them with unclean water, manufacturing widespread joblessness, or managing mass death for the sake of the economy during a pandemic. The State's need for any particular group to serve its role of distraction while the actual crime of dispossession and extraction is arbitrary. While the fabricated society only knows how to parrot what the State wishes it to, the distraction is always the focus. The fabricated society is always "dependent upon the *permanence* of certain groups' criminalization…[and made functionally] ineligible for personhood" (Cacho, 2012, p. 6). In an act of astounding puppeteering, the State then responds to the demands of the fabricated society for public policy to enforce the order at ever-increasing strength and potency, an act the State was going to do regardless. Assimilation and conformity proffer the possibility for inclusion into the fabricated society, and the potential to be a principal actor for the State. We consent to this coercion in both explicit and subtle ways. The very ride-sharing apps bias users of racialised populations and the spaces that they select to be picked up from or taken to (Pandey & Caliskan, 2020). These function as literal consensus-building cultivators of the racialisation of people and places they inhabit, but "only by conforming to those U.S. heteronormative 'morals' and 'standards of living' that, ironically, have been defined over and against their very communities and their communities' survival strategies" (p. 129). Survival and dissent demand retribution by the State on behalf of the fabricated society.

And so, with the decline of public executions in the late 1700s and early 1800s, the need for the police came into existence for the sake of the order (Wilf, 1993). With the 1960s and 1970s, the need for greater policing came into existence. Policing beyond just traffic stops, helicopters, and heavy assault units was deployed with precision: Remarley Graham in the bathroom; Aiyana Stanley-Jones laying on the couch, probably waiting for her grandmother to bring some Kool-Aid; and Breonna Taylor lying in bed after a long day at work or being intimate with her partner, but each in a targeted neighbourhood for a certain type of policing and a certain type of governance. The State knows that no one of importance to the fabricated society lives in over-policed neighbourhoods. The order is restored through their policing. But policing is not at the site of the officer. Policing is at the site of the zoning law, the city ordinance, and the court decree. All the officers can do is shrug their shoulders, beat us to submission, or shoot us until there is no more to shoot. But with surplus populations, there are always a steady supply of people to shoot. The police are not authority; they execute the will of authority. They execute State governance, and governance, as is policing, is inherently violent.

Capitalism, despite its perceived longevity and permanence, is a tenuous order and a necessary impetus to govern. Our ability to focus on its operations constantly shifts and is obscured because it creates disorder. As capitalism destabilises both our cognition of reality and our social interactions, the police are required to maintain order (Seigel, 2018). Since the order is tenuous, discourse is needed to gin up the fabricated society. The "criminal" and "crime" must be hallmarks of news coverage, political campaigns, and representations of governing. Policing, not the cop, the law, and the will of the State to subjugate, dispossess, and extract is what is obscured when epitomising the cop as police. What Seigel (2018) does in *Violence Work* is to more directly (and profoundly) link policing with the State and not the cop by way of following how and where the cop functions. The cop is not a civilian in spite of collecting a check, clocking in and out, and shopping at the grocery store. The powers given to the cop render them within the apparatus of the State but above all other apparatuses with their dispatching of force and death. The cop is not a public employee despite tax dollars paying for their uniform, car, gun, and bullets, but instead a servant of the public-private partnership to defend property and the flow of wealth from the accumulation of capital. The TV mythmaking of creation of special victims' units (*Law & Order SVU*) runs against the actual defence of property and order. The cop is not a local actor, or representative of government, but actually a functionary that can and has been dispatched across state lines, at borders, across borders, and in other States. Thus, the connection between the violence from the police, violence from the State, and violence that is fundamentally a part of racialisation is the same violence, one violence by the State in the sole interests of capital. The way that racialisation has always operated, "how it disposes of bodies, how it appropriates their products, and how it fixes them in a visual grid" of the city (Hartman & Wilderson, 2003, p. 191). And as Seigel (2018) gives a reader pause,

> In other words, the more unequal are social relations, the more violence is required to preserve social hierarchies, and a cycle of exacerbated inequality and corresponding greater violence can ensue as elites attempt to keep other people from leaving or revolting. [...] This is precisely what has happened over the last forty years in the United States, as [*Violence Work*] has observed. As neoliberalism exacerbated inequality, police-inflicted violence expanded and intensified. Police forces mushroomed, budgets spreading like stains, and their fatal impact followed suit. How much, how badly? As with violence overall, police violence is somewhere between difficult and impossible to quantify. How should we think about police violence in a way that allows us to appreciate its magnitude? (p. 182)

*Violence work,* unlike any other discussion on policing, other than *Policing the Crisis* (Hall et al., 1978), cuts at the heart of what policing is and does by presenting a philosophical understanding of what policing is by examining what policing has done. Hall et al. (1978) posit that a crisis is always needed for the deployment of force and of violence and contextualises it as a moral panic among the populace of a Society. Crisis is a production of the State, so the very real harm of rape in the city is manipulated as an "allegory of Empire" (Sharpe, 1993). The surveillance camera won't stop the rape, nor is it truly meant to, although that is what we are instructed to believe. The camera and the policing that produces it will only be used to arrest a bunch of non-rapists under the auspices of the public safety. Sexual assault is anti-democratic. It disrupts the use of spaces and leads to a social death for survivors. Worse of all, the manipulative emphasis ny media on White women and their

screams against "dark" men is also anti-democratic and leads to the elimination of them. And this too is patriarchy.

And as a deliberately developed discursive term, "moral panic" spread across cities in the United States throughout the 1960s and 1970s, to eventually find its way into cities across the United Kingdom in the 1980s, where it spread to a host of European cities in the 1990s and early 2000s. Moral panic occurs,

> When the official reaction to a person, groups of persons, or series of events is *out of all proportion* to the actual threat offered, [and] when "experts," in the form of police chiefs, the judiciary, politicians, and editors [of media sources] *perceive* the threat in all but identical terms, and appear to talk "with one voice" of rates, diagnoses, prognoses and solutions, when the media representations universally stress "sudden and dramatic" increases (in numbers involved or events) and "novelty", above and beyond that which a sober, realistic appraisal could sustain, then we believe it is appropriate to speak of the beginnings of a *moral panic*. (p. 16; emphasis in the original)

Again, the State derives its sole power only in association to "persons, places, and activities":

> The "power of the State" is a resultant, not a cause, an outcome of the composing and assembling of actors, flows, buildings, relations of authority into relatively durable associations mobilized, to a greater or lesser extent, towards the achievement of particular objectives by common means. This is not a matter of the domination of a "network" by "the State" but rather a matter of translation. The translation of political programmes articulated in rather general terms – national efficiency, democracy, equality, enterprise – into ways of seeking to exercise authority over persons, places and activities in specific locales and practices. The translation of thought and action from a "centre of calculation" into a diversity of locales dispersed across a territory – translation in the sense of a movement from one place to another.

**Fig 4.29** An Aerial View of the São Paulo favela of Paraisópolis and Its Wealthy Neighbour Morumbi, 2004 (Photo Credit: Tuca Vieira, https://en.tucavieira.com)

Through a multitude of such mobile relays, relations are established between those who are spatially and temporally separated, and between events and decisions in spheres that none the less retain their formal autonomy. (Rose, 1996, p. 43)

We outsource the matter of harm and safety to police, policing, and policy as we are so concerned about crime while we shop at the mall and drink our lattes. We are too busy indulging in our lifestyles of fabricated society to truly care about "crime", harm, and public safety. The favela sits next to the luxury apartment complex (see Fig. 4.29), the 'hood is across the street from the stadium, the barrio is just on the other side of the interstate from the mall, and the township is right at edge of the city.

### 4.8 A Fourth Conclusion

The State governs through "crime", making use of the geographic spaces of cities to foster this entrenched political practise that has been built over decades. The infrastructure of the city both supports

the myth of moral panic (the 'hood, the projects, and the ghetto) and hides the myth by use of the features of amusement and leisure (the plaza, the canal walk, the riverfront festival, the recreation in the public park). In this fabricated society, all

the fears and anxieties of those who first imagined, and then discovered him [the young Black male]...threatening the traditional peace of the streets...[where he is] embodying in his every action and person, feelings and values that were the opposite of those decencies and restraints which England what she is. (pp. 161–162)

And this, too, is patriarchy. The systematic oppression of (gendered) women and the systematic elimination of particularly "Othered" (and gendered) men. And an examination of the city as the articulation of State power challenges past and present "existing theory attributed women's domination by men either to nature or social necessity rather than to social structural processes, unequal power, or exploitation" (Acker, 1989, p. 235). And patriarchy and racial supremacy within the State disrupts our political life, but the sanctity for the social life we have conjured into being in the spaces of the city extends our devotion to them and the State that has given them to us as patronage. Roller blading, walking the dog, bird watching, etc., all support the myth in some way and deepen our embrace of it. Love of this life serves death dealing in the life of others, in particularly in their potential interruption of it due to their "criminal behaviour". Linebaugh's thanatocracy (rule by violence, killing, and death) is wielded in everyday governance by an understanding of Achille Mbembe's (2009) *necropolitics* (socio-political power of life and death for some and not others). Surplus populations that have grown in access by the needs of capitalism, are now managed to death due to their uselessness – except their death (or violence that renders death) is useful by the State. Some deaths are immediate (for example, the refugees fleeing the sanctioned warfare by vigilantes in towns and cities across Central and South America). Seigel's violence work is the functional glue in Mbembe's necropolitics that articulates how Linebaugh's thanatocracy exists, and all three give the third part of the conceptualisation in the "Geographies of Threat", the **identification for violence**, its credence.

The history of the city, of cities, lies within the historical origins of the colonial city and the revision of the social and geo-spatial arrangements of the imperial city that form the basis for the creation of society as a fabrication. Space is the site of murder, killing, and genocide. Some deaths are with deliberate speed (for example, life on a reservation, bantustáns, or marginalised neighbourhoods). Space is the site of restraint, order, or social control in access and movement. Some deaths are managed (for example, concentration camps or refugee camps). Space is the site of condemnation, perpetual harassment, and selective death. And lastly, some deaths are concealed (for example, jails and prisons). Space is the site for slow death and carefully governed dead cities.

Under the auspices of security, populations are identified, populations are targeted as threats, and populations are set up for violence. Security theatre, a performance if you will, is performed to give us false confidence in the State within the city. The

rolling police car, the racial profiling of dangerous populations, the police dog as checkpoint, and the blinking blue police light of a surveillance camera put us at ease. In reality, they put land, buildings, property, and those who own and govern over them at ease. There are no dangerous neighbourhoods as personal harm is produced by a small network of individuals in any given city who engage in their activities when and where their activities take them (Weisburd, 2015). However, Geo-spatial harm of dramatic rent increases, exposure to toxins, and State violence are never the matter and order of the day. The very founding of the police is based on a property regime. It is no wonder that police support increases with wealth, regardless of Race (Elkins, 2016; Motley & Joe, 2018). Yet again, the focus on the cop hides the State. The community concern of the acquisition of Bearcats and MRAPS as examples of militarisation in smaller towns and cities is a distraction from the reasons for the use of their purchase and later deployment in a nearby city (re: Ferguson uprising). But those community concerns also distract and hide how insidious policing is. The police are given the license to kill by the State, and the acquisition of such equipment does not change their function. The acquisition is not sending a message that disturbs your peace in your café. They (the State through the cop) do not have to send a message because they are the message, and they always have been.

The State inflicts violence through dispossession and extraction. The State responds violently to objection and defiance to that dispossession and extraction. The State institutes violent measures that the Society embraces and earnestly braces for its implementation. The State strangles Society for more complicity through lower and lower wages, and high costs of living that necessitate violent responses to debt collection and property eviction. The State also targets housing, the site of domestication and the family, as a performed gender violence by actually targeting households (the people, women, within the home) (Brickell, 2020). The State responds with violence to "Black" market enterprises that created alternative markets and incomes to offset the substandard living with violence.

**Fig 4.30** 60th and Sheridan, in Kenosha, Wisconsin, the Location of Kyle Rittenhouse Shooting and Killing of Anthony Huber and Joseph Rosenbaum, and the Shooting and Maiming of Gaige Grosskruetz on 25 August 2020. (Photo Credit: Lightburst/Wiki Commons)

The State encourages the people of the fabricated society to call for greater State violence. The State's monopoly of violence means that the violence performed by the State is both judicial and extra-judicial, too. As Society's vigilante and volunteers are encouraged, condoned, and deputized for the work of extra-judicial (Hinton, 2020). Known Nothings, the White Caps, The first Klan, Red Shirts, Bald Knobbers, The Regulators, The Horse Thief Detective Associations, Vigilance Committees, Peace Societies, ethnic athletic associations, the second Klan, "White Citizens' Councils", Citizens' Council of America, White Hats, the third Klan, Committee of Ten Million, United Citizens for Community Action (also known as the United Coon Control Association), Traditionalist Worker Party, Proud Boys, III Percenters, and civil guards are just some of those groups that were formed to fulfil the need and to heed the call. The State reacts to the populace who finally opt-out off complicity with utter violence. The State renders all life as a carceral state within the enclosure of cities with the shiny veneer of the fabricated society. The State's monopoly of violence means that the violence performed by the State is extra-judicial, too. And that Society's vigilante and volunteered violence is not and never was extra-judicial. To protect property and exact vengeance against protestors who may threaten it, teenagers and their mothers can travel miles away and be deputized (see Fig. 4.30). Any violence that occurs is only allowed because the State allows it to. Violence, and the space where it has occurred, the necessary "out-of-control momentum of extreme violence of unlimited warfare [that] fueled [and fuels] race hatred" (Dunbar-Ortiz, 2014, p. 59). The State renders all life as a carceral state within the enclosure of cities with the shiny veneer of the fabricated society. There was never (Native) removal; there was always expulsion, deportation, and extermination. There was never a legal basis; there was only chicanery (Saunt, 2020). The violence from the army and the violence from the settler was one and the same.

As historian Roxanne Dunbar-Ortiz (2014) in *An Indigenous People's History of the United States*, corroborated and quoted fellow historian

John Grenier, the "Indian Wars" were exceptionally one-sided forms of colonial violence that were falsely attributed to,

> racism. [As] Grenier argued that rather than racism leading to violence, the reverse occurred: the out-of-control momentum of extreme violence of limited warfare fuelled Race hatred. "Successive generations of Americans, both soldiers and civilians, made the killing of Indian men, women, and children a defining element of their first military tradition and thereby part of a shared American identity... later generations of 'Indian haters,' men like Andrew Jackson turn the Indian wars into Race wars". By then, the indigenous peoples' villages, farmlands, towns, and entire nations formed the only barrier to the settlers' total freedom to acquire land and wealth. (pp. 58–59)

And it is with this understanding that the United States' Second Amendment had less to do with the right of individuals to bear arms, but instead with the right and need to form militias in defence of themselves (as settlers) and to the State (as the law granting and protecting political body), "a well regulated Militia, being necessary to the security of a free state". Hidden from both the "fallism" of statue toppling and flag waving in pro-gun rallies is the true nature from the settler colony of the United States to operate as military dispossession machine under the guiding principles of the Constitution as a fiscal military document. The sudden demise of a statue does not quite get us to confronting that reality, nor does the refusal to acknowledge one's desire to kill people within the guise of defence. Dunbar-Ortiz (2018) followed up with,

> The U.S. Constitution formally instituted "militias" as state-controlled bodies that were subsequently deployed to wage wars against Native Americans, the voluntary militias described in the Second Amendment entitled settlers, as individuals and families, to the right to combat Native Americans on their own. (p. 53)

The Second Amendment of the Constitution did two important things: 1) it forbade Black and indigenous populations from being accounted amongst the members of a militia; and 2) it empowered settlers to wantonly kill indigenous populations (and Black people involved in insurrections).

The city, a settler colonial base, a seat of the imperium, a site of violence condoned by the State and later memorialised in monument form as a mode of continued pedagogy upon the populace of what is allowed and what is the order of the day. A monument like that of the aforementioned Henry Grady (see Fig. 4.31), a fierce proponent of racial violence and bondage, that also served as shrine to further violence during the 1906 Race Massacre as,

> Another ragtag collection of Whites marched up Marietta Street to a barbershop across from the post office.... Armed with assorted weapons and their bare hands, the White men forced themselves through the shop ...killing...instantly. After vandalizing the shop and stripping the slain...of their clothes, the White men dragged their bodies face-first from the shop. A short distance [away]... another [was killed]. The three corpses were heaped together at the base of the famous Henry Grady Monument. (Godshalk, 2005, p. 93)

In and with this fabrication, the populace of society fights not only over space and territory, but also about the sort of reality that the space constitutes in their lives. We are trapped in the stories we tell ourselves. Our cities...wait, let me stop and correct myself, the cities of the State, are settlements – settlements of the old, new order to dispossess and extract. To exploit labour. To subjugate through processes of "Othering". To gender and engender oppression and elimination. And "any settlement is an inscription in space of the social relations in the society that built it...our cities are patriarchy written in stone, brick, glass and concrete" (Darke, 1996, p. 88). The "Other"-ing of N.H.I. (the judicial system designation – No Humans Involved), wildlings, and savages is the counter to "ones humanness and North Americanness [or Britishness, Frenchness, etc.] are always defined, not only in optimally White terms, but also in the optimally middle-class...variants of these terms" (Wynter, 1994, p. 44). Once a group has been culturally identified as

**Fig 4.31** The Erection and Unveiling of the Henry W. Grady Statue. Atlanta, Georgia, 1891. (Kenan Research Center at the Atlanta History Center)

the "Other" through both media practises, policy declarations, and the outcries of the conditioned public, the deployed forces have been given clearance and discretion to do a range of actions with the use of a range of tools. But immediate force deployment results in quick death; slow death requires violence from the moving gesture of the pen: Drucker's (1999) *Organized Abandonment*, no economic infrastructure for thriving, closing schools, little to no health care infrastructure, etc. So, the only encounter with government then becomes public works (at best) and police (at worst). For police to become trusted, it would actually require government to become trusted and for government to do trusting things. The basic principle for cities to be at their maximum potential as a sphere of operation, they must regularly assess, identify, and abandon things that are no longer profitable to the maximisation of the future; thus, they have been identified for the work of violence to be employed. And this is the third and final conceptualisation of the "Geographies of Threat", the **identification for violence**.

"…irrepressible violence is neither sound and fury, nor the resurrection of savage instincts, nor even the effect of resentment: it is man re-creating himself".

– Jean-Paul Sartre, 1967, preface to *Wretched of the Earth*, p. 18

"As much as guns and warships, maps have been the weapons of imperialism".
– Brian Harley, 1988 in *Maps, Knowledge and Power*, pp. 282–283.

## References

Acker, J. (1989). The problem with patriarchy. *Sociology*, *23*(2), 235–240.

Agnew, J. (1994). The territorial trap: The geographical assumptions of international relations theory. *Review of International Political Economy*, *1*(1), 53–80. http://www.jstor.org/stable/4177090

Alexievich, S. (2006). *Voices from Chernobyl: The oral history of a nuclear disaster* [Trans. by K. Gessen]. Picador.

Anderson, B. (1983). *Imagined communities. Reflections on the origin and spread of nationalism.* Verso Books.

Anguelovski, I., Triguero-Mas, M., Connolly, J. J., Kotsila, P., Shokry, G., Del Pulgar, C. P., Garcia-Lamarca, M., Argüelles, L., Mangione, J., Dietz, A., & Cole, H. (2020). Gentrification and health in two global cities: A call to identify impacts for socially vulnerable residents. *Cities & Health*, *4*(1), 40–49. 10.1080/2374 8834.2019.1636507

Applebaum, A. (2017). *Red famine: Stalin's war on Ukraine.* McClelland & Stewart.

Beck, B. (2020). Policing gentrification: Stops and low–level arrests during demographic change and real estate reinvestment. *City & Community*, *19*(1), 245–272. 10.1111/cico.12473

Beckert, S. (2015). *Empire of cotton: A global history.* Alfred A. Knopf.

Belletto, S. (2009). The game theory narrative and the myth of the National Security State. *American Quarterly*, *61*(2), 333–357. 10.1353/aq.0.0074

Belew, K. (2018). *Bringing the war home: The White Power Movement and paramilitary America.* Harvard University Press.

Benbow, M. E. (2010). Birth of a quotation: Woodrow Wilson and "like writing history with lightning". *The Journal of the Gilded Age and Progressive Era*, *9*(4), 509–533. http://www.jstor.org/stable/2079940

Berlet, C. (2001). Hate groups, racial tension and ethnoviolence in an integrating Chicago Neighborhood, 1976-1988. In B. A. Dobratz, L. K. Walder, & T. Buzzell (Eds.), *Research in Political Sociology, Vol.9: The Politics of Social Inequality* (pp. 117–163). Oxford Elsevier Science.

Berr, J. (2017, August 17). *PayPal* cuts off payments to right-wing extremist. *CBS News.*

Bhandar, B. (2018, December 3). Organised abandonment: The meaning of Grenfell. *The Sociological Review.* https://www.thesociologicalreview.com/organised-state-abandonment-the-meaning-of-grenfell/

Bhatnagar, R. D., Dube, R., & Dube, R. (2005). *Female infanticide in India: A feminist cultural history.* State University of New York Press.

Billingham, C. M. (2017). Waiting for bobos: Displacement and impeded gentrification in a midwestern city. *City & Community*, *16*(2), 145–168. 10.1111/cico.12235

Blee, K. M. (1991). *Women of the Klan: Racism and gender in the 1920s.* University of California Press.

Blee, K. M. (2002). *Inside organized racism: Women in the hate movement.* University of California Press.

Blum, E. D. (2008). *Love canal revisited: Race, class, and gender in environmental activism.* University Press of Kansas

Bodansky, D. (2004). Nuclear reactor accidents. In *Nuclear energy: Principles, practices, and prospects* (pp. 411–438). Springer. 10.1007/0-387-26931-2_15

Boswell, A. A. & Spade, J. Z. (1996). Fraternities and collegiate rape culture: Why are some fraternities more dangerous places for women?. *Gender & Society*, *10*, 133–147.

Brenner, N. & Elden, S. (2009). Henri Lefebvre on State, space, territory. *International Political Sociology*, *3*(4), 353–377. 10.1111/j.1749-5687.2009.00081.x

Brickell, K. (2020). *Home SOS: Gender, violence, and survival in crisis ordinary Cambodia.* John Wiley & Sons, Inc.

Bromwich, J. E. (2017, August 9). *Airbnb cancels accounts linked to White Nationalists rally in Charlottesville. The New York Times.*

Brown, K. (2015). *Plutopia: Nuclear families, atomic cities, and the great Soviet and American plutonium disasters.* Oxford University.

Buirski, N., Hubbard, B., Chandler, C. L., Margolin, S. (Producers). & Buirski, N. (Director). (2017). *The rape of Recy Taylor [Documentary].* U.S.A.: Augusta Films.

Bullard, R. (Ed.). (1983). *Confronting environmental racism: Voices from the grassroots.* South End Press.

Bullard, R. D. (1994). The legacy of American apartheid and environmental racism. *Journal of Civil Rights and Economic Development*, *9*(2), 445–474.

Bullard, R. (2004). *Environment and Morality: Confronting Environmental Racism in the United States.* United Nations Research Institute for Social Development, Programme Paper Number 8.

Cacho, L. M. (2012). *Social death: Racialized rightlessness and the criminalization of the unprotected.* New York University Press.

Cardona, G. (2007, March 19). Denver's crime rankings to change. *The Denver Post.* https://www.denverpost.com/2007/03/19/denvers-crime-rankings-to-change/

Carnoy, M. (1986). *The state and political theory.* Cambridge University Press.

Chaison, G. (2014). *The unions' response to globalization.* Springer.

Cobb, J. (2017, February 6, 2017). *Inside the trial of Dylann Roof. The New Yorker.*

Cohen, Z. (2017, August 19). *Trump's mixed messaging sparks concerns of 'emboldened' White Supremacists. CNN.*

Colver, J. (2016). *Riot. Strike. Riot.: The new era of uprisings.* Verso.

Covington, J. & Taylor, R. B. (1989). Gentrification and crime: Robbery and larceny changes in appreciating Baltimore neighborhoods during the 1970s. *Urban Affairs Quarterly*, *25*(1), 142–172. 10.1177/004208168902500109

Cresswell, T. (1996). *In place/out of place: Geography, ideology, and transgression.* University of Minnesota Press.

Darke, J. (1996). The man-shaped city. In C. Booth, J. Darke, & S. Yeandle (Eds.), *Changing places: Women's lives in the city* (pp. 88–100). Sage.

Davis, M. (2006). *City of quartz: Excavating the future in Los Angeles.* Verso Books.

Davis, M. (2017). *Planet of slums.* Verso Books.

Day, W. R. & Supreme Court of The United States. (1917). *U.S. Reports: Buchanan v. Warley, 245 U.S. 60.* [Periodical]. https://www.loc.gov/item/usrep245060/.

Denvir, D. (2020). *All-American nativism: How the bipartisan war on immigrants explains politics as we know it.* Verso.

Detroit Edison & Page, E. M. (1976) *We did not almost lose Detroit: A critique of the John Fuller Book: "We Almost Lost Detroit"*. University of Michigan Press.

Donaldson, G. A. (1984). A window on slave culture: Dances at Congo square in New Orleans, 1800–1862. *Journal of Negro History, 69*(2), 63–72.

Donovan, D. (2010, September 12). Voices of reason: An open response to the Kansas City Star article "the new militia." *Ad Astrum.* http://adastrum.kansascity.com/?q=node/1026

Downs, D. A. (1985). *Nazis in Skokie: Freedom, community and the First Amendment.* University of Notre Dame Press.

Drucker, P. (1999). *Management challenges for the 21st Century.* Harper Collins.

Dubey, D. (1977, July 14). *No swastikas allowed: Lift march injunction. The Skokie Life.* Chicago Historical Museum Archives.

Du Bois, W. (1926). The shape of fear. *The North American Review, 223*(831), 291–304. http://www.jstor.org/stable/25110229

Dunbar-Ortiz, R. (2014). *An Indigenous people's history of the United States.* Beacon Press.

Dunbar-Ortiz, R. (2018). *Loaded: A disarming history of the Second Amendment.* City Lights Books.

Duvall, T. & Bailey, P. M. (2020, July 5). Breonna Taylor warrant connected to Louisville gentrification plan, lawyers say. *Louisville Courier Journal.* https://www.courier-journal.com/story/news/crime/2020/07/05/lawyers-breonna-taylor-case-connected-gentrification-plan/5381352002/

Elkins, E. (2016, December 7). *Policing in America: Understanding public attitudes toward the police. Results from a national survey.* Cato Institute. https://www.cato.org/survey-reports/policing-america

Engels, F. (1972). *The origin of the family, private property and the State* [Edited by E. B. Leacock]. International Publishers.

Ezer, T., Joyce, A., McCalley, & Pacamalan, N. (2011). Protecting women's human rights: A case study in the Philippines. *Human Rights Brief, 18*(3), 21–27.

Fanon, F. (1963). *The wretched of the earth [Trans. C. Farrington].* Grove Press.

Freeman, L. (2006). *There goes the 'Hood: Views of gentrification from the ground up.* Temple University Press.

Fine, S. (2007). *Violence in the model city: The Cavanagh Administration, Race relations, and the Detroit Riot Of 1967.* Michigan State University Press.

Fortune, T. T. (1884). *Black and White: Land, labor, and politics in the South.* Fords, Howard, & Hulbert.

Foucault, M. (1972). *The archeology of knowledge and the discourse on language.* Pantheon Books.

Foucault, M. (1978a). *The history of sexuality.* Vintage Books.

Foucault, M. (1978b). *Power/Knowledqe* [Edited by Colin Gordon]. Pantheon Books.

Foucault, M. (1991a). *Discipline and punish: The birth of the prison.* Penguin Books.

Foucault, M. (1991b). Governmentality [trans. R. Braidotti and revised by C. Gordon]. In G. Burchell, C. Gordon & P. Miller (Eds.), *The Foucault effect: Studies in governmentality* (pp. 87–104). University of Chicago Press.

Foucault, M. (2000). Truth and juridical forms. In J. Faubian (Ed.), *Power: Essential works of Foucault 1954–1984, Volume 3.* The New Press.

Fuller, J. G. (1975). *We almost lost Detroit.* Reader's Digest Press.

Gamson, W. A. & Modigliani, A. (1989). Media discourse and public opinion on nuclear power. A constructionist approach. *American Journal of Sociology, 95*(1), 1–37. 10.1086/229213

Gandolfo, D. (2009). *The city at its limits: Taboo, transgression, and urban renewal in Lima.* University of Chicago Press.

German, D. & Latkin, C. A. (2016). Exposure to urban rats as a community stressor among low-income urban residents. *Journal of Community Psychology, 44*(2), 249–262. 10.1002/jcop.21762

Gibson, M. (2007). *Culture and power: A history of cultural studies.* Berg Publishers.

Gibson, T. A. (2004). *Securing the spectacular city: The politics of revitalization and homelessness in downtown Seattle.* Lexington Books.

Gibson, R. & Zambrano, M. (1986, June 29). Marquette hostilities boil. *The Chicago Tribune.* http://articles.chicagotribune.com/1986-06-29/news/8602160298_1_klan-rally-ku-klux-klan-supremacist-group

Gilbert, P. (2017, October). A monumental decision: What to with Confederate monuments?. *Parks & Recreation Magazine,* 36–39. http://www.nrpa.org/parks-recreation-magazine/2017/october/a-monumental-decision/

Gillham, P. F. & Noakes, J. A. (2007). "More than a march in a circle": Transgressive protest and the limits of negotiated management. *Mobilization: An International Journal, 12*(4), 341–357.

Gilmore, R. W. (2008). Forgotten places and the seeds of grassroots planning. In C. R. Hale (Ed.), *Engaging contradictions: Theory, politics, and methods of activist scholarship* (pp. 31–61). University of California Press.

Gilmore, R. W. (2015, November 9). *Organized abandonment and organized violence: Devolution and the police* [Keynote]. The Humanities Institute at UCSC.

Godshalk, D. F. (2005). *Veiled visions: The 1906 Atlanta Race Riot and the reshaping of American Race srelations*, University of North Carolina Press.

(2017, August 14). *Google* cancels Neo-Nazi site registration soon after it was dumped by *GoDaddy. Reuters.*

Gordon, L. (2017). *The second coming of the KKK: The Ku Klux Klan of the 1920s and the American political tradition.* Liveright Publishing Corporation.

Gramsci, A. (1980). *Selections from the prison notebooks.* Wishart Publications.

Gramsci, A. (1996). *Prison Notebooks, Volume 2* [Edited and Trans. by J. A. Buttigeg]. Columbia University Press.

Grenier, J. (2005). *The first way of war: American war making on the frontier, 1607–1814.* Cambridge University Press.

Griggs, B. (2017, May 15). Protests over Confederate statue shake Charlottesville Virginia. *CNN.* http://www.cnn.com/2017/05/15/us/charlottesville-lee-monument-spencer-protests-trnd/index.html

Gurney, M. (2012, March 25). Would the last person out of Detroit turn out the lights? Oh, wait, too Late. *National Post.* https://nationalpost.com/opinion/would-the-last-person-out-of-detroit-turn-out-the-lights-oh-wait-too-late

Habermas, J. (2001). *The structural transformation of the public sphere: An inquiry into a category of Bourgeois society.* MIT Press.

Hadacheck v. Sebastia, 239 U.S. 394, 36 S. Ct. 143, 60 L. Ed. 348 (United States Supreme Court 1915).

Hall, S., Critcher, C., Jefferson, T., Clarke, J., & Roberts, B. (1978). *Policing the crisis: Mugging, the state, and law and order.* Palgrave.

Hall, S. (1996). The West and the Rest: Discourse and power. In S. Hall, D. Held, D. Hubert, and K. Thompson (Eds.), *Modernity: An introduction to modern societies* (pp. 184–228). Blackwell.

Hall, S. (1993). Culture, community, nation. *Cultural Studies, 7*(3), 349–363. 10.1080/09502389300490251

Hall, S. (1997). Culture and power [Interview by P. Osborne & L. Segal]. *Radical Philosophy, 86,* 24–41.

Hall, S. & Schwarz, B. (2007). Living with difference: Stuart Hall in Conversation with Bill Schwarz. *Soundings, 37,* 148–158.

Hardin, G. (1968). The tragedy of the commons. *Science, 162*(3859), 1243–1248.

Hargreaves, A. (2017). *Violence against indigenous women: Literature, activism, resistance.* Wilfrid Laurier University Press.

Harland Bartholomew & Associates. (1932). *The Negro Housing Problem in Louisville.* Harland Bartholomew & Associates Collection, University Archives, Department of special Collections. Washington University Libraries. St. Louis, MO.

Harvey, D. (2004a). The "new" imperialism: Accumulation by dispossession. *Socialist Register, 40,* 64–87.

Harvey, D. (2004b). *The new imperialism.* Oxford University Press.

Harvey, D. (2009). *Social justice and the city.* The University of Georgia Press.

Hartman, B. (2011, July 24). Norway attack suspect had anti-Muslim, Pro-Israel views. *Jerusalem Post.*

Hartman, S. V. & Wilderson, F. B. (2003). The position of the unthought. *Qui Parle, 13*(2), 183–201. http://www.jstor.org/stable/20686156

Herbert, C. W. (2021). *A Detroit story: Urban decline and the rise of property informality.* University of California Press.

Herring, C. (2019). Complaint-Oriented Policing: Regulating Homelessness in Public Space. *American Sociological Review, 84*(5), 769–800. 10.1177/0003122419872671

Hinton, E. (2020). *America on fire: The untold history of police violence and Black rebellion since the 1960s.* Liveright.

Hise, G. & Deverell, W. (2000). *Eden by design: The 1930 Olmsted-Bartholomew Plan for the Los Angeles region.* University of California Press.

Horton, J. O. (2004). Urban alliances: The emergence of Race-based populism in the age of Jackson. In J. W. Trotter, E. Lewis, and T. W. Hunter (Eds.), *African American Urban Experience: Perspectives from the Colonial Period to the Present* (pp. 23–34). Palgrave Macmillan.

Hwang, J. & Sampson, R. J. (2014). Divergent pathways of gentrification: Racial inequality and the social order of renewal in Chicago neighborhoods. *American Sociological Review 79*(4), 726–751.

Intondi, V. J. (2015). *African Americans against the bomb.* Stanford University Press.

James, J. (Ed.). (2007). *Warfare in the American homeland: Policing and prison in a penal democracy.* Duke University.

Mowatt, R. A. (2012). Lynching as leisure: Broadening notions of a field. *American Behavioral Scientist, 56*(10), 1361–1387. 10.1177/0002764212454429

Kaplan, J. S. (Ed.). (2000). *Encyclopedia of White power: A sourcebook on the radical racist right.* AltaMira Press.

Kelling, G. L. & Wilson, J. Q. (1982, March). Broken windows: The police and neighborhood safety. *The Atlantic.* https://www.theatlantic.com/magazine/archive/1982/03/broken-windows/304465/

Kern, L. (2020). *Feminist city: Claiming space in the man-made world.* Verso.

Kikuchi, C. T. (1976). We Didn't Almost Lose Detroit [Partial meltdown, Oct. 5, 1966 at Fermi-1]. *Electric Perspectives, 4,* 6–11.

King, T. L. (2019). *The black shoals: Offshore formations of Black and native studies*. Duke University Press.

Kittrie, O. F. (2016). *Lawfare: Law as a weapon of war*. Oxford University Press.

Kirshenbaum, A. M. (1998). The vampire that hovers over North Carolina: Gender, White Supremacy, and the Wilmington Race Riot of 1898. *Southern Cultures*, *4*(3), 6–30.

Kneeland, D. E. (1978, July 10). 72 seized at rally of Nazis in Chicago. *The New York Times*. http://www.nytimes.com/1978/07/10/archives/72-seized-at-rally-of-nazis-in-chicago-police-keep-2000-under.html

Koerner, C. L. (2014). Media, fear, and nuclear energy: A case study. *The Social Science Journal*, *51*(2), 240–249. 10.1016/j.soscij.2013.07.011

Kyne, D. & Bolin, B. (2016). Emerging environmental justice issues in nuclear power and radioactive contamination. *International Journal of Environmental Research and Public Health*, *13*(7), 700. 10.3390/ijerph13070700

LaDuke, W. (1999). *All our relations: Native struggles for land rights and life*. South End Press.

Laniyonu, A. (2018). Coffee shops and street stops: Policing practices in gentrifying neighborhoods. *Urban Affairs Review*, *54*(5), 898–930. 10.1177/1078087416689728

Lawson, E. W. (1939, Mat 21). "The Slave Market," Today in St. Augustine. Public Market Clippings File, St. Augustine Historical Society Research Library.

Lee, C. (1992). *Proceedings: The First National People of Color Environmental Leadership Summit*. United Church of Christ Commission for Racial Justice.

Lefebvre, H. (1976–1978). *De L'E'tat*, Four Volumes. UGE.

Lefebvre, H. (1991). *The production of space* [Trans. by D. Nicolson-Smith]. Blackwell.

Lefebvre, H. (2009). *State, space, world: Selected essays* [Edited by N. Brenner & S. Elden; Trans. by G. Moore, N. Brenner, & S. Elden. University of Minnesota Press.

Lerner, S. (2010). *Sacrifice zones: The front lines of toxic chemical exposure in the United States*. MIT Press.

Levine, L. (2009, April 17). Skokie to open new Holocaust Museum: Site of Neo-Nazi march that launched Shoah Education. *The Jewish Daily Forward*.

Lewis, B. R. (2009). *Mapping the trail of a serial killer: How the world's most infamous murderers were tracked down*. Lyon Press.

Leyser, H. (1995). *Medieval women – A social history of Women in England 450-1500*. Weidenfeld & Nicolson.

Ley, D., & Dobson, C. (2008). Are there limits to gentrification? The contexts of impeded gentrification in Vancouver. *Urban Studies*, *45*(12), 2471–2498. 10.1177/0042098008097103

Linebaugh, P. (1991). *The London Hanged: Crime and civil society in the eighteenth century*. Allen Lane.

Lipstein, E. (2019, May 24). You're not mapping rats, you're mapping gentrification. *Deadspin*. https://theconcourse.deadspin.com/you-re-not-mapping-rats-you-re-mapping-gentrification-1835005060

Lybeck, R. (2015). The rise and fall of the U.S.–Dakota War Hanging Monument: Mediating old-settler identity through two expansive cycles of social change. *Mind, Culture, and Activity*, *22*(1), 37–57. 10.1080/10749039.2014.984311

Makhijani, A., Smith, B., & Thorne, M. C. (2006). *Science for the vulnerable setting radiation and multiple exposure environmental health standards to protest those most at risk*. Institute for Energy and Environmental Research.

Marwick, A. E. (2012). The public domain: Surveillance in everyday life. *Surveillance & Society*, *9*(4), 378–393. http://www.surveillance-and-society.org

Marx, K. (1976). *Capital: A critique of political economy*, Vol. 1. Penguin.

Mazin, C. (Producer) & Renck (Director). (2019). *Chernobyl*. HBO and Sky UK.

Mbembé, J. A., & Meintjes, L. (2003). Necropolitics. *Public Culture 15*(1), 11–40. https://www.muse.jhu.edu/article/39984.

Mbembe, A. (2019). *Necropolitics (Theory in forms)* [Trans. by S. Corcoran]. Duke University Press.

McCarthy, C. & Dimitriadis, G. (2000). Governmentality and the sociology of education: Media, educational policy and the politics of resentment. *British Journal of Sociology of Education*, *21*(2), 169–185. 10.1080/713655350

McCoy, T. S. (2009). Hegemony, power, media: Foucault and cultural studies. *The European Journal of Communication Research*, *14*(3), 71–90. 10.1515/comm.1988.14.3.71

McGuire, D. L. (2010). *At the end of dark of the street: Black women, rape, and resistance – A new history of the City Rights Movement from Rosa Parks to the rise of Black Power*. Vintage.

McKean, B. L. (2016). Toward an inclusive populism? On the role of Race and difference in Laclau's politics. *Political Theory*, *44*(6), 797–820. 10.1177/0090591716647771

McKenzie, B. (2017, August 7). City says permit will only be ok'd if rally is moved to McIntire Park. *The Daily Progress*. http://www.dailyprogress.com/news/local/city-says-permit-will-only-be-ok-d-if-rally/article_29f8e566-7baa-11e7–906d-63c9ea503128.html

McKittrick, K. (2006). *Demonic grounds: Black women and the cartographies of struggle*. University of Minneapolis Press.

McWhirter, C. (2011). *Red Summer: The summer of 1919 and the awakening of Black America.* Henry Holt and Company.

Metzl, J. M. (2019). *Dying of Whiteness: How the politics of racial resentment is killing America's heartland.* Basic Books.

Miller, S. C. (1982). *Benevolent assimilation: The American conquest of the Philippines, 1899-1903.* Yale University Press. (1988, August 29). Mob attacks Black man at Klan rally. *The Washington Post.*

Moore, K. S. (2009). Gentrification in Black Face?: The return of the black middle class to urban neighborhoods. *Urban Geography, 30*(2), 118–142. 10.2747/0272-3638.30.2.118

Motley, R. O. & Joe, S. (2018). Police use of force by ethnicity, sex, and socioeconomic class. *Journal of the Society for Social Work and Research, 9*(1), 49–67. 10.1086/696355

Mowatt, R. A. (2012). Lynching as leisure: Broadening notions of a field. *American Behavioral Scientist, 56*(10), 1361–1387. 10.1177/0002764212454429

Mowatt, R. A. (2018). Black lives as snuff: The silent complicity in viewing Black death. *Biography: An Interdisciplinary Quarterly, 41* (4), 777–806. 10.1353/bio.2018.0079

Mullins, P. R. (2021). *Revolting things: An archaeology of shameful histories and repulsive realities.* University of Florida Press.

Mundigo, A. I. & Crouch, D. P. (1977). The city planning ordinances of the Laws of the Indies revisited. Part I: Their philosophy and implications. *The Town Planning Review, 48*(3), 247–268. https://www.jstor.org/stable/40103542

Nadesan, M. (2013). *Fukushima and the privatization of risk.* Palgrave.

National Socialist Party of America v. Village of Skokie on petition for writ of certiorari to the supreme court of Illinois citations, 432 U.S. 43 97 S. Ct. 2205; 53 L. Ed. 2d 96; 1977 U.S. Lexis 113, 2 Media L. Rep. 1993. docket no. 76-1786 (June 14, 1977).

Noakes, J., Klocke, B., & Gillham, P. F. (2005). Whose streets? Police and protesters struggle over space in Washington, DC, 29-30 September, 2001. *Policing and Society, 15*(3), 235–254. 10.1080/10439460500168576

Nolan, D. (2009, September 27). Slaves were sold in Plaza Market. St. Augustine Record.

Oliver, P. & Myers, D. J. (2003). The coevolution of social movements. *Mobilization: An International Journal, 8*(1), 1–24. 10.17813/maiq.8.1.d618751h524473u7

Osborne, P. & Segal, L. (1997). Culture and power: Interview with Stuart Hall. *Radical Philosophy, 86*, 24–41.

Ostrom, E. (1990). *Governing the commons: The evolution of institutions for collective action.* Cambridge University Press.

Paes, E. (2012, February). The 4 commandments of cities. *TED.* https://www.ted.com/talks/eduardo_paes_the_4_commandments_of_cities?language=en

Pandey, A. & Caliskan, A. (2020). Iterative effect-size bias in ridehailing: Measuring social bias in dynamic pricing of 100 million rides. *Computer and Society, 1.* arXiv:2006. 04599

Papachristos, A. V., Smith, C. M., Scherer, M. L., & Fugiero, M. A. (2011). More coffee, less crime? The relationship between gentrification and neighborhood crime rates in Chicago, 1991 to 2005. *City & Community 10*(3), 215–240.

Parekh, T. (2015). 'They want to live in the tremé, but they want it for their ways of living': Gentrification and neighborhood practice in Tremé, New Orleans. *Urban Geography 36*(2), 201–220.

Patterson, O. (1982). *Slavery and social death: A comparative study.* Harvard University Press.

Patterson, W. C. (1983). *Nuclear power.* Penguin Books Ltd.

Pelisek, C. (2017). *The Grim Sleep: The lost women of South Central.* Counterpoint.

Povinelli, E. A. (2011). *Economies of abandonment: Social belonging and endurance in late liberalism.* Duke University Press.

Proctor, J. (2004). *Stuart Hall.* Routledge. (2000, June 30). Profile: Copeland the killer. *BBC News.*

Ramírez, M. M. (2020). City as borderland: Gentrification and the policing of Black and Latinx geographies in Oakland. *Environment and Planning D: Society and Space, 38*(1), 147–166. 10.1177/0263775819843924

Reese, L. A. (2006). Economic versus natural disasters: If Detroit had a hurricane….". *Economic Development Quarterly, 20*(3), 219–231. 10.1177/08912424062 89344

Regencia, T. (2010, October 25). Students urged to fight bullying scourge. *Skokie Patch.*

Rockwell, G. L. (1966/2016). *White power.* Sandycroft Publishing Limited.

Rose, N. (Ed.). (1996). Governing 'advanced' liberal democracies. In A. Barry, T. Osborne, & N. Rose (Eds.), *Foucault and political reason: Liberalism, neo-liberalism and rationalities of government* (pp. 37–64). University of Chicago Press.

Rothstein, R. (2017). *The color of law: A forgotten history of how our government segregated America.* Liveright Publishing Corporation.

Rowan, C. T. (1996). *The coming race war in American: A wake up call.* Little, Brown, and Company.

Said, E. W. (1978). *Orientalism.* Pantheon Books.

Samara, T., & Chang, G. (2008). Gentrifying downtown Miami. *Race, Poverty & the Environment, 15*(1), 14–16. http://www.jstor.org/stable/41554577

Saunders, P. & Kirby, J. (2010). Move along: Community-based research into the policing of sex work in

Washington, D.C. *Social Justice*, *37*(1(119)), 107–127. http://www.jstor.org/stable/41336938

Saunt, C. (2020). *Unworthy republic: The dispossession of Native Americans and the road to Indian territory*. W.W. Norton.

Scott-Heron, G. & Jackson, B. (1977). *We Almost Lost Detroit"*, track #6 on *Bridges*. Arista Records.

Schneider, J. C. (1980). *Detroit and the problem of order, 1830 -1880: A geography of crime, riot, and policing*. University of Nebraska Press.

Scutt, J. A. (2016). *Women and the Magna Carta: A treaty for rights or wrongs?*. Palgrave MacMillan.

Seigel, M. (2018). *Violence work: State power and the limits of police*. Duke University Press.

Sharpe, J. (1993). *Allegories of empire: The figure of women in the colonial text*. University of Minnesota Press.

Shrubsole, G. (2019). *Who owns England? How we lost our green & pleasant land & how to take it back*. William Collins.

Silk, M. L. (2007). Come downtown & play. *Leisure Studies*, *26*(3), 253–277. 10.1080/02614360601053889

Simmons, W. J. (1923). *The Klan unmasked*. W. E. Thompson Publishing Co.

Skokie Park District. (1976a, October 4). Letter from Frank Collin to Skokie Park District. *Skokie Park District / Minutes of the Board Meeting of October 25, 1976, Skokie Park District Board of Park Commissioners Archives*.

Skokie Park District. (1976b, October 25). Skokie Park District Board of Park Commissioners (Ordinance Attached). *Skokie Park District / Minutes of the Board Meeting of October 25, 1976, Skokie Park District Board of Park Commissioners Archives*.

Silver, C. (1997). The racial origins of zoning in American cities. In J. M. Thomas & M. Ritzdorf (Eds.)., *Urban planning and the African American community: In the shadows* (pp. 23–42). Sage Publications.

Smith, K. R. (1988). Perception of risks associated with nuclear power. *Energy Environment Monitor*, *4*(1), 61–70.

Sovacool, B. (2009). The accidental century: Prominent energy accidents in the last hundred years. *Exploration & Production: The Oil and Gas Review*, *7*(2), 132–137. http://sro.sussex.ac.uk/id/eprint/58149

Spivak, G. C. (1988). Can the subaltern speak?. In C. Nelson & L. Grossberg (Eds.), *Marxism and the Interpretation of Culture* (pp. 217–313). Macmillan Education.

Stapley, G. (2017, August 14). 'This is a huge victory.' Oakdale White Supremacist revels after deadly Virginia clash. *The Modesto Bee*. http://www.modbee.com/news/article167213427.html

Stone, P. R. (2013). Dark tourism, heterotopias and post-Apocalyptic places: The case of Chernobyl. In L. White and E. Frew (Eds.), *Dark Tourism and Place Identity* (pp. 1–10). Routledge.

Stovall, T. (2006). Race and the making of the nation: Blacks in modern France. In M. A. Gomez (Ed.), *Diasporic Africa: A reader* (pp. 200–218). New York University Press.

Strum, P. (1999). *When the Nazis came to Skokie: Freedom for speech we hate*. University Press of Kansas.

Stuart, F. (2016). *Down, out, and under arrest: Policing and everyday life in Skid Row*. The University of Chicago Press.

Sugrue, T. J. (1996). *The origins of the urban crisis*. Princeton University Press.

Sullivan, D. M. (2006). Assessing residents' opinions on changes in a gentrifying neighborhood: A case study of the Alberta neighborhood in Portland, Oregon. *Housing Policy Debate*, *17*(3), 595–624. 10.1080/1 0511482.2006.9521583

Supreme Court of Appeals of Virginia. (1915, September 9). Hopkins et al. v. City of Richmond. (No. 1.) Coleman v. Town of Ashland. (No. 2.). [86 S. E. 139].

Taliman, V. (1992). Stuck holding the Nation's Nuclear Waste. *Race, Poverty and Environment*, *3*(3), 6–9. https://www.jstor.org/stable/41554076

Taylor, S. (2007). *Privitisation and financial collapse in the nuclear industry: The origins and causes of the British energy crisis of 2002*. Routledge.

Thomas, L. L. (2018). Neutral ground or battleground? Hidden history, tourism, and spatial (in)justice in the New Orleans French Quarter. *The Journal of African American History*, *103*(4), 1548–1867. 10.1086/699953

Thomas, S. W. (1978). *Louisville since the twenties: Views two, A sequel to views of Louisville since 1766*. The Courier Journal.

Thompson, L. (2020, September 14). The cop who quit instead of helping to gentrify Atlanta. *Mother Jones*. https://www.motherjones.com/crime-justice/202 0/09/the-cop-who-quit-instead-of-helping-to-gentrify-atlanta/

Throgmoton, J. A. (2004). Where was the wall then? Where is it now?. *Planning Theory and Practice*, *5*, 349–365.

Travieso, C. (2020, September). A nation of walls: The overlooked history of Race barriers in the United States. *Places Journal*. https://placesjournal.org/article/a-nation-of-walls/ (1925, August 10). 200 join as fiery cross lights capital. *The New York Herald*.

Tyner, J. A. (2012). *Space, place, and violence: Violence and the embodied geographies of Race, sex, and gender*. Routledge

Uitermark, J., Duyvendak, J. W., & Kleinhans, R. (2007). Gentrification as a governmental strategy: Social control and social cohesion in Hoogvliet, Rotterdam. *Environment and Planning A: Economy and Space*, *39*(1), 125–141. 10.1068/a39142

United State Census Bureau. (1970). Census of population and housing, 1970. In *Vol. 1 Characteristics of the Population, Michigan.* U.S. Department of Commerce. https://www2.census.gov/prod2/decennial/documents/1970a_mi-01.pdf

United State Census Bureau. (1981). *1980 Census Report.* U.S. Census Population Division. Retrieved from https://www2.census.gov/prod2/statcomp/documents/1981-02.pdf

United State Census Bureau. (2001). *2000 Census Report.* U.S. Census Population Division. Retrieved from https://www2.census.gov/prod2/statcomp/documents/1981-02.pdf

United States Supreme Court. (1895). *U.S. Reports: Plessy v. Ferguson, 163 U.S. 537.* https://www.loc.gov/item/usrep163537/.

Van Dyke, A. (2013, February 7). Topeka police seek donations to fund stolen property tracking. *The Topeka Capital-Journal.* https://www.cjonline.com/news/2013-02-07/topeka-police-seek-donations-fund-stolen-property-tracking

Village of Euclid v. Ambler Realty Co., 272 US 365 (United States Supreme Court, 1926).

Vidal, G. (2002). *Perpetual war for perpetual peace: How we got to be so hated.* Thunder's Mouth Press.

Vitale, A. S. (2008). *City of disorder: How the quality of life campaign transformed New York politics.* New York Univ. Press.

Walker, S. J. (2004). *Three Miles Island: A nuclear crisis in historical perspective.* University of California Press.

Wallace, D. H., & Kreisel, B. (2003). Martial Law as a counterterrorism response to terrorist attacks: Domestic and international legal dimensions. *International Criminal Justice Review, 13*(1), 50–75. 10.1177/105756770301300103

Warren, L. (2014, June 9). *'The dawn of a new day…may all out sacrifices be worth it': Chilling online messages of White Supremacists couple. Daily Mail.*

Weeks, L. (2015, March 19). When the Klan was mainstream. *NPR.* https://www.npr.org/sections/npr-history-dept/2015/03/19/390711598/when-the-ku-klux-klan-was-mainstream

Weisburd, D. (2015). The law of crime concentration and the criminology of place. *Criminology, 53*(2), 133–157. 10.1111/1745-9125.12070 (1925, August 9). White-robbed Klan cheered on march in nation's capital. *The Washington Post.* https://www.washingtonpost.com/news/retropolis/wp/2017/08/17/the-day-30000-white-supremacists-in-kkk-robes-marched-in-the-nations-capital/?utm_term=.b3330f23a90c

Wilf, S. (1993). Imagining justice: Aesthetics and public executions in late eighteenth-century England. *Yale Journal of Law & the Humanities, 5*(1), 51–78. https://digitalcommons.law.yale.edu/yjlh/vol5/iss1/3

Wright, W. J. & Herman, C. (2018). No "black canvas": Public art and gentrification in Houston's third ward. *City & Society, 30*(1), 89–116. 10.1111/ciso.12156

Wynter, S. (1994). No humans involved – An open letter to my colleagues. *Knowledge on Trial, 1*(1), 42–73.

Yankovska, G. & Hannam, K. (2014). Dark and toxic tourism in the Chernobyl Exclusion Zone. *Current Issues in Tourism, 17*(10), 929–939. 10.1080/13683500.2013.820260

Zupello, S. (2016, August 18). 'Grim sleeper' serial killer: Everything you need to know. *Rolling Stone.* https://www.rollingstone.com/culture/culture-features/grim-sleeper-serial-killer-everything-you-need-to-know-252246/

# 5.
# THE CITY BETWEEN US: A CONCLUSION

**Fig 5.1** Mowatt Peace Park, Formerly Astor Park at the Corner of Brunswick and Cumberland in Spanish Town, Jamaica. 2001. (The Author)

"…like everything that 'exists,' the State was born, and grew up. One can assume that it will decline and disappear."
— Henri Lefebvre (2003, p. 62).

"Abolition is a totality and it is ontological. It is the context and content of struggle, the site where culture recouples with the political; but it is not struggle's *form. To have form,* we have to organize. Organize…"
–Ruth Wilson Gilmore, "What Is To Be Done?" given as the 2011 Presidential Address for the American Studies Association, p. 258.

In this reading of the city as a text, the social forces that bring about so much misery and so much suffering all come down to the ways in which the city serves that very function. This is why Soja (1989) argued that any modern theorising of geography requires a "radical deconstruction and reconstruction" to resist the rigidity of historical geography that does provide an outward critical social theorising that does not adjust to "contemporary reassertion of space" (p. 45). Such an undertaking would involve "a resistance to paradigmatic closure and rigidly categorical thinking; the capacity to combine creatively what… was considered to be antithetical/uncombinable"

DOI: 10.1201/9781003149545-5

(Soja, 1989, p. 73). What Wynter (2006) in "On How We Mistook The Map For The Territory" noted as a "reluctance to see a relationship so global in reach – between the epistemology of knowledge and the liberation of people – a relationship that we are not properly able to theorize" (p. 113). But it is the map and its depiction of a territory, and how this map maps us, plots us, situates us, and identifies us in such a way that creates the *désêtre*, wrongness of being imposed by the State. This reading fits within the function of the *undercommons*, a cognitive space in academia for the subversion of the status quo and the order (Harney & Moten, 2013), not focused on the lived life that has been stolen but instead on the life of the thief. This line of work still comes from a person, myself, who occupies the position of the modern *unthought*, resisting the urges of affirmation in hopes of transformation (Hartman & Wilderson, 2003). The city was the text in which dispossession and extraction were read upon its formation. Instead of asking "why do cities exist?" or "what is a city?", the explanandum in search for an explanans (the explanation), the study here was on the explanans of dispossession and extraction evident in the cities of 2020, where people could be killed for a fake $20 bill while sleeping in an apartment, being dually overexposed to a pandemic and under-vaccinated against a disease, and made unhoused in an instant. And instead of drawing a conclusion that conceptions of systematic and systemic racism as well as patriarchy do or do not exist, the conclusion here is that a State of dispossession and extractivism is far worse. So instead, this reading of the city began with that conclusion and moved in reverse to the explanandum, "what in fact do cities do and do quite well?" A city is a machine of the State. Within the city as a "capitalist spatiality", the State is restructuring itself through the urban form (see Fig. 5.2). An evolution that occurs within the enclosures called cities. This evolution marshals the forces of dispossession, extraction, exploitation, and violence work, a group of forces whose terrifying magic stuns and dazzles an unsuspecting populace, day in and day out. This populace is trapped within the thrall of the splendour of the city, the day-to-day labour extraction of the city, and the brutality of the city, all because the modern city is "an iron cage – one that imprisons disoriented, labouring

animals" that was designed for disorder with the violence of maintaining that order (Sendra & Sennett, 2020, p. 20). The city has historically identified and situated populations into their proper place in service to the order. The city by design has taken those identified populations and has discursively framed them as threats to the safety of the remaining populace, when in actuality they are merely the threat of a surplus population on the operations of the order. And the city has dealt with and continues to deal with those populations deemed violent with continued blows of violence with social, psychological, and physical death of their person and the people and spaces that they have held dear – a settler colonial city project that continues its occupation of stolen lands and dispossession of stolen peoples. The settler occupation maintains its original manifestation in the present and will continue to echo into the future (Dorries et al., 2019). The city reminds us that we will perpetually be owned if we continue the "legal, political, and ideological performance of ownership and belonging" (Estes, 2019a, p. 53). (Fig. 5.2)

The fabrication of life called Society is the construct that most functions within the bright lights and dim alleys of the city infrastructure, creating a triad of spaces that have never been neutral and never have been empty containers for us to inhabit: to be subjected through the spatial practises of the State (concentration, city-splitting, slum clearance); to become subjects through the State discursive representations of space (the hood, ghetto, rez, barrio, or trailer park; place-making; urban renewal); and to be moulded and remade as a citizen, friend, and villain as useful agents of the State in the lived experiences of representational space (the native, savage, or criminal; the labourer, city planner, or looter; the settler militia, officer, or rioter). The State constructs the city by way of occupying and dispossessing indigenous land and populations and revises this construction over and over, but with fresh properties and new bodies to satisfy its consumptive hunger. The city is a colonial settlement, because where it is situated has always been a settler colony – the border town with the explicit purposeful spatial formation to murder. Border towns with bright lights encircle the indigenous towns, reservations, reserves, and townships in the settler cities of

**Fig 5.2** The Art and Poetry of Hugo Gellert, "The Distribution of Wealth (The Lion and Other Beats A-Hunting", Depicting a Vacuum Cleaner Sucking Up Cities in Their Entirety. 1936. (Mary Ryan Gallery)

Ciudad de Juárez, Halifax, Jakarta, Lagos, Phoenix, and São Paulo, among others. The city is also of imperial dominion, propped up by its people and lands in its possession. The castle fed by the people beyond its-walls with the intent to maim through a life devoted to subservience. The "Municipal Darwinistic" machines consuming the lesser cities of the world to maintain its lustre, prominence, and the cityscape of Amsterdam, Copenhagen, Istanbul, London, Madrid, and Tokyo. But this hunger cannot be quenched as the State utilises the city to extract resources from the land it now possesses as territory, labour from the populace it encloses, wealth of the city to fill the coffers of the elites and ruling classes, and if necessary, extraction itself. Capitalists classes, protected by the State from disasters and pandemics, are the only ones to prosper (see Fig. 5.2). Gellert's lion consumes all of the spoils of the hunt even though it was aided by other beasts of the hunt. This is the project of deracination at its best (Gahman & Hjalmarson, 2019). And it is with violence that the business of capitalism is regulated and it is with disaster that the accumulation of wealth from capital thrives (see Fig. 5.3). Regulated through land removals, slum clearances, forced expulsions, execution of eminent domain, evictions, street harassments, Stop & Frisk, Traffic Stops, civil forfeiture, work terminations with police escort, Castle laws/Castle Doctrines/Defence of Habitation laws, Stand-Your-Ground Laws, warrants, raids, tactical manoeuvres, summary executions, extra judicial executions, and so forth.

The project of deracination in the accumulation of wealth and capital in the contemporary period since the 1970s has ushered in a 50-year campaign that intensified the overpopulation of cities through forced concentration and the complete extraction of resources for rural areas that has necessitated flight to the cities. This same 50-year campaign has resulted in the overaccumulation of wealth and capital in cities that signals the waves of worsening economic recessions to come and the volatility and devaluation of production everywhere, leaving dispossession the last viable source of accumulation that must engender greater amplitudes of force. This same 50-year campaign has led to the over-carcerality of cities that bloat the cells in prisons, camps, jails, and detention centres in the world based on exclusionary and selective lawfare and warfare actions that have turned those centres of concentrations into dead cities of the degenerate and deviant populace. The identification of populations, the identification of threats, and the identification of violence will likely transform over the next 50 years

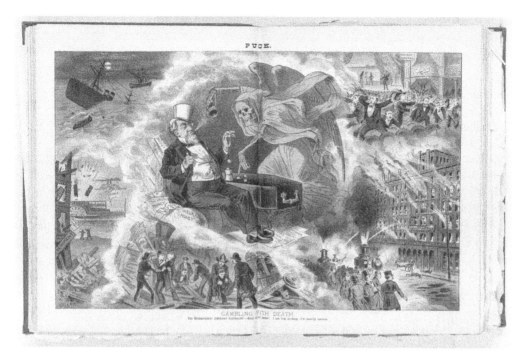

**Fig 5.3** "Gambling to Death: Too Enterprising American Capitalist – Keep Up The Game! I Can Lose Nothing – I'm Heavily Insured" in Puck Magazine, January 24, 1883. (Library of Congress/Public Domain)

into the overpopulation of cities, the over-accumulation of wealth and capital in cities, and the over-carcerality of cities. The "War on Alcohol" in the 1920s and the "War on Marijuana" in the 1930s jointly birthed the "War on Crime" in the 1970s and the "War on Drugs" in the 1980s (Balto, 2019), and they all set the stage for the "War on Terror" in the 2000s and all of the increases in dispossession, incarceration, and anti-immigration that came with the calls for these public policies.

The transformational intensification of the endeavours of the State works through the network of and around the site of cities as the "Geographies of Threat", the looming threat that the well is becoming drying. During the 1970s, the city had been used as the "spatial-temporal fix", with the manufactured crisis of the urban Black Riot in the United States and in the United Kingdom to avert our attention from the drying up of resources and coming labour shortages in the 1980s. During the 1980s, the city was particularly used as the "spatial-temporal fix" with the instigation of State instability in cities throughout Latin America to avert our

attention from the shoring up of wealth amongst a small elite class in the 1990s. During the 1990s, the city was heavily used as the "spatial-temporary fix" by way of the urban crime "moral panic" throughout cities in the European, British, and U.S. world to avert our attention from the coming collapse of the property values in the 2000s. During the 2000s, the city was used as the "spatial-temporal fix" in response to "wars" on terror and insurgency in the Middle East to avert our attention from the increased unification of the elite and ruling classes as a hoarding collective in the 2010s. And during the 2010s, the city was used as the "spatial-temporary fix" that re-affirmed the control of cities in order to avert our attention from the reconstruction of Anderson's (1975) *Absolutist States* throughout the world in order to prepare for global dissent. Harvey's (2004) *New Imperialism* is the last dying phase of the structure of governance through imperialism by the State as there is simply not enough juice left to squeeze from the fruit that was plucked through the creation of the colonial city and revision of the imperial city.

The new imperialist and the returned absolutist State of the present era are grounded in an understanding of history:

> Secular struggle between classes is ultimately resolved at the *political* – not at the economic or cultural – level of society. In other words, it is the construction and destruction of State which seal the basic shifts in the relations of production, so long as classes subsist. A "history from above" – of the intricate machinery of class domination – is thus no less essential than a "history from below".... (Anderson, 1975, p. 11)

The end of feudalism brought the end of absolute monarchy and the divine right of kings and queens through the revolts of the noble bourgeoisie. The end of a scale of colonialism brought the end of the absolute rule of the bourgeoisie and lords of wealth through the revolts of landowners and land-possessing commoners. We are now in the period of the end of a scale of imperialism, and the forces that shall bring its end have not yet surfaced or revealed their full representation. A technocracy, an assembly of racially and gender-diverse members from the elite and ruling classes that re-assemble as a managerial (and not governing) class ruling what is left of the resources and populace that are available? An oligarchical plutocracy, an assembled structure of power of an even smaller group of wealthy individuals who will systematically preside over a few important cities of accumulations leaving the rest in anarchy as extractive sources for scraps? Or, a totalitarian fascist regime, a coalescing of rivalling political parties under one ruling regime that is absent of limits to infringements on rights and exercises of violence with absolute control of production and commerce? The options as you can see are not viable (or they should not be). This time of transition brought about through capitalist upheaval presents opportunities for the State or the populace, but not for both. History has always shown us the recurrence of power maintenance, whether it is of "strongmen" (Ben-Ghiat, 2020), "iron ladies" (Hall, 1988), or "post-racial" hip hop presidents (Coates, 2017). A new Round Table to replace the old, a multi-cultural and gender-diverse Round Table to replace the Anglo-American hegemony

of the British, the settler colony of Canada, the settler colony of Newfoundland, the settler colony of New Zealand, the settler colony Union of South Africa, and the settler colony of the United States in 1908 (Kirkwood, 2021).

What we are experiencing during COVID-19 has been exacerbated by the pandemic, and what we are experiencing are these forces assembling. The elite and ruling classes, alongside the aspiring classes at the beginning of the pandemic, were longing to embrace a return to normalcy – because for them the fabricated society maintained the illusion of stability that was in every cup of latte, was on every re-creation trail for rollerblading, was in every shopping bag at the mall. The eye rolls levied against the non-maskers were inconveniencing their lifestyle return, not the prevention of millions of deaths. A return to normalcy was no different from the era of fierce retaliation that was bounded up and hidden within the push for a certain "quality of life" free of undesirables. The freedoms in normalcy and quality were at the cost of others. The freedoms in normalcy and quality were giving additional freedoms to the State to create cities of disorder (Vitalie, 2008). The freedoms of the State to function in ongoing response to the issues presented to them during the 1970s are determining the form in which the State will take shape in a realignment of both global power throughout the world and within their respective territories and cities of governance. And the only alternative realignment beyond the aforementioned three options of a technocracy, an oligarchical plutocracy, and a totalitarian fascist regime is the abolition of the State from those who do not compose those assemblies and do not aspire to maintain the order of dispossession, extraction, and accumulation.

In the milieu of abandonment, dereliction, dispossession, and violence, there is the possibility of Gilmore's (2017) *Abolition Geography* – an abolition and that must first take effect "at the level of the map rather than at the level of the territory" (Wynter, 2006, p. 118). Thus, power maps become crucial to activism and organising not just in determining the limits and possibilities of one's agency, but also in understanding the space in which you dwell. Hidden in those cells and halls of prisons, jails, camps, and detention centres are examples of what the world could become from of the rule of the present States and the potential re-emergence of an "absolutist state". Behind their walls are James' (2016) *Captive Maternal,* yet again working to make due and undue their lived experiences, but this time working to resist rather than just negotiating ways of getting by psycho-socially: the projects of mutual aid among the incarcerated in the midst of no or little resources; the pooling together of funds to create collective pots of currency for necessary purchases from the commissary, most especially medication; non-familial and gender non-conforming caregiving for the sick and elderly in the absence of adequate health care; collective and sustaining modes of education and artistic performance for creative expression in coping with trauma. This same technology of living is then transported to sites beyond the dead cities that are prison, to the neighbourhoods that the formerly incarcerated are from or where their families reside. Community free farms, food pantries, carpools for the elderly, neighbourhood day cares, Saturday schools, and dance and theatre production in the public view are just a few examples, when politically formed, of the true commons, like the Jane Collective around abortion and health care in the 1960s and 1970s, and the Debt Collective of the contemporary period. The abandoned spaces of *les damnés* (the invisible, forgotten damned) are spaces of possibility (McKittrick & Woods, 2007). The imagination of self-determination that was and still remains in the lessons of *marronage* from enslaved Africans, the re-imagined space and society of self-determination separate from the established order contained within the fabricated-Soceity of the State (Bledsoe, 2017).

The free spaces and mobilities are contained in political-creative thoughts that defy State, nation, and borders as *floating borderlands* where new identities can thrive and emerge for action (Flores, 1998). In abandonment, you and your neighbourhood are left alone, with no aid or resources, and with police presence managed through rotating shifts throughout the day of the vast city. There is no economic infrastructure for thriving, closing schools, little to no health care infrastructure, etc., so the only encounter with government then becomes public works (at best) and police (at worst). For

police to become trusted requires government to become trusted, and for government to do trusting things. The basic principle is for cities to be at their maximum potential, they must regularly assess, identify, and abandon things that are no longer profitable to the maximisation of the future; thus, they have identified violence work to be employed. And that work, beyond maiming and killing, is to perpetually beat into our psyche misogyny and racialisation that is necessary.

Abandoned neighbourhoods are artlessly modernised into abandoned indigenous reservations, bantustáns, and ghettos for the greater purpose of operating as camps for the concentration of populations within an enclosed city rather than solely within the expanse of a territory like the West, the Saharra, the Negev, the Transvaal, the Amazon, the Yukon, the Outback, or the Bush. The conditions in abandoned neighbourhoods mimic the long-abandoned rural towns that have perpetually lived in states of Statelessness with limited running water, irregular shipments of supplies, and the absence of political representation that cares or harms. The rural towns, which have been converted to Stateless-beyond-city cities, alongside the dead cities that are prisons, both respectively represent Gilmore's notion of "forgotten places" beyond the eyes and ambitions of the State.

Because, again, the State only exists within the city and is only composed of the network of cities that are connected to the arteries of circulation of capital and wealth that are the highways and interstates that connect the network of those cities (see Fig. 5.4). All that exists between and beyond cities will become increasingly abandoned by the State (i.e., indigenous "protected areas", reservations, and preserves of Australia, Brazil, Canada, and the United States; Gaza and the West Bank in Israel/Occupied Palestine; the Appalachia Mountain region of the United States; northern parts of the Federalist District of Siberia in Russia; the Canadian Yukon; the Kurdish settlements and habitations that defy borders of Armenia, Iran, Iraq, Syria, and Turkey). By extension, with dwindling resources to manage the vast and complicated city, all that exists between and beyond the city prime (the capitol, the downtown, the commerce district) will become increasingly abandoned by the State also. As a result, Santiago de Chile sends its people to

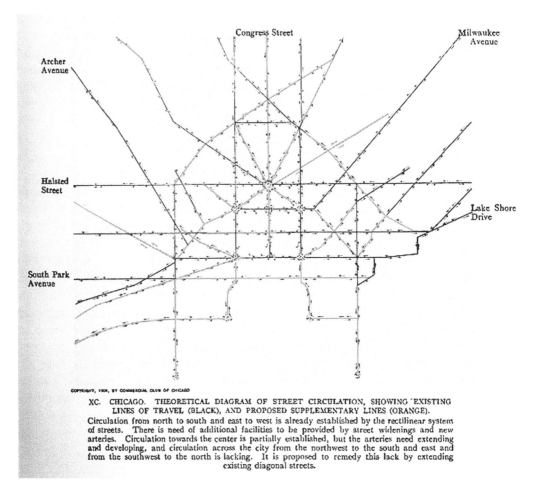

XC. CHICAGO. THEORETICAL DIAGRAM OF STREET CIRCULATION, SHOWING EXISTING
LINES OF TRAVEL (BLACK), AND PROPOSED SUPPLEMENTARY LINES (ORANGE).
Circulation from north to south and east to west is already established by the rectilinear system
of streets. There is need of additional facilities to be provided by street widenings and new
arteries. Circulation towards the center is partially established, but the arteries need extending
and developing, and circulation across the city from the northwest to the south and east and
from the southwest to the north is lacking. It is proposed to remedy this lack by extending
existing diagonal streets.

**Fig 5.4** The Daniel Burnham and Edward Bennett's Plan of Chicago, and the Theoretical Diagram of Street Circulation, Showing Existing Lines of Travel (Black), and Proposed Supplementary Lines (Orange). 1909. (Public Domain)

Ciudad de México, who sends its people to El Paso, Texas, who sends its people to Louisville, Kentucky, who sends its people to Chicago, Illinois, who sends its people to Toronto, Canada. The great migration of surplus populations!

Abolition geographies require a variety of *abolitionisms* (Joy James) to tackle the worsening conditions of living in abandonment but also stridently ushering in a new and counter world by noticing and recognising each other in the struggle to commit to collective action as we are all that we have. The collective action must overcome the State mediated conditioning for *entrepreneurial activism* that emphasises individual action, individual agency, and individual gratification. The recycling practies that

are falsely given as a solution to climate colonialism (*nee* climate change), the individualised arguing with a boss that never results in a pay raise, the hashtagging of "metoo" that never ends sexual assault in the workplace or marketplace of the everyday person, or the holding of a Black Lives Matter in one's hands or one's lawn in front of a home that never stops the killings. But also, collective action that does not imitate the culture of the order and control of the oppressive State by constructing organisations governed by *feudal activism*, governed by a cult of personality or a cult leader, or nationalised system of authority that peddles social or fiscal dependence with the control of information or a collective pot of funds under the authority of a central schema and influencing brand. The lands that we wish to re-imagine are vast and should not be restricted to narrow understandings of territory nor limited to phraseological singularities. Thus, a collective action has and will continue to result in the joining of forces of seemingly disparate and potentially ideologically opposed collectives, as the greater plight of overpopulation, overaccumulation, and over-carcerality comes for all of us (Braz & Gilmore, 2006). This has also led to *plural resistance* as a logic to tackle multiple modes of interconnections and interworking violence (gender violence, specifically) as an enactment of the State functioning through its cities like Seattle in the United States and the city of Hyderabad in India, and the fabrications of society that it enacts in both cities and all cities (Piedalue, 2016). Such work results in the creation of "geographies of peace" (Piedalue, 2015). Fundamentally, a re-envisioned and "truly sustainable society is one where wider questions of social needs and welfare, and economic opportunity are integrally related to environmental limits imposed by supporting ecosystems" (Agyeman et al., 2002, p. 78). But it needs to be clear to us that a requisite of abolition is and always has been total (community) control. One cannot abolish what one does not control.

We cannot think of freedom as an idea; "freedom is a place" (Gilmore, 2017, p. 226). The current State as constituted is not the "only possible orientation of desire", and realities are birth-desired states of being and *Desired States* of justice-oriented geographical governance (Frazier, 2020, p. 4). The place or space of contention is the city; it is where Hall's (1988) analysis of class struggle is forged on the "open terrain" of its streets, property, and infrastructure, not the often focused-on economic conditions in the sites of production. The creation of the idea of male to operate as a buffer division between public space and property ownership. The creation of the racialised idea of White to operate as buffer class between the revolting classes and the elite. City maps merely "depict a region of superabundance adjacent to a region of brutal poverty" that becomes our cognitive map that makes the fabrication a social fact (Bunge, 1975, p. 150). The "open terrain" formulates the fabricated society into

something to win the populace's hearts and minds that they then tolerate the abandonment among the disposable classes, the exploitation of labour among the working classes, and the "great moving nowhere show" of government among the aspiring classes (Hall, 1988, 1998). Hall et al. (1978) said that "Race [is] the modality in which class is lived" (p. 394). And if gender cannot be disentangled from Race, the coming over-cacerality of the city via the existing apparatuses and processes of "mass incarceration is class war" (Gilmore, 2017, p. 230). The city is the ideal site to confront the conflict of revolting classes (*dangereuses*) through their revolting modalities of being oppositional (the basis for gendering) and "criminal" (the basis for racialisation) to the order. The city is the site in which all of these forces have come to a head. Because the "politics to come", the politics that are already here, indicate that "*place* will supercede position" (Torino & Wohlleben, 2019).

## 5.1 Schemes and Schemas

Thus, it is the abolishment of property that must bear the most space in our imaginations to consider and to achieve as as an intermediate aim (Walcott, 2021a). For it is insufficient to abolish police, prisons, rents, or the wage systems without doing so. Policing serves the purpose of corralling all process and apparatuses that subjugate a designated and given population as formal (slaves) and informal (workers) properties of the State. Police officers are merely the janitors and custodians of the property system that the State is built upon, they serve violence and carry forth violence for the aim of protecting property and protecting property ownership. The greater conception of policing requires the interlocking systems that organise "the economy", centres of education, political affairs, and halls of criminal justice to be tied to the de jure and de facto processes of a State, and that are socially encouraged and supported through various institutions of the media, various denominations of religiosity, and numerous social systems that give the luster to the illusions of the fabricated society. This is the contemporary manifestation of Wynter's (1995) long analysis of the historical entanglement that began in

1492. It is not only this history that we are bound to, but it is also the present that it has birthed. As McKittrick (2013) soundly stated, the past can be exceptionally traced "to the present and the present to past through geography" (p. 7). The produced violence is the infrastructure that in turn produces the social relationships of hierarchical mirages, sudden dislocations, perpetual dispossessions, irreparable extractions, and the spectacular deaths and injuries of those bonded and bounded to the State. Thus, it is only in the State can violence erupt at any point to remind us of the only truly acceptable status quo. And it is only the city that is now the truest representation of the enclosure instead of the commons (Class), the home (Gender), and the plantation (Race). It is undeniable that the very true act of disobedience within McKittrick's (2013) inventory can initiate a rebirth of what it means to be Wynter's (1995) human. It is also understood that the plantation logics of the plantation town are what cultivated the development of what we now know of and think of as a city (McKittrick, 2013). But the aim throughout this book was to situate the violence that is produced by the production of the space that it occurs. However, this violence is enacted only out of inconvenience, as the true and sole aim has always been accumulation wealth (not the subjugation of people and the exploitation of land). In the present, the city is the only site of both micro- and macro-level gendering and racialisation. This is why it is geography that must be abolished in the Ruth Wilson Gilmore sense. *Geographies of Threat, Cities of Violence* and the conceptual frameworks of "Geographies of Threat" connected the everyday lived experiences in the space of the city (domestically, in the United State and globally, in cities within each continent) with an analysis of those field observations that tied relevant matters of spatiality: policing, gentrification, sexual assault, protests, riots, borders, and environmental racism; and argued that they all exist within one central context, the social order of the will of the State that required (and continues to require) spaces of domination and subjugation, for "practices of subjugation are also spatial acts" (McKittrick, 2006, p. xix). However, we should be clear that freedom and liberation are not the same thing. As freedom services the old call

of finishing the emancipation of State subjectified and desubjectified peoples, liberation is an entire other endeavor and is comprised of the stuff of what has yet to take place in this moment of human history (Walcott, 2021b). And dreams of liberation must take over space as much as the mind. And again (as it needs to be re-stated), freedom and liberation are not the same thing. The illusiveness of freedom is only so because the State can adjust as it sees fit. Freedom can be given and had. So, the State can squirm and albeit reluctantly, proffer freedom to individuals or large portions of the subjugated. But the State will never capitulate and will only vehemently fight against anything that will lead to its ruin. With the occupation of space comes "the power to suspend the suspensions that defin[ed] our metropolitan social separation", the fabricated society and the State-produced city (Torino & Wohlleben, 2019). The logic of this book and the conceptualisation of the "Geographies of Threat" target the State's use of the spatial arrangements of a city to do violence. Violence is delayed in facilities and spaces of prisons, of housing, of health care, and of education. Just as Chapter 1 opened with a personalised account from my youth, and how it informed this present-day line of questioning that the book pursued, the book concludes with the same reflection. There I stand in the northern end of Spanish Town, Jamaica (the former Spanish settlement in 1534 and the former British colonial capital in 1692) (see Fig. 5.2).

I stand next to a bust of Andrew Duffus Mowatt, my paternal great grandfather and my father's namesake, that sits at the corner of Brunswick St. and Cumberland Rd. in what was once named Astor Park but now is known as Mowatt Peace Park. For you see, the importance of this man known as "Father Mowatt" was in the mission of the organisation he founded, the Jamaican Burial Scheme Society and the collective actions of its members in bringing dignity to the dead. Caribbean, Central, and South Americans both in their States and in the States that migrated too were known to create these "schemes", such as the Onward and Upright Society, the Forward Growth Society, the People's Progressive Relief Society, La Costa Rica Burial Scheme Association, the Jamaica Relief Association, the Jamaica Women's Association, and one that most may be familiar with, the Universal Negro Improvement Association (Carnegie, 1987; Sherlock, 1973). And just as I indicated in Chapter 1 that there would be no further stories of myself, to centre myself in the discussion of (societal) oppression, it remains the same for the conclusion with the integration of this image and my great grandfather. The Society, a society not fabricated by the State but by the common people, was founded on February 18, 1901, as the first benevolent society of any kind in Jamaica. Those who laboured on the plantations of the British elites and in the factories of the British business class worked for pittance. With little for food, shelter, and education, at the time of their death their body was condemned to squalor just as in life. The dead were flung into pits with lime sprinkled on top. The living went door to door begging for any support to cover the costs of a burial, and no landowner, business owner, or philanthropic society of England would ever consider giving any funds to those who laboured for them. Just like in the midst of a pandemic with an ever-increasing rate and total of deaths, the price of colonialism and imperialism is the ravages upon the lives of the dispossessed. Certain populations are simply too poor to live and even too poor to die. Their labour extraction on the territories of resource extraction should require no expense from the owners. Yet, they are consigned to a dumping into a pauper's grave. This insufferable indignity heaped onto the dead and the living was the basis for my great grandfather to found the Society in collaboration with other labourers like himself (a cooper by trade). With a donation of six cents per week, the collective pooling of funds paid for a mortician, casket, a plot, the digging of the plot, a service, and the burial with a marker for every single member of the family. This fabrication of society spread from city to city, town to town, and island to territory with over 160 branches as near as Cuba and Panama and as far away as Costa Rica and Trinidad. And there I stand in this image, taken on the 100<sup>th</sup> year anniversary of its founding, a Society that is still in operation today because the need still remains.

As a schema, the city and the space within it are all representations and articulations of State power. With a conceptualisation of the "Geographies of Threat", space is no longer conceived as being individually distinct and cognitively different by persons occupying those spaces. As State power via the ideologies of White Supremacy, imperialism, patriarchy, capitalism, and settler colonialism have dominated peoples and places, all space is thus under its authority. Even our cognition of space is under this same authority, as we go along with State commands of use or negotiate with how we operate with the State depending on our own basic needs. We even contend with State conceptions of space as we completely reject those commands and struggle to establish alternative spaces. Space as a *location schema* is the processes and apparatuses in the co-ordination of State activities, not merely the site for the coordination of those activities. The perception of our own agency in coordinating our own activities and coordinating our own space is bounded by what the State allows in a given space. As Zierhofer (2005) posed, "space, conceived as a cognitive tool, like any other cognitive instrument, cannot be but a historically, culturally, socially, biographically and situationally contingent entity" (p. 30).

And from this emerging perspective on the city, specifically the colonial city project, the analysis of the history of these cities directs us to situate a notion that space can hardly be seen as empty or neutral, and never be seen under any State authority due to the overwhelming dominance of the State. City-splitting techniques only broaden our cognition of the more specific ways that space has been ordered as a component of power through systems of rulership. Our entire social reality is bounded by this authority even if we seek alternative systems through political struggle. The sites of contestations are still spaces under State rule; it is just that the sheer mass of space, the numbers of peoples within spaces, and the quantity of things to be ordered enable vacancies in power articulation to arise. With those vacancies, absences, and abandonment, the possibilities to occupy and challenge State power in redefining the control of those spaces emerges. Whose space and what spaces are for are possibilities, but they are not "definites" or readily available opportunities for anyone to wield. There is one dominant schema. There is one (type of) location that is unpretentiously duplicated in new territories, cities. The city is a colonial, imperial, Stateless-beyond-city, and dead city, with its set function. Within the concept of space, all social activities and social institutions occupy space at the decree of the State. And with an analysis informed by State power, the concept of place is the stuff of imagination and cognition convened and curated by the State with complicity by us as the State constitutes. Space as a *location schema* in the Zierhofer sense does not mean that it is an epistemic category generated by knowledge production. It is not necessarily a location with multiple schemas having equal claims on its cognition, and it is not necessarily a schema with multiple locations as its physical representation of various theories. State power forbids this differentiation and variety, because State power has also produced all space and the varieties in which we witness and experience.

Once again, *the modern city* is a conglomeration of the lessons learned from: 1) what I term here as *the empty city* as a construct represented by the long disposed, old, indigenous populations and spaces that are now sites for extraction of resources, culture, and histories with 2) *closed cities* functioning as border towns (Estes, 2019b; Galli, 2010); 3) *the colonial city* principally introduced the methods of congregating populations within its geographical space; 4) *the imperial city* that devised the procedures to separate those populations within its limits as a capital for administration or a network of cities as the State; respectively the "forgotten places" of 5) the *Stateless-beyond-city* (the rural town) to manage through the abandonment of management surplus and disposable spaces, and 6) *the dead city* (the prison) to handle surplus and disposable people, as outgrowths of both the *Welfare State* and the *Shadow State* (Wolch & Dear, 1989). Neil Smith's (1996) 7) the *revanchist city* reveals efforts to recapture the inner and central city through fiscal reinvestment, administrative redevelopment, and social revalorisation efforts formerly "unavailable" that are the actual phenomenon of gentrification of the *Real Estate State* (Stein, 2019). There is the possibility to return to 8) *fortress cities,* with their fortified walls and armaments that once populated territories in the settler colony and imperium; and 9) *private cities,* where profit and not needs rule through selective ownership, registration,

and access. The combined lesson of all nine yields the production of 10) the *apartheid city* as the most ideal geographical and spatial response for the necessary use of the current and coming overpopulation, overaccumulation, and over-carcerality. The apartheid city effectively separates populations in new arbitrary and morphing groupings of ethnic identity in underinvested spaces and prioritises investment in areas deemed the dominant, ruling, and elite classes (Simon & Christopher, 1984; Wilson, 2019). The contemporary period in response to "crisis", in particular the "War on Terror" and the COVID-19 pandemic, has resulted in the restructuring of the public sphere and of urban space based on that fear (Mowatt, 2020). The schema of fear that is articulated through the "Geographies of Threat" is:

1. The distillation of the actual deindustrialisation of the economy in the 1970s (Clover, 2016).
2. The rampant rise of austerity measures like organised abandonment via the implementation of neo-liberalism in the 1980s (Brown, 2019).
3. The revanchist policies of retaliation to dissent and opposition in the 1990s (Smith, 1996).
4. The fabricated-Society's embrace of a culture of fear and moral panic of the 2000s.

## 5.2 Ideas and Ideologies

The only resolution appears to be is a process of separation from the fabrication that has been a conceptualised construct by the State. Not the naïveté that lies within the wishful thinking and individualised escape to the woods, the forrest, or one's goat farm, but a process that begins with the decoupling of one's aspirations, imaginations, pride, and articulations of life from the construct of the order. While the denizens of the city expand these social activities, they are ultimately nurtured, allowed, and managed by the State. Society is nothing more than the sum of all of the social activities that the State has produced and sanctioned. Since the State governs a massive populace and a vast territory, we live under constant abandonment or constant enforcement, and this is society. So, while society is a separate conceptual enterprise for thinking of

**Fig 5.5** Unknown Woman Struggles With Police During the Summer 1967 Unrest in Milwaukee, WS. (Photo Credit: Bettmann / Getty Images)

spaces, in its function there is no separation or distinction of society, space, and the State. "Geographies of Threat" points us to analysing social conditions, social activities, and the power play (relations) that occurs in city space. Space may inform our everyday actions, and the actions of the past, but State power is actually doing the informing via space. Where the need to decouple one's self from the fabricated-Society is necessary and births a perpetually evolving alternative or counter ideology produced from the shared experience and desire to dictate another life in the abandoned spaces.

Ideologies are the ways we talk about the world as we experience it. Ideologies are not a science; ideologies are an approximation. Transparent spaces, empty of ideological interrogation, need to be ruptured by the infusion of a critical analysis and then creation of a critically responsive viewpoint. Some spaces for criticality, radicalism, and dissent are illusions of underground or counter activity that serve as traps set by the State. Some spaces for criticality, radicalism, and dissent are secret places that lead to the development of the commune but are absent of the political progression that started with the riot. Some spaces for criticality, radicalism, and dissent are operating within and outside traditional places as the distillation of organised abandonment or the production of the captive maternal. But they all serve State power in some manner. White Supremacy, patriarchy, imperialism, settler colonialism, and capitalism as well as the functional categorisations of

class, gender, and Race require space and the geographies it works within to be conceived and actualised. As threats, gender and Race attract their own modes of violence. But unlike Race, the violence of gender is performed through processes and apparatuses of management rather than as a system of responses to a mass threat (see Fig. 5.5). For as we looked back at the disruption of property ownership by women, there was nothing in that property ownership to suggest that slavery would not have been interjected into the various European economies that then enabled the transition from feudalism to capitalism. Equality in ownership would not/will not bring equality in society for all peoples. The very private ownership of property is the corrupting element. Thus, it is the question of property and the abolition of it that offers the greatest possibility. However, it is not to say that such gendered diversity in property ownership does not present any threat.

Gender threat is handled through a patriarchal management structure that operates at the microlevel and upon groupings of individuals, most often in four ways (stages of violence, theoretically, socially, and physically to control ownership and instruct future labour of social order – childbearing women, Race production, class production):

1. *Property/Land Discrimination* – The State (over history has been the Crown-Church, Crown-Nobles, and Government-Private Interest) holds dominion over property. This

determines who can possess it, and under what restrictions. Property is wealth and control. Discrimination counters forces in the populace that challenge the practical existence and function of marriage – which leads to economic independence and inheritance of wealth. (e.g., include Magna Carta of 1215, the 1782 Flannagan's Lessee v. Young case in British American Colonies, Married Women's Property Act of 1848 in the settler colony of the United States, and the Law of Succession Act of 1972 in Kenya)

2. *Business/Organisational Property Ostraciza tion* – The State in matters of governance produces policy that is regulated by the force of lawfare. It is not just that property is wealth, it is what can be produced with and on it. Ostracization here is not a feeling of being excluded, it is the actual force of exclusion (language in policy, loan giving, denial of suffrage, fair representation, and reproductive control). Ostracization counters the forces in the populace that would bring about inclusion in roles of leadership that would threaten the false unification of gendered men in decision-making. (e.g., the Great Reform Act of 1832 in Great Britain, Aba Women's War of 1929 in Nigeria, the police repression of the Jane Collective from 1969-1973 and the increased provision of Norplant to Black women in the 1990s in the settler colony of the United States)

3. *Social Impacts of Spatial Policy Restrictions* The State empowers its representation (bureaucrats and law enforcement) regulate policy through the force of warfare. This results in intentionally disproportionate violence to be inflicted upon gendered women as a pedagogical tool to snuff opposition. Force is directed at repression of the right to assemble and organize. But force also results in the over-policing and over-carcerality of neighbourhoods predominantly comprised of women of colour. (e.g., the Peterloo Massacre of 1819 in Great Britain – repression of strikers of the Uprising of the 20,000 in 1909 in the settler colony of the United States, and the Pass Laws Act of 1952 in Apartheid South Africa; see Fig. 5.6)

4. *Actual and Perceived Spatial Violence* – The State empowers vigilante, State actors, and off-duty State actors to engage in violence by way of abandoning laws of protection and defence. The abandonment of protections from harm that results in our perception of what gender is and what gender roles are. This also elicits terrors in the social sphere/space and the absence of specific laws of protection from partners and strangers but also snuffs out women-led political opposition. (e.g., the Grim Sleeper killings from 1985-2007 and the 2013-2015 sexual assaults of Black women by police officer Daniel Holtzclaw in the settler colony of the United States, the 2016 murder of Berta Cáceres and other environmental activists by representatives associated with private companies like DESA - Desarrollos Energéticos, and the 2018 assassination of Marielle Franco by members of the federal police and vigilante police militias in Brazil – and the thousands of missing and murdered indigenous women – MMIW of the settler colonies of Canada and United States, and Mexico; see Fig. 5.7).

Spaces become intensified with the influx of ideology that shapes, feeds, and contextualises it. The movement of people in those spaces becomes inscribed with those ideologies. And in the fashion of Fanon's *corporal schema*, the body is rendered in a way that it becomes just a target that elicits a response from fellow citizens. The State controls all bodies because it identifies all persons, the spaces they occupy, and the line of thinking they wish to make manifest as a material reality (Pile, 2011). But in the influx of a constantly changing and evolving ideology, the crack in the system or order comes into play, and dissenting opportunities present them. In the need to shape and maintain everything and everyone, the system becomes overburdened, and in that slip up or crack, an alternative is seen.

State actors have disproportionately targeted Black, Latinx, indigenous, immigrant, and poor White citizenry with incrementally heavy police repression. Whether a person is compliant or dissents, he or she will experience State actions. Just like looting was a particular response to other triggering

**Fig 5.6** The Peterloo Massacre in St. Peter's Square in Manchester, England on 16 August 1819. Protesters holding banners with descriptions "Universal Suffrage" (commoner men) and "Female Reformers of Roynton – Let Us Die Like Men and Not Be Sold Like Slaves" are depicted. Thousands were attacked and many were trampled by Manchester and Cheshire Yeomanry Calvary. 20 were killed and hundreds more serious injured. Henry Hunt, esq., is also depicted and was the main speaker for the rally as well as a supporter for women's suffrage. (Public Domain)

moments, both the drowning *and* the stoning were the respective triggering moments, the "enough is enough", for the 1919 Chicago Race Riot. The shooting of Latasha Harlins in 1991 and the verdict of the Rodney King trial in 1992 were the triggering moments for the Los Angeles Rebellion in 1992. And preceding this, the beating of Rena Price with a blackjack by police who challenged the arrest of her sons in front of her fellow residents of Watts was the triggering moment for the Watts Riot turned rebellion in 1965 (see Fig. 5.8). The social psychological triggering moments are felt and experienced, but those triggering moments also have geo-spatial component to them: on the sidewalk, on the street,

**Fig 5.7** The Poster Reads: "I am because we are". A Picture of Rio de Janeiro's City Councillor Marielle Franco, 38, Who Was Shot Dead, Is Seen Outside the City Council Chamber in Rio de Janeiro, Brazil, 15 March 2018. (Photograph: Pilar Olivares)

**Fig 5.8** "Turn Left or Get Shot", in the Watts District of Los Angeles, 1965. (Photo Credit: Getty Images)

and on the curb. We see the State exerting its will in a way that vacates any illusion. We see the State exerting its will with immediacy and impunity that vacates any niceties. We also see the State allowing some forms of violence to occur, to take shape, and to occupy a space. In the end, can one really burn down and destroy that which never belonged to you in the first place? Never belonged to you due to the dispossession in living. Never belonged to you due to forces that constantly seek to dispossess because (the production of) space is always of some eventual value to the State. And, never belonged to you due to the reality that it was never really the State's property to begin with.

What is key are the motivations that were there before the (racialised) target ever appeared. Moving beyond an explanation of racially "Other" people in Black geographies and racial geographies, the focus here is on the State that construes and shapes those experiences and the basis for them. Most perniciously are the experiences of violence. The racial "Other" is threatened through the lenses of "The Geographies of Threat" through an 11-stage continuum for White Supremacy and white supremacy. This continuum situates violence undertaken to keep racialised populations in place, in order to maintain the social order by determining what modes of violence are utilised:

1. *Race Massacres/Riots* – to maintain mass social order of a racialised population for spatial domination through a mass, large-scale events of violence by sanctioned vigilantes and State officials (e.g., the initial phases of the 1921 Tulsa Race Massacre in Oklahoma or 1946 Calcutta Massacres of roughly 7,000–10,000 Hindus and Muslims).

2. *Racial Coups* – to maintain mass or localised order of a racialised population for socio-political control through a concentrated event by sanctioned vigilantes and possibly State officials (e.g., the 1876 Hamburg Massacre of South Carolina - see Fig. 5.9, the 1898 Wilmington Race Massacre in North Carolina or the 2019 Bolivian Political Coup that forced Evo Morales and several indigenous leaderships to resign from office and be removed from the country).

3. *Mass Lynchings* – to maintain mass or localised order of a locally racialised population through a series of events of violence on a representative racialised group for social control by sanctioned vigilantes (e.g., 1891 Lynching of 11 Italian Americans in New Orleans, Louisiana, or 1919 Elaine Massacre in Arkansas during "Red Summer" that resulted in 237 people lynched over the span of three days).

THE HAMBURG RIOT, JULY, 1876

**Fig 5.9** Political cartoon decrying the Hamburg Massacre (South Carolina) of July 1876 in Harper's Weekly. The goal of the state-wide series of White Democrat-led massacres through their paramilitary social club, the Red Shirts, was the suppression of Black political organising that included running candidates, forming coalitions, voting, and secret meetings. (Public Domain)

4. *Individualized or Small-Group Lynchings* – to maintain localised order of a locally racialised population through a singular, ongoing events of violence for social control by sanctioned vigilantes, sustained over time and significant in the volume of those events (e.g., various examples throughout history and globally, but most prominently, the 1915 Lynching of Leo Frank in Marietta, Georgia, or the 1916 Lynching of Jess Washington in Waco, Texas, with a crowd of nearly 15,000 people).

5. *Gun Violence* – to maintain localised and national order of various locally racialised populations through ongoing events of violence that are condoned for the purpose of geo-spatial marginalisation and abandonment by the State (e.g., the emphasis on policing low-level non-violent drug offences and not solving homicides suggests an allowance of those murders, the neighbourhood area of Englewood in Chicago, Illinois, or São Paulo, Brazil).

6. *State Executions* – to maintain localised and national order of a racialised population through official singular events of violence for geopolitical control by State officials (e.g., Dakota Wars of 1862, 38 Lakota in Mankato, Minneapolis, or the last publicly attended execution, the execution of Rainey Betha in 1936 in Owensboro, Kentucky).

7. *Police Killings* – to maintain localised order of a localised population for socio-economic control by State officials (i.e., since 2013 roughly 7,700 people have been killed by police in the United States, with nearly 3,000 killed by police in the state of Rio de Janeiro in Brazil within one year).

8. *Racialised Recreational Murder* – to maintain order of a locally racialised, population for geo-social control by a combination and coordination of vigilante, State officials, and off-duty State officials, for display (i.e., the alleged hate crimes of the 1981 Michael Donald case in

Mobile, Alabama, or 1998 Matthew Shepard case in Fort Collins, Colorado).

9. *Racial Hunting* – to maintain order of a racialised population for spatial domination by a combination and coordination of vigilantes, State officials, and off-duty State officials, in secrecy (i.e., aforementioned 1982 Murder of Vincent Chin in Detroit, Michigan, and the 2020 case of Ahmaud Arbery of Brunswick, Georgia, both of whom were targeted, or the 2017 hunting of Black men by James Harris Jackson in New York City, New York).

10. *Ethnic Cleansing* – to maintain order for the geo-spatial elimination of a racialised population by the systematic coordination of State officials and vigilantes in targeted areas that includes forced expulsions and murder (e.g., the Indian Removal Act of 1830 in the United States, the Armenian Genocides of the 19th and 20th century, the plan and execution of Jewish extermination in Europe during WWII, the Cambodian Genocide from 1975 to 1979, or the 1994 Rwandan Genocide).

11. *Race War* – to maintain order for the total geo-spatial elimination of a racialised population by the State influencing its entire population for action at a mass scale with aim of eradication of a racialised population (e.g., the series of pogroms in Europe from 1821 in Odessa, Ukraine, to Kristallnacht in Danzig, Germany, in 1938 for the systematic elimination of Jewish populations, the Anfal Genocide of 1986 in Kurdistan, Iraq, of nearly 182,000 Kurds, and as an articulated concept and aspirational future in White Nationalist fiction of *The Camp of Saints* (Raspali, 1975) and *The Turner Diaries* (Pierce, 1978).

The continuum, as presented, considers the suppression or promotion of racial violence in order to deter or foster contagious ideas of social ordering. Ordering has always been the way of the city, but as surplus populations abound, the necessity for order is at an all-time high. And the order is violent, so a discussion and theory of city must also be a theory of violence, its management, its avoidance, its inevitability, and its needlessness. In response, "a theory of

riot is a theory of crisis…ongoing and systemic capitalist crisis" (Clover, 2016, p. 1). The very phenomenon of violence – in lynching that formed the basis for the Great Migration of Black citizenry, the post realities of the 4-year federal internment of Japanese citizenry, the erection of border walls with strategically placed openings into dangerous spaces of Central and South American migrants and refugees, and the forced exodus of indigenous populations across the contiguous United States – highlights a norm, a standard, a dominant way. With the use of coded language of "dirty", "unsafe", "violent", "savage", "beastly", etc., threats are identified, and forces are deployed.

The fabricated society has taught us that it is acceptable "to shrug our shoulders at genocide" (Lindqvist, 1996, p. 130). We know the state of things. We have always known, and "it is not knowledge we lack. What is missing is the courage to understand what we know and draw conclusions" (Lindqvist, 1996, p. 172).

## 5.3 Discursions and Practicalities

And so, this brings us to the summer of 2020 as the triggering moment was not only the 9 minutes and 29 seconds of the slow death of George Floyd on camera but also the reason for his death, an alleged fake $20 bill, the generative basis for this book. This and the lived realities of COVID-19 that have taken our loved ones, health, employment, and for many, their homes. The lived realities of COVID-19 have resulted in other deaths due to loss in wages and home, and in consequence have led to further compounded triggers. The vigilante or thrill style of death of Ahmaud Arbery of Brunswick, Georgia, in February 2020; the gentrification instigated raid of the apartment of Breonna Taylor of Louisville, Kentucky, in March 2020; and the backdrop of the inability of the formerly incarcerated to get hired for steady lines of work that results in Rayshard Brooks of Atlanta, Georgia, in June 2020 asleep in his car in the parking lot of a fast-food restaurant and then shot and killed running for his life. And these triggering moments open the doorway for us to know of the legions of others who have been killed, and to question those killings for not just what occurred but also why. In the contemporary era and in the city, "the riot begins now not at the granary [of the 1700 and early 1800s] but at the police station" (Clover, 2016, p. 10). Once, "*riot* [was] *the setting of prices for market goods, while strike* [was] *the setting of prices for labor power*" as a practical response to the condition of shared dispossession or of shared economic circumstance (Clover, 2016, p. 15). The triggering moments in the contemporary are the vehicle to voice the people's disdain in State's closure of schools, provision of inadequate health care, and the maintenance of policies that incentivizes corporate production of unemployment and joblessness for increased values in stock shares and revenue generation. For Clover (2016), "the global *classes dangereuses* are not united by their role as producers but by their relation to state violence" (p. 165). Because these triggering moments, initiated by State violence, are the necessary order-maintaining tactics by a State through its cities to chill the populace, to maintain a different fear amongst the disposable at the behest of the fears of the essential.

This was always inevitable; capitalism has been struggling and will not return to some golden age to save us. Post-1970s, it is ever truer now that,

> Capitalism has retained as a constant the extreme poverty of three quarters of humanity, too poor for debt, too numerous for confinement: control will not only have to deal with erosions of frontiers but with the explosions with shanty towns or ghettos. (Deleuze, 1992, pp. 6–7)

The State is going to, and has been preparing to, do violence, or as the character of Matt Graber as played by Josh Brolin in the 2015 film *Sicario* articulated about the nature of their mission in the "War on Drugs" turned "War on Terror", to "dramatically overreact". For the film, overreaction by the United States was to be done in Ciudad Juárez in México and not in El Paso, Texas. In reality, overreaction is to be done everywhere because there is complete embrace by cities of "a punitive approach to social problems" (Vitalie, 2008, p. 2). Since capitalism is no longer able to "purchase the social

peace", then force is necessary, and overreaction is necessary because the competence to do right has never been a skill that the State has been willing to learn (Clover, 2016, p. 165). Overreaction at the border, in settlements or encampments, and on the streets of the city, hence the procurement of military transport vehicles and the swiftness in which they have been quite prominently deployed in places like Ferguson, Missouri, for a protest that only occurred in a half mile radius with no citizen weaponry. The surplus of populations is a global surplus of populations. When the State engages in "cleans[ing] the large cities...you cleanse the entire country" (Barthelemy on the Haussmannisation of Paris, as quoted by Wright, 1991, p. 15). As settler colonial cities like Tel Aviv and the Jaffa region are geographic representations of the governed, "belief that the 'new Israel' could only be erected on a *vacant* site" that then must also be viciously revised in its historiography and public memory to prevent a joint Arab and Jewish co-imagined and co-inhabited city (Levine, 2005, p. 23). This Tel Aviv also works at the international level as well, which is "why Tel Aviv is not considered a 'national' space in the way that *The New York Times* conceives of Jerusalem", although the city most embodies Zionism and a Jewish utopia (Levine, 2005, p. 219). In some respects, certain thoughts and behaviours have become proscribed; certain modes of living have long been socially conditioned inclusive of memory. New modes must take into account the dominant modes that maintain certain narratives and memory. And having certain modes of living and memory become outlawed or forbidden grants the State the authority to prescribe the maintenance of old erasures or creates new ones in the future.

If you move into spaces not for your designated group, and you question and challenge the system, then incarceration and death await you. This is the same for Palestinians and other populations as a racialized ethnic identity in Israel/Occupied Palestine, as it pertains to the free mobility of Palestinian Muslims, Jews, and Christians within the entire land that they once inhabited or the Falasha Jew who has immigrated, as well as for any ostracised political Jewish opinion that considers violating the borders for humanitarian relief, political solidarity, or anything other than pro-settlement. This is the same for any other racialised ethnicity that has faced violence for violating separation in Los Angeles during the 1940s Zoot Suit Riots grounded in anti-Mexican sentiment but based on job competition and city land expansions; in San Francisco during the Chinatown Riots of 1877 and then again in 1907, spawned by anti-Chinese sentiment in order to seize prime real estate in the heart of the burgeoning downtown; or in South Dakota during the Wounded Knee Massacre of 1890 to extract revenge and further quests of land seizures on already designated reservations of resettlement. The very presence of the racial "Other" and the protest of the racial "Other" under these economic conditions are premised by the need for capitalism to grow in theory and in space. On this front, in response to violence erasures of personhood and memory, much can be learned from Black feminist geography in drawing our attention to "the spatial dilemma – between memory and forgetfulness" as it has produced "a Black absented presence" due to "processes of displacement [that] erase histories and geographies" but are in fact, "present, legitimate, and experiential" (McKittrick, 2006, p. 33).

Black people are determined to maintain a Black *Lieux de Mémoire* (site, space of memory) to preserve what has faced erasure due to closure of public memory, the reframing work of "geographies of crime", and the "postracial romanticism" as false benignity infotainment (re: tourism in the lower 9$^{th}$ Ward in New Orleans; Thomas, 2014). But the ideological function of White Supremacy is to determine which White people in the fabricated-Society of the settler colony of the United States United States will be Supreme. Uppercase White Supremacy is for those who truly wield it, and lowercase white supremacy is for those who aspire to be given it. The right is always reserved for some and not for others. Racism then is merely an actionable cause, not a happenstance phenomenon of ponderance and curiosity. Racism is for relegation and regulation. Racism is a process that regulates White behaviour to never align with the non-White. There is no such thing as racial tensions, racial strife, and race relations. The only relationship is racism, which is capitalism, which means there is a class struggle that is dealing with all

things about Race (control of movement), by extension all things about Gender (control of property control), and obviously all things about Class (division of labour). The State's spatial evisceration of populations and the territories they are relegated to through the use of "crisis" is but "a screen for political desires and identifications as well as fears" (Aretxaga, 2003, p. 393).

The show of force throughout 2020 was to invoke riot as well as to repel it. The provocation of riot was to justify force and to create crisis, as Ella Baker on April 24, 1968, at the Southern Conference Education Fund dinner in honor of her, New York City, three weeks after the assassination of Martin Luther King Jr, remarked.

> The burning at the school took place about four hours after [H Rap Brown] had been shot in the arm by a deputy and after he had left. And that the people in the community really came out and tried to help put out the school blaze. But there is the possibility that the chief of police had decided that he was ready for a riot, and, so help him, there had to be one. Those of who are not ready for the burning will go down to our halls, go down to our mayors and our governors, and even to our federal government, and question who so much artillery is being brought and stocked, to deal with people who are fighting against a repressive system that they have become victim to. The voice of those who believe that life is more sacred than property must be heard now, if at no other time. (Ellis & Smith, 2010, p. 99; see Figs. 5.10 and 5.11)

Riots serves a purpose, so they are instigated, stoked, and quelched with purpose.

And therein lies the dance that the State traps the populace in engaging in. As Harcourt (2018) outlined, counter-insurgency strategies from military campaigns in foreign cities have been brought to domestic cities and the State works to 1) achieve total knowledge through mass data collection; 2) continuously isolate and eliminate small dissent; and 3) garner mass public support for the first two. The agents and owners of capital will react because their way of life will come to an end at some point. Capitalism is not a forever mechanism for

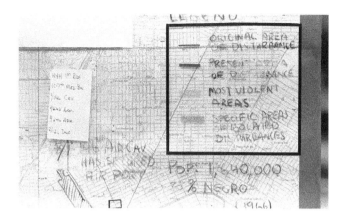

**Fig 5.10** Map of the 1966 Detroit Riot and the Military and Police Staging. The Fairgrounds Became the Landing Zone for Paratroopers, the City Airport was the Main Base, and 17,000 Troops Were Brought to Quell the Discontent of Detroit Residents. (DETROITography)

governance and wealth generation, and this "end of the world" directly leads to more aggressive forms of wealth and resource hoarding. The hoarding of wealth leads to more poverty and hunger, and this leads to greater protest and unrest. The hording of resources necessitates more cheap labour and more

unemployment to refill those positions in labour upon death, disability, or dissent. The populace is at surplus levels, and they can no longer be taken care of by the insufficient employment opportunities, inadequate housing, abandonment of services, and corrupt bureaucracies of the city. After all, the city

**Fig 5.11** In Front of a Building at 14th and Pingree, in Detroit's Riot Area, July 28, 1967, as Police and National Guard Conduct a Search for Arms. (AP Photo/Julian C. Wilson)

was merely a distracting spectacle, an empty image and not a tangible reality. The city, especially during this pandemic, is no longer a safe haven for a better quality of life from the horrors of rural death. The people have begun to react via protest because wages no longer stop, calm, or slow death. Illusions are not as effective as they once were, and especially so in a pandemic that has been poorly handled by various States throughout the world. It has made many aware of the illusions that had previously coerced the populace. But awareness is not the same as "having enough". Awareness often engenders a different set of thoughts and actions than no longer tolerating the conditions in which you have been placed within – illusions that are represented by the sad and comical attempts to pacify through procla-mations of care, as sad and comical as the names of victims of State power labelled on the back of jer-seys, sports helmets, and parquet floors. This is a capturing of the city riot by elites and aspiring elites for their own ends of identity-based social mobility advancement, at the sacrifice of those most apt to be placed on the hood of a police car likely dead, evicted from their homes, terminated from their jobs, or serving a life sentence. This is elite capture coupled with the canard of wealth (Ball, 2020; Táíwò, 2020). What Clover considers the clarity and honesty in the looting riot (the acquiring of practical needs – food, medicine, water, TVs for trade from the convenience store) is deftly different than the potential obscuring in rally, vigil, or march, because in the contemporary period,

> The spaces and activities that surround social movements and activism might best be understood as events, or at least as activities shaped by the corporate events against which people are pro-testing. (Lamond & Spracklen, 2014, p. 93)

In the city park, plaza, square, and street, festivals and events have become a thing for the populace of the fabricated society to participate in because "events [have] become a mark of responsible citizenship" a discursive display of who you are and what you aspire to be" and the protest has become another event that has been manipulated by the State, by corporate in-terest, and by social media platforms (Rojek, 2013,

p. vi). And this stands in stark contrast to "a populace seething with rancour, rage and resentment, not to mention material needs" that are not met by events of illusion (Brown, 2019, p. 85). Like a pandemic un-leased upon the fabricated society, the allure and lulling of events like the Olympics infect some of the populace, and within others, an immunity builds into dissent (Fig. 5.12). Thus, dissent is such a break from this conditioned existence that calls "up a different history than the plazas and squares of the large cities" (Torino & Wohlleben, 2019).

As the illusions disappear, our criticism and actions become clearer and honest. The right to the city is the right to see and use public spaces as important "protest platforms" and "staging grounds" that function as a pseudo- "liberated zone" from "within which political action could [can] be organized" (Mitchell, 2003, pp. 104–105). Why protest? To dissent to the social order of the day. People protest where they are, and the fact that they do so reflects something much more than the ease of location. Where they are also reflects the location of many of their own issues – issues tied to market forces that have made living insufferable, but more important issues tied to the ever presence of State violence. Is there a relationship between restrictive covenants, redlining, urban renewal, highway con-struction, zoning, and gentrification? Why rally or march? To engage in a discourse for the redress of grievances, either to another, to authority, or to them-selves as an ongoing mass protest of the abuses and actions of the Special Anti-Robbery Squad (SARS) of Lagos, Nigeria. Why strike? To stop production or to receive fair shares as an ongoing united mass organi-sation and mobilisation effort of farmers in Delhi and throughout rural India. Why riot? To disobey the un-lawful law as an ongoing response to police violence in Minneapolis-St. Paul. Joshua Clover in a 2018 interview commented that protest has a logic to it, an in-tentionality, what is done and how it is done:

> People do make considered choices about whether they want to fight, and how, and they do so from disparate circumstances. But I think there are two important frameworks in which those choices get made. One, their degree of immiseration. The greatest predictor of who will engage in criminal activity is

**Fig 5.12** Exigimos dos governantes eleitos uma trégua nas ambicoes em algum momento zelem por nossos dreitos ("We demand from elected officials an end to ambitions and at some point to watch over our rights") and Olympiada trodei a pandemia de coruptodos os podepes ("The Olympics is the most corrupting pandemic of all powers"), message in a demolished favela before the 2016 Summer Olympics, 16, July 2015. (Photo Credit: Kyodo via Associated Press)

poverty, which tells us that the decisions people make about how unlawful they're willing to be are decisively based in their own experience of immiseration. The second framework is that when people choose to act, they inevitably act where they are. (Chelgren, 2018)

In *Riot. Strike. Riot: The New Era of Uprisings,* Clover (2016) is emphatic in 1) maintaining that riot is still a fundamentally necessary term to study and to explain a reaction and response to the State and to the living conditions of the times (the response to the circulation and production of goods, and the employment or lack thereof in relationship to that production); 2) contextualising the actions of riot and strike as protests in dissent; and 3) noting that protest, riot, and strike are in direct relationship to economic growth (or lack thereof).

The protest only loses because of what Clover described as the distinctive difference between discursive and practical protest. Where the practical protest settles itself on challenging the State, the shop, and the block because it acknowledges that the State will never change and never care about everyday people, discursive seeks to do something else. Discursive protests seek to explain, point out, and articulate their demands to the State, the shop, and the block. Therefore, during the Summer of 2020, the after-release of the recordings and images of the death of Elijah McClain of Aurora, Colorado, in 2019; the already-mentioned death of Ahmaud Arbery; the death of Daniel Prude of Rochester, New York; and the death of Maurice Gordon of Poughkeepsie, New Jersey, all in 2020, resulted in retrograde outrage once those recordings were released but not when their deaths were first reported in the general associated press. These outrages also mask aspects of gendered selections of focus, notoriety trends in social media, and propensity to respond to visual stimuli, and thereby merit continued scrutiny and critique due to elements of attention to spectacle (Mowatt, 2018). Little to no national outcry is extended to police shootings of indigenous populations (Loreal Juana Barnell-Tsingine of Winslow, Arizona, in 2016 and Clarence Leading Fighter of Rushville, Nebraska, in 2019), Latinx populations (Sean Monterrosa and Andres Guardado of Los Angeles, California, in 2020), and Asian populations (Kuanchung Kao of Rohnert Park, California, in 1997 and Voua Vang of Saint Paul, Minnesota, in 2006). Little to no national outcry is also sustained for unresolved cases of police shootings of anyone (Kenneth Chamberlain, Sr., of White Plains, New York, in 2011 and Harith Augustus of Chicago, Illinois, in 2019) and suggests a conditioning of the populace in a city to solely protest in the direction that the media outlet's trending news cycle, editorial directives, and social media algorithms are steering us to protest. This also forecloses the possibility for us to ever examine what is happening in our own geographic proximity. So, re-imagined *memory work*, *civic guerrilla journalism*, *sousveillance* or *inverse surveillance* (watching the State), or the powerful frequency of free radio and news are not just used in protest but in everyday re-imaginations of a better life (Moorman, 2019; Mowatt, 2019) – to report the world that one wishes to see from the imaginations of abolition.

## 5.4 A Final Conclusion

What is there to see in the image of a 5-year-old little boy walking in a protest in 1977 in the city of Shikaakwa? A once indigenous space of the Myaamiaki-Illiniwek nation and confederation? A space that represents notions of the the "geography of social control", the "geography fear", "geography of crime", the "contrapuntal geographies of threat and security", the "geography of violence", and the "geographies of deracination"? A space that articulates this notion of the "Geographies of Threat"? A space that illuminates the possibility of an abolitionist geography of possibilities? Liberation thought of geographically and spatially asks who did the State kill today and where, and what are we going to do about it. A focus on the production of space and the functionality of cities aids efforts to return to a political economic/structural critique that provides a

theoretical framework for understanding State anti-Black discourse, indigeneity erasure, among many other articulations of oppression (Burden-Stelly, 2016). It removes the niceties of thinking that there is a peaceful world, that actions of peace will not solicit repression. The "riot, the blockade, [the barricade,] the occupation and at the far horizon, the commune" are here (see Fig. 5.13; Clover, 2016, p. 31). And they have been here all along, respectively in the spatial formations of the summer of 2020, but most especially in the Watts Rebellion in 1968 (Davis & Weiner, 2020); the Dakota Access Pipeline action of 2016 (Estes, 2019b); the Young Lords garbage offensive of 1969 (see Fig. 5.14; Fernández, 2020); the Occupy Wall Street movement of 2011; and the Capitol Hill Autonomous Zone/Organised Zone of Seattle (see Fig. 5.15), the urban Quilombos of São Paulo, the Association Habita! of Lisbon, Portugal, and *Okupas* of Barcelona, Spain (Mendes, 2020; see Fig. 5.16). In the city, new possibilities of destitution have created new possibilities of re-imagination. All that is between us is the city. That is all.

From this spatial re-imagination, a new personhood that illuminates the possibility of an abolitionist sociology of possibilities. A personhood that is birthed from the process of *desubjectification*, to accept the ways that the State fails you and abandons you and produce the ways to remake oneself, "a subject that resists and evades biopolitical control" (Lund, 2009, p. 76). To make oneself a subject of one's own imagination. So, it does not matter if a person engages in protests or not. And it does not matter how one may protest. But to protest invokes the fury of the State, even in co-opted and diluted forms. It is in the study of the State's intensity in response to riot that reveals the banal responses to its citizens in their everyday living that results in many of the same actions and ends as in the repression of riot. It is not just the State or the city that stands between us; we are the enemy that stands in the way of ourselves (Di Prima, 1969). The Pyrrhic victories of getting everyone to proclaim that Black Lives Matter in society today; to be prideful in the diasporic student protests to end Apartheid in another distant State of the 1980s and 1990s; to be happy with (only) the legislative successes of the

**Fig 5.13** A Defended Barricade Protecting the Paris Commune of 18 March 1871. (Public Domain)

modern Civil Rights Movement of the 1950s and 1960s, absent of successes to material conditions; to be virtuously and individually affirmed by the radical imaginations of Radical Feminism instead of collectively affronted enough for collective organising (Davis, 1969); to know of a place called Palestine and that the place of Palestine should be free, but only on your t-shirt and social media post; and to be content with the alterations to the work day and incremental occupational safety from the work of the Labour Movement but care nothing for unions, each are mere examples that do not result in a changed reality, just a changed emotionality. Each reveals an idea vacant of meaningful action, an act of virtue signalling that keeps us busy being too busy to self-care our way out of any actual reality of living in the merciless city. Each results only in the State forming and reforming itself in even uglier and deadlier fashion to offset the coming dangers of over-population, over-carcerality, and overaccumulation that are leading to socio-environmental upheavals. A reality that far right and far left, everyday folx and activist, and volunteers and organisers have

responded to in the moments of the Parisian *Gilets jaunes* ("Yellow Vests") and during *El Esallido Social* ("Social Outbreak") most prominently in Santiago de Chile. Thus, a spatial re-imagination is a desubjectified re-making of oneself as ungovernable. Like a Soul City, conceived of and created by people rather than the State (see Fig. 5.17).

As this book came to a close and this concluding chapter is being drafted, a new regime in the settler colony of the United States had come to power. There have been other transitions in power that have reverted to legitimate indigenous imaginations, as in Bolivia, and the mass support for the constitutional restructuring for equality rather than autocracy in Chile (see the cover of this book and Fig. 5.18). As the epnonymous character in the first season and fifth episode ("Sources and Methods") of the show *Jack Ryan* is told, "geography is destiny, my friend. The world is the kiln, we are the clay". The city presents the possibility of new political horizons for the "downpressing" State or for the resisting people. The phenomena of decolonisation, for Fanon, is and only is "the spectacular flight of capital" (Fanon,

**Fig 5.14** During the "Garbage Offensive", the Streets of Spanish Harlem at the Intersections of 3rd Avenue and East 110 Street Were Blocked With Trash Cans, Some of Which Were Set on Fire. c. July 1969. (Photo Credit: Bev Grant via Getty Images)

**Fig 5.15** "Welcome to the CHAZ" or the CHOP, Seattle, Washington, 13 June 2020. (Photo Credit: Derrick Simeone/ Wiki Commons)

**Fig 5.16** Casa de Okupas ("the house of the squatters"), La Okupa "Blokes Fantasma" en La Salut (Gràcia), Barcelona/ Okupa y Resiste Located in the Gràcia District of Barcelona, Spain, 2007. (MickStephenson/Wiki Commons)

**Fig 5.17** Soul City, North Carolina. Picture of Sign Near Soul City Boulevard in 2006. (Photo Credit: Tijuana Brass/ Public Domain)

**Fig 5.18** Santiago, Chile. La Marcha más grande de Chile of 1.2 million people (3 million across Chile) for a new Chile (also captured as the cover for this book). The image shows people in the distance amassed on top of the stature of General Baquedano in Plaza de la Dignidad/Dignity Square (formerly, Plaza Baquedano and Plaza Italia). The mass protest was in opposition to President Sebastián Piñera's austerity measures, privatization of basic utility services, and the maintenance of long-standing material conditions that have led to income equality and violation of indigenous rights. 25 October 2019. (Photo Credit: Francisco Javier Ramos Rosellon/Alamy)

1963, p. 103). Because decolonisation is "an agenda for total disorder" (Fanon, 1963, p. 3). The type of an agenda that curries a type of fury of the contemporary moment. Because fury never abstains, never recoils, never reverses course. The threat to person, profit, and property fuels that fury of the State, but also the populace of cities. The city can be ours for the taking.

(For a liberating society) We need to birth the dreamers who will grow up in a just society that we have wrestled from the State.

So, our work should be clear…it is to at least build the just society that makes all other futures possible.

> if what you want is jobs
> for everyone, you are still the enemy,
> you have not thought thru, clearly
> what that means

if what you want is housing,
industry (G.E. on the Navaho reservation)
a car for everyone, garage, refrigerator,
TV, more plumbing, scientific
freeways, you are still
the enemy, you have chosen
to sacrifice the planet for a few years of some
science fiction utopia, if what you want
still is, of can be, schools
where all our kids are pushed into one shape,
are taught
it's better to be "American" than Black
of Indian, or Jap, or PR, where Dick
and Jane become and are the dream, do
look like Dick's father, don't you think
your kid
secretly wishes you did
if what you want
is clinics where the AMA
can feed you pills to keep you weak, or sterile

shoot germs into your kids, while Mercke
& Co.

grows richer
if you want
free psychiatric help for everyone
so that the shrinks
pimps for this decadence, can make
it flower for us, if you want
if you still want a piece
a small piece of suburbia, green lawn
laid down by square foot
color TV, whose radiant energy
kills brain cells, whose subliminal ads
brainwash your children, have taken over
your dreams
degrees from universities which are nothing
more than slum landlords, festering sinks
of lies, so you too can go forth
and lie to others on some greeny campus
THEN YOU ARE STILL
THE ENEMY, you are selling
yourself short, remember
you can have what you ask for, ***ask for***
***everything***.
–Diane Di Prima, "Revolutionary Letter #19 (for
the Poor People's Campaign)", in *Revolutionary*
*Letters*
(1969) [bold and italic emphasis added].


Imagine,
 A city without prejudice.
 A city without poverty.
 A city without slums.
 A city tailor-made for industry.
 A city with a booming economy.
 A brand new shining city.
With open spaces. Trees and grass. Rolling
hills. Soft winds.
 Fresh air. Clear skies. Where stars and moon
are visible. Clean
 water. Lakes. Creeks. Ponds. Springtime
weather. Hardly any
 snow. Yet distant mountains. Ample schools,
hospitals, parking,
 recreation. Well built, stylish housing. A
master plan. But not
 sterile and cold. For a city conceived with just
an eye for bricks
 and mortar is a city without a soul. Call the
bold alternative

SOUL CITY.
–*Soul City: The Bold Alternative,* published by
The Soul City Company (1971).


## References

Agyeman, J., Bullard, R., & Evans, B. (2002). Exploring the nexus: Bringing together sustainability, environmental justice and equity. *Space and Polity, 6*(1), 70–90.

Anderson, P. (1975). *Lineages of the absolutist state.* New Left Books.

Aretxaga, B. (2003). Maddening states. *Annual Review of Anthropology, 32,* 393–410. http://www.jstor.org/stable/25064835

Ball, J. (2020). *The myth and propaganda of Black buying power.* Palgrave MacMillan.

Balto, S. (2019). *Occupied territory: Policing Black Chicago from Red Summer to Black Power.* University of North Carolina Press.

Ben-Ghiat, R. (2020). *Strongmen: Mussolini to the present.* W.W. Norton & Company, Inc.

Bledsoe, A. (2017). Marronage as a past and present geography in the Americas. *Southearn Geographer, 57* (1), 30–50. 10.1353/sgo.2017.0004

Braz, R. & Gilmore, C., (2006). Joining forces: Prisons and environmental justice in recent California organizing. *Radical History Review, 1*(96), 95–111. 10.1215/01 636545-2006-006

Brown, W. (2019). *In the ruins of neoliberalism: The rise of antidemocratic politics in the west.* Columbia.

Bunge, W. (1975). Detroit humanly viewed: The Americanurban present. In R. Abler, D. Janelle, A. Philbrickm & J. Sommer (Eds.), *Human geography in a shrinking world* (pp. 149–181). Duxbury Press.

Burden-Stelly, C. (2016). *The modern capitalist State and the Black challenge: Culturalism and the elision of political economy* [Unpublished dissertation]. University of California Berkeley.

Carnegie, C. V. (Ed.) (1987). *Afro-Caribbean villages in historical perspectives.* African-Caribbean Institute of Jamaica.

Chelgren, J. (2018, January 1). The causality runs both ways: A conversation with Joshua Clover. *The Rumpus.* https://therumpus.net/2018/01/the-rumpus-interview-with-joshua-clover/

Clover, J. (2016). *Riot. Strike. Riot.: The new era of uprisings.* Verso.

Coates, T. (2017). *We were eight years in power: An American tragedy.* One World Publishing Co.

Davis, A. (1969, October 6). Philosophical themes in Black literature. *Angela Davis Ad Hoc Committee Papers.* University of California at Los Angeles.

Davis, M. & Weiner, J. (2020). *Set the night on fire: L.A. in the sixties*. Verso.

Deleuze, G. (1992). *Postscript on the Societies of Control. October, 59,* 3–7. https://www.jstor.org/stable/778828

Di Prima, D. (1969). *Revolutionary Letter #19 (for the Poor People's Campaign). In Revolutionary Letters.* The Ann Arbor Sun & Artists Workshop Press.

Dorries, H., Henry, R., Hugill, D., McCreary, T., & Tomiak, J. (Eds.). (2019). *Settler city limits: Indigenous resurgence and colonial violence in the urban prairie west.* University of Manitoba Press.

Ellis, C. & Smith, S. D. (Eds.), (2010). *Say it loud!: Great speeches on civil rights and African American identity.* The New Press.

Estes, N. (2019a). Anti-Indian common sense: Border town violence and resistance in Mni Luzahan. In H. Dorries, R. Henry, D. Hugill, T. McCreary, & J. Tomiak (Eds.), *Settler city limits: Indigenous resurgence and colonial violence in the urban prairie west* (pp. 44–69). University of Manitoba Press.

Estes, N. (2019b). *Our history is the future: Standing rock versus the Dakota Access Pipeline, and the long tradition of indigenous resistance.* Verso.

Fanon, F. (1963). *The wretched of the earth* [Trans. by C. Farrington]. Grove Weidenfeld.

Fernández, J. (2020). *The Young Lords: A radical history.* University of North Carolina Press.

Flores, L. (Eds.). (1998). *Floating borderlands: 25 years of U.S. Hispanic literature.* University of Washington Press.

Frazier, L. J. (2020). *Desire states: Sex, gender, and political culture in Chile.* Rutgers University Press.

Gahman, L. & Hjalmarson, E. (2019). Border imperialism, racial capitalism, and geographies of deracination. *ACME: An International Journal for Critical Geographies, 18*(1), 107–129.

Galli, C. (2010). *Political spaces and global war* [Edited by A. Sitze and Trans. E. Fay]. University of Minnesota Press.

Gilmore, R. W. (2017). Abolition geography and the problem of innocence. In C. T. Johnson & A. Lubin (Eds.), *Futures of Black radicalism* (pp. 224–241). Verso.

Hall, S. (1988). *The hard road to renewal: Thatcherism and the crisis of the left.* Verso.

Hall, S. (1998). The great moving nowhere show. *Marxism Today.*

Hall, S., Critcher, C., Jefferson, T., Clarke, J., & Roberts, B. (1978). *Policing the crisis: Mugging, the state, and law and order.* Palgrave.

Harcourt, B. E. (2018). *The counterrevolution: How our government went to war against its own citizens.* Basic Books.

Harney, S. & Moten, F. (2013). *The undercommons: Fugitive planning & Black study.* Autonomedia.

Hartman, S. V. & Wilderson, F. B. (2003). The position of the unthought. *Qui Parle, 13*(2), 183–201. http://www.jstor.org/stable/20686156

Harvey, D. (2004). The 'new' imperialism: Accumulation by dispossession. *Socialist Register, 40,* 63–87.

Kirkwood, P. (2021). A war time love affair: The Round Table and The New Republic, c.1914–1919. *The Journal of the Gilded Age and Progressive Era, 20*(1), 44–65. 10.1017/S1537781420000754

James, J. (2016). The womb of Western theory: Trauma, time theft, and the captive maternal. In P. Zurn & A. Dilts (Eds.), *Challenging the punitive society: The carceral notebook, volume 12* (pp. 253–296). Columbia University.

Lamond, I. & Spracklen, K. (2014). *Protests as events.* Rowman & Littlefield International Ltd

Lefebvre, H. (2003). *The urban revolution.* University of Minnesota Press.

Levine, M. (2005). *Overthrowing geography: Jaffa, Tel Aviv, and the struggle for Palestine, 1880-1948.* University of California Press.

Lindqvist, S. (1996). *"Exterminate all the brutes": One man's odyssey into the heart of darkness and the origins of European genocide* [Trans. by J. Tate]. The New Press.

Lund, J. (2009). Biopolitical Beckett: Self-desubjectification as resistance. *Nordic Irish Studies, 8*(1), 67–77. https://www.jstor.org/stable/25699543

McKittrick, K. (2006). *Demonic grounds: Black women and the cartographies of struggle.* University of Minnesota Press.

McKittrick, K. & Woods, C. A. (Eds.). (2007). *Black geographies and the politics of place.* South End Press.

Mendes L. (2020). How can we quarantine without a home? Responses of activism and urban social movements in times of COVID-19 pandemic crisis in Lisbon. *Tijdschr voor Economische en Sociale Geografie, 111*(3), 318–332. 10.1111/tesg.12450

Mitchell, D. (2003). *The right to the city: Social justice and the fight for public space.* Guilford Press.

Moorman, M. J. (2019). *Powerful frequencies: Radio, State power, and the Cold War in Angola, 1931-2002.* Ohio University Press.

Mowatt, R. A. (2018). Black lives as snuff: The silent complicity in viewing Black death. *Biography: An Interdisciplinary Quarterly, 41* (4), 777–806. 10.1353/bio.2018.0079

Mowatt, R. A. (2019). Events of dissent, events of self: The liminality of protest images. In I. R. Lamond & J. Moss (Eds.), *Liminality and critical event studies: Borders, boundaries, and contestation* (pp. 223–245). Palgrave MacMillan.

Mowatt, R. (2020). A people's future of leisure studies: Leisure with the enemy under COVID-19. *Leisure Sciences*. 10.1080/01490400.2020.1773981

Piedalue, A. (2015). *Geographies of peace & violence: Plural resistance to gender violence and structural inequalities in Hyderabad and Seattle* [Unpublished dissertation]. University of Washington

Piedalue, A. (2016). Beyond 'culture' as an explanation for intimate violence: The politics and possibilities of plural resistance. *Gender, Place and Culture: A Journal of Feminist Geography, 24* (4), 1–12. 10.1080/0966369X.2016.1219323

Pierce, W. L. (1978). *The Turner diaries*. National Vanguard Books.

Pile S. (2011). Skin, race and space: The clash of bodily schemas in Frantz Fanon's *Black Skins, White Masks* and Nella Larsen's *Passing. Cultural Geographies, 18*(1), 25–41. 10.1177/1474474010379953

Raspali, J. (1975). The camp of the saints. *Scribner.*

Rojek, C. (2013). *Event power: How global events manage and manipulate.* Sage Publications.

Sendra, P. & Sennett, R. (2020). *Designing disorder: Experiment and disruptions in the city.* Verso.

Sherlock, P. M. (1973). *West Indian nations: A new history.* Macmillan.

Simon, D. & Christopher, A. J. (1984). The apartheid city. *Area, 16*(1), 60–62. https://www.jstor.org/stable/20001997

Smith, N. (1996). *The new urban frontier: Gentrification and the revanchist city.* Routledge.

Soja, E. W. (1989). *Postmodern geographies: The re-assertion of space in critical social theory.* Verso.

Stein, S. (2019). *Capital city: Gentrification and the real estate State.* Verso.

Táíwò, O. O. (2020, May 7). Identity politics and elite capture. *Boston Review.* http://bostonreview.net/race/olufemi-o-taiwo-identity-politics-and-elite-capture

Thomas, L. L. (2014). *Desire and disaster in New Orleans: Tourism, Race, and historical memory.* Duke University Press.

Torino, P. & Wohlleben, A. (2019, February 26). Memes with force – lessons from the Yellow Vests. *Mute.* https://www.metamute.org/editorial/articles/memes-force-%E2%80%93-lessons-yellow-vests

Vitalie, A. S. (2008). *City of disorder: How the quality of life campaign transformed New York City politics.* New York University Press.

Wilson, B. M. (2019). *America's Johannesburg: Industrialization and racial transformation in Birmingham.* The University of Georgia Press.

Wolch, J. & Dear, M. (Eds.). (1989). *The power of geography: How territory shapes social life.* Routledge.

Wright, G. (1991). *The politics of design in French colonial urbanism.* University of Chicago Press.

Wynter, S. (2006). On how we mistook the map for the territory, and re-imprisoned ourselves in our unbearable wrongness of being, of Désêtre: Black studies toward the human project. In L. R. Gordon & J. A. Gordon (Eds.), *Not only the master's tools* (pp. 107–169). Routledge.

Zierhofer, W. (2005). State, power and space. *Social Geography, 1,* 29–36. www.social-geography.net/1/29

# INDEX

For Product Safety Concerns and Information please contact our EU
representative GPSR@taylorandfrancis.com
Taylor & Francis Verlag GmbH, Kaufingerstraße 24, 80331 München, Germany